# Pennsylvania Fiduciary Guide

*A Handbook for Executors and Administrators*

---

**Seventh Edition**

*by*

M. PAUL SMITH

RICHARD L. GROSSMAN

*and*

JAMES L. HOLLINGER

*Members of the Montgomery County Bar*

**GEORGE T. BISEL COMPANY, INC.**

**710 S. WASHINGTON SQUARE**

**PHILADELPHIA** **PENNSYLVANIA**

**www.bisel.com**

Printed in United States of America

Library of Congress Catalog Card Number: 2007941856

ISBN: 0-9755281-8-1

## HOW TO USE

First refer to main text herein, then check any current supplement, using same reference numbers. New material subsequent to publication of original text is contained in later supplements and text revisions. SINCE LAWS AND CODE REFERENCES CHANGE QUITE FREQUENTLY, ALWAYS CHECK THE TIMELINESS AND APPLICABILITY OF THE STATUTES AND CODE CONTAINED HEREIN.

FOR QUESTIONS ABOUT THIS PUBLICATION,
CALL TOLL FREE 1-800-247-3526

# FOREWORD

This seventh edition of Fiduciary Guide, like the first six editions, is based primarily upon research involved in the production of the *Fiduciary Review*, to which frequent references are made. Amendments to the Pennsylvania Inheritance and Estate Tax Act, substantial changes in Federal tax laws, changes in the Supreme Court Orphans' Court Rules and continuing amendments to the Probates, Estates and Fiduciaries Code made it advisable to incorporate many changes reflected in the annual supplements for the convenience of those who use this publication.

M. Paul Smith, founding editor of *Fiduciary Review* and originator of the concept for Fiduciary Guide, died in August 1998 but much of the format developed by him and original material included in the early editions is incorporated in this revision.

The current editors, as in the past, are committed to retaining the format of the *Fiduciary Guide* as a handbook; the references to the *Fiduciary Review* and other sources point the user to resources for further research.

October 2012

Richard L. Grossman
James L. Hollinger

# TABLE OF CONTENTS

## CONDENSED

---

# *APPENDICES*

## Chapter 5

# THE GRANT OF LETTERS TESTAMENTARY

## Chapter 6

# DUTIES FOLLOWING GRANT OF LETTERS

## Chapter 7

# FAMILY EXEMPTION



## Chapter 8

# ELECTIVE SHARE OF SURVIVING SPOUSE

## Chapter 9

# ADMINISTRATION OF REAL ESTATE



## Chapter 10

# DEBTS AND CLAIMS AGAINST THE ESTATE

## Chapter 11

# SURVIVAL, ABATEMENT AND CONTROL OF ACTIONS



## Chapter 12

# INVENTORY

## Chapter 13

# PENNSYLVANIA INHERITANCE, ESTATE AND INCOME TAXES



## Chapter 14

# FEDERAL ESTATE AND INCOME TAXES

### A. Federal Estate Tax

## Chapter 15

# ACCOUNTING



## Chapter 16

# DISTRIBUTION

## Chapter 17

# WILL CONTESTS



# *APPENDICES*

# Chapter 1

# STEPS PRELIMINARY TO PROBATE AND GRANT OF LETTERS



## § 1.1 THE PERSONAL REPRESENTATIVE

The law requires that when a person dies his assets shall be collected and, after the payment of his debts and death taxes, distributed to those entitled under his will or under the intestate laws. This is performed by a personal representative of the decedent. In Pennsylvania, the court of Common Pleas of each county has jurisdiction over this process of liquidation and distribution. Of the sixty-seven counties of the Commonwealth, twenty counties have separate orphans' court divisions through which the jurisdiction of the common pleas court is exercised.[1] Jurisdiction is exercised over the "personal representative," who is either an ex-

§ 1.1

1. Separate orphans' courts in the more populous counties existed between the Constitution of 1874 and the 1968 revision of Article V of the Constitution. The jurisdiction of decedents' estates formerly exercised exclusively by those courts is now exercised through the orphans' court divisions of the common pleas courts of those twenty counties which are: Allegheny, Beaver, Berks, Bucks, Cambria, Chester, Dauphin, Delaware, Erie, Fayette, Lackawanna, Lancaster, Lehigh, Luzerne, Montgomery, Philadelphia, Schuylkill, Washington, Westmoreland and York. See *Fiduc. Rev.* March 1970, Aug. 1971, March 1972 p. 3, Dec. 1972 p. 3, Dec. 1973, April 1977, p. 3, July 1978.

ecutor named in the decedent's will or an administrator appointed by the register of wills[2] if the decedent has died without a will or has named no executor. There are several types of personal representatives, and these are discussed in Sections 3.2 and 5.2. The authority of the personal representative to act for a decedent is evidenced by letters granted by the register of wills. Letters granted to an executor are known as letters testamentary, and those granted to an administrator are known as letters of administration. In special situations, dealt with in Chapter 2, the appointment of a personal representative may be dispensed with, but in most situations letters are advisable.

Since the duties of the personal representative accrue from the grant of letters, those duties cannot ordinarily be imposed upon him otherwise, and he should proceed cautiously until he obtains letters.[3] However, if the decedent is known to have left a will and named an executor therein, there are several preliminary matters—for example, funeral and burial instructions—which the nominee can and should attend to in anticipation of formal appointment. It is therefore desirable to search for the will and related documents as soon as possible. If no will is found, or if no executor is named in the will that is found, these preliminary matters should be attended to by a member of the family, preferably one who can be expected to qualify for appointment as administrator.

In unusual circumstances, the court's aid has been obtained both before death (*Dettra Will (No. 2)*, 13 Fiduc. Rep. 463), and after (*King Will*, 3 Fiduc. Rep. 435), to protect assets of a testator when no qualified fiduciary exists. In *Dettra Will*, upon the advice of the President Judge of the Philadelphia Orphans' Court, an official examiner of the court, accompanied by the person named executor of a dis-

§ **1.1**

**2.** The register of wills is an elected county official before whom wills are probated and who grants letters testamentary or of administration. For the history of the office, see *Fiduc. Rev.* Aug. 1952.

**3.** If prior to the grant of letters the personal representative performs some act which the law regards as evidence of his acceptance of the responsibilities, he may find he has incurred legal obligations. Cf. *Ralston Estate*, 158 Pa. 645. See also Section 1.4.

puted will (the probate of which, incidentally, was later set aside: 415 Pa. 197) and by his attorney, investigated the assets of a seriously ill person including the cash in her safe deposit box which was carefully counted and listed. This action was later approved by the court en banc, where Judge Lefever, 13 Fiduc. Rep. at p. 466, stated that "This course of procedure was proper. It is a proud tradition of this court that the judges and the law clerks are available to aid counsel in perplexing problems."

In *Commonwealth v. Sourbeer*, 492 Pa. 17, annot. *Fiduc. Rev.* June 1980, the action of the named executor in authorizing a search of the premises of his murdered mother prior to the grant of letters to him was approved. However, a widow in *Fitterer v. Laudermilch*, 15 Fiduc. Rep. 2d 183, who "never probated her husband's will and had herself formally appointed the personal representative of the estate" could not commence suit for breach of contract to purchase his chiropractic equipment and to lease premises or for wrongful appropriation of clientele. See annotation *Fiduc. Rev.*, June 1995.

## § 1.2 SEARCH FOR WILL AND RELATED DOCUMENTS

In searching for the will and related documents,[1] the safe deposit boxes of the decedent should first be opened. Banks recognize the right of the family, next of kin or executor, if known, to search the contents of a decedent's safe deposit box for such documents as wills, codicils, testamentary memoranda, trust instruments, life insurance policies, lodge or veterans' benefit memoranda and cemetery deeds. The restrictions imposed upon entry into safe deposit boxes by Subchapter L of the Inheritance and Estate Tax Act do not alter the practice regarding search for the will or cemetery deeds and in any event do not apply to safe deposit boxes in the joint

§ 1.2

1. These may include documents not physically a part of the testator's formal will or not executed with the requisite formalities but which are nevertheless entitled to probate because they are incorporated by references or are testamentary in character. See Section 4.4.

names of husband and wife. Section 1792(e) thereof allows the bank to permit removal of such documents provided a bank employee certifies that they, but no other assets, have been removed. See Section 6.6. The testamentary writings can be removed for inspection, but the bank may insist that they remain in its custody until lodged with the register of wills. A search should also be made of other places where the decedent may have kept important papers, such as his desk and his office files. His attorney and financial advisors should be consulted to determine whether they have custody or knowledge of any writings which may constitute his will.

Authority to search decedent's premises prior to the grant of letters has been given in limited circumstances. In *King Will*, 3 Fiduc. Rep. 435, where the decedent, "an eccentric bachelor aged about 76 years, lived the life of a partial recluse in his secluded mountain farm home protected by his ever present dogs and shot gun . . . the Orphans' Court directed the Sheriff and Clerk of the Orphans' Court to . . . conduct a thorough search of the premises, which resulted in finding" cash, bonds and four holographic wills.

## § 1.3 FUNERAL AND BURIAL

The duty of the personal representative with regard to funeral arrangements is primarily one of payment rather than of selection of the burial site or of employment of the undertaker: *Hodge v. Cameron*, 132 Pa. Super. 1, annot. *Fiduc. Rev*. Sept. 1938; 13 Temp. L.Q. 258. The extent of the estate's liability is discussed in Section 10.2. The individual who expects to be appointed personal representative should consider advising those ordering the funeral that their right to reimbursement from the estate is limited to what will be regarded as a reasonable expenditure in light of the decedent's assets and his station in life. If the funeral is too elaborate, the person ordering it takes the risk of personal liability for the excessive cost: *Fiduc. Rev*. Feb. 1942; *Andrews Est*., 20 Fiduc. Rep. 163; *Righi Est*., 9 Fiduc. Rep. 511. Special care must be exercised in ordering the funeral if there is any likelihood that the estate may prove to be insolvent, for in that event only a nominal sum will be allowed: *Bracken Est.*, 9 Fiduc. Rep. 49. Generally, the funeral is ordered either by one of the decedent's family or by a personal friend, so that the principal hazard is in the disallowance of the excessive cost as an inheritance tax deduction.

For liability of estate for funeral ordered by friend and neighbor, see *Bruninghaus Est.*, 26 Fiduc. Rep. 178, annot. *Fiduc. Rev*. April 1976, p. 3. Funeral expenses of the life income beneficiary of a trust are sometimes payable by the trust. See *Frank Trust*, 26 Fiduc. Rep. 267; *Gallinger Trust*, 26 Fiduc. Rep. 622.

Under section 3101 of the PEF Code, funds remaining in the patient's care account of the recipient of medical assistance from the department of Public Welfare may be available for funeral expenses.

If the testamentary papers can be produced and examined prior to burial, the wishes of the decedent concerning his funeral and the cost thereof should be followed, if any have been expressed: *Lauro Est.*, 11 Fiduc. Rep. 567; cf. *Baccaro Est.*, 4 Fiduc. Rep. 46. Such wishes are entitled to great weight. If a dispute arises as to the disposition of the decedent's remains, it is useful to have in mind the following order of preferences recognized in ordinary cases: (1) the wishes of the surviving spouse if a normal marriage relationship existed at death; (2) the wishes of the decedent, particularly if strongly and recently expressed; (3) the wishes of the next of kin according to their relationship or association with the decedent: *Pettigrew v. Pettigrew*, 207 Pa. 313. However, there is no rule applicable to all situations, and each must be considered on its merits: see *Fiduc. Rev*. Sept. 1938 and *Santus Est.*, 1 Fiduc. Rep. 3d 1, annot. *Fiduc. Rev*. Feb. 2011, p. 3. Sec. PEF 305 and *Weiss Est.*, 29 *Fiduc. Rep*. 2d 479, annot. *Fiduc. Rev.*, Dec. 2009 p. 4 and *Weiss Est.*, 1 Fiduc. Rep. 3d 270, annot. *Fiduc. Rev*. July 2011, p. 2.

Chapter 86, of the PEF Code, which is the Pennsylvania version of the Uniform Anatomical Gifts Act, took effect in Pennsylvania on January 1, 1970; *Fiduc. Rev*. Feb. 1970, p. 3; 21 U. of Pitts. L. Rev. 523; 111 Trusts and Estates 16. It authorizes gifts of "all or any part" of a body for medical and dental education, research, advancement of medical and dental science, therapy and transplantation. Such gifts can be made by any decedent who was of sound mind and at least 18 years old, but gifts of the entire body are invalid unless made in a writing executed at least 15 days prior to death. Provision is also made for gifts of the body or body parts to be made by surviving relatives where the decedent had not made such arrangements prior to his death, and the Act sets forth in detail the procedures to be followed in connection with gifts by the decedent or by his survivors. PEF § 8619 (b), effective June 23, 2006, authorized electronic access by federally designated organ procurement organizations to Pa. DOT driver license database to confirm donor status.

For criminal and civil liability for improper disposition of a decedent's body, see *Fiduc. Rev*. Aug. 1982, p. 4.

If a dispute arises concerning the interment of the decedent's body, legal counsel should be consulted at once. The orphans' court division has exclusive jurisdiction of the "control of the decedent's burial." PEF 711(1); cf. *Russell v. Laier*, 3 Fiduc. Rep. 557; *Knox Burial*, 21 Fiduc. Rep. 448.

Act 99 of 1998, effective January 16, 1999, added a new Section 305 to the PEF Code setting forth rules for "determination of the final disposition of a decedent's remains . . ." to apply in the absence of "waiver or agreement," but subject to the provisions of a "valid will" and of PEF 8611(a). In general, priority is given first to the surviving spouse, then to next-of-kin, and provision is made for court proceedings instituted within 48 hours of death or later discovery of the body. Compare *In re Ebert*, 27 Fiduc. Rep. 2d 317, annot. *Fiduc. Rev.* Sept. 2007, p. 1, where bigamous wife was preferred over separated wife and children to make disposition of decedent's remains.

For consideration of the situation where a medical school to which decedent has given her body refuses to accept it, see *Holland v. Metalious*, 198 A.2d 654 (N.H.) With respect to a request for reinterment, see *Zale v. Koons*, 16 Fiduc. Rep. 70, where daughter's request was denied, the widow and mother having agreed upon the place of burial. See *Shipley Estate*, 20 Fiduc. Rep. 171, for conflict between wishes of decedent and his widow. See also *Ronick v. Lynn*, 2 Fiduc. Rep. 2d 396. Cremated remains of unmarried son could not properly be divided between different sites selected by father and mother over father's objection. *Kulp v. Kulp*, 920 A.2d 867.

## § 1.4 MEASURES TO PROTECT ESTATE

The register of wills will not ordinarily grant letters prior to the funeral: cf. *Comfort Est.*, 12 C.C. 571. In most cases a delay of several days may be expected. In the meantime, while no one has lawful authority to act for or on behalf of the estate, there may be matters that require immediate attention—such as perishable property, livestock, growing crops or the operation of the decedent's business. If the circumstances warrant immediate action, the register may make an exception to the "no funeral no letters" policy, and issue letters. Usually, however, a member of the family to whom letters will be granted in the event of intestacy, or the executor, if known, is willing to assume the responsibility of bypassing this formality and to take whatever action is necessary to prevent loss or waste of the estate's assets. He and parties dealing with him will be assuming some risk if it is subsequently found that his acts did not benefit the estate, and, in any event, there is the possibility of being held responsible as an "executor de son tort" who has all the liabilities but none of the rights of a legally appointed representative. However, if the person who assumes such responsibility is eventually granted letters, his previous acts are validated if otherwise reasonable and proper: *Purman Est.*, 334 Pa. 238, 244. Such acts, even when taken by someone other than the personal representative subsequently appointed, give rise to no personal liability but bind the estate if they are reasonable in the circumstances and benefit the estate: *Cooper v. Eyrich*, 6 Pa. Super. 200; cf. *Sherly Est.*, 19 Erie 486. See Sections 1.1 and 1.2 for search of decedent's premises and safe deposit box prior to grant of letters.

## § 1.5 EMPLOYMENT OF LEGAL COUNSEL

The administration of most estates will require the services of an attorney sooner or later, and it is advisable to consult one immediately so as to have the benefit of legal advice during the initial stages. For example, it is preferable to know before the petition for probate is filed what writings or memoranda in fact constitute the decedent's will.

The personal representative is entitled to employ any qualified attorney he wishes, and this is so regardless of any contrary direction in the will or contract made by the decedent with an attorney: *Krieder Est.*, 426 Pa. 617, aff'g per cur. 17 Fiduc. Rep. 290; see 10 Ala. L. Rev. 241. In the absence of special circumstances, it is advisable to employ the attorney who served the decedent during his lifetime, or who drafted his will,[1] since presumably he is best informed about the decedent's affairs. Reasonable attorneys' fees are proper expenses of administration: Section 13.10. If more than one personal representative is appointed, each has the right to employ his own attorney, but total counsel fees should not exceed what one attorney would have charged in settling the estate: see *Fischer Est.*, 1 Fiduc. Rep. 83; *Williams Est.*, 9 Fiduc. Rep. 681; *Grier Est.*, 13 Fiduc. Rep. 502; *Fiduc. Rev.* Aug. 1977, p. 4.

A personal representative, being a fiduciary, will not be personally liable if he relies in good faith on the advice of his attorney on any legal question, even though the advice proves unsound: *Henry Est.*, 341 Pa. 439, 444; *Fiduc. Rev.* May, 1942, Sept. 1975, p. 3. This is especially true when the personal representative employs the same attorney who served the decedent: *Dempster Est.*, 308 Pa. 153, 158. However, with respect to questions not legal in nature, the personal representative must use his own business judgment, and as to these matters the attorney's advice offers no protection: *Gilbert Ap.* 78 Pa. 266; *Rohrbaugh Est.*, 3 Fiduc. Rep. 225; cf. *Fiduc. Rev.* May, 1942.

## § 1.6 PRELIMINARY PLANNING

It is usually advisable that certain other preliminary matters be looked into by the person or persons anticipating

---

**§ 1.5**

**1.** For possible liability of attorney for error in will drafting, see *Fiduc. Rev.* July 1983

appointment as personal representative and their attorneys. One is to ascertain the approximate size and nature of the decedent's estate with a view to charting in advance the course of his administration and, more specifically, to determine whether application for letters should be made. See Appendix 4 regarding post-death tax planning; see also 65 Dick. L. Rev. 113. In some circumstances, notably when the estate is small, the appointment of a personal representative may not be necessary. See Chapter 2; David, *Independence from the Probate Court*, 3 Real Property, Probate and Trust Journal 181. Another step is to ascertain in what county application for letters should be made. This will be the county where the decedent had his last family or principal residence, but if he was not domiciled in Pennsylvania the proper county must be determined in accordance with the rules set forth in Sections 3.8 and 5.1. It is helpful to obtain at an early date as much information as can be assembled concerning the decedent's assets and liabilities and also the names, ages and relationship of the next of kin or distributees under the will. If these matters are attended to promptly, valuable time can be saved.

Essential to the preliminary planning is a review of the initial duties of the personal representative and his counsel as set forth in Chapter 6. Of particular importance is an analysis of the will (Section 6.3) and related documents including inter vivos trusts and of the problems which may arise in the distribution of estate assets as related in Chapter 16. Also, the initial planning should include an evaluation of the possibilities in post-death tax planning. Included therein may be a consideration of the elective rights of a surviving spouse (*Fiduc. Rev.* Oct. 1980) and of disclaimers authorized under Chapter 62 of the PEF Code (*Fiduc. Rev.* Oct. 1980, p. 4, Aug. 1981, p. 2).

Assembling available information for the attorney's check sheet in Appendix 1 or on a similar data sheet should prove helpful in preliminary planning for the administration of the estate. It also will prove helpful to obtain the Social Security numbers of the decedent and all distributees as soon as they are available. Any questions concerning the residence of the decedent should be resolved without delay. It is "incumbent upon the administrator to make every reasonable effort to ascertain where decedent was domiciled when she died." *Jens Est.*, 30 Fiduc. Rep. 551. See *Urban Will*, 2 Fiduc. Rep. 2d 313, annot. *Fiduc Rev*. Nov. 1982, p. 3.

Consideration should be given to past actions and possible future aid of anyone who has served under decedent's power of attorney, especially if such person was granted the enlarged powers possible under Chapter 56 of the PEF Code as revised.

Since the law and practice in Pennsylvania illustrate that an estate in many instances can be administered independently of court supervision or even grant of letters by the register of wills, it is important to decide initially what measure of protection is required or desired by the personal representative. In reaching his conclusion, the personal representative must, of course, consider the rights of the taxing authorities, claimants and distributees under the will or intestate laws, who rightfully can hold him accountable for failure to perform any duty owing to them. See Appendix 7 for statutory provisions which protect fiduciaries, including personal representatives, when they take "shortcuts." As stated in *Fiduc. Rev*. Sept. 1967, p. 4:

> ". . . Pennsylvania provides several plateaus at which formal administration of a decedent's estate can rest or proceed further depending on the measure of protection required for personal representatives, or those acquiring assets as distributees or purchasers. The requirements of the Pennsylvania and federal governments in regard to death taxes must be met without fail. Additional steps in administration are dependent on the degree of security desired by the personal representative and distributees and the insistence of unpaid claimants in the enforcement of their demands. If all creditors have been paid and there is no dispute concerning distribution to be made of the net estate among the parties in interest, it is suggested that steps in estate administration in many instances, where a member of the family is the personal representative, might proceed only to the extent required to accomplish the objectives desired."

The various plateaus in avoiding full administration of a decedent's estate might be illustrated by the following steps which should be taken to a higher altitude only when the personal representative is able and willing to take the risk, if any, involved in leaving the more firmly established lower plateau. The chart should be read from the bottom to the top and in connection with Section 2.1.

All lower steps can be omitted only when no taxable assets exist. This can happen in smaller estates consisting of life insurance and entireties property. See Chapters 13 & 14.

(2), (3), and (4) cannot all be omitted if any difficulty is experienced in obtaining custody or control of estate assets. However in smaller estates they can still be omitted with aid of the court. See Chapters 2 & 7. Beware of unknown assets.

Skipping (3) and (4). Particular care must be exercised to consider rights of creditors before this step is taken. Beware of unknown claimants.

Skipping only (4) and substituting a family settlement agreement. The validity of the will, if any, the agreement of the beneficiaries and family harmony are essential for omission of (4).

Complete administration including:
(1) all tax returns and tax clearances;
(2) obtaining letters from register of wills;
(3) advertising grant of letters;
(4) filing inventory and court accounting, making distribution and filing satisfactions of award.

This firm foundation should not be avoided and a higher step taken without considering the risk involved.

Chapter 2

# DISPOSITION OF ESTATES INDEPENDENT OF LETTERS



## § 2.1 IN GENERAL

It is possible to dispense with administration in some situations, so that the grant of letters is not necessary for the distribution of the estate to the decedent's family or for the payment of claims. See Section 2.4. Moreover, there are various kinds of property which form no part of the decedent's estate except for tax purposes, and for which, consequently, administration is not required. See Section 2.2. Accordingly, before application is made for the grant of letters testamentary or of administration, the size and nature of the decedent's estate should be reviewed carefully to determine whether letters are necessary or advisable.

The two general situations in which the appointment of a personal representative is unnecessary or undesirable are (1) where the estate may be less than $25,000 (see Section 2.4) and (2) where all the interested parties can resolve their conflicting interests by agreement among themselves (see Section 2.5). In such situations there is little justification for subjecting the estate to the usual expenses of administration or for withholding the transfer of assets until the expiration of the ordinary period for full administration.[1]

Except in the first of these two situations, attempts to dispense with the appointment of a personal representative in the process of liquidating and settling a decedent's estate can give rise to a number of problems. These problems can best be understood by keeping in mind the purpose and effect of the various decrees of the register of wills and of the court in the formal procedure. Thus, the decree of probate establishes the legality of the testator's will and forms an important link in the title of the decedent's real estate. See Chapter 4. The grant of letters conclusively establishes the authority of the personal representative to take possession of the decedent's property and to administer it. See Chapters 3 and 5. The court's confirmation of the personal representative's account frees him from future liability for anything the account discloses. See Chapters 15 and 16. Finally, the decree of distribution relieves the personal representative of the risk of liability for distributing to the wrong person and also fixes the relative interests of creditors and distributees. See Chapter 16. If the parties proceed without the benefit of any one or more of these decrees, they assume the risks involved, especially in the following areas:[2]

(1) *Collection of assets*. Banks or persons owing money to the estate may refuse to permit withdrawals or to pay claims since they are entitled to know with certainty that the payment will operate to discharge the obligation. Likewise, a debtor who pays the heirs of the decedent directly may remain liable to a personal representative if one is subsequently appointed, and for this reason he may be unwilling to pay one who is not the personal representative. If a suit for collection must be brought because a debtor of the estate refuses to pay,

---

§ 2.1

**1.** General discussion of the administration of small estates may be found in *Fiduc. Rev.* April 1947, Dec. 1949; Proc. A.B.A., Section of Real Property, Probate and Trust Law 102 (1946–1947); 45 Mich. L. Rev. 898; 49 id. 111; 68 Ill. Bar J. 248; 84 Dick. L. Rev. 37.

**2.** See Tharp, *Hazards of Short Cuts*, 29 Trust Bull. 10 (Oct. 1949), and Appendix 7, for statutory provisions which protect fiduciaries when they take shortcuts.

the appointment of a personal representative is necessary. Moreover, transfer agents and others who have custody of the decedent's property will hesitate to make payment or delivery to anyone other than a duly appointed personal representative. See Section 6.12. However, as a practical matter, persons or institutions owing small amounts to a decedent often can be persuaded to make payments to the widow or other person entitled even when no personal representative has been appointed.

(2) *Payment of debts.* In many situations, the existence of the decedent's debts can be determined and their payment provided for only through the machinery of a formal administration. This is especially true if the assets of the estate are not sufficient to pay all obligations in full.

(3) *Distribution.* If assets of the decedent are taken in distribution without administration, they remain subject to the claims of the decedent's unpaid creditors as well as to the claims of unsatisfied distributees. A creditor, for example, is entitled to compel the appointment of a personal representative who will recover the assets; likewise, a creditor may hold a taker in distribution responsible on the basis that by intermeddling with the decedent's assets the taker has made himself executor de son tort.

(4) *Death taxes.* It must be remembered that in all instances the obligation to discharge the Pennsylvania inheritance and Federal estate tax liabilities must be met irrespective of whether or not letters are obtained. If letters are not granted, inheritance and estate tax forms may be signed by an interested party.

## § 2.2 PROPERTY AND CLAIMS WHICH MAY PASS WITHOUT ADMINISTRATION

Various kinds of property either form no part of the decedent's estate or can be disposed of without formal administration.

(1) *Wages, salary or employee benefits.* If wages, salary or employee benefits were owing the decedent, his employer *may* pay to the decedent's family up to $5,000 (provided the decedent-employee was domiciled in Pennsylvania), without regard to the size of the estate or whether a personal representative has been appointed: PEF 3101. The employer, without regard to his own residence or to the location of the place of employment, is protected as though he had made payment to a duly appointed personal representative. The person receiving the payment is "answerable therefor to anyone prejudiced by an improper distribution." If the amount owing is in excess of $5,000, the employer, nevertheless, may make payment thereof but must assume the risk involved in paying the excess to one who may prove not to have been entitled. Payment may be made only to the following relatives of the decedent, and in the following order: (1) surviving spouse; (2) insofar as is practicable, any child;[1] (3) father or mother; (4) sister or brother. It should be noted that Section 3101 empowers, but does not compel, payment by the employer. Employment benefits passing to a designated beneficiary under a plan established by an employer for the benefit of its employees and their beneficiaries (e.g., pension or profit sharing trusts or death benefit plans) may be paid directly to the beneficiary designated. In the absence of court orders, such payments can be made directly to the beneficiary even if another person such as a surviving spouse is claiming adversely to the named beneficiary: PEF 8704; *Fiduc. Rev.* Sept. 1967, p. 3. Notwithstanding these permissive rules, the employer may await appointment of a personal representative or the entry of a court decree under the provision for settling small estates without administration before making payment. See Section 2.4; PEF 3102.

(2) *Automobile.* The Bureau of Motor Vehicles will permit transfer of title to a decedent's automobile to the person or persons entitled without the appointment of a personal representative if certain requirements are fulfilled—for example, submission of a death certificate or other proof of death

§ 2.2

1. Distribution to minors or incapacitated persons should, of course, be avoided, and it would seem that payment need not be made to more than one of the class involved.

and form MV-39. Transfer can be made in this manner to a surviving spouse or his or her nominee even when decedent is survived by minor children: 75 Pa. C.S. § 1114(b). A sales tax return (form MV-4ST) is also required, although the transfer will be exempt from tax. Detailed instructions under current regulations and forms to fit the particular case can be obtained by writing to the Bureau of Motor Vehicles, Department of Transportation, Harrisburg, Pennsylvania. See *Fiduc. Rev*. Feb. 1956, p. 3. For discussion of estate administration aspects of registration of a vehicle in joint names of husband and wife and registration in decedent's name alone, see *Fiduc. Rev*. Jan. 1969, p. 3.

75 Pa. C.S. 1315 provides:

"When the owner of a vehicle is deceased, the vehicle may be operated by or for any heir or personal representative of the decedent for the remainder of the current registration period and throughout the next following registration period, provided that the registration is renewed in the name of the decedent's estate as otherwise required by this chapter. Registration may continue to be renewed thereafter in the name of the decedent's estate by any person entitled to the family exemption until the final account is approved by the court."

(3) *Other property*. Certain property, either because of its nature or because of statutory provisions relating thereto, is not part of the decedent's estate (except for tax purposes) or may be transferred without the grant of letters.

A common instance of property not part of the decedent's estate (in the sense that that word is used here) is property which is owned as a joint tenant or as a tenant by the entireties. Bank accounts, shares of stock and savings bonds are frequently so held, and title thereto passes automatically to the other tenant or tenants upon the decedent's death. See Hunter—Gifts Inter Vivos. The same also is true of so-called tentative trusts. See Section 6.9. Frequently, property is kept in a joint safe deposit box with the intent that the entire contents pass to the survivor. If this device is legally effective in the circumstances, the contents form no part of the decedent's estate except perhaps for tax purposes. See Hunter—Gifts Inter Vivos, § 14(d); *Fiduc. Rev*. May 1962, Oct. 1968.

Chapter 63 of the PEF Code dealing with multiple-party bank accounts is annotated in the September 1976 issue of *Fiduciary Review*. It deals particularly with rights of survivorship in joint and trust accounts. See also *Fiduc. Rev.* January 1982, p. 3.

Household goods and furnishings acquired in anticipation of or during marriage and used by both spouses are presumptively owned by the entireties: *DiFlorido v. DiFlorido*, 459 Pa. 641.

The right of the surviving spouse, child or parent to retain or claim, as a family exemption, real or personal property not exceeding $3,500 in value is independent of the grant of letters: PEF 3121. Procedure for obtaining the exemption is discussed in Chapter 7.

A liquor license can be transferred by the widow-administratrix to herself as an individual pursuant to Section 468 of the Pa. Liquor Code. A "liquor license is an asset of decedent's estate for inheritance tax purposes but not for distributive purposes": *Kauffman Est.*, 29 Fiduc. Rep. 229.

The grant of letters is not a prerequisite to the payment or reissue of United States savings bonds belonging to the estate of an individual who is deceased. In such circumstances, the bonds may be paid to, or reissued in the names of, the persons entitled, pursuant to an application signed by all persons entitled to share in the estate: 31 CFR, Part 315. Forms for use in executing the agreement are obtainable from any Federal Reserve bank or branch or from the Treasury Department, Bureau of Public Debt, Parkersburg, West Virginia 26101-1328. Form PDF 5336-E, Application for Disposition, is used for cases of settlement without administration. Strict compliance with the instructions on the forms will prevent delay in processing the case.

Under PEF 3101 funds in the patient's care account of a recipient of medical assistance may be available for payment to a licensed funeral director for decedent's burial expenses and to the decedent's family. But see Section 10.3 re lien for medical assistance payments. Also, under the same section, life, endowment, accident or health insurance of $11,000 or less payable to the decedent's estate may be acquired by a member of the decedent's family without risk to the insurance company. Unclaimed property of $11,000 or less held by the State Treasurer may be paid to family members provided no personal representative has been appointed or more than five years have elapsed since appointment. PEF 3101(e). Likewise, enumerated banking institutions may pay the amount held if the total does not exceed $3,500 to designated relatives of a decedent, provided an affidavit or receipted funeral bill is presented.

Claims for life insurance proceeds (unless paid to the estate), social security, employees', lodge and veterans' benefits likewise form no part of the decedent's estate, except possibly for tax purposes. The procedures for obtaining payment of such claims are included in Sections 6.10 and 6.11.

## § 2.3 REAL ESTATE

Although the Fiduciaries Act of 1949 brought real estate into administration and for many purposes abolished the distinction between real and personal property, there still remains a substantial difference in the way the two types of property are treated, particularly in the situation where no personal representative is appointed. Three sections of the PEF Code are of particular importance in this connection. Section 301(b) provides that legal title to real estate passes to a decedent's heirs or devisees, "subject, however, to all the powers granted to the personal representative by this code and lawfully by the will and to all orders of court." Section 3385 provides that if no letters are taken out within a year of the decedent's death or thereafter prior to the time his interest is acquired, a bona fide[1] purchaser, mortgagee, or lien holder of the heir or devisee takes clear of all claims which are not liens of record at the time of the decedent's death. Section

§ 2.3

1. A purchaser or holder of a lien probably could not be considered bona fide if a claim against the decedent had been filed with the clerk of the orphans' court prior to his acquisition of his interest: cf. PEF 3532.

3546 provides a procedure for establishing the title of the heir or devisee by court decree without the appointment of a personal representative.

The principal effects of the three foregoing sections can be enumerated as follows:

(1) If the family wishes to sell or encumber a decedent's real estate before the expiration of a year from the decedent's death, the appointment of a personal representative is essential, because prior to that time even a bona fide purchaser would not be protected if a claimant appeared within the year and compelled the grant of letters, under which the personal representative could reach the property to satisfy any claim that was due and that could not be paid from other assets.

(2) If the heir or devisee wishes to keep title to the realty, but there is danger that someone will make a claim against the estate, it usually will be advisable to take out letters, administer the estate and have the realty awarded in distribution. Instead of a court accounting, the heir or devisee could accept a deed from the personal representative. Title so acquired would be free of all claims except those as to which a written notice had been filed with the clerk. See Section 10.12. In the alternative, the heir or devisee, instead of taking out letters, could wait a year and proceed under Section 3546 to have the property awarded to him free of all claims.

(3) If there is a possible question as to who is entitled to the property under the will or intestate law, and if the heir or devisee wishes the matter cleared by court decree, he must either pursue the entire process of formal accounting or wait a year and proceed under Section 3546.

(4) If there is no question as to the right of the heir or devisee to the property, and if he is not concerned about possible claims of real or supposed creditors, he need do nothing. While he continues to hold the property, it will be sub-

ject for an indeterminate period to the claims of possible creditors (subject to ordinary statutes of limitations); and, even if he sells the property, he will continue to be liable personally for such claims. After a year has expired, however, he can pass clear title if he wishes to sell it and has cleared death taxes if no letters were granted prior thereto: PEF 3385. For rights of judgment creditors of other distributees if distribution is made to fewer than all heirs or devisees, see *Fiduc. Rev.* Nov. 1967, p. 4.

(5) If the property is rented and no letters are obtained, a problem arises as to who is entitled to the rents. A personal representative, if appointed, clearly is entitled to rents of property not in the possession of an heir: PEF 3311. But prior to the appointment of a personal representative, the heir or devisee has all the incidents of title, including the right to possession: PEF 301(b). Hence it would seem that the tenant would be safe in paying the heir or devisee as long as the identity of the heir or devisee is clear and no personal representative has been appointed. If a personal representative subsequently is appointed, the heir or devisee would be accountable for the rents received if needed to pay debts, but it would seem that the tenant's obligation would be satisfied.

A spouse, child or parent may elect to take all or part of a decedent's real estate as a family exemption and, as an alternative to PEF 3546, may establish title free of other claims under family exemption procedures whether or not a personal representative has been appointed. See Chapter 7; PEF 3123. However, the procedure under Section 3123 is usually more cumbersome than proceeding through regular administration and having the real estate sold or awarded under Section 3534.

Title to real property held by the decedent as a joint tenant with another, or as a tenant by the entireties with his spouse, passes automatically to the survivor or survivors without the necessity of administration.

## § 2.4 STATUTORY PROCEDURE FOR PERSONAL ESTATE OF $25,000 OR LESS

Section 3102 of the PEF Code provides a procedure for settling small estates of personal property not exceeding $25,000 by a single petition[1] and decree which take the place of all the steps of formal administration from the grant of letters through accounting and distribution. Under that section, the court may order distribution of the estate upon petition of a distributee or claimant, without regard to whether a personal representative has been appointed: *Bliem Est.*, 8 Fiduc. Rep. 131; *Bussler Est.*, 12 Fiduc. Rep. 281. The wording of the section must be read with care. Real estate is not affected by the procedure: its value is ignored in determining whether the section is applicable, and its distribution is not affected by the decree. Furthermore, wages, salary, employee benefits, deposit accounts, patient's care accounts or insurance proceeds paid under Section 3101 of the PEF Code (see Section 2.2(1)) are excluded in determining whether the estate falls within the $25,000 limit. Assets not part of the estate (see Section 2.2) are also excluded.

The filing of a separate inventory under PEF Code 3301 is not required when the small estate petition under PEF Code 3102 is used: *Estates of Kruth, Kelly and Adams*, 19 Fiduc. Rep. 2d 213, annot. *Fiduc. Rev.*, Nov. 1999. See Chapter 12.

The following illustration shows the manner in which Section 3102 operates:

| | | |
|---|---|---|
| Assets not part of the estate | | |
| Insurance payable to widow | $15,000 | |
| Bank account passing to widow by right of survivorship | 1,000 | $16,000 |
| Estate assets | | |
| Real estate | 10,000 | |
| Furniture | 3,000 | |

§ 2.4

1. Under PEF 761, the petition may be verified by statement or affidavit.

| | | |
|---|---|---|
| Watch | 10 | |
| 20 shares XYZ Corp. | 14,830 | |
| Insurance | 10,500 | |
| Bank Deposit | 1,200 | |
| Cash | 10 | |
| Salary and employee benefits due decedent | 5,800 | |
| Note due decedent | 300 | 45,650 |
| Total assets | | 61,150 |
| Exclude | | |
| Assets not part of estate | 16,000 | |
| Real Estate | 10,000 | |
| Insurance paid to widow | 10,500 | |
| Bank deposit paid to widow in reimbursement for funeral expenses | 1,200 | |
| Salary paid under § 3101 | 5,000 | |
| Total exclusions | | 42,700 |
| Balance of assets (including $800 of salary in excess of § 3101 limitation) | | $18,950 |

It should be observed that the decree governs $25,000 of assets ("exclusive of real estate and of property payable under Section 3101, . . . but including personal property claimed as the family exemption"). If the employer does not voluntarily pay salary as authorized by Section 3101, it must be included in calculating the $25,000 limit. In the case supposed, it is assumed that the devisee of the realty does not wish to sell the real estate within a year of the decedent's death and is satisfied to rely on Section 3385 or 3546 of the PEF Code for its future marketability. See Section 2.3.

Application of Section 3102 of the PEF Code and the question of compliance with the requirements as to notice or appraisement are entirely within the discretion of the orphans' court: *Trusky Est.*, 52 Lanc. 31. See *Fiduc. Rev.* March 1970, p. 4, which discusses circumstances not justifying the award of distribution under small estate procedures and *Rybak Est.*, 424 Pa. 470, annot. *Fiduc. Rev.* April 1967, where the lower court's decree of distribution was set aside because of an alleged indebtedness of $11,000 owing decedent which should not be disposed of in such a proceeding. For constitutionality of provisions for distribution such as those in PEF 3101 and 3102, in absence of notice, see 60 *Minn. L. Rev.* 317 (1976). The claimant or distributee presenting his petition should exercise care to comply with local rules of court and should set forth information which will answer the following questions as completely as possible:

(1) Does the personal estate, exclusive of payments under PEF 3101 have a value which does not exceed $25,000?

(2) Is all of the decedent's property known, or is it likely that other property will be discovered at a later date?

(3) Is the value of the property apparent or should an appraiser or appraisers be appointed by the court?

(4) Are all claimants and distributees known, have they joined in the petition, and are their respective rights clear or agreed upon?

(5) Are family exemption rights involved (see Chapter 7), and if so, is adequate provision made therefor?

(6) Is a hearing required, and if so, what notice thereof should be given?

(7) Has any inheritance tax which may be due been paid or has provision been made for its payment?

(8) Is there a will, and if so, has it been probated or submitted with the petition?[2]

The foregoing questions are not the only ones to be considered, but they are illustrative of the kinds of questions which are likely to pass through a judge's mind before he ex-

§ 2.4

**2.** It should be noted that the decedent's will can be probated without obtaining letters. See Section 4.1

ercises his discretion to order distribution. See form of petition and decree in Partridge-Remick, O.C. Practice § 1.04; 8 Dunlap-Hanna, Pennsylvania Forms 75.16-1. Obviously the court will not exercise its discretion in favor of an abbreviated administration unless it is reasonably assured that it knows the facts and that the requested short cut is the advisable procedure in the interests of the Commonwealth, as well as of creditors and distributees.

## § 2.5 SETTLEMENT OF PERSONAL ESTATE BY AGREEMENT

Complete administration of an estate may properly be avoided if all the parties concerned can agree to dispense with it and if the distribution agreed upon is feasible. When an estate is small, the family often is willing to forego the protection of formal administration and in the interest of economy to assume whatever risks are involved in settling the estate by agreement, without any procedure before the register or orphans' court. In spite of the difficulties and problems outlined in Section 2.1, family arrangements for this purpose are looked upon favorably by the law, and, when fairly made, they cannot be disturbed subsequently by the parties thereto: *Kurek Est.*, 8 Fiduc. Rep. 287. However, such an arrangement should not be carried out unless the decedent had no unpaid creditors (otherwise, creditors should join in the agreement, *Morgan Est.*, 8 Fiduc. Rep. 86) and unless he left only assets which can be transferred by delivery, e.g., cash, furniture, bearer bonds. Care should be taken to protect any share distributed for the benefit of a minor. Problems that arise with respect to real estate owned by the decedent, other than in joint tenancy and tenancy by the entireties, are considered in Section 2.3. See Section 15.5 concerning representation of charities.

If the assets of a decedent can be collected without encountering the difficulties outlined in Section 2.1, the member of the family or other person who obtains custody of the assets is in the position of an executor or administrator de son tort. In spite of the uncomplimentary appellation, the position involves no liability if in fact the assets are administered and distributed correctly so that no one is harmed. On the other hand, the person assuming the responsibility will be liable, regardless of good faith, if the distribution is erroneous. Hence it is essential (1) to determine who is entitled to the assets collected, (2) to keep an accurate record of everything that is done, and (3) to secure the written agreement of all possible parties in interest. See *Fiduc. Rev.*, Oct. 1997 for a discussion of family agreements.

With respect to the first point, Section 3392 of the PEF Code, governing preference in claims against the estate, is of primary importance because in most estates where administration is by-passed, preferred claims will exhaust or nearly exhaust the estate. If there is anything left after the family exemption has been paid (see Chapter 7) and claims against the estate settled, the persons entitled will be determined by the intestate laws or by the will. The order of abatement provided in Section 3541 of the PEF Code will be important if the decedent left a will. Moreover, an inheritance tax return must be filed and the tax due, if any, paid. The Pennsylvania inheritance tax return may be executed by a party in interest if there is no personal representative. If the assets exceed the amount required for filing a federal estate tax return, it must be executed, filed and tax due, if any, paid.

With respect to records, although no formal court accounting is required, there is always the risk that someone will demand one in the future: cf. *Hammer Est.*, 389 Pa. 78. Hence a record of all receipts and payments should be carefully preserved—either in the form of a court accounting or in such form that a court accounting could be prepared easily therefrom.

Finally, the execution of written receipts, releases and consents is all-important when this type of estate settlement is employed. Receipts of the funeral director, doctor, and other creditors should be carefully preserved, and those who receive any part of the assets should be asked to sign a paper acknowledging the payment, releasing all concerned from any further claim and agreeing to refund pro rata the amounts received in the event that payment turns out to be erroneous. If there are other parties who in fact receive nothing but who may have a real or supposed claim, depending on the construction of the will and statutes, they should be asked to agree in writing to the distribution insofar as practical. The drafting of these agreements should not be attempted without the aid of a lawyer. It must be emphasized that the execution of these agreements offers no safeguard against unexpected creditors' claims. For form of family settlement agreement, see 8 Dunlap-Hanna Pennsylvania Forms at 76.13-3. Although it is neither good practice nor recommended, an oral settlement of dispute over the amount of the decedent's estate has been enforced without a signed release. *Daggett Est.*, 25 Fiduc. Rep. 2d 92.

All papers should be kept in a safe place for an indefinite period, because parties using short cuts forsake the protection that would otherwise be afforded by the various limitations on claims provided for estates which are fully administered. See Chapter 10. Consideration should be given to filing under PEF 3532(c) which provides that: "The personal representative may file with the clerk receipts, releases and refunding agreements which he may have received from persons to whom he has made a risk distribution, or from other parties in interest. Receipts, releases and refunding agreements so filed shall be indexed under the name of the estate. Their acceptance shall not be construed as court approval of any act of administration or distribution therein reflected."

Presumably this statutory provision is available to personal representatives who have not qualified as such before the register of wills.

For effectiveness of receipts, releases and refunding agreements, see *Fiduc. Rev.* Sept. 1977; *Horton Est.*, 2 Fiduc. Rep. 2d 89 and editors' note thereto.

# Chapter 3

# THE GRANT OF LETTERS OF ADMINISTRATION



## § 3.1 IN GENERAL

If the decedent died without a will, or if he died leaving a will which cannot be probated, or one which names no executor, and if, further, it has been decided that administration is necessary (see Chapter 2) or advisable, the first step in the settlement of the decedent's estate is to secure the appointment of an administrator. The administrator is appointed by the register of wills, usually upon the petition of a person entitled to become administrator. That person is usually one of the next of kin. See Section 3.4. Letters of administration are granted by the register to the administrator and are his official certificate of authority to represent the decedent's estate. In addition, the register will issue as many "short certificates" as are requested to evidence the administrator's authority to collect or deal with estate assets. See Section 3.12.

Application for letters should be made as soon as practicable after the funeral. It is customary to delay application therefor until after burial "in the absence of some imperative necessity shown." *Comfort Est.*, 12 C.C. 571. In the absence of the consent of the surviving spouse and of those entitled to intestate shares, letters cannot be granted to other persons within seven days of the decedent's death: PEF 3155. Letters may not be granted by the register after expiration of twenty-one years from the decedent's death, except upon order of the court, upon cause shown: PEF 3152; *Ginsberg Est.*, 31 D.&C. 2d 623. For form of petition after twenty-one years, see Partridge-Remick, O.C. Practice § 6.11.

## § 3.2 TYPES OF LETTERS OF ADMINISTRATION

Although the usual situation in which letters of administration are granted exists when the decedent has left no will, such letters are also granted in other circumstances. If the will names no executor, or if the executor therein named renounces, or is unable or unwilling to serve, letters of administration with the will annexed (c.t.a.—cum testamento annexo) are applied for. See Section 5.2; PEF 3158. If the executor named in the will is appointed but subsequently dies, resigns or is removed before his duties are completed, the register of wills will grant letters of administration d.b.n.c.t.a. (de bonis non cum testamento annexo). If there is no will and the administrator duly appointed has died, resigned or been removed without having completed his administration, an administrator d.b.n. (de bonis non) is appointed in his place. See Section 5.2; PEF 3159.

There are also various types of temporary letters of administration which are necessary when, for any reason, letters of administration or letters testamentary cannot be granted immediately. Thus, an administrator pendente lite may be necessary in the event of a will contest in order to conserve the assets of the estate. See Section 3.13. If the named executor or the next of kin of an intestate is a minor when the decedent dies, an administrator durante minoritate may be appointed. See Section 3.13; PEF 3160. If the named executor or the next of kin of an intestate is absent from the jurisdiction and cannot return within a reasonable time, letters durante absentia will be granted. See Section 3.13; PEF 3160. See PEF Code, Chapt. 43 for appointment, powers, duties and relationships established when a temporary fiduciary is appointed because of the nonfunctioning of the original fiduciary occasioned by his absence in military or other government service or his conflicting interest.

## § 3.3 FACT OF DEATH OR PRESUMED DEATH

In many counties no formal proof of death is required prior to the grant of letters other than a statement of such fact in the petition for letters. In some counties a death certificate or a separate affidavit of death is required. The ordinary case presents no problem, but when there is any question whatsoever about the fact of death, the petition for the grant of letters should be delayed until a court having jurisdiction to do so has established the fact of his presumed death and the date thereof. Upon application of a party in interest, the court can establish such fact either from an unexplained absence of at least seven years (cf. *In re Windsor*, 28 Fiduc. Rep. 184) or from exposure "to a specific peril of death." PEF 5701. See Uniform Determination of Death Act: Act 323 of 1982, 35 P.S. § 10201 et seq. Under the latter circumstances, death can be established before expiration of the seven-year period. In no event will the court establish death upon a presumption in the absence of notice by advertisement and otherwise, as the circumstances of the case may require. PEF 5704. In all cases when death has been found by court decree from absence, distribution of the estate will be conditioned upon the giving of refunding bonds. See Section 16.5. If letters are granted without prior court decree establishing death upon a presumption, and if the "decedent" is in fact alive, any letters granted will be absolutely void, regardless of the good faith of the applicant: *Devlin v. Commonwealth*, 101 Pa. 273. See generally *Fiduc Rev.* Nov. 1945; 53 Dick. L. Rev. 108; 51 Pa. C.S. § 9401. Pending expiration of the seven-year period, the estate of the absentee can be safeguarded by appointment of a trustee, as provided in PEF 5702. For extensive discussion and forms, see Partridge-Remick, O.C. Practice, Chapter 86. For the grant of letters in the estate of an unborn child, for the purpose of bringing suit for the death, see *D'Antonio Est.*, 11 Fiduc. Rep. 425; *Pillsbury Est.*, 12 Fiduc. Rep. 325. See Section 11.1 regarding whether or not liability exists for injury to an unborn child.

## § 3.4 PETITION FOR LETTERS—PERSONS ENTITLED TO LETTERS OF ADMINISTRATION—ORDER OF PREFERENCE

The register of wills determines whether or not letters of administration will be granted, and if so to whom, primarily on the basis of the statutory preferences and of his examination of the petition submitted to him by the party or parties seeking letters. Petitions are filed on forms supplied by the register. In the case of intestate decedents, the petitioner should state under oath the following facts, insofar as they are known: (1) the decedent's name, age, state or country of domicile, his last family or principal residence and the place and day of his death; (2) the name and residence address of the surviving spouse, if any, and the names, relationships and residence addresses of his issue or other next of kin; (3) if the decedent was domiciled in Pennsylvania, the estimated value of *all* his personal property and the value and location of real estate in Pennsylvania; if the decedent was domiciled elsewhere, the estimated value of personal property in Pennsylvania and in the county where letters are sought and the value and location of real estate in Pennsylvania; (4) other facts necessary to entitle the petitioner to letters, such as the death or incapacity of persons having a right to letters superior to that of the petitioner: PEF 3153. Registers of wills in some counties now require pre-registration by counsel to use the online probate process and then completion of required probate information online. Others are using computer-assisted probate which removes the necessity to complete a petition for probate and letters testamentary or of administration. However, it is still helpful to complete the petition prior to arriving for probate so that information required is readily available.

The order in which parties interested in an intestate estate are preferred in appointment is set forth in PEF 3155. The right to administer is based upon the size of the interest of the applicant and not upon the closeness of his relationship: *Buell Est.*, 2 Fiduc. Rep. 10. Thus, if the interest in the estate has been forfeited for any reason (see PEF 2106), the right to letters is also lost: *Odiorne Ap.*, 54 Pa. 175. The register exercises his discretion only within the classes named, except for good cause; once exercised, it is not subject to review except for abuse of such discretion. See Section 3.9; *Buell Est.*, 2 Fiduc. Rep. 10. Where the interests of those entitled to letters are equal, none may be granted to one without notice to the others: *Nearhoof Est.*, 6 Fiduc. Rep. 209. However, the fact that notice was not given to one of the class of persons entitled who lived in New York was held to be "without material error" in *Coolidge Est.*, 16 Fiduc. Rep. 404. In *Frantz Est.*, 14 Fiduc. Rep. 93, annot. *Fiduc. Rev*. May 1964, p. 3, the court stated "We do not find it obligatory on the register to give notice to heirs who are non-residents of the county of administration prior to an initial grant . . . but such heirs are proper parties to a petition to revoke once a dispute has arisen." Where the parties in interest who are entitled equally cannot agree upon an administrator, the register can grant letters to one of them (*Marshman Est.*, 3 Fiduc. Rep. 2d 270 annot. *Fiduc. Rev.*, Oct. 1983) or to a competent disinterested person: *Schulz Est.*, 392 Pa. 117, aff'g 56 Lanc. 5.

The order of preference, when there is no will, is:

(1) Surviving spouse. Mere separation without fault does not deprive widow of right to letters and letters granted to another without prior renunciation of widow will be revoked: *Strickland Est.*, 74 D. & C. 2d 550; *Nilles Est.*, 27 Fiduc. Rep. 289. It should be noted that a widow who has released her intestate interest by a postnuptial agreement loses her right to letters: *Kowtko Est.*, 2 Fiduc. Rep. 651; and see *Wilson Est.*, 52 Berks 67. Desertion for more than one year precludes a spouse from receiving letters of administration:

*Johnson Est.*, 5 Fiduc. Rep. 2d 199. The full faith and credit clause of the U.S. Constitution may prevent a divorced spouse from collaterally attacking a foreign divorce decree for the purpose of securing letters: *McKaig Est.*, 12 Fiduc. Rep. 155. See also *Fiduc. Rev*. Aug. 1967; *Carr Est.*, 30 Fiduc. Rep. 136.

Although common law marriage was abolished, such marriages contracted on or before January 1, 2005 are valid and wife entitled to letters of administration: *Dennis Est.* 1 Fiduc. Rep. 3d 288, annot. *Fiduc. Rev*. July 2011, p. 1.

(2) Those who are entitled under the intestate laws[1] and who the register, in his discretion, shall judge will best administer the estate. Preference is given, as stated above, according to the sizes of the shares of those in this class. In *Zaleski Est.*, 28 Chester 420, parents of decedent were not removed on petition of decedent's divorced wife who asserted right to letters as natural guardian of decedent's only child, a minor. In *Weaver Est.*, 19 Fiduc. Rep. 2d 236, letters of administration granted to intestate's ex-wife (mother of minor daughter) were revoked and decedent's parents were appointed.

(3) Principal creditors of the decedent at the time of his death (hence excluding undertakers). See Section 3.7. The grant of letters to a creditor, without prior notice to the Commonwealth, as sole heir, may be revoked: *Springer Est.*, 5 Fiduc. Rep. 528, annot. *Fiduc. Rev*. Oct. 1955; *Cleaver Est.*, 8 Fiduc. Rep. 546; *Barnhart Est.*, 9 Fiduc. Rep. 487; cf. *Tierney Will*, 10 Fiduc. Rep. 310. See *Stephenson v. Wildasin Estate*, 20 Fiduc. Rep. 100, where a plaintiff, who did not know of the defendant's death until one day before the statute of limitations expired, brought suit against the person to whom he requested letters to be granted, which request was made on the last day for suit permitted by the statute of limitations. The action was held to have been begun in timely fashion, because the subsequent grant of letters related back to the date of application for such letters. Letters may be granted to create a party defendant: *Johnston, Admrx. v. Johnston, Executrix*, 71 D. & C. 2d 745.

---

**§ 3.4**

**1.** For those entitled under the intestate laws, see Appendix 5.

(4) Other fit persons. Regardless of the usual requirement of notice to those having prior right to letters, in *Collossa Est.*, 21 Fiduc. Rep. 77, it was held that the Commonwealth was not entitled to notice as statutory heir before the register appoints other fit persons, with the court making some scathing comments about political patronage.

The register will not be enjoined from granting letters of administration to other than agents or nominees of the Commonwealth in estates of decedents without known heirs: *In re Costigan*, 26 Fiduc. Rep. 126; *Yakowicz v. Costigan*, 17 Pa. Cmwlth. Ct. 287, annot. *Fiduc. Rev.* Nov. 1975.

Decree of lower court refusing to interfere with intended action of register to appoint an "impartial third party" as administrator was affirmed. The persons seeking appointment were a 19 year old son and an 18 year old daughter: *Millar Est.*, 483 Pa. 274, 396 A.2d 639.

(5) A guardianship support agency serving as guardian of an incapacitated person who dies during its administration was added in 1992 as a proper appointee in last position.

For Supreme Court Orphans' Court Rules on registers' form and annotation thereon, see *Fiduc. Rev.* June 1979.

The order of preference in granting letters of administration c.t.a. or d.b.n.c.t.a. (see Section 3.2) is the same as when there is an intestacy, except that those entitled to the residuary estate under the will have a preference over the others listed above: PEF 3155; *Nichols Est.*, 11 Fiduc. Rep. 153 (ancillary letters—creditor). Nonresidence of a residuary beneficiary is not itself sufficient cause to refuse him letters of administration c.t.a. *Kiker Est.*, 7 Fiduc. Rep. 232.

Renunciation and nomination of another by one entitled to be an administrator are discussed in Section 3.6.

## § 3.5 PERSONS NOT QUALIFIED TO BE ADMINISTRATORS

Section 3156 of the PEF Code states:

No person shall be qualified to serve as personal representative who is:

(1) Under 18 years of age [see *Woods Ap.*, 55 Pa. 332, regarding nominee of minor's guardian];

(2) A corporation not authorized to act as fiduciary in the Commonwealth;

(3) A person, other than an executor designated by name or description in the will, found by the register to be unfit to be entrusted with the administration of the estate [see *Kravitz Est.*, 9 Fiduc. Rep. 425];

(4) The nominee of any beneficiary, legatee or person having any interest whatsoever, when such beneficiary, legatee or person is a citizen or resident of any country outside the territorial limits or possessions of the United States, when it shall appear doubtful to the register that in the distribution of the estate any such person will have the actual benefit, use, enjoyment or control of the money or other property representing his share or interest therein. See Section 16.12; Cf. *Martinzik Est.*, 2 Fiduc. Rep. 496.

In addition, the register in his discretion may refuse letters of administration to nonresidents of Pennsylvania: PEF 3157; *Adams Est.*, 20 Fiduc. Rep. 88; cf. *Kiker Est.*, 7 Fiduc. Rep. 232. Nonresidents have been appointed to secure diversity jurisdiction in the federal courts, e.g., *D'Antonio Est.*, 11 Fiduc. Rep. 425. The appointment of a nonresident "manufactured" for purpose of diversity is now disapproved: *Fiduc. Rev.* Nov. 1968; 14 Villa. L.R. 727; 73 Dick. L. R. 562. Potential debtor of estate is not a party in interest who may object to issuance of letters of administration: *Terzini Est.*, 39 Beaver 136.

## § 3.6 RENUNCIATION AND NOMINATION BY PARTIES

Ordinarily, when a person entitled to act as administrator is competent but does not wish to act in that capacity, he should execute a renunciation stating his desire not to act. He may, if he wishes, nominate a substitute. It is sometimes advisable to renounce in favor of a corporate fiduciary in order to save the cost of a bond. See Section 3.10. Letters should be granted to the nominee of all parties interested in the estate as residuary beneficiaries or next of kin: *Coover Est.*, 52 Pa. 427. If one of those in the preferred list of those entitled to administer renounces his right to letters, the register, in his discretion, may appoint a nominee of the person so renouncing in preference to persons having rights inferior to the renouncing parties: PEF 3155(b)(6).[1]

One who is unfit under Sections 3156(3) and 3156(4) of the PEF Code cannot nominate another to act in his stead: *Kravitz Est.*, 9 Fiduc. Rep. 425. See Section 3.5. No general form of renouncing is prescribed, but renunciations are usually made on forms provided by the register; they also may be made by oral declarations or conduct: *Weidner Est.*, 39 Pa. Super. 120. In some counties it is required that the renunciation be acknowledged before a notary. When the circumstances warrant, a renunciation improperly obtained may later be repudiated: *Bechtold Est.*, 57 Montg. 295. An executor who renounces his right to serve does not have the power to nominate another person to serve as administrator. *Estate of Tigue*, 926 A.2d 453 (Pa. Super.) annot. *Fiduc. Rev.* Oct. 2007, p. 3.

## § 3.7 PROCEDURE TO COMPEL ADMINISTRATION

Occasionally, the surviving spouse or next of kin of an intestate decedent neglects or refuses to petition for letters of administration. In such circumstances a creditor of his estate may petition the register, who will then hold a hearing and thereafter grant letters to a member of the decedent's family, who appears and qualifies, or to a qualified creditor. The creditor may at that time renounce in favor of some other

**§ 3.6**

**1.** The appointment of daughter of surviving husband who was sole beneficiary of decedent wife to act as personal representative is proper where husband died and daughter was sole beneficiary of his estate. *Fluellen Est.*, 2 Fiduc. Rep. 3d 323, annot. *Fiduc. Rev.* July 2012, p. 3.

fit person. See Section 3.6; PEF 3155(b); Partridge-Remick, O.C. Practice § 2.06.

The timely appointment of a personal representative on application of a creditor, including a tort claimant, can be important when the statute of limitations might bar the claim (*Stephenson v. Wildasin Estate*, 20 Fiduc. Rep. 100), but the attorney for such a created party should not continue to represent the estate: *Johnston, Admx. v. Johnston, Executrix* (O.C. Div. Forest), 71 D. & C. 2d 745; see Section 10.14.

## § 3.8 COUNTY WHERE LETTERS ARE GRANTED

Letters of administration of the estates of decedents domiciled in Pennsylvania can be granted only in the county where the decedent had his last family or principal residence.[1] A nursing home which is decedent's sole residence for several years may be her residence: *Seager Est.*, 4 Fiduc. Rep. 2d 179, annot. *Fiduc. Rev.*, June 1984. If the decedent had no domicile in Pennsylvania, either original or ancillary letters may be granted in any county wherein property of his estate is located. Such letters when granted are exclusive throughout the Commonwealth: PEF 3151. It is the situs at death which is important (cf. *Somerset Coal Co. v. Diamond State Steel Co.*, 224 Pa. 217). The office location of the attorney who wrote the will or the residence of the executor does not give a Pennsylvania court jurisdiction of the estate of a person not domiciled in Pennsylvania (*Delgado Est.*, 38 Beaver 82), but a Pennsylvania court can determine ownership of Pennsylvania bank accounts following death of a nonresident former owner: *D'Urbano Est.*, 29 Fiduc. Rep. 557. A claim under a simple contract has its situs at the debtor's residence (*Sayre v. Helm*, 61 Pa. 299), and one under a promissory note or specialty at the locus of the document (*Lang Est.*, 301 Pa. 429; *Viosca Est.*, 197 Pa. 280), while a chose in action represented

**§ 3.8**

**1.** The problem of what constitutes domicile is discussed in Section 4.7; *Fiduc. Rev.* Nov. 1982, p. 3, April 1983, p. 3.

by a judgment has its situs where the judgment is entered (*Lang Est.*, 301 Pa. 429), and one represented by a mortgage, where the land is located (*Brooks v. Litchfield*, 19 Dist. 40). See also *Appleton Est.*, 1 Fiduc. Rep. 475. Regarding the necessity of ancillary administration, see *Parkhurst Est.*, 8 Fiduc. Rep. 442; *Fox Est.*, 55 Montg. 110.

If the decedent had no domicile or property within Pennsylvania, and it is desired to serve process upon his personal representative as authorized by law (e.g., suits relating to nonresident operators of aircraft and motor vehicles), letters may be granted by the register of any county as provided in PEF 3151. See Section 11.1.

## § 3.9 CONTEST OF LETTERS

Anyone entitled to letters of administration who is apprehensive that they may be granted to someone not entitled thereto may file a caveat with the register. See Section 17.5. In the first instance, the caveat may be made informally by any written notice filed with the register, but the register may not delay grant of letters for more than ten days thereafter or ten days after the filing of a petition for letters, whichever is later, unless a bond is given for payment of any costs which may be decreed against the caveator: PEF 906. During the ten-day period the register is without capacity to grant letters: *Phillip Est.*, 293 Pa. 351. Cf. *Sheerin v. Beattie*, 365 Pa. 510, annot. in *Fiduc. Rev.* Jan. 1951, p. 3.

Following receipt of a caveat, the register will appoint a time for hearing the claims of all applicants. The caveat may be followed by a more complete petition at or before the hearing, depending upon the requirements of the register. A party dissatisfied with the register's appointment (regardless of whether he had earlier filed a caveat) may appeal therefrom within one year to the orphans' court: PEF 908; *Buck Est.*, 14 Fiduc. Rep. 201. In some instances, the register (without deciding the issue) may certify, or the orphans' court may direct him to certify, the entire record to the orphans' court division for its determination: see *Fiduc. Rev.* Feb. 1961, p. 2; *Milgrom Will*, 13 Fiduc. Rep. 153; *Lockett Will*, 13 Fiduc.

Rep. 160. No letters pendente lite may be granted without leave of court once the record has been certified to the orphans' court. See Section 3.13.

Letters of administration may not be collaterally attacked: *Chambers v. Bash, Jr.*, 30 Fiduc. Rep. 456.

For discussion of will contest, see Chapter 17.

## § 3.10 BOND REQUIRED—CHANGING THE AMOUNT THEREOF

An individual who is a resident of Pennsylvania and is either the sole next of kin or the nominee of all next of kin who are adult and sui juris need not give a bond before obtaining letters of administration: PEF 3174(b). See *Fiduc. Rev.* April 1982. Any other individual not named in the will as a personal representative must execute and file a bond before letters will be granted to him. No bond is required of resident corporate fiduciaries and of foreign corporate fiduciaries in states which have enacted reciprocal exemptions to Pennsylvania corporate fiduciaries: PEF 3174(a). The court upon application may direct a surety bond or increase or decrease the amount of an existing bond: PEF 3175. For discussion of whether a bond should be required of administrators in absence of a request therefor, see *Fiduc. Rev.* Oct. 1976, p. 4. Should the register grant letters without the required bond, both the register and his surety become liable to pay all damages which accrue to anyone by reason thereof: PEF 3172.

The bond, executed on a form supplied by the register, is in the name of the Commonwealth "with sufficient surety, in such amount as the register considers necessary, having regard to the value of the personal estate" only. The bond is customarily twice the estimated value of the personal estate, and either a corporate surety or two individuals usually serve as surety. In the case of individual sureties, at least one of them should own real estate sufficient in value above encumbrances to meet the penal amount of the bond. The condition of the bond depends on whether there is more than one administrator: PEF 3171. The purpose of the distinction is to ensure that an administrator will not be liable as surety for his co-administrator. Since no bond is required with respect to real estate, the statute provides that no proceeds of sale of real estate may be paid to a personal representative who has been required to give bond "until the court has made an order excusing him from entering additional security or requiring additional security, and in the latter event, only after he has entered additional security": PEF 3351. See generally *Fiduc. Rev.* May 1962.

Although the amount of bond is required to be fixed in the first instance by the register and cannot be determined by the court before grant of letters (*Stuckert Est.*, 3 Fiduc. Rep. 179), the court upon cause shown has power to increase or decrease the amount of the bond already fixed: PEF 3175; cf. *Pantazis v. Fidelity & Deposit Co. of Maryland*, 369 Pa. 221; *Patterson Est.*, 5 Fiduc. Rep. 122. For form of petition, see Aker, PEF Code Annot. § 3175; Partridge-Remick, O.C. Practice § 7.07. Since bonds are conditional upon the personal representative's performance of his duties, without regard to particular assets, it is customary for the court to require that, if possible, the surety on any additional bond be the same as on the original bond: cf. Montg. O.C. Rule 12.10 C. Additional bond may be required by the court upon application: *Twining Est.*, 8 Fiduc. Rep. 224. For rights and duties of a surety, see PEF Code, Chapt. 45; *Commonwealth v. Aetna Casualty & Surety Co.*, 11 Cumb. 162; cf. *Marshall Est.*, 403 Pa. 348.

When the decedent was a fiduciary, the register in his discretion, upon application of any party in interest, may require that a separate bond be given by the personal representative, with sufficient surety to safeguard property of such estate or trust: PEF 3173.

## § 3.11 OATH OF ADMINISTRATOR

Before letters may be granted to a personal representative, an oath must be administered to him by the register that he will "well and truly administer the estate according to law": PEF 3161. Failure to make such an oath would not per se void the letters granted, but "persistent neglect or refusal of an administrator would justify an order" revoking such letters (*Beeber Ap.*, 99 Pa. 596), especially if a bond also were not given: *Henry Est.*, 30 Dist. 945. The oath of a corporate personal representative may be given by any of its officers: PEF 3161. The oath is administered on the form supplied by the register, which recites that the personal representative will "well and truly administer the estate according to law."

## § 3.12 GRANT OF LETTERS; SHORT CERTIFICATE

When the petition for letters, renunciations (if required), bond (if required) with surety and oath of office have been received and filed, the appropriate fees of the register paid, and the caveats (if any) disposed of, the register will grant letters of administration in the form required to the person entitled: PEF 3155(b). The document, issued over the register's seal, states that the register thereby grants to the designated person letters of administration. The grant of letters is a judicial act and will not be set aside in a collateral proceeding, *Freer Est.*, 353 Pa. 351, annot. *Fiduc. Rev.* Feb. 1946; *West v. Young*, 332 Pa. 248, 251. As already stated, the grant of letters in one county is exclusive throughout the Commonwealth: PEF 3151; *Brown Est.*, 105 Pa. Super. 236. Hence the appointment of a personal representative in more than one county is neither required nor permitted. Letters testamentary issued in another county automatically supersede letters of administration issued earlier or on the same day: *Jackson Est.*, 35 Dauph. 432.

The administrator has no powers in any state other than in the state of his appointment, except as he may be given them by the statute of the other state. Consequently, if the decedent left assets in more than one state, it is frequently necessary for an administrator to be appointed in each such state. See Section 3.16.

The letters granted to the administrator are his official certificate. Since it is frequently necessary for him to evidence his authority with numerous people and institutions to collect and deal with estate assets, provision is made for issuance of "short certificates" which state in brief language over the seal of the register that the designated person has been named administrator and that his letters have not been revoked. "Short certificates" can be obtained in any number at any time for a modest charge. If a period of time has elapsed since their issuance, persons relying upon them may insist on certificates with a current date of issuance. This can be accomplished by having the register stamp a current date on the certificates earlier issued. Since there is often a charge for such updating, it is unwise to order more short certificates than will be needed for current use.

## § 3.13 TEMPORARY LETTERS

When the decedent's will is contested (see generally Chapter 17), it frequently becomes necessary to appoint an administrator pendente lite to protect the assets of the estate pending the outcome of the litigation. Cf. Section 3.2; PEF 3160. It is not an abuse of discretion for the register to appoint as administrator pendente lite a bank named as coexecutor in the contested will where such bank was also named co-executor in an earlier will which the contestant is seeking to establish: *Townsend Est.*, 16 Fiduc. Rep. 250. The primary duty of such an administrator is to file an inventory, care for the assets and collect debts. Seldom does his authority extend to the payment of creditors, never to distribution: *Katz Est.*, 49 D. & C. 215; *Fiduc. Rev.* Aug. 1959. No letters pendente lite may be granted without leave of court once the record has been certified to the court: PEF 907; cf. Section 3.9. The grant of letters testamentary by the register automatically revokes the authority of the administrator pendente lite, even though there is an appeal being taken from probate. *Gorsuch Est. (No. 1)*, 7 Fiduc. Rep. 31. When there is no need for further administration, the balance accounted for by the administrator pendente lite may be awarded directly to the distributees: *Pozner Est.*, 17 Fiduc. Rep. 220. See Administrator Pendente Lite—Appointment, Powers, Duties, Liabilities, Discharge, *Fiduc. Rev.* Aug. 1959.

An attorney, appointed administrator pendente lite, acted properly in employing legal counsel and in proceeding with exceptional caution in keeping all parties in interest informed as to what was being done in the administration of the estate. Expenditures made in preparing real estate for sale were approved as were substantial copying and mailing costs and the fees of the administrator and counsel: *Oberrender Est.*, 29 Fiduc. Rep. 87, annot. *Fiduc. Rev.* May 1979, p. 4.

An administrator pendente lite is not required to have an interest in the estate. *Witherspoon Est.*, 30 Fiduc. Rep. 2d 423, annot. *Fiduc. Rev.* Nov. 2010, p. 2.

When the next of kin of an intestate are minors, temporary letters may be granted by the register of wills to "any fit person or persons, after such notice, if any, as the register shall require." PEF 3160. Application may be made by any party in interest, and the register of wills is not limited in his appointment to the order of preference indicated by PEF 3155(b). Security is required as in other cases. Such letters are called "durante minoritate." The duties of such an administrator are generally similar to those of an administrator pendente lite. The appointment terminates upon the coming of age of the eldest next of kin, at which time the temporary administrator should file his account and the amount so determined be turned over under a proper award to the administrator.

When the next of kin are absent from the jurisdiction and cannot return within a reasonable time, temporary letters durante absentia will be granted upon appropriate application to any fit person as in the case of letters durante minoritate: PEF 3160. The duties of such a temporary administrator cease with the return of the next of kin and qualification thereof as administrator.

Chapter 43 of the PEF Code sets forth provisions for appointment of temporary fiduciaries if "any fiduciary is in military service, in other government service, in a position of conflicting interest or in any situation where his functioning as a fiduciary for a temporary period may not be in the best interests of the estate." An example of such an appointment is *Smith Est.*, 29 Fiduc. Rep. 175, where the widow-executrix had elected against the will and it was to her interest to have stock valued for death tax purposes at a value which would reduce capital gain tax payable by her individually, the court appointed an administrator pro tem under PEF 4301(2) to negotiate liability of estate for federal estate and state death taxes. In "all other respects the duties and powers" of the executrix were directed to "remain as heretofore."

## § 3.14 REVOCATION OF LETTERS AND THE EFFECT THEREOF

"The register may revoke letters of administration[1] granted by him whenever it appears that the person to whom letters were granted is not entitled thereto": PEF 3181(a). This may be done in instances when letters were originally granted without notice to others having a superior or equal right thereto, and the action of the register in revoking letters will not be set aside on appeal, except for abuse of discretion. *Nearhoof Est.*, 6 Fiduc. Rep. 209; *Buell Est.*, 2 Fiduc. Rep. 10. The most frequent occasion for revoking letters of administration is the discovery of a will: *Waltz's Ap.*, 242 Pa. 167. However, letters of administration should not be revoked and the will probated without first giving proper notice to the administrator, his surety and other parties in interest: *McQuade Est.*, 1 Fiduc. Rep. 579; cf. *Riggin Est.*, 16 Fiduc. Rep. 431; *Mullen Est.*, 22 Fiduc. Rep. 639; see generally Section 17.5.

The procedure for securing revocation of letters is by a petition for citation filed with the register, to which an answer can be filed. For form of petition, see Partridge-Remick, O.C. Practice §§ 2.07, 8.05. Thereafter, the issue will be decided by the register. In appropriate circumstances, the court will revoke the grant of letters of administration without requiring that application therefor be first directed to the reg-

**§ 3.14**

1. But not letters testamentary: PEF 3181(b).

ister: *Lowry Est.*, 2 Fiduc. Rep. 2d 403, annot. *Fiduc. Rev.* Dec. 1982, p. 4.

PEF 3329 provides that "No act of administration performed by a personal representative in good faith shall be impeached by the subsequent revocation of his letters or by the subsequent probate of a will, of a later will or of a codicil: Provided, That regardless of the good or bad faith of the personal representative, no person who deals in good faith with a duly qualified personal representative shall be prejudiced by the subsequent occurrence of any of these contingencies." That third persons can rely on the authority of the administrator to act for the estate until his letters are revoked is further emphasized by three other statutory provisions. PEF 908(c) states that "no appeal from a decree of the register shall suspend the powers or prejudice the acts of" the personal representative to whom letters have been granted. *Kravitz Est.*, 9 Fiduc. Rep. 425; *Abercrombie Est.*, 9 Fiduc. Rep. 539 (O.C. Allegh.). PEF 3357 provides that sales, mortgages and conveyances made by a personal representative shall not be prejudiced by the terms of a will thereafter probated or by the revocation of letters. PEF 793 provides that an appeal to an appellate court shall not suspend the powers or prejudice the acts of the personal representative.

## § 3.15 REMOVAL, DEATH OR DISCHARGE

The court has exclusive power to remove a personal representative who is unfit or who is improperly managing the estate. The specific grounds for removal and the procedure to be followed, whether the action be summary or upon petition with notice, are outlined in some detail in PEF 3182 and 3183. Examination of these sections and of the cases decided thereunder discloses that the court has adequate power to remove a personal representative whenever it is essential for the estate that he be removed: *Gontovich Est.*, 14 Fiduc. Rep. 582; *Quinlan Est.*, 441 Pa. 266; cf. *DiMario Est.*, 435 Pa. 428; *Costello Est. (No. 2)*, 28 Fiduc. Rep. 515; see 3 Hunter O.C. Commonplace Book (2d ed.), Fiduciaries, § 12(b). For circumstances where personal representative was removed, see

*Sloan Est.*, 25 Fiduc. Rep. 324 (failure to carry out duties and hostility to sole beneficiary); *Roadcap Est.*, 26 Fiduc. Rep. 26 (conflicting interests). Conviction of administratrix for minor crimes connected with drugs was no basis for her removal where the crimes had no bearing on her honesty and ability to administer the estate: *Scavello Est.*, 70 D. & C. 2d 615. The court will act summarily when occasion demands: *Gernand Est.*, 8 Fiduc. Rep. 395. Summary removal may take the form of a revocation of letters improperly obtained by the administrator: *Lowry Est.*, 2 Fiduc. Rep. 2d 403, annot. *Fiduc. Rev. Dec.* 1982, p. 4. Any orders or decrees necessary to protect estate assets made in connection with the removal can be enforced under the powers granted to the court in PEF 781 through 786. Compensation may be awarded to counsel for a personal representative who has been removed: *Taulane Est.*, 408 Pa. 19.

When an entire vacancy occurs in the office of personal representative before the administration of an intestate estate is completed, the register is required to grant letters of administration d.b.n. to the person entitled thereto: PEF 3159. See Sections 3.2, 3.4. An administrator d.b.n. has power to recover the assets of the estate from his predecessor in administration, or from the personal representative of such predecessor, and he stands in the predecessor's stead for all purposes, except that he is not personally liable for his predecessor's acts: PEF 3326. It should be noted that the personal representative of a deceased fiduciary does not succeed to the administration of any asset of an estate which was being administered by his decedent except to protect it pending its delivery to the person entitled. The court may direct the personal representative of a deceased fiduciary to make distribution and to make the transfers and assignments necessary to carry into effect a decree of distribution: PEF 3324. Similar provision is made for situations in which the personal representative is adjudged incapacitated.

The termination of the administrator's duties or the approval of his final account does not operate as an automatic discharge of the personal representative or relieve him from responsibility as to anything not embraced in his accounting.

See Chapter 15. An individual administrator who has given surety and wishes to be relieved from future liability may take appropriate steps to be discharged as provided by PEF 3184. Rule 12.7 of the Supreme Court Orphans' Court Rules outlines the minimum requirements of the petition which may be filed by a fiduciary and his surety, or by the surety alone. Provision for discharge of the surety alone, as authorized by PEF 3184, as well as by the Supreme Court Orphans' Court Rules, makes it possible to eliminate the cost of continuing the surety bond while at the same time rendering it possible for the personal representative to continue to act for the estate; for example, to execute papers or conclude ministerial acts in order to perfect transfers made during administration. When the surety but not the personal representative is discharged, the personal representative is not entitled to receive further assets until he files another bond with sufficient surety, as required by the register.

## § 3.16 ANCILLARY ADMINISTRATION

Since the administrator is the "hand of the court" that appoints him, his powers necessarily stop at state lines.

When the decedent is a resident of Pennsylvania and leaves property outside the state, it is sometimes necessary to have an ancillary administrator appointed in the foreign jurisdiction. Except in a state which requires that a personal representative be a person residing in that state, or a corporate fiduciary authorized to do business in that state, the Pennsylvania personal representative can be appointed ancillary administrator. However, in many instances the Pennsylvania personal representative is permitted by the laws of the foreign jurisdiction to take the required action without first securing ancillary letters. Cf. PEF Chapt. 41 for comparable Pennsylvania law.

The expenses of ancillary administration may be such that it should be avoided. If the assets in the foreign jurisdiction are not substantial, it may be to the advantage of the estate in some instances to abandon them. Cf. PEF 3312. See

*Parkhurst Est.*, 8 Fiduc. Rep. 442, refusing a foreign fiduciary permission to obtain Pennsylvania assets naming Pennsylvanians as surviving joint tenants. And see *Fiduc. Rev.* April 1961, concerning the grant of ancillary (or "non-domiciliary") letters in Pennsylvania; 39 Trust Bull. 30 (June, 1960) regarding problems in administration and estate planning where assets are located in several states. For refusal to audit account of administrator c.t.a. who obtained letters based on manufactured jurisdiction, see *Grimani Est.*, 1 Fiduc. Rep. 2d 204. As to claims in ancillary administration, see Section 10.15; as to distribution by Pennsylvania ancillary personal representative, see Section 16.35.

## § 3.17 FOREIGN PERSONAL REPRESENTATIVE

See the discussion in Section 5.9, which is equally applicable to an administrator appointed in a foreign jurisdiction.

# Chapter 4

# PROBATE OF WILLS



## § 4.1 NECESSITY FOR PROBATE

Probate establishes that the decedent's will has been duly executed, published and attested as required by law, and that the testator was of sound and disposing mind. Without probate it is not a will in the legal sense (*Toner v. Taggart*, 5 Binn. 489), and it has no effect as an instrument of title or for vesting powers in the executor. Hence probate is a prerequisite to the grant of letters testamentary. The probate of wills is governed primarily by PEF Code Chapter 9 and Chapter 31, Subchapter C.

The executor or executors named in the will are generally the person or persons who initiate its probate, although they are under no legal duty so to do, either at common law or by statute: *Yontz v. Yontz*, 42 D. & C. 182. Probate also may be initiated by any party in interest.

In many instances the probate of a will is neither necessary nor advisable. Care should therefore be exercised at the outset to determine whether a will should be probated. See Chapter 2. When title to real estate is involved, it is sometimes advisable to probate the will but not to petition for letters. See Section 2.3.

It has been held that a revocable trust to which a will poured over must be probated to commence the one-year appeal period limitation. *Estate of Pew*, 655 A.2d 521; *Estate of Newhart*, 833 A.2d 1153, annot. *Fiduc. Rev.* Oct. 2003, p.1. However, the official comment to PEF 7754 notes ". . . this subchapter is intended to eliminate any need to probate the trust instrument . . .". See *Fiduc. Rev.*, Nov. 2011, p. 4.

## § 4.2 FACT OF DEATH

The fact of death is a prerequisite to probate proceedings. See Section 3.3. It is normal practice to refuse probate of a will until the decedent has been buried. In absence of unusual circumstances, the registers of many counties accept the petitioner's allegation of death as adequate proof thereof. However, in many other counties (e.g., Montgomery and Philadelphia) a death certificate is a prerequisite for probate of the will or grant of letters.

## § 4.3 PRODUCTION OF WILL AND RELATED DOCUMENTS

The foundation of the probate proceeding is the will itself, and it is therefore obvious that the first step is to produce the will and related documents before the register. Usually production of the will is accomplished without difficulty. If the personal representative has the will in his possession, he should produce it, and if in the custody of another, he should obtain possession of it or compel its delivery to the register. Anyone having custody of testamentary papers is legally bound to produce them for probate and can be compelled to do so by the register of wills: PEF 903(1), 905, 3137; *Clunen Est.*, 34 D. & C. 490; *Fiduc. Rev.* Nov. 1954, p. 3. See generally Partridge-Remick, O.C. Practice §§ 3.03–3.05. It should be noted that any person who with intent to injure anyone "destroys, removes or conceals any will" is guilty of "a felony of the third degree" and as such could be subject to an imprisonment of up to seven years and a fine of not more than $15,000. Crimes Code, 18 Pa. C.S. §§ 4103, 1101(2) and 1103(3).

## § 4.4 DOCUMENTS WHICH CONSTITUTE A WILL

(1) *Incorporation by reference.* As stated in Section 1.2, a will may include prior wills partially or ineffectively revoked, codicils and memoranda not duly executed but which are a part of the will by virtue of "incorporation by reference." *Dreisbach Est.*, 384 Pa. 535; *Fiduc. Rev.* April 1959, p. 3; cf. *Clapphanson Est.*, 9 Fiduc. Rep. 328. It is essential that all documents purporting to dispose of the decedent's property be carefully scrutinized with a view to determining which ones should be offered for probate: *Callin Est.*, 12 Fiduc. Rep. 92; *Meyer Est.*, 17 Fiduc. Rep. 454; cf. *Wright Trust*, 12 Fiduc. Rep. 158. Where the apparently testamentary writings consist of unconnected sheets found either loose or in an envelope, it is most important for care to be exercised in noting the order of the several pages and refraining from disturbing such order: see *Van Gilder Est.*, 421 Pa. 520, annot. *Fiduc. Rev.* June 1966. In *Nicholas Est.*, 86 Montg. 49, a will was construed solely by its own language unaffected by a "letter of instruction" written by the decedent to his attorney after he executed his will but before he executed a codicil. Cf. *Azinger Will*, 1 Fiduc. Rep. 2d 325, annot. *Fiduc. Rev.* Sept. 1981, p. 4. Documents (such as a trust to which will assets pour over) incorporated by reference in a will should be submitted for probate. *Pew Trust*, 440 Pa. Super. 195, 665 A.2d 52.

(2) *Old wills or codicils.* Even an old will or codicil is important, for frequently such a document may have been re-

voked ineffectively or only in part. Sometimes also an old will that has been revoked will be republished or revived in whole or in part by a subsequent instrument: see *Houlihan Will*, 10 Fiduc. Rep. 660, annot. *Fiduc. Rev*. Jan. 1961, p. 3; *Kretz Trust*, 410 Pa. 590, annot. *Fiduc. Rev*. Nov. 1963. See *Johnson Est.*, 435 Pa. 303, annot. *Fiduc. Rev*. Aug. 1969, p. 3 to the effect that a second codicil expressly ratifying and republishing a will, but omitting any mention of a first or intermediate codicil, nevertheless republishes the will with every codicil which has been added to it, unless there is evidence of a clear contrary intention. If the documents to be offered for probate contain deletions or interlineations, such changes or attempted revocations may bring into play the doctrine of "dependent relative revocation." *Braun Est.*, 358 Pa. 271, annot. *Fiduc. Rev*. Feb. 1948; *Shelly Will*, 484 Pa. 322; 82 Dick L.R. 305; *Fiduc. Rev*. Sept. 1971; Aker, Law of Wills in Pennsylvania, § 4.13. Careful consideration should be given to writings which at first glance might not appear to be wills, such as bank account signature cards (*Bartkus Est.*, 17 Fiduc. Rep. 364, annot. *Fiduc. Rev*. Aug. 1967, p. 4) and beneficiary forms under employment plans: *Blair Est.*, 17 Fiduc. Rep. 231, annot. *Fiduc. Rev*. May 1967, p. 4. Extrinsic evidence may establish that a note giving directions to a relative is a will: *Sedmak Est.*, 467 Pa. 379; *Laurin Will*, 492 Pa. 477. Writings signed informally such as "mother" may be a will; *Heffner Will*, 1 Fiduc. Rep. 2d 300.

A review of the document or documents which purport to be the decedent's will may disclose that none of them is entitled to probate because improperly executed: *Pavlinko Will*, 394 Pa. 564, annot. *Fiduc. Rev*. Feb. 1959, p. 3, 107 U. of Pa. L. Rev. 1237; *Glace Will*, 413 Pa. 91; 67 Iowa L.R. 205. For validity of a will on which signature is pasted, see *Wells Will*, 15 Fiduc. Rep. 557, annot. *Fiduc. Rev*. Nov. 1965, p. 3. See also Section 17.4. Concerning the location of the testator's signature, see *Miller Will*, 414 Pa. 385, annot. *Fiduc. Rev*. June 1964; *Proley Will*, 30 Fiduc. Rep. 74, aff'd 492 Pa. 57, annot. *Fiduc. Rev*. Feb. 1981, p. 4. Special problems exist in the probate of wills executed by mark (*Fiduc. Rev*. Nov. 1977, p. 4; *Bottari Will*, 2 Fiduc. Rep. 2d 246; *Kajut Will*, 2 Fiduc. Rep. 2d 197) or by a blind person: *Kajut Will*, 2 Fiduc.

Rep. 2d 197, annot. *Fiduc. Rev.* June 1983. For possible liability of attorney when will has been improperly executed, see *Fiduc. Rev.* Jan. 1980, Oct. 1982, July 1983.

If the will, duly executed, names an executor (or testamentary guardian, *Pagel, Minor*, 8 Fiduc. Rep. 338), but is totally ineffective to dispose of the decedent's property, probate may nevertheless proceed: *Sando Will*, 362 Pa. 1; cf. *Fiduc. Rev.* Sept. 1955; Oct. 1981, p. 4.

There is authority to delete libelous material in the probate of the will and impound the original will: *Schell Will*, 10 Fiduc. Rep. 123, annot. *Fiduc. Rev.* Feb. 1960; 32 Pa. Bar Assn. Q. 248.

(3) *Copy fair—Cancellations and interlineations.* Since the probate record must set forth the wording accepted by the register as the will of the testator, it should show clearly how the register has dealt with the items submitted for probate. This is especially important in the case of cancellations and interlineations. As to these, a record should be made of all pertinent facts, such as whose handwriting is involved, where the will was kept or found, and who other than the testator had access to it. As suggested in *Rockett Will*, 348 Pa. 445, annot. *Fiduc. Rev.* Feb. 1944, a "copy fair" illustrating what constitutes the will should be made. It is appropriate for the proponent to submit a version of a "copy fair" to the register for his approval. See *Fiduc. Rev.* May 1966, p. 2, June 1966; *Werkley Will*, 27 Fiduc. Rep. 530; *Lansinger Est.*, 26 Fiduc. Rep. 554; *Lutz Est.*, 102 Montg. 293; cf. *Alwine Est.*, 28 Fiduc. Rep. 340. For finality of "copy fair" and complications which arise when the record is not clear, see *Gallagher Est.*, 485 Pa. 61, annot. *Fiduc. Rev.* June 1979, p. 4.

## § 4.5 PROOF OF LOST WILLS OR PARTS THEREOF

If a will cannot be produced because it is lost, or accidentally mutilated or destroyed, or destroyed maliciously by one other than the testator, it nevertheless may be entitled to probate if the following can be proven: (1) the will was duly executed by one having testamentary capacity, (2) a diligent search has been made since the testator's death and the will has not been found, and (3) the contents of the will are as stated. These matters must be proved by two witnesses, "each of whom must separately depose to all the facts necessary to complete the chain of evidence, so that no link in it may depend on the credibility of but one": *Hodgson Est.*, 270 Pa. 210, 213; *Fiduc. Rev.* Jan. 1956, p. 3. In addition to proof of execution and contents, it is incumbent on the proponent to overcome the presumption that the will which cannot be found was revoked by the decedent, and it must therefore be shown that someone other than the testator destroyed it, or that the decedent did not have access to it, or that the decedent made statements up until the time of his death indicating continued existence of the will: *Dalbey Est.*, 326 Pa. 286; *O'Neill Est.*, 58 D. & C. 351; *Tribit Est.*, 2 Fiduc. Rep. 213; Brégy, Intestate, Wills and Estates Acts of 1947, p. 2313; Hunter, Lost Wills; *McCaffrey Will*, 16 Fiduc. Rep. 604, annot. *Fiduc. Rev.* Jan. 1967, p. 3, 22 Fiduc. Rep. 551, annot. *Fiduc. Rev.* Oct. 1972, rev'd 453 Pa. 416; *Walters Will*, 26 Fiduc. Rep. 2d 397, annot. *Fiduc. Rev.* Oct. 2006, p. 4; *Banus Will*, 27 Fiduc. Rep. 2d 341; *Yeager Est.*, 3 Fiduc. Rep. 386, cf. *Scheib Will*, 11 Fiduc. Rep. 132. See 75 Harv. L. Rev. 432 regarding probate of an accidentally destroyed will.

See also *Lockett Will*, 13 Fiduc. Rep. 160, refusing probate of a duplicate original of a will, and imposing the costs on the widow-caveator where there was "room for suspicion" that she destroyed the original will. An unopened envelope given to a friend to hold contained only a copy of the will. Since there was no explanation concerning the missing original which had been in testator's possession, probate of the copy was reversed. *Leone Will*, 2 Fiduc. Rep. 3d 189, annot. *Fiduc. Rev.* June 2012, p. 4. In *Ervien Will*, 427 Pa. 64, probate of a conformed but unsigned copy of a will executed by the decedent in 1956 was sustained, even though witnesses had not seen it following its execution. The evidence was held to have rebutted the presumption that the testatrix revoked the original, which was apparently inadvertently destroyed when she moved from her home to an apartment.

If a page or other part of a will is missing, a similar problem arises, and the foregoing discussion is applicable.

It is not permissible to show by oral testimony against an existing will in writing that there was another will which has been lost and which revoked the existing will: *Ewing Est.*, 498 Pa. 141. A writing declaring the revocation must be produced: *Koehler Est.*, 316 Pa. 321; *Shetter Est.*, 303 Pa. 193; cf. *Fiduc. Rev.* Jan. 1961, p. 3; *Fisher Est.*, 13 Fiduc. Rep. 530. See *Florish Will*, 16 Fiduc. Rep. 443, annot. *Fiduc. Rev.* Sept. 1966, where an unsigned carbon copy of a will, the execution of the original of which was proven by testimony, was held sufficient to revoke an earlier will and thereby result in the estate passing by intestacy. See *Leonard Est.*, 427 Pa. 363, annot. *Fiduc. Rev.* Jan. 1968, p. 4, following the rule of *Koehler Estate* and *Shetter Estate* in a situation where the alleged lost will would have, if properly proven, revoked an earlier will containing charitable bequests, which was relied upon to sustain similar charitable gifts in the last will executed within thirty days of death. An earlier will cannot be probated even though the later signed will has not been probated: *Clark Will*, 25 Fiduc. Rep. 457. See *McCaffrey Will*, 22 Fiduc. Rep. 551, annot. *Fiduc. Rev.* Oct. 1972 (rev'd 453 Pa. 416), regarding conformed copy of lost will which revoked a prior will and the utility of parol evidence. However, revocation of later will does not revive earlier will: *Entinger Will*, 471 Pa. 118, 369 A.2d 1223, aff'g per cur. 26 Fiduc. Rep. 412.

## § 4.6 WILLS IN A FOREIGN LANGUAGE

If a will, codicil or other testamentary document is written in any language other than the English language, a sworn translation must be attached to the original and both filed together: PEF 3135. The correctness of the translation is a question of distribution and not of probate: cf. *Harris Estate*, 351 Pa. 368; *Lipman Est.*, 31 D. & C. 122. See *Mannarelli Est.*, 436 Pa. 141, where writings partly in Italian and partly in English were held not to constitute a will, because by their terms they were clearly not a testamentary disposition.

## § 4.7 WHERE WILL MUST BE PROBATED

If the decedent was domiciled in Pennsylvania, jurisdiction of the probate of the will is in the register of wills in the county where the decedent had his "last family or principal residence." If the decedent was not domiciled in Pennsylvania, then the "will may be probated before the register of any county where any of his property is located": PEF 3131. Compare *Melesky Est.*, 26 Fiduc. Rep. 2d 257 where probate occurred in Maine where decedent's real property and most of her personal property was located and the Orphans' Court which had determined her to be a domiciliary of Chester County granted deference to that probate.

The domicile of the decedent therefore plays a critical role in determining the jurisdiction of the register of wills and the place of probate: see *Finkel Est.*, 42 Wash. 37. The evidentiary factors to be weighed and considered in determining domicile can entail a vexatious problem: cf. *Publicker Est.*, 385 Pa. 403; *Dorrance Est.*, 309 Pa. 151; *McFadden Will*, 177 Pa. Super. 37. In general, domicile is acquired by actual residence in a given place, coupled with the intention to reside there. When once acquired, it continues until by free choice another is substituted therefor: *Loudenslager Will*, 430 Pa. 33. For change of residence when decedent is located elsewhere because of illness or has insufficient mental capacity to change domicile, see *Mader Est.*, 16 Fiduc. Rep. 81, aff'd per cur. 423 Pa. 639, annot. *Fiduc. Rev.* March 1967, p. 4. For jurisdiction when decedent had moved to a retirement home (*Schellentrager Will*, 30 Fiduc. Rep. 169) or nursing home (*Urban Will*, 2 Fiduc. Rep. 2d 313), see *Fiduc. Rev.* Nov. 1982, p. 3, April 1983, p. 3.

A person cannot, by any wish, declaration or intent, inconsistent with the dominant facts of where he actually lives and what he actually means to do, retain a domicile in one place when he has moved to another and intends to reside there indefinitely: *Dowling Est.*, 12 Bucks 439. If doubt as to domicile appears, a careful investigation should be made immediately to determine the facts. A recital in a will setting forth the domicile of the decedent is given little or no weight in comparison with the evidence supplied by the daily life of the individual and his acts and conduct: *Leser Est.*, 10 Fiduc. Rep. 411; *Dreer Est.*, 9 Fiduc. Rep. 660.

The register of wills may not appeal if the will is probated in another county (*Cameron Est.*, 12 Fiduc. Rep. 586), but a party in interest may do so (*Burke Est.*, 1 Fiduc. Rep. 260).

In the statutory phrase "last family or principal residence," the terms "family" and "principal" are not used alternatively, but as explanatory of one another (*Gundy Est.*, 37 Berks 37), and the word "residence" is synonymous with domicile as opposed to temporary residence (*Obici Est.*, 373 Pa. 567; *Corne Est.*, 66 York 22; *Frazier Est.*, 75 D. & C. 577).

## § 4.8 MANNER OF PROBATE

Probate proceedings are begun by a petition to the register, generally on a printed form which he supplies, signed and sworn to by the applicant and setting forth the age, domicile and residence of the decedent, the place and day of his death, the estimated value of his property, the location of his real estate and whether or not he was married, divorced or had children born or adopted after the execution of the will, also whether he was the victim of a killing or was ever adjudicated incompetent. Usually, the petition for probate is also a petition for the grant of letters testamentary. The Supreme Court Orphans' Court Rules include approved forms to be employed by Registers of Wills. See *Fiduc. Rev.* June 1979. See § 3.4 concerning computer-assisted probate in some counties. Ordinarily, the proceeding before the register is informal, but it becomes complicated if a caveat is filed.[1] See Chapter 17.

It is necessary to prove that the instrument or instruments offered for probate were executed by the decedent. The requirements as to valid execution are set forth in PEF 2502 and 3132. *Pendergrass Will*, 30 Fiduc. Rep. 2d 430, annot. *Fid. Rev.* Oct. 2010, p. 3 determined that signature by

---

§ 4.8

1. Questions as to the validity of the will prior to probate are raised through a caveat requesting the register not to probate a will or grant letters testamentary: PEF 906.

an agent under a power of attorney did not qualify. See *Fiduc. Rev.* April 2012, p. 3. Appeal quashed 26 A.3d 1151.

A will is "proved" by the oaths or affirmations of two competent witnesses who appear before the register: PEF 2504. Subscribing witnesses to the will are normally called upon and are preferred to the extent they are readily available: PEF 3132(1). See § 4.10, infra, for "self-proved" wills which do not require the attendance of the witnesses before the register, absent a will contest. Procedures exist for compelling the attendance of witnesses and also for taking their depositions: PEF 903; Partridge-Remick, O.C. Practice § 3.08. Most registers will send deputies outside their offices for probate upon payment of additional fees. If the subscribing witnesses cannot be found, or if they are unable to attend because of absence from the jurisdiction, the testator's signature may be proved by others without resort to proof of the witnesses' signatures: PEF 3132(1).

When a will is signed by a mark or by another on behalf of the testator, the will must be proved by the subscribing witnesses, unless the register is satisfied that such proof cannot be adduced. In that event, other proof of the execution of the will may be accepted, and proof of the signature of a witness who has subscribed to an attestation clause is prima facie proof of the facts there recited: PEF 3132(2). See Brégy, Intestate, Wills and Estates Acts of 1947, § 4.2(b). In the event of contest, the procedure before the register is as outlined in Chapter 17. For discussion of writings which should be probated, see Section 4.4. For discussion of procedures for probating will and codicils—and the rules applicable where the subscribing witnesses to the codicil are not the same as those to the will, see *Fiduc. Rev.* Nov. 1972, p. 3.

## § 4.9 LIMITATION OF TIME FOR PROBATE

A will may be offered for probate at any time (PEF 3133(a))[1] but a will that is not offered for probate within one

§ **4.9**

**1.** If a will has been previously probated and one year has elapsed, the right to probate a later will may be barred: see Chapter 17.

year of the testator's death has no effect upon a bona fide conveyance or mortgage of real estate of the decedent recorded prior thereto: PEF 3133(c). It is no longer possible to prove a nuncupative (oral) will.

## § 4.10 SELF-PROVED WILLS

The concept of a self-proved will originated from the Uniform Probate Code (§ 2-504). It permits probate in uncontested cases without the required attendance of the subscribing witnesses before the register of wills. It was adopted in Pennsylvania in 1976 by the addition of section 3132.1 to the PEF Code which includes a suggested form, amended in 1982 to remove any suggestion that three witnesses are required and amended in 1984 to provide that wills signed by mark or by another do not qualify as self-proved wills. Acknowledgment of testator and affidavit of witnesses may be taken before an attorney-at-law pursuant to the Uniform Acknowledgment Act. See *Fiduc. Rev.* July 1976 and *Flynn Will*, 2 Fiduc. Rep. 2d 124, annot. *Fiduc. Rev.* May 1982, for an understanding of its origin and its operation.

## § 4.11 DECREE OF PROBATE

If the will has been duly proved, and no question raised at the hearing as to its validity, a decree of probate will be entered. This is so even though the will contains not a single dispositive provision capable of being carried out: cf. *Sherman Est.*, 5 Fiduc. Rep. 497, annot. *Fiduc. Rev.* Sept. 1955; Section 4.4.

A register, in deciding whether to probate or refuse probate of a will, acts as a judge, and the admission of a will to probate is a judicial act: see *Szmahl Est.*, 335 Pa. 89. Once a will has been probated or refused probate, the decree establishes conclusively the validity or invalidity of the will: PEF 3133(b). The decree in absence of fraud can be attacked only by an appeal to the court within one year of its entry (*Farley Will*, 1 Fiduc. Rep. 2d 49), and it is not subject to collateral attack: *Mangold v. Neuman*, 371 Pa. 496. In the limited circumstances described in PEF 3138, the probate record can be opened in order to probate a will or codicil discovered after the original will has been probated, and in those limited circumstances, an appeal to the court is no longer required: see *Fiduc. Rev.* Jan. 1970, p. 4.

The personal representative has no standing to appeal, unless he is an heir or beneficiary: PEF 908. But see *Gulden Will*, 3 Fiduc. Rep. 627, annot. *Fiduc. Rev.* Dec. 1953, p. 3; *Underdown Will*, 24 Fiduc. Rep. 311. Probate, unappealed from, establishes the fact of the decedent's death and unless he was domiciled outside the Commonwealth, of his residence in the county of probate: *Freer Est.*, 353 Pa. 351, annot. *Fiduc. Rev.* Feb. 1946. Probate also establishes that it is the will of the deceased person whose estate is under consideration and that the will was duly executed in accordance with statutory requirements as to execution, capacity, proper age and freedom from undue influence: *Smith Est.*, 308 Pa. 265. See *Schell Will*, 10 Fiduc. Rep. 123, annot. *Fiduc. Rev.* Feb. 1960, regarding deletion of libelous material from a will.

It is not within the scope of the probate proceedings to construe or interpret a will or any of its provisions, or to distinguish between valid and void, feasible and impossible dispositions. These are matters for the orphans' court: see *Rockett Est.*, 48 D. & C. 6, 13–14. If, however, there is uncertainty in the probate record as to what text was in fact probated as a will—for example, whether a clause or marginal markings form part of the will—the decree of probate is equivocal and can be declared void: *Rockett Will*, 348 Pa. 445, annot. *Fiduc. Rev.* Feb. 1944; *Mayor Will*, 12 Fiduc. Rep. 151. See Section 4.4(3), supra, for "copy fair" to establish the exact wording of the probate record.

All probated wills are required to be indexed and recorded by the register and must "remain in his office, except for the period required to be in the custody of a higher court": PEF 921.

## § 4.12 REFUSAL OF PROBATE

The register may refuse probate of a proffered instrument or any part thereof: cf. *Casto Est.*, 1 Fiduc. Rep. 37.

Refusal of probate can be important in will contests because, although the fact of the probate of a will does not have any evidentiary value, it does have procedural importance in that it raises a presumption of the will's validity, and this presumption must be overcome by one seeking to attack it. *Geho Est.*, 340 Pa. 412. See Chapter 17.

## § 4.13 OPENING THE DECREE OF PROBATE

Sometimes, after the probate decree has been entered, a later will is found; more commonly, a codicil is discovered which should have been probated with the will. If the codicil is submitted to the register within three months of the death of the testator, the register after such notice as he deems advisable can open and amend the probate record: PEF 3138. Codicils offered for probate after the three-month deadline of PEF 3138 but before expiration of one year from probate may be probated. *Snyder Will*, 29 Fiduc. Rep. 2d 187, annot. *Fiduc. Rev.* Aug. 2009, p. 3. In all other circumstances, an appeal to the court must be taken to authorize the register to open the decree of probate: PEF 908; 3133(b); *Fiduc. Rev.* April 1959, p. 3, May 1966, p. 2, Jan. 1970, p. 4. The procedure therefor is similar to that followed in will contests. See Chapter 17. It should be noted that if the will first probated disposed of the decedent's entire estate, a later discovered will or codicil cannot be probated after one year from the time of original probate. Cf. Sections 4.9, 17.6.

## § 4.14 ANCILLARY PROCEEDINGS

Since the personal representative is the "hand of the court" that appoints him, his powers stop at state lines. Hence, when the testator who was a resident of Pennsylvania leaves assets in other states, it is sometimes necessary to have appointed a personal representative in such other states. What has been said with respect to ancillary administration (see Section 3.16) is also applicable when the decedent died leaving a will. See Section 5.8, infra.

## § 4.15 PROBATE OF WILL OF NONRESIDENT

When a decedent was not a Pennsylvania resident, and the grant of letters locally is necessary (such as when there are unpaid Pennsylvania creditors), probate in Pennsylvania is essential. A duly authenticated copy of the will probated in the foreign jurisdiction may be offered for probate "as though the original will had been offered before [the] register"; and if accompanied by the probate record, such a copy is entitled to probate "without the production or examination of the witnesses to prove such will": PEF 3136. If the probate record of a will probated outside of the United States discloses that an essential requirement of Pennsylvania law is missing, then such probate record may be supplemented by the submission of additional evidence. For wills not in English, see Section 4.6.

The will of a nonresident testator may be probated in Pennsylvania before it has been probated in the state of his domicile: see *Kortright Est.* (*No. 1*), 237 Pa. 138; *Lockett Will*, 13 Fiduc. Rep. 160.

See Aker, Law of Wills in Pennsylvania § 1.7, and *Mathiot Estate*, 23 Fay. 163, regarding separate wills disposing of property in different jurisdictions.

## § 4.16 CONTRACT TO WILL

While contracts to make (or refrain from making) wills to favor a contracting party are a frequent cause of litigation, which is dealt with at length in 1 Hunter O.C. Commonplace Bk. (2d ed.), Contract to Make a Will, the probate of the will cannot be restrained because of a violation of the contract, since this presents a question of distribution rather than a question of probate. See *Fiduc. Rev.* Sept. 1952, Jan. 1955. For claims under contract at audit of personal representative's account, see *Fiduc. Rev.* April 1978, Nov. 1982; *Rust Est.*, 1 Fiduc. Rep. 2d 183; *Lichtenfeld Est.*, 1 Fiduc. Rep. 2d 141. See PEF 2701 for contracts made on or after January 1, 1993 concerning succession, such as a contract to will.

# Chapter 5

# THE GRANT OF LETTERS TESTAMENTARY



## § 5.1 APPLICATION FOR LETTERS TESTAMENTARY

If it has been determined that the appointment of an executor is advisable (see Chapter 2), letters testamentary should be applied for by the executor or executors named in the will and as soon as "practicable" after the burial of the decedent (see Sections 3.1, 4.2). If no executor named in the will qualifies, letters of administration c.t.a. should be applied for. See Sections 3.1, 3.2; PEF 3158, 3325. The order of preference in granting said letters is set forth in Section 3.4. Application is made to the register of wills, usually as a part of the petition for probate,[1] and should state the facts with respect to the decedent as described below. Generally a printed form of petition will be supplied by the register. Proof of ex-

§ 5.1

1. When title to real estate is involved, it is sometimes advisable to probate the will but not to take out letters. See Sections 2.3, 2.4.

ecution of a valid will, established by the decree of probate, is a prerequisite to the granting of letters testamentary. Letters testamentary cannot be granted by the register after the expiration of twenty-one years from the decedent's death without an order of the court, upon cause shown. See Section 3.1; PEF 3152; *Miller Est.* 30 Fiduc. Rep. 391, annot. *Fiduc. Rev.* Nov. 2010, p. 1.

The executor or executors named in the will should either take out letters or renounce. He may be bound by provisions in the will specifying his compensation: *Goodhart Est.*, 12 D. & C. 2d 403; *Bell Est.*, 7 Fiduc. Rep. 1. See Section 5.3.

As in the case of letters of administration, if the decedent was domiciled in Pennsylvania, application for letters testamentary should be made to the register of the county where he had his "last family or principal residence." See Sections 3.8, 4.7; PEF 3151. If he was not domiciled in Pennsylvania, ancillary letters may be granted by the register of any county "wherein property of the estate shall be located": PEF 3151. Although the will of a nonresident decedent may be probated in any county where property is located and thus conceivably could be probated in several counties, letters granted in any county are exclusive throughout the state: PEF 3151. See Section 11.1.

The petition for letters testamentary must set forth:

(1) The decedent's name, age, state or country of domicile, last family or principal residence, and place and date of his death;

(2) Whether the decedent has married, was divorced, or has had or adopted any child since execution of his will, was the victim of a killing or was ever adjudicated incompetent.

(3) The estimated value of personal property and the estimated value and location of real property in Pennsylvania: PEF 3153.

The oath of the executor "that he will well and truly administer the estate according to law" must be taken before letters are granted: PEF 3154, 3161.

## § 5.2 RIGHT TO LETTERS TESTAMENTARY OR OF ADMINISTRATION C.T.A.; TEMPORARY LETTERS

The person or persons entitled to letters testamentary are the executor or executors named in the decedent's will. If none are named, or those named are unable or unwilling to act, an administrator c.t.a. or administrator d.b.n.c.t.a. is appointed. See Section 3.2. The first right to letters of administration c.t.a. is given to those entitled to the residuary estate under the will: PEF 3155(b); *Buck Est.*, 14 Fiduc. Rep. 201. Nonresidence of a residuary beneficiary (*Kiker Est.*, 7 Fiduc. Rep. 232) or release of rights under a postnuptial agreement (*Fratoni Est.*, 13 Fiduc. Rep. 10) is not sufficient cause to refuse letters c.t.a. Conviction of voluntary manslaughter, like conviction of murder (cf. *Kravitz Est.*, 418 Pa. 319), disqualifies the slayer from serving as the named executor of the victim's will: *Craig Est.*, 27 Fiduc. Rep. 102, annot. *Fiduc. Rev*. April 1977. Query as to effect of acquittal: *Gabel Est.*, 27 Fiduc. Rep. 322; *DeMatteo Est.*, 1 Fiduc. Rep. 2d 57. Attorney who mishandled other estates and had been suspended from practice of law (*Sulecki Est.*, 11 Fiduc. Rep. 2d 32), person found to have exercised undue influence regarding later will (*Flock Est. No. 3*, 22 Fiduc. Rep. 2d 344), and person convicted of bribery and tax fraud (*Katz Est.*, 11 Fiduc. Rep. 2d 408) were not permitted to serve as executor. A divorced spouse is not entitled to letters testamentary by virtue of an appointment in a will executed prior to the divorce: PEF 2507(2); *Domanyi Est.*, 30 Fiduc. Rep. 133, annot. *Fiduc. Rev*. April 1980, p. 3. Whenever the circumstances require and letters testamentary cannot be granted immediately, temporary letters durante minoritate, durante absentia or pendente lite may be granted. See Sections 3.2, 3.13.

## § 5.3 RENUNCIATION

The executor named in the decedent's will may be unwilling for a variety of reasons to undertake the duties of that office. In such circumstances he should formally renounce his right to act in a writing addressed to the register. See Section 3.6. Application should then be made by a party in interest for the appointment of an administrator c.t.a. See Sections 3.4, 5.2.

Grant of letters testamentary to one of two executors without renunciation by the other named executor cannot be attacked collaterally: *Bochniowich Est.*, 26 Fiduc. Rep. 584.

## § 5.4 BOND

An individual resident executor is not required to give bond unless it is required by the will or ordered by the court: PEF 3174(b); *McCloskey Est.*, 6 Fiduc. Rep. 197; *Lazar Est. (No. 2)*, 15 Fiduc. Rep. 605. No bond is required of a bank and trust company or of a trust company incorporated in the Commonwealth, or of a national bank having its principal office in the Commonwealth.[1] An individual nonresident executor need not file a bond if the testator expressly so directed in his will, unless the register, for cause, deems it necessary: PEF 3174(c). See *Fiduc. Rev.* April 1982.

The register of wills has the exclusive authority to fix the amount and pass upon the sufficiency of the surety in the first instance. See Section 3.10. Once the bond has been fixed, the court, upon cause shown, may change the amount of an existing bond, if it appears that bond is excessive or inadequate: PEF 3175; *Stuckert Est.*, 3 Fiduc. Rep. 179. For form of petition to change amount of bond, see Aker, PEF Code Annot. § 3175; Partridge-Remick, O.C. Practice §§ 7.06, 7.07. For

---

§ **5.4**

**1.** In the discretion of the register of wills, a bond may be required of a foreign corporation or a national bank having its principal office outside the Commonwealth: PEF 3174(a). See Banking Code of 1965, § 106(b) (7 P.S. § 106) for reciprocal law applicable to foreign corporate fiduciaries.

an action against the surety of a nonresident executor to recover the balance of a funeral bill, see *Shindler v. Wright*, 14 Fiduc. Rep. 309. See generally *Fiduc. Rev.* May 1962, p. 2.

## § 5.5 GRANT OF LETTERS; SHORT CERTIFICATES

When the petition for letters, any required renunciations and bond (if any) with surety have been filed, the oath of office (PEF 3161; see Section 3.11) has been taken, the appropriate fees of the register have been paid and the caveats (if any) disposed of, the register will grant letters testamentary in the form required to the person entitled (PEF 3155(a)). The executor, like the administrator, should, after the grant of letters, obtain from the register of wills "short certificates" showing his authority to act. See Section 3.12. These will be needed to collect assets of the estate and to transfer securities.

## § 5.6 REVOCATION OF LETTERS TESTAMENTARY AND THE EFFECT THEREOF

The register of wills may revoke letters of administration granted by him whenever it appears that the person or persons to whom they were earlier granted are not entitled thereto. See Section 3.14. However, he can revoke letters testamentary only when they are not in conformity with the provisions of a will admitted to probate: PEF 3181(b). When a will is probated after an earlier grant of letters and the person earlier appointed is the executor named in the later probated will, the original letters may be amended to provide continuity of administration: cf. *Friese Est.*, 317 Pa. 86, 91.

The procedure for securing revocation of the grant of letters testamentary and the effect of such revocation on acts earlier performed by the executor are the same as that outlined in regard to an administrator in Section 3.14. See *Navitsky Est.*, 13 Fiduc. Rep. 14, where the executor of an invalid will was directed to surrender unconverted assets to the administrator prior to audit of his accounts.

## § 5.7 REMOVAL OR DEATH OF EXECUTOR

Sections 3182 and 3183 of the PEF Code set forth the grounds for removal of the executor by the court, together with the procedure for and the effect of such removal. See Section 3.15. For discharge of executor, see PEF 3184. For rules applicable to removal of an executor, see *Fiduc. Rev.* Dec. 1968, May 1980. For designation of a successor fiduciary, see *Fiduc. Rev.* May 1975, p. 3; *Bailey Trust*, 25 Fiduc. Rep. 388. Petitioner for removal of executor must have standing. Specific legatee whose bequest has been paid in full lacks standing. *Schaffer Est.*, 29 Fiduc. Rep. 121.

When an entire vacancy occurs in the office of personal representative before administration is completed, the register is required to grant letters d.b.n.c.t.a. to the person or persons entitled thereto. See Section 3.2; PEF 3159. Such an administrator has power to recover the assets of the estate from his predecessor in administration, or from the personal representative of such predecessor, and he stands in the predecessor's stead for all purposes, except as the decedent's will provides otherwise, except that he is not personally liable for his predecessor's acts: PEF 3326. See, however, *Fiduc. Rev.* March 1964, p. 3, as to the duty of a successor fiduciary to take action against the predecessor fiduciary for any wrongdoing. See also *Nolen Est.*, 14 Fiduc. Rep. 379; 107 Trusts & Estates 197. For effect of appeal to Supreme Court upon power of removed executor to continue in office, see *Fiduc. Rev.* April 1978, p. 4.

The statute makes it clear that the personal representative of a deceased fiduciary does not succeed to the administration of any asset of an estate which was being administered by his decedent except to protect it pending delivery to the person entitled. The account of the deceased fiduciary may be filed by his personal representative, and it must be filed if the court so directs. The court may order the representative of the deceased fiduciary to make distribution and to make the transfers and assignments necessary to carry into effect a decree of distribution: PEF 3324. The situation where the personal representative is adjudged an incapacitated person is similar to the case of a deceased personal representative: PEF 3324; *Rosenstein Est.*, 7 Fiduc. Rep. 181. A personal representative who incurs fees and expenses in resisting an unfounded attempt to remove him is entitled to reimbursement from the estate: *Coffin Est.*, 16 Fiduc. Rep. 627.

## § 5.8 ANCILLARY ADMINISTRATION

What is said in Section 3.16 with respect to the territorial limits of the personal representative's powers and the necessity of having appointed a personal representative in states other than the domicile where the decedent left assets, is equally applicable when the decedent left a will.

## § 5.9 FOREIGN PERSONAL REPRESENTATIVE

A foreign fiduciary is a personal representative, guardian of a minor or incapacitated person, trustee or one performing the functions of any such fiduciary, who is subject primarily to the control of the court of another jurisdiction and who has not received ancillary authority in Pennsylvania: PEF 102.

A foreign fiduciary may exercise all the powers of a similar local fiduciary, provided that there is no administration in Pennsylvania, in which event he has no such powers unless he is the appointed ancillary fiduciary. The only limitations on the general powers of a foreign fiduciary are set out in PEF Chapter 41 and in 7 P.S. 106 (b) which requires foreign corporations to provide written notice to the Pennsylvania Department of Banking "at least thirty days prior to the commencement of fiduciary activities" which notice must be accompanied by specified documents. See annotation *Fiduc. Rev.* June 2001, p. 4.

Pennsylvania is especially lenient in granting powers to foreign fiduciaries in dealing with bank accounts in Pennsylvania and in transferring securities of Pennsylvania corporations: PEF 4102. Regarding foreign personal representatives of nonresident motorists, see Section 11.1.

## Chapter 6

# DUTIES FOLLOWING GRANT OF LETTERS

## § 6.1 INTRODUCTION

The executor or administrator, as a result of the grant of letters, obtains title to all personal property of the decedent as of the date of his death: PEF 301(a). He has a duty to collect the assets, recover debts, pay creditors and ultimately distribute the balance to those entitled.[1] In the course of administering the estate, he may have to bring or defend actions or substitute himself as a party to litigation in which the decedent was involved in his lifetime. See Chapter 11. At the outset, the personal representative should familiarize himself not only with the extent and character of the decedent's property, his debts and liabilities, but also with the family situation as it existed at his death. Prior to his appointment, if an administrator, he will have ascertained whether or not the decedent left a surviving spouse and children and, if not, will have taken steps to identify the next of kin. If there is a will, he will have ascertained whether the decedent has married, or remarried, or children have been born or adopted since the date thereof, and whether the decedent was the victim of a killing or ever adjudicated incompetent. He should also find out at an early date whether the surviving spouse of the decedent will elect to take against the will and inter vivos transfers even though the effect of the election relates primarily to distribution. See Chapter 8.

The personal representative is required to take possession of, maintain and administer all the real and personal estate of the decedent, except real estate occupied by an heir or devisee. Even such realty may be administered, if the court so directs, if necessary to protect the rights of claimants or other parties: PEF 3311. He is required to collect the rents and income of each asset in his possession until it is sold or distributed, and during the administration of the estate he has the right to maintain any action with respect to it and to make all reasonable expenditures necessary to preserve it. Unfinished

---

**§ 6.1**

**1.** Title to real estate passes to the decedent's heirs or devisees, but the personal representative nevertheless has duties with respect thereto. See Sections 6.21, 9.1 et seq.

contracts of the decedent may be carried out or abandoned according to the best interests of the estate: *Allam Est.*, 199 Pa. 573. The administration of valueless property may be renounced under authorization of the court: PEF 3312; *Fiduc. Rev.* May 1971, p. 3. Except as otherwise provided by the decedent's will, the personal representative may sell, at a public or private sale, any personal property whether specifically bequeathed or not, any real property not specifically devised, and real property specifically devised with the joinder of the devisee: PEF 3351. However, upon application of any party in interest, he may, in the discretion of the court, be restrained from making any sale under an authority not given by will: PEF 3355. He also has power to make contracts which are within his authority as personal representative (cf. PEF 3331) and to lease real or personal property which he is entitled to possess (PEF 3352). These and other powers of the personal representative are frequently qualified or enlarged by the decedent's will.

Among the duties of the personal representative following his appointment and the grant of letters are an examination of the decedent's papers and a search for the assets and liabilities of the estate. See Section 6.6 et seq. The information so assembled will form the basis of the inventory, tax reports and account, and it is therefore essential that such work be performed diligently, accurately and with dispatch. Preliminary steps in this direction may already have been taken in anticipation of the appointment. See Sections 1.2, 1.4. Care should be taken to distinguish assets which form no part of the estate except for tax purposes. See Section 6.11. Specific duties arise out of these general initial obligations, and care should be exercised to see that they are performed in the manner prescribed.

The personal representative should make prompt application for the estate's "employer identification number," which will be needed for the tax returns required to be filed during administration of the estate. Even if it is anticipated that the estate will not have sufficient income to file an income tax return, a number may be required to be furnished to those making payments (e.g., dividends) to the estate. The application is to be made on Form SS-4 (obtainable from any

Social Security or Internal Revenue office) and is to be filed with the District Director at the personal representative's residence. See *Fiduc. Rev.* Nov. 1962, p. 4.

Some of the duties of the personal representative which are set forth in this chapter are discussed at greater length in the four succeeding chapters dealing respectively with the family exemption (Chapter 7), the administration of real estate (Chapter 9), debts and claims against the estate (Chapter 10) and survival actions (Chapter 11). It must be borne in mind that, although in many respects the administration of an estate must follow a procedural timetable, many of the personal representative's duties are continuing and must be carried out simultaneously with others. The order of discussion in this chapter and those that follow therefore should not be regarded as necessarily prescribing the order in which those duties should be accomplished. There is a distinct advantage to all parties in interest when all steps in the administration of the estate are anticipated and promptly carried out to the extent possible. See Estate Settlement Timetable, Appendix 2; Prac. Law. 73 (Nov. 1958).

See Chart, Principal Duties of an Efficient Executor or Administrator in Administering an Estate, at the end of this Chapter.

A Chart entitled "Distribution of Decedent's Assets" appearing at the beginning of Chapter 16 sets out in graphic form the order of availability of assets for payment of claims and for distribution to those entitled under the will or by intestate succession.

## § 6.2 ADVERTISING THE GRANT OF LETTERS

Notice of the grant of letters testamentary or of administration should be advertised immediately, once a week for three successive weeks, in the legal publication, if any, of the county where letters were granted and also in a newspaper published at or near the place where the decedent resided: PEF 3162. In every such notice the personal representative is required to request all persons having claims against the estate of the decedent to make them known, and all persons indebted to the decedent to make payment without delay. It is important that the advertisement appear promptly, because the personal representative's account cannot be filed for audit and confirmation by the court until four full months have elapsed "after the first complete advertisement of the grant of letters": PEF 3501. See generally Chapter 15. Promptness in advertisement is also important in cutting off the rights of creditors against distributees and the personal representative: PEF 3532. See generally Chapter 16. If the advertisement appears in the public newspaper on January 2, 9 and 16, and in the legal publication on January 4, 11 and 18, the "first" complete advertisement is considered to have appeared on January 4. If publication in the newspaper is the only publication that is possible because there is no legal publication in the county, the first complete advertisement is January 2: PEF 102.

After the advertisement has appeared for the required three successive weeks, the personal representative should procure from the publications involved what is known as a "proof of publication," that is, an affidavit showing a copy of the notice and setting forth the time and manner of its publication. It is the accepted practice of the courts to require the proofs of publication when the personal representative's account is audited. See Chapter 15.

It should be noted that the personal representative of a minor is not excused from the requirement of advertising the grant of letters since the minor's estate might still be liable for necessaries furnished to the minor, even though the minor could not contract for indebtedness: *Bradley Est.*, 15 Fiduc. Rep. 177.

## § 6.3 ANALYSIS OF THE WILL

If the decedent left a will, an early and careful analysis thereof is essential to a proper administration of the estate. This is particularly true if any uncertainty exists as to the testator's meaning, if the estate appears inadequate to meet the apparent plan of the will, or if there is some likelihood that a will contest will develop. As already stated, a will may consist of several documents, and advice of counsel in determining the dispositive documents is accordingly important. See Section 4.4. The analysis also will assist the surviving spouse in determining whether to elect to take under or against the will (PEF 2203), and the personal representative should consider whether the surviving spouse should be advised to seek separate counsel to protect his or her rights in respect thereto (*Fiduc. Rev.* March 1967, Nov. 1969). See Chapter 8. In appropriate circumstances a written opinion from the personal representative's attorney (see Section 1.5) or a declaratory judgment should be sought.

## § 6.4 ASSISTANCE TO SURVIVING MEMBERS OF FAMILY

The rendering of financial assistance to the surviving spouse or family of the decedent is a problem which arises frequently and which must be handled promptly by the personal representative with great care and tact. The problem is especially urgent when there is any basis for believing that distribution will be held up because of a possible contest of the will or when the estate appears to be insolvent. Salary due should be collected (see Section 2.2) and employees' or lodge benefits applied for (see Section 6.10). In many instances, examination of estate assets will disclose that the decedent owned a joint savings or checking account which, because of his death, passes to the survivor. Sufficient funds may be available from such sources to provide for the immediate needs of the family. There also may be life insurance payable directly to the spouse, in which event the personal representative should make his service available in counseling re selection of available options provided in the insurance policy and in obtaining the proceeds, or in securing a loan in anticipation of payment thereof. Unless the estate is insolvent, a loan usually can be arranged with the decedent's bank.

If the surviving members of the family are entitled to the family exemption, the personal representative should explore the advisability of those entitled claiming it at once, and he should bear in mind that there is a right to "retain" as well as a right to "claim" the exemption. See Chapter 7.

## § 6.5 CARE AND DISPOSITION OF ANIMALS

It is essential that an early determination be made of the care and disposition of animals on the premises of the decedent. In many instances this may have been a matter of considerable importance to the decedent who directed their destruction or the setting aside of funds for their future care: *Mateer Est.*, 18 Fiduc. Rep. 354, annot. *Fiduc. Rev.* Aug. 1968; *Hackett Est.*, 30 Fiduc. Rep. 237; *Stewart Est.*, 30 Fiduc. Rep. 68. On occasion, the animals will be disposed of in the same manner as tangible personal property. See *Fiduc. Rev.* Dec. 1982. In at least one instance, the direction of the testatrix for their destruction has been vetoed by court decree on the ground of public policy: *Capers Est.*, 15 Fiduc. Rep. 150, annot. *Fiduc. Rev.* March 1965. See also Destruction of Pets, 16 Real Property, Probate and Trust J. 894.

Section 7738 of the PEF Code validates a trust established for care of an animal subject to the court's power to limit the value of the trust if it exceeds the amount required for the intended use. See annotation *Fiduc. Rev.* Dec. 2006, p. 4.

## § 6.6 OPEN AND LIST CONTENTS OF SAFE-DEPOSIT BOXES

As stated in Section 1.2, it is important that others, preferably a member or members of decedent's immediate family, be present when the contents of the safe-deposit box are first examined and before any contents thereof are removed. However, the safe-deposit "freeze" imposed by Article XI of the Inheritance and Estate Tax Act of 1961 (now Part XII, 72 P.S. § 9191 et seq.) would seem to minimize the dangers formerly attendant upon an entry without the presence of such persons.

An Inheritance Tax Bulletin 2011-02 issued May 11, 2011 and effective immediately authorizes entry by "estate representatives," after notice, who will then make and file an inventory, without the need to be accompanied by a bank employee or attorney. Representatives of the Department will no longer be available to attend and make the inventory.

A seven day notice to the Department under 72 P.S. § 9193 is required.

(1) The Notice must include:

a. the name of estate and person entering the box,

b. the name and street address of the financial institution in which the box is located, and

c. the date and time of entry.

(2) The Notice must be:

a. delivered via United States Postal Service, return receipt service,

b. copied to the financial institution in which the box is located,

c. sent at least seven days in advance to:

PA Dept. of Revenue
Safe Deposit Box Unit
P.O. Box 280601
Harrisburg, PA 17128-0601

(3) At the time of entry, the estate representative must also provide a statement to the financial institution attesting that the notice was sent to the department, with the following or similar language:

> Under penalties of perjury I swear that I gave the notice required under Section 2193 of the Inheritance and Estate Tax Act, 72 P.S. § 9193, to the Pennsylvania Department of Revenue, via United States

Postal Service, of my intention to enter this safe deposit box on today's date.

(4) Within 20 days of the entry, the estate representative must also return a completed Safe Deposit Box form REV-485 to the department's Safe Deposit Box Unit.

It will be noted that the procedure is announced with respect to Section 9193 of the Act, which establishes a method of entry "when [it] is not, or cannot be made under" subsections (a), (b), (c) or (d) of Section 9192. Thus, those methods (with bank employee, under court order, under business box certification) would seem to remain viable. The subsection (b) procedure—with a Department representative—is clearly suspended.

The program initiated in 1998 under which the District office of the Department of Revenue authorized estate counsel as the Department's appointee to inventory the box and complete the inventory forms apparently has been discontinued. *See Fiduc. Rev.*, June 2011, p. 4.

For bank practices for entry to safe-deposit boxes, *see* § 9192 of Grossman and Smith, Pa. Inheritance and Estate Tax (Fifth Ed. 2002).

The "freeze" is not applicable to boxes "in the names of the decedent and his or her spouse" (1963 P.L. 21) although the addition of a third name to the box will invoke the "freeze."

If the safe-deposit box is no longer required, it either should be released to avoid future rental charges or should be transferred to a member of the decedent's family. If needed to safeguard estate assets, it should be retained as long as required. Once the "freeze" has been broken by an entry under any provision of the Inheritance and Estate Tax Act of 1991, other than Section 9192(e) (see Section 1.2), subsequent entries may be made free of all restriction.

If the safe-deposit box was rented jointly by the decedent and a surviving party, the survivor usually has sole right of access thereto following the decedent's death: see *Stevenson v. Economy Bank of Ambridge*, 413 Pa. 442. However, the "freeze" provisions of the 1991 statute apply to such a box, and the foregoing procedure will be applicable thereto.

See also Section 13.3.

Compare *Cochran Est.*, 9 Fiduc. Rep. 229, and *Rodenheiser Est.*, 76 Montg. 78, with *Lowell Est.*, 9 Fiduc. Rep. 235. See *Fiduc. Rev.* Nov. 1957, p. 2; *Stewart Est.*, 8 Fiduc. Rep. 615. See *Christie Est.*, 436 Pa. 101, concerning the rights of the survivor where the safe-deposit box contract was signed by both the decedent and the survivor.

## § 6.7 PERSONAL EFFECTS AND PAPERS

Another important step which the personal representative should take as soon as possible is to visit the decedent's place of residence and his place of business for the purpose of gathering together his personal effects and papers not found in his safe-deposit box. These will include copies of tax returns, tax receipts, deeds, business records, checkbooks, savings bankbooks, bills paid and unpaid, cancelled checks, bank statements, insurance policies, securities, jewelry, contracts and cash. In exceptional circumstances, such as if the decedent lived alone and there is a suspicion that he may have concealed important papers or cash, it is advisable that the search of the premises be conducted under supervision of the court: cf. *King Will*, 3 Fiduc. Rep. 435; *Dettra Will (No. 2)*, 13 Fiduc. Rep. 463.

Care and diligence should be exercised in searching for the decedent's assets and liabilities. It is seldom that a decedent has "set his house in order" in anticipation of death, and disorderliness may be expected. Neatness and thoroughness often are not found, since occasional notations and memoranda usually suffice during life. Hence conferences with those familiar with the decedent's affairs—his immediate family, his lawyer, his broker, his insurance agent and tax consultant are essential. Evidence of all forms of inter vivos gifts and of the existence of powers of appointment should be sought. A sum of money found in the decedent's house is presumed to belong to the decedent's estate: *Karch Est.*, 133 Pa. 84; *Moyer Est.*, 2 Leb. 188. Assets, personal effects and papers, as they are found, should be taken into custody and kept separate from the personal representative's own property and that of others.

All personal effects of the decedent found in his place of residence[1] and the business should be listed and valued with a view to preparing the inventory (see Chapter 12) and tax returns (see Chapters 13, 14). Assets of the estate which are specifically bequeathed or devised should be appraised separately. Articles which are not specifically bequeathed or which are not to be distributed in kind should be sold promptly to minimize storage and insurance charges. If there is to be a public sale thereof, it may be advisable for the auctioneer to be present for the listing and valuation; and in this event, the latter can serve as an appraiser. If antiques or valuable jewelry is involved, it is advisable to have an expert appraiser whose valuations will be accepted without question by the taxing authorities. See Section 12.5.

If among the decedent's effects there is found any article which clearly did not belong to him, it should be delivered to the owner upon proof of title, and a receipt therefor should be obtained. If the decedent's will makes specific bequests of household furniture, jewelry or personal effects, serious consideration should be given to their early delivery to the persons entitled. See Chapter 16. Early delivery of property to those ultimately entitled thereto whether under the

---

§ 6.7

1. Household goods and furnishings acquired in anticipation of or during marriage and used by both spouses are presumptively owned by the entireties: *DiFlorido v. DiFlorido*, 459 Pa. 641. For prior law, see *Fine v. Fine*, 366 Pa. 227; *Dura Seal Products Co. v. Carver*, 186 Pa. Super. 425; *Gumbes Est.*, 172 Pa. Super. 59; *Schwartz Est.*, 166 Pa. Super. 459; *Matheny Est.*, 164 Pa. Super. 18; *Kincaid Est.*, 8 Fiduc. Rep. 537; *Shain v. Didio*, 15 D. & C. 2d 173; *McGee Est., 56 Lanc. 253; Rapkin v. Israel*, 4 Fiduc. Rep. 57; *Campbell Est.*, 20 Fiduc. Rep. 81. Regarding cash found in the home, see *Lauro Est.*, 11 Fiduc. Rep. 567.

will or otherwise may reduce administration expenses for insurance and storage charges and relieve the personal representative of responsibility for its safekeeping. But note that I.R.C. § 663(a)(1) may cause undesirable income tax consequences. Any such distribution is made at the risk of the personal representative, and it cannot be done safely if there is any question concerning the solvency of the estate or the interpretation of the will, or when there is any likelihood of a will contest. See Section 17.3. The hazards of early distribution frequently can be reduced by demanding refunding bonds or by securing the written agreements of the distributees: cf. PEF 3533. However, care should be exercised to have the approval of taxing authorities before property is removed from the premises. See Sections 13.2, 14.1. The risk of advance distribution is lessened where other assets eventually distributable to the distributee remain in the hands of the personal representative: cf. *Campion Est.*, 2 Fiduc. Rep. 54.

## § 6.8 BOOKS OF ACCOUNTS, FILES, RECORDS

Among the most important of the decedent's effects at the initial stage of administration are his checkbooks, books of accounts, files and records. These should be carefully assembled and examined, and the accuracy of all open items should be verified with debtors and creditors. Letters, papers and even photographs may be important if the decedent died intestate and there is doubt as to the existence or identity of the next of kin. Such materials, in those circumstances, should be carefully preserved. See *Garrett Est.*, 372 Pa. 438, annot. *Fiduc. Rev.* Feb. 1953. Particular care should be exercised to acquire the decedent's copies of his income and other tax returns in order to ascertain assets and obligations of the estate (see Sections 6.15, 10.8) and to aid in the preparation of tax returns (see Chapters 13, 14).

The decedent's checkbooks and account books will also provide evidence of whether salary, royalties or commissions are due but have not been paid, and in this event steps should be taken to obtain payment. See Section 6.23. Examination of decedent's files will also be helpful in disclosing the existence of fiduciary relationships which may result in fees owing to the estate (*Manning Trust*, 15 Fiduc. Rep. 293) and of trusts under which the estate may be entitled to accrued income, apportionments (*Fiduc. Rev.* May 1969, p. 4; April 1970, p. 3, May 1972) or transmissible remainder interests (*Smyth Trust*, 9 Fiduc. Rep. 340; *Streuber Est.*, 9 Fiduc. Rep. 407).

## § 6.9 BANK ACCOUNTS

Notice of the decedent's death and of the intention to close bank accounts should be given immediately after the grant of letters. This is particularly important because of a provision in the Commercial Code permitting a bank to pay or certify checks for a ten-day period.[1]

The "short certificates," referred to in Sections 3.12 and 5.5, are usually required to obtain funds in bank accounts. In most instances, it will be advisable to close existing checking accounts and to transfer all balances to an estate bank account: cf. *Caplan Est.*, 19 Fiduc. Rep. 207, holding that a bank need not deliver the remaining balance in the decedent's checking account to the personal representatives where the decedent was indebted to the bank in a greater amount and the solvency of the estate had not yet been established: *Dillon Est.*, 20 Fiduc. Rep. 151 annot. *Fiduc. Rev.* March 1970, p. 3, aff'd, 441 Pa. 206. Credit balances with brokerage houses also should be withdrawn.

Deposit accounts in a financial institution with balances not exceeding $3,500 may be obtained by close relatives of the decedent who have paid the funeral bill. See PEF 3101(b). If the decedent had savings or share accounts, notice of the decedent's death and of the intention to close them should also be given, but it may be advisable to leave such

§ **6.9**

**1.** U.C.C. § 4-405(2). "Even with knowledge a bank may for ten days after the date of death pay or certify checks drawn on or prior to that date unless ordered to stop payment by a person claiming an interest in the account." [Pa: 13 Pa. C.S. § 4405(b)].

monies on deposit until needed so that they will continue to earn interest.

*New estate account.* If all estate funds are deposited in an estate checking account and payments made therefrom, confusion in preparing subsequent court accountings will be avoided. In making deposits into an estate account, care should be exercised to maintain a record of the source of the deposits. For example, in depositing dividend checks, statements thereon or therewith should be noted so that it is clear whether they represent a dividend to stockholders prior to the date of death and therefore are to be included in the inventory, and so that they are reported for the proper period in the income tax returns and to insure that stock certificates conform to the number of shares evidenced by the check.

When the personal representative is an individual, as opposed to a corporate fiduciary, and he employs an attorney, it is usually advisable that all deposits be made through the attorney, and that checks for withdrawals be prepared in his office for signature by the personal representative. In this way both the personal representative and his attorney will have full knowledge about the funds of the estate and there will be less possibility for confusion in the estate records. If there is more than one personal representative, all should sign checks. See *Fiduc. Rev.* Sept. 1945. Some banks when authorized by the personal representatives to do so will honor checks signed by fewer than all of them. Disagreements between or among personal representatives are dealt with in PEF 3328; cf. *Fiduc. Rev.* June 1959, p. 2.

*Multiple party accounts.* When a bank account or savings account is in the name of the decedent "in trust" for another (a so-called "tentative trust"—see 6 Hunter, O.C. Commonplace Book (2d ed.), Trusts Inter Vivos, § 12(a)), or when it is a joint account with right of survivorship (see 3 Hunter (2d ed.), Gifts Inter Vivos, §§ 13, 15(a)), it normally forms no part of the estate except for death tax purposes and usually can be drawn upon by the surviving beneficiary or surviving co-owner without difficulty. See Sections 2.2, 6.11. Compare, however, *Brose Est.*, 416 Pa. 386, annot. *Fiduc. Rev.* Feb. 1965, holding that a tentative trust deposit does not exist unless all the funds in the account were the property of the trustee; *Waligora Est.*, 22 Fiduc. Rep. 603, where the funds were traceable to the beneficiary; see *Fiduc. Rev.* April 1971, p. 2, annotating *Howanec Est.*, 21 Fiduc. Rep. 221, which held that a tentative trust designation was not revoked by an express clause in a will, which will was in turn revoked by the testatrix-trustee. See *Agostini Est.*, 457 A.2d 861 (Pa. Super.), for revocation by letter of tentative trust account in Florida bank.

Chapter 63 of the PEF Code was enacted in 1976 to determine "the property rights among multiple-party accounts and all claims made through them." It has no effect as to the rights and liabilities between the parties and the financial institution or as to inheritance tax. See *Fiduc. Rev.* Sept. 1976; *Layman v. Western Savings Bk.*, 302 Pa. Super. 433. The additional step suggested in *Fiduciary Review* articles of January 1973 and September 1976 to clarify the intention of the parties when the multiple-party account is opened has not yet been taken and consequently unnecessary intra-family squabbles continue. See *Fiduc. Rev.* Nov. 1978, Nov. 1980, p. 3 and Jan. 1982, p. 3. Until this situation is clarified, the personal representative must be extremely diligent in clarifying the intention of the decedent, the rights of the parties and the possibility of compromising differences. A number of cases dealing with PEF Code 6304 have concluded that evidence was not sufficient to overcome the statutory presumption that multiple party accounts, including joint accounts, pass to the surviving joint owner unless there is "clear and convincing evidence of a different intent at the time the account is created." *See Fiduc. Rev.* Dec. 2009, p. 3; *Novosielski Est.*, 992 A.2d 89; *Piet Est.*, 997 A.2d 338; *Pagnotti v. Old Forge Bank* (Pa. Super.), 631 A.2d 1045, annot. *Fiduc. Rev.* April 1994; *Meyers Est.* (Pa. Super.), 642 A.2d 525; *Heske Est.* (Pa. Super.), 647 A.2d 243; *Strahsmeier Est.* (Pa. Super., 9/7/12); *Longstreet Est.*, 13 Fiduc. Rep. 2d 342; *Mainiero v. Ward*, 14 Fiduc. Rep. 2d 373; *Haller Est.*, 16 Fiduc. Rep. 2d 33. Chapter 63 of the PEF Code applies to joint brokerage accounts notwithstanding the limited definition of joint accounts in § 6303. *Deutsch, Larrimore & Farnish P.C. v. Johnson*, 791 A.2d 350.

The law requires that for tax purposes notice of the death of the co-owner of a joint account (other than husband and wife) or of the trustee of a tentative trust bank account be given by the financial institution to the Department of Revenue in Harrisburg within ten days of knowledge of death, if the balance exceeds $300: Inh. & Est. Tax Act, § 9147; Grossman and Smith, Pa. Inheritance Tax, § 9147 (Fifth Ed. 2002).

## § 6.10 LIFE INSURANCE AND DEATH BENEFITS—SOCIAL SECURITY—MEDICARE—VETERANS' BENEFITS—PENSION BENEFITS

*Life insurance*. Life insurance payable to a named beneficiary who survives the decedent is not part of the decedent's estate except for federal estate tax purposes. Review of all life insurance policies to determine the interests of the estate, if any, is essential. In many instances when the proceeds are payable to a named beneficiary the personal representative will wish to confer with him or her as to the rights under the policy and the options exercisable. If a portion of the estate tax may be attributable to life insurance, consideration thereof should be given when the policy is delivered to the beneficiary. See Section 14.7.

If the beneficiaries predecease the decedent or no beneficiary is named, the insurance is payable to the estate and must be administered. It is the duty of the personal representative to file proof of death and to collect the proceeds. The decedent's insurance agent will be glad to help with the collection unless the personal representative prefers to deal directly with the home office of the insurance company. The company will supply forms to be completed and executed by the beneficiary and the attending physician. Often a death certificate can be substituted for the physician's statement. Some companies require that other forms be executed by one who is not the beneficiary but who is familiar with the facts. Proceeds paid to a son under a facility of payment clause, there being no agreement that they were to be used for decedent's expenses, are not part of decedent's estate: *Witcofskie Est.*, 57 Schuyl. 177.

If there are employees' or lodge benefit policies, it frequently is advisable to urge the obligor to make payment directly to the undertaker, to the person named in the agreement or to the person or persons entitled to the residuary estate. Assets subject to administration expenses can thus be reduced: Cf. *Mellor Est.*, 286 Pa. 149; *Hampton Est.*, 9 Fiduc. Rep. 313; *Dunkle Est.*, 16 D. & C. 45; *Southard Est.*, 16 D. & C. 751. When a federal estate tax return is to be filed, Form 712 should be requested from all insurance companies. See Section 14.4.

Survivors of firefighters (paid and volunteer), certified hazardous material response team members, National Guard member, ambulance service and rescue squad members or law enforcement officers killed in the performance of duty may obtain the sum of $100,000 adjusted for inflation after 2005 as provided by Act of 1976 as amended (53 P.S. § 891). In addition a payment to the survivors of public safety officers, including law enforcement officers, fire fighters (paid and volunteer) and correctional, parole, probation and judicial officers, killed in the performance of duty on or after September 29, 1976, is available from the federal government under the Public Safety Officers' Benefits Act of 1976.

Possibilities for obtaining increased benefits for accidental death should not be overlooked. See *Roque v. Nationwide Ins. Co.*, 292 Pa. Super. 117, where insured's death occurred as result of being shot by policeman while insured apparently was burglarizing an unoccupied home and the beneficiary was held entitled to the accidental death benefit. Death was considered accidental even though it resulted from the insured's criminal conduct.

In some limited circumstances, life insurance proceeds payable to minors may be used for the insured's funeral expenses. In *Borkowski Est.*, 109 Montg. 446, the guardian of estates of minors was directed to pay the balance of the funeral cost for the minors' father from proceeds of a life insurance policy and to lend sufficient funds without interest to their mother to complete necessary repairs for the home property.

*Social security benefits.* If the decedent was insured under Social Security, notice of death and application for benefits thereunder should be made immediately, either by the personal representative or a member of the decedent's family, to the nearest Social Security Administration field office: 42 U.S.C. § 402j(1). The law provides that a lump sum is payable to the surviving spouse in addition to the monthly payments made to designated survivors. The lump sum is paid only if application therefor is filed within two years of the death of the insured: 42 U.S.C. § 402(i). The Social Security death benefit is not subject to inheritance tax, and the full funeral expense is deductible: Inh. & Est. Tax Act, §§ 9111(p), 9127(4).

*Medical insurance and benefits.* It is important for the personal representative and his attorney to review medical and hospital bills which have been paid by the decedent prior to his death, as well as those bills which arise after death, to ascertain whether reimbursement should be sought for the former, and whether the latter should be submitted to Medicare and other insurance carriers for payment. The same is true, of course, as to any private hospital or accident insurance policies which the decedent may have. With respect to the procedures for filing claims under Medicare, see *Fiduc. Rev.* Nov. 1967, p. 3. Generally, the hospital will submit bills unpaid at death so that the personal representative need not do so; if decedent had "65 Special" coverage, the entire bill will be paid (Medicare Part A pays 80% and "65 Special" pays 20%). As for physician's bills, he or she often bills direct and is paid by Medicare and other insurance coverage; if not, the personal representative will have to make the request. Generally, the deductible amount is paid by the patient and thereafter Medicare Part B pays 80% and "65 Special" pays 20%.

Under Section 1729(k) of the Pennsylvania Inheritance and Estate Tax Act, medical expenses are not deductible if paid by Medicare or insurance coverage, reversing the decision in *Goldberg Est.*, 486 Pa. 507, annot. in *Fiduc. Rev.* Dec. 1979. See *Fiduc. Rev.* Jan. 1983.

*Veterans' benefits*. If the decedent was a veteran, a review should be made of insurance, burial and other benefits to which his family or the estate may be entitled. For a chart of such benefits, see Appendix 3 and *Fiduc. Rev*. Mar. 1975, p. 3. Claims for veteran's benefits must be made within two years of his death. Claims for county burial benefits must be made within one year. For benefits to dependents of Pennsylvania National Guard members who died from injuries received in active service or who were killed in active service, see 51 Pa. C.S. § 3502.

*Employee benefits*. The personal representative should contact the decedent's employer, if any, to determine what salary or wages may have been owing at death. Cf. Section 2.2. In addition, he should ascertain whether there are any benefits or insurance to which the decedent's estate or his family may be entitled by reason of his employment. Payments from pension and profit sharing plans may be made directly to the named beneficiary despite the existence of a controversy between adverse claimants: PEF 8704, annot. *Fiduc. Rev*. Sept. 1967, p. 3. For accrued unemployment compensation benefits, see 43 P.S. § 803. For worker's compensation, death benefits for survivors, see 77 P.S. §§ 541 and 561, and for worker's compensation burial benefit, see 77 P.S. § 561.

See *Fiduc. Rev*. March 1973, p. 2, for chart "Corporate-Owned Life Insurance on Life of Employee Shareholder Where Corporation Pays Premiums."

## § 6.11 PROPERTY NOT PART OF DECEDENT'S ESTATE

Various types of property, some of which are referred to in the preceding sections, are not part of the decedent's estate but are associated with it either because they are subject to death taxes or because they come into enjoyment by reason of the decedent's death. See also Section 2.2. The personal representative is under a duty to ascertain the existence of such property and should make memoranda thereof. Although he may be required to value it for tax purposes, he is not required to inventory or account for it. See Sections 12.8, 15.4.

These nontestamentary assets may include:

(1) Insurance payable to a named beneficiary who survives the decedent or to a trustee of an insurance trust;

(2) Property held in joint tenancy or by the entireties (as distinguished from that held in common), which passes by right of survivorship;

(3) Remainder interests in trust or legal estates which come into enjoyment at the decedent's death;

(4) Tentative trusts;

(5) Gifts made in contemplation of death;

(6) United States savings bonds registered in the name of the decedent "or" another, or "payable on death to" another;

(7) Employee benefits payable to designated beneficiaries;

(8) Securities registered in transfer on death form.

It is often difficult to determine whether a particular item of property is part of the decedent's estate or falls into one of the above categories.[1] Even when it is clear that property is not part of the decedent's estate, there is the further question of whether it is subject to death taxes—federal, state or, as is frequently the case, both. See further, Chapters 13 and 14. Tax liability may attach to the personal representative for failure to keep watch over nontestamentary assets:

---

**§ 6.11**

**1.** For some discussion and references to other authorities and texts on the nature of such property, see Atkinson on Wills § 116 (2d ed.); Brégy, Intestate, Wills and Estates Acts of 1947, pp. 64 et seq.

For tax questions, see *Fiduc. Rev*. Aug. 1949, p. 3; Nov. 1943, p. 3 (entireties ownership); Oct. 1953, p. 3 (employee's trust); Aug. 1936, p. 3 (joint tenancy).

Inh. & Est. Tax Act, § 1746. If there is any reasonable doubt as to whether the property belongs in the estate, the personal representative should of course take the position that it should be included, make claim for any such property not in his possession and retain possession of that which he has—unless the court directs otherwise or unless all parties claiming through the estate agree that the estate's claim should be abandoned: cf. PEF 3312; *Miller Est.*, 3 Fiduc. Rep. 279; *Leichner Est.*, 2 Fiduc. Rep. 361. For inventory of such items, see Section 12.8.

The procedure for gaining possession of nontestamentary interests and making the necessary changes in any registered or recorded titles is primarily a matter of establishing the fact of the decedent's death. Each bank, transfer agent, insurance company and title company will have its own requirements.

Life insurance payable to a named beneficiary is not a part of decedent's estate except for federal estate tax purposes: see Section 6.10, supra.

When real estate held by the entireties passes by survivorship, nothing need be done with respect to the record title[2] until the property is sold, at which time the presentation of a simple affidavit usually will be sufficient as proof of death of the deceased owner. There is no Pennsylvania inheritance tax payable on entireties property. On the other hand, when shares of stock pass by right of survivorship, the registration of the stock should be corrected promptly, so that subsequent dividend checks will be properly issued. This does not affect the right to choose alternate valuation date for federal estate tax purposes. A registered mail letter should be sent to the transfer agent whose name appears on the stock certificate, enclosing the stock certificates, a death certificate and an affidavit as to domicile. If, before this is done, a dividend check is received made out to both the deceased and surviving own-

---

§ 6.11

2. The insurance policies related to the property should be changed to eliminate the decedent's name as one of the insured.

ers, it belongs to the survivor, regardless of the declaration or record date, because the right to the unpaid dividend is itself joint or entireties property and hence passes by survivorship just as the stock does. Several courses are open: either the check can be returned to the company, together with the proof required for transfer of the stock, so that the check can be reissued to the survivor; or the check can be deposited in any existing joint account of the decedent and the surviving joint owner, deposited in the estate account after endorsement by the surviving co-owner or cleared for payment to the survivor by the endorsement of the survivor and the personal representative of the decedent, together with a short certificate from the register of wills to show the latter's authority. Household goods and furnishings acquired in anticipation of or during marriage and used by both spouses are presumptively owned by the entireties: *DiFlorido v. DiFlorido*, 459 Pa. 641. For severance of entireties ownership, see *Fiduc. Rev.* Feb. 1976.

Note, however, that a right of survivorship cannot exist in connection with a tenancy in common of unequal interests, even if the deed creating the interests sets forth an intent to create a right of survivorship. Three-fifth interest conveyed to a husband and wife as tenants by the entireties cannot have survivorship rights with one-fifth interests conveyed to two others: *Edel v. Edel*, 283 Pa. Super. 551. On the other hand, where decedent and his wife, designated as sellers in the agreement of sale, sold real estate (and business conducted thereon by them jointly) owned in part by decedent alone, the agreement of sale created a chose in action in personalty held by the entireties which vested in the wife upon the husband's death: *Croce Est.*, 19 Leb. 115.

The accounting and distribution of a remainder interest in a trust is part of the administration of the trust estate. It is the responsibility of the trustee, who can be cited to account in court if he fails to do so. The personal representative of a deceased trustee is responsible for custody and care of the assets until they are delivered to those entitled. Legal remainders in real estate, when there is no trustee, vest immediately and automatically so that the legal remainderman, like the joint tenant, need do nothing other than pay death taxes: *Fiduc. Rev.* Sept. 1946.

A legal future interest in securities or cash created prior to 1948 is an entirely different matter. If, prior to that date, a testator's will bequeathed personal property "to A for life, remainder to B," B is not considered to have a remainder, but is treated as a creditor of the estate of the life tenant for the amount of principal he originally acquired. B's claim is enforced like any other creditor's claim against the personal representative of the life tenant's estate: see *Fiduc. Rev.* April 1943, Dec. 1950, p. 4; *Gramm Est. (No. 2)*, 15 Fiduc. Rep. 105. However, if the decedent has a life estate with the power to consume, the debtor–creditor relationship does not arise and the personal representative of the life tenant need turn over only what is left of the principal: see *Fiduc. Rev.* Feb. 1943. Since January 1, 1948, it has been impossible to create legal future interests in personalty because the statute changes all such estates into trusts, with the life tenant, or another person appointed in his stead by the court, as the trustee: PEF 6113; see *Morris Est.*, 12 Fiduc. Rep. 142. Hence the distribution of a remainderman's interest under an instrument that took effect on or after January 1, 1948, is a matter of trust administration and is enforced by citing the trustee or his personal representative to account for the trust rather than by proceeding against the life tenant's individual estate.

Other types of property which pass to another without passing through the decedent's estate raise no serious problem of procedure. Donees of inter vivos gifts, even when made in contemplation of death, usually will be in possession of the property. Each bank will have its own requirements for withdrawing the amount which passes by law to the beneficiary of a tentative trust. United States savings bonds registered in the name of the decedent "or" another and bonds registered in the name of the decedent "payable on death to" another can be cashed by the survivor or reissued in the survivor's name upon presentation of a certificate evidencing the decedent's death. For income tax consequences of cashing Series E bonds, see *Fiduc. Rev.* March 1960, p. 3. Transfer on death security registrations can be transferred promptly to the designated beneficiary subject to PEF 6411 requirements including clearance of Pennsylvania inheritance tax.

## § 6.12 SECURITIES

The early acquisition and safeguarding of securities is essential, especially when they are negotiable. "Short certificates," referred to in Sections 3.12 and 5.5, will be required to transfer securities from the decedent's name. They should be transferred to the name of the personal representative promptly, especially if they are not to be sold immediately. If a corporate fiduciary is the personal representative, or agent for the personal representative, the transfer should be made to its nominee: PEF 3321. For requirements to place securities in the name of the personal representative or his nominee, see *Fiduc. Rev*. Oct. 1960. Securities in the possession of banks and brokers should be taken into custody, and any collateral loans should be paid in order to release pledged securities. In listing securities, it is well to do so in a manner which will supply the requisite information for the inventory, and also allow sufficient space for listing valuations. See Chapter 12. It is important to check the dividend record to make certain that certificates for small stock dividends and shares acquired under reinvestment of cash dividends have not been overlooked: *Crawford Est.*, 468 Pa. 381. Accrued interest should be calculated to the decedent's death and entered, and dividends should be listed in a manner which will facilitate their apportionment between principal and income. When the circumstances are such that ownership of securities may be claimed by others, care should be exercised to preserve the securities and the envelopes and papers associated therewith in the form in which they were left by the decedent. Particular care is required in respect to securities of a close corporation which may have been the subject of a buy-sell agreement: *Lied Est. v. Lied Est.*, 487 Pa. 333, annot. *Fiduc. Rev.* Mar. 1980, p. 3; *Richman Est.*, 2 Fiduc. Rep. 2d 321; *Dobson Est.*, 29 Fiduc. Rep. 339.

The personal representative of a deceased owner of shares in a statutory close corporation (15 Pa. C.S. § 2301 et seq.) may require the corporation to purchase the shares, or to cause the purchase of the shares by others, or to be dissolved, unless the by-laws provide otherwise: 15 Pa. C.S. § 2325.

Early review of securities should be made to determine whether they are to be sold (*Cooperman Est.*, 487 Pa. 148) or held for distribution (cf. *Niessen Est.*, 28 Fiduc. Rep. 362), and steps should be taken to comply with anticipated requirements of transfer agents, and to ensure that future dividend checks will be sent to a convenient address. If a corporate change has occurred in respect to securities specifically bequeathed, care must be exercised in considering the rights of the legatee in assets traceable therefrom: PEF 2514(17); *Fiduc. Rev.* Dec. 1976. In addition, consideration should be given to the need to continue any existing Subchapter S elections (to be taxed as "partnership") applicable to stock owned by the decedent: see IRS Reg. § 1.1372-3(b).

As stated in Section 6.1, the personal representative has broad powers of sale, and, unless the decedent's will provides otherwise, he may sell at a public or private sale personal property whether specifically bequeathed or not: PEF 3351. It is the duty of the personal representative to convert into cash within a reasonable time personal property not specifically bequeathed, but it may be advisable to secure the written consent of parties in interest who may prefer distribution in kind: see Section 16.1; *Crooks Est.*, 7 Fiduc. Rep. 677. Absent consent to retain, the personal representative may be surcharged for failure to sell securities: *Fiduc. Rev.* April 1974, p. 2. If the securities are to be held for any period of time, it may be advisable to prepare a card for each security upon which interest or dividends when received can be posted. This method preserves a clear record of the income on each asset. Attention should also be given to the need for exercising stock rights or conversion privileges. Disagreements between or among personal representatives are dealt with in PEF 3328; see also *Fiduc. Rev.* June 1959.

Chapter 63 of the PEF Code applies to joint brokerage accounts notwithstanding the limited definition of joint accounts in § 6303. *Deutsch, Larrimore & Farnish P.C. v. Johnson*, 791 A.2d 350.

## § 6.13 UNITED STATES SAVINGS BONDS

United States savings bonds in the name of the decedent alone present no particular problem and may be considered the same as any other security: see *Fiduc. Rev.* July 1952; cf. *Fiduc. Rev.* Oct. 1960, p. 4; July 1967. However, care should be exercised to follow federal regulations in the case of bonds which can be surrendered without discount upon the death of the owner. Registered U.S. bonds cannot be given without complying with federal regulations: *Drachenberg Est.*, 30 Fiduc. Rep. 203, annot. *Fiduc. Rev.* May 1980, p. 4; *DeSantis v. Prothero* (Pa. Super.), 916 A.2d 671. See *Fiduc. Rev.* March 1960, p. 3, for a discussion of the option, granted by IRC § 454 to accrue annually the increased redemption value of Series E savings bonds, and its effect upon personal representative, co-owners and beneficiaries.

Sales of Series E and Series H savings bonds have ended, but all unredeemed bonds will continue to earn interest until they reach final maturity. For instance, Series E bonds issued in 1941 matured in 1981; Series H bonds issued in June 1952 matured in 1982. Since no interest is earned after maturity date, matured bonds should be cashed promptly.

Frequently, United States Government bonds are registered in the name of the decedent "payable on death" to another or registered in two names in the alternative. Except in unusual circumstances, such bonds become the property of the surviving beneficiary or co-owner (see *Horstman Est.*, 398 Pa. 506; *Neglia Est.*, 403 Pa. 464; *Lingousky v. Gillespie,* 7 Fiduc. Rep. 489; cf. *Free v. Bland*, 369 U.S. 663; *Yiatchos v. Yiatchos*, 376 U.S. 306; *Hetrick Est.*, 17 Fiduc. Rep. 317, annot. *Fiduc. Rev.* July 1967), but if there is any dispute as to ownership, delivery thereof to the survivor should be delayed until the audit of the personal representative's account. See Chapter 15. Care should of course be exercised to make certain whether there is any obligation on the part of the personal representative to collect taxes thereon: Inheritance and Estate Tax Act § 1746. Co-ownership bonds, unless held by husband and wife, are subject to Pennsylvania inheritance tax: Inheritance and Estate Tax Act § 1708.

## § 6.14 INVESTMENTS

PEF 3316 states that the personal representative (subject to his duty to liquidate assets for prompt distribution, and to the provisions of the will) ". . . may invest the funds of the estate but shall have no duty to do so." If the funds are substantial, the personal representative may decide to invest them as provided by the will, or in certain government obligations and savings accounts, but usually he is under no duty to invest: *Fiduc. Rev.* June 1970, p. 2; *Arney Est.*, 23 Fiduc. Rep. 272; *Groesch Est.*, 13 Fiduc. Rep. 65; *Bellian Est.*, 11 Fiduc. Rep. 137.

Investment in U.S. Treasury Notes is not improper: *Burke Est.*, 2 Fiduc. Rep. 2d 259. However, when administration of the estate is likely to be delayed for an extended period of time, it is incumbent on the personal representative to invest the funds and not to permit them to lie idle: *Pitone Est.*, 489 Pa. 60, annot. *Fiduc. Rev.* May 1980, p. 2; see *Lare Est.*, 436 Pa. 1; *Brunner Est.* (Pa. Super.), 691 A.2d 530; *Carson Est.*, 14 Fiduc. Rep. 420. See also Banking Code of 1965, § 404, 7 P.S. § 404; cf. PEF 7314 regarding investments by corporate fiduciary in common trust fund. Investments should not be purchased on margin: *Shaner Est.*, 11 Fiduc. Rep. 648; cf. *Lychos Trust*, 1 Fiduc. Rep. 2d 254. The attorney's advice may be no excuse for failure to invest: see *Birely Est.*, 30 Fiduc. Rep. 522. See *Knipp Est.*, 489 Pa. 509, where it was held that it is not per se imprudent for an executor "vested with absolute discretion" to diversify immediately a large block of stock received at the commencement of administration.

## § 6.15 TAXES DUE OR OWING

The personal representative should ascertain the amount of any taxes owed by the decedent, including federal income and gift taxes, real and personal property taxes and wage or similar assessments. Returns should be prepared, and any tax shown due must be paid: *Fiduc. Rev.* Oct. 1958, p. 3. Such taxes are distinct from the estate and inheritance taxes discussed in Chapters 13 and 14. It is advisable that such returns be prepared early in the administration so that the schedule of debts can be completed. See Section 10.8. In this connection the personal representative will find it helpful to consult with the person, if any, whom the decedent employed to prepare his returns.

Copies of the decedent's federal income tax returns for the preceding three years should be examined. If the decedent died without having filed a return for the preceding year, the personal representative should determine if a return is required and, if so, file it. A federal tax return must be filed for the period beginning January 1 of the year the decedent died (or with the beginning of his fiscal year) and extending to the date of his death. See Section 14.9. When the returns have been filed, the personal representative, in appropriate cases, should consider requesting the District Director of Internal Revenue to make an early audit of these returns so as to shorten the three-year statute of limitations to eighteen months and thus expedite the administration of the estate: IRC § 6501(d); *Fiduc. Rev.* Oct. 1958, p. 3. If the personal representative is unable to meet a due date, he should request an extension so as to avoid, or at least minimize, any penalties.

## § 6.16 INSURANCE OF DECEDENT'S PROPERTY

Under PEF 3313, an important power is granted to the personal representative which enables him to protect himself, his employees and the beneficiaries of the estate from liability to third parties by taking out public liability insurance at the expense of the estate: see *Anderson Est.*, 1 Fiduc. Rep. 449; *Brooks Est.*, 2 Fiduc. Rep. 57, annot. *Fiduc. Rev.* Feb. 1952, p. 3. It is imperative that the personal representative make an early appraisal of the assets of the decedent's estate to determine whether public liability insurance carried by the decedent is adequate. If existing insurance is inadequate, or if no insurance was carried by the decedent, the personal representative should consider the advisability of having the coverage increased or a policy issued.

Fire insurance is a necessity, and the personal representative will be held responsible for failure to obtain it. Even if the decedent carried no fire insurance, the personal representative is under a duty to maintain an adequate amount: see *Brooks Est.*, supra. The cost of premiums for fire insurance, unlike that of public liability, is neither chargeable to the estate as an expense of administration nor deductible for inheritance tax purposes; but it is considered an income expense and chargeable to the heirs and devisees, since it is primarily for their benefit: *Anderson Est.,* 1 Fiduc. Rep. 449, annot. *Fiduc. Rev.* Sept. 1951. Act 98 of 1992, 40 P.S. § 636.1, requires continuation of "basic property insurance" coverage for 180 days after death of the insured or until sale if earlier, provided premiums are paid. However, note the provisions of the standard policy regarding vacancy of more than sixty days. 40 P.S. § 636.

In deciding what types and amounts of insurance should be obtained, the personal representative is held to the standard of conduct of ordinarily prudent businessmen who own property of the type considered: *Fiduc. Rev.* Dec. 1941. See *Lychos Trust*, 2 Fiduc. Rep. 2d 40; *Andrulewicz Est.*, 52 Northum. 109.

In all cases, the designation of the insured should be broadened to include the personal representative and those interested in the estate "as their interests may appear": see *Kyle v. National Ben-Franklin Ins. Co.*, 11 Fiduc. Rep. 556.

## § 6.17 INSURANCE AGAINST A DECEDENT'S PROFESSIONAL LIABILITY

Earlier, a professional such as a physician, accountant, lawyer, insurance agent, etc., carried professional liability or errors and omissions insurance which covered claims rising from negligence for the policy year in which the negligence occurred. Thus, insurance could be cancelled at death without negating the pre-death coverage even though the claim was not presented until after death.

The trend toward issuing professional liability insurance on a "claims made" basis, so that one must have coverage when the claim is made, regardless of whether he was insured when the negligence occurred, suggests that the personal representative consider maintaining in force the decedent's professional liability policy during the course of administration, or purchasing coverage for decedent's past professional acts, assuming the insurance company is willing to issue such policy.

For possible liability of attorney for services re execution of will, see *Fiduc. Rev.* Jan. 1980.

## § 6.18 CONTINUATION OF DECEDENT'S BUSINESS

The function of administration is to wind up the estate as promptly as possible and to make distribution. Thus, absent a provision in the will or specific statutory authority, the personal representative has no right to continue the decedent's business: *Kurkowski Est.*, 487 Pa. 295, annot. *Fiduc. Rev.* Feb. 1980, p. 3; 104 U. of Pa. L.R. 679. If he does so, he proceeds at his own peril; he will be surcharged for any losses, and all benefits and profits will inure to the estate. *Fiduc. Rev.* Sept. 1941, p. 4; June 1952. A testator may, of course, authorize or direct his executor to continue a trade or business: cf. *Jones Marketing Service v. Stotz*, 8 Fiduc. Rep. 620. Under PEF 3314, the orphans' court may authorize a personal representative "to continue any business of the decedent for the benefit of the estate," and in exercising this power the court may disregard the provisions of the will. For form of petition, see Partridge-Remick, O.C. Practice § 14.07. The court order may provide:

(1) For the conduct of the business by the personal representative alone, or jointly with others;

(2) For the conduct of the business as a corporation to be incorporated;

(3) The extent of the liability of the estate or of the personal representative for obligations incurred in the conduct of the business;

(4) Whether liabilities incurred are to be chargeable to the estate as a whole or solely to the part of the estate set aside for use in the business;

(5) The period of time the business may be conducted;

(6) Such other rules and regulations as the court deems suitable and proper.

Provision is made in PEF 3315 for the court to authorize the personal representative to organize a corporation to carry on the business of the decedent. For form of petition, see Partridge-Remick, O.C. Practice § 14.07.

One of the initial duties of the personal representative is to consider whether the estate will be enhanced by continuance of the decedent's business and, if so, to take immediately such steps as may be required to obtain court authorization. For reference to the matter of rentals, see Section 9.4.

The duty to safeguard assets of a business sometimes has unusual aspects. See *Mitchell Est.*, 20 Fiduc. Rep. 591, for a situation where the executors prevented seizure of an asset by the State Police.

## § 6.19 PARTNERSHIP INTERESTS

Where the decedent was a member of a partnership, the personal representative is confronted with problems which require careful consideration and handling. Basically, the interest of a decedent in a partnership business, like other assets, ordinarily is to be liquidated with reasonable promptness to the best advantage of the estate. However, surviving partners and partnership creditors have rights and interests which must be taken into account. Initially, the personal representative should acquaint himself with the liabilities of the estate by familiarizing himself with the partnership agreement, if any, and ascertain whether any provisions exist in the partnership agreement concerning appraisal or valuation of a deceased partner's share, or what arrangements and provisions are set forth concerning purchase of the deceased partner's interest: cf. *Lee v. Dahlin*, 399 Pa. 50; *Volpe Est.*, 10 Fiduc. Rep. 262, annot. *Fiduc. Rev.* Nov. 1960, p. 4; *Glenn Est.*, 5 Fiduc. Rep. 545; *Fiduc. Rev.* June 1952. For effect of a buy-and-sell agreement on death tax valuation, see Grossman and Smith, Pennsylvania Inheritance and Estate Tax § 9121(f) (Fifth Edition). Early consideration should be given to the advisability of incorporating if the business interest is to be retained.

The orphans' court division has initial jurisdiction to decide whether a partnership existed: *Fiduc. Rev.* March 1970. Regarding the extent of court jurisdiction over accounting by the surviving partners, see *Fiduc. Rev.* Feb. 1964, p. 4; *Jones Est.*, 13 Fiduc. Rep. 583; *Goodman Est.*, 25 Fiduc. Rep. 322. Where the executor himself is a surviving partner, no sale of the decedent's interest in the partnership may be made to him without court approval under PEF 3356: *Stauffer Est.*, 10 Leb. 114. In *Powell Est.*, 19 Fiduc. Rep. 140, annot. *Fiduc. Rev.* April 1969, the court determined that a judgment held by the decedent against her partner and herself individually and trading as a partnership "is not a first lien against the real estate of the decedent, and further, we conclude that the effect thereof, if such a judgment were considered to be a valid lien, would be to inequitably advance the status of the common creditors at the expense of junior lien creditors" of the partnership.

## § 6.20 REMOVAL OF FICTITIOUS NAME

When any person has registered a fictitious name and later dies, Section 2 of the Fictitious Names Act of 1982, P.L. 1309, 54 Pa. C.S. § 313, makes it the duty of his personal representative to file a statement of withdrawal and have the

Department of State make a notation of the withdrawal on the public records in order to avoid continuing liability: see *Willey v. Kaiser*, 86 D. & C. 209.

## § 6.21 REAL PROPERTY AND DUTIES WITH RESPECT THERETO

The personal representative has the right and duty to take possession of, maintain and administer all real property of the decedent except that occupied by an heir or devisee: cf. *Malinowski Est.*, 9 Fiduc. Rep. 44. Extended discussion of the administration of real estate including initial duties of the personal representative in regard thereto will be found in Chapter 9. Reference also should be made to Section 2.3.

## § 6.22 TANGIBLE PERSONAL PROPERTY AND DUTIES WITH RESPECT THERETO

The personal representative acquires the title (PEF 301(a)) and the right and duty (PEF 3311) to take possession of, administer and dispose of the decedent's tangible personal property at the time of his death. Its early disposal by sale (PEF 3351) or distribution to persons equitably entitled thereto discharges his responsibility concerning its value and its safety. However, the identification of the property given and of the legatee may be unclear: see *Fiduc. Rev.* Nov. 1981; *Rudy Est.*, 2 Fiduc. Rep. 2d 250; *Baker Est.*, 495 Pa. 522, annot. *Fiduc. Rev.* Nov. 1981. Exceptional care must be exercised when claims of a live-in partner of the decedent are involved: *Toloczko Est.*, 2 Fiduc. Rep. 2d 418, annot. *Fiduc. Rev.* Dec. 1982; *Brown Est.*, 28 Fiduc. Rep. 623; cf. *Banko v. Malanecki*, 499 Pa. 92, annot. *Fiduc. Rev.* March 1983. PEF § 3534.1, effective Sept. 5, 2006, provides:

"Except as otherwise provided in the will, if any, the personal representative shall pay as an expense of administration the reasonable expenses of storage, insurance, packing and delivery of tangible personal property to a beneficiary."

If the decedent owned an automobile which he did not specifically bequeath, the personal representative should give prompt consideration to having the title, registration and insurance changed from the decedent's name so that the car can be operated by a surviving member of the family. See Section 2.2; *Fiduc. Rev*. Feb. 1956, p. 3. For operation of car after death, see Act of 1976, P.L. 162, 75 Pa. C.S. § 1315.

If the personal representative or his attorney is to become the purchaser of any such property, it is essential that prior approval of all parties in interest, after full disclosure, be obtained. A purchase at public auction is not of itself sufficient protection: *Berzinsky Est.*, 40 Som. 11, annot. *Fiduc. Rev*. Feb. 1982, p. 4.

## § 6.23 DEBTS DUE THE ESTATE

A personal representative has not only the power but also the duty to collect all indebtedness owing the estate within a reasonable time, and he may proceed by suit if necessary to collect such obligations. All debts owing the decedent must be included in the inventory of the estate. See Section 12.1. His power to collect is as broad as was the decedent's in his lifetime. Carelessness or negligence in the performance of or failure to perform this duty may not only harm the estate but may render the personal representative personally liable. The personal representative should, in the course of his examination of the books of account of the decedent, ascertain all debts, such as salaries, royalties, rents, commissions, claims, judgments, accounts receivable, and so forth, and he should proceed to notify each debtor of the estate to make payment to him as personal representative. A corporate fiduciary is responsible for "ordinary prudence" not "special skill" in collecting estate assets: *Brickajlik Est.*, 29 Fiduc. Rep. 372. See Section 6.8. For general discussion of survival of claims, actions and judgments, see Chapter 11. Life Insurance, pensions and annuities should also be ascertained. See Section 6.10.

When a claim seems doubtful or is controverted, the personal representative should obtain legal advice as to whether it can be legally enforced. Advice of counsel in this regard will be evidence that the personal representative exercised the care and prudence of a reasonable man in the event that a surcharge is subsequently attempted: *Fiduc. Rev.* May 1942. In *Cooperman Est.*, 3 Fiduc. Rep. 2d 327, leave was granted under PEF 3312 to abandon a malpractice suit against attorneys in circumstances where the court was convinced it was a valueless asset.

The duty to collect debts includes debts owed by heirs, legatees (*Zavelle Est.*, 7 Fiduc. Rep. 638), agents (*Pierce Est.*, 1 Fiduc. Rep. 2d 342, annot. *Fiduc. Rev.* Oct. 1981, p. 3) and the personal representative himself, even though the statute of limitations thereon has run: *Woodruff Est.*, 7 Fiduc. Rep. 270, see Inh. & Est. Tax Act § 1711(o). However, the orphans' court division has no jurisdiction to determine whether the indebtedness of a beneficiary exceeds his beneficial interest in the estate: *Wharton Est.*, 17 Fiduc. Rep. 275. The appointment of a personal representative does not operate as a discharge of his indebtedness to the decedent, and any party in interest may, if necessary, bring an appropriate action to revive and continue the lien of a judgment which the decedent held on property of the personal representative: PEF 3304, 3318, Section 12.7. For claims against non-residents of Pennsylvania, see *Schumann Est.*, 27 Fiduc. Rep. 617, annot. *Fiduc. Rev.* Jan. 1978, p. 3.

## § 6.24 DECEDENT'S MAIL

It is advisable that the local post office be given a short certificate and be requested to forward to the personal representative all mail addressed to the decedent. Thus, a considerable amount of needed information with respect to the decedent's affairs may be secured easily and promptly, with the result that the task of accounting for dividends, for example, is simplified. The personal representative also will be in a position to advise business correspondents and transfer agents of the decedent's death and thus help to reduce the amount of mail received, and to ensure receipt of important mail.

## § 6.25 NOTICE OF GIFT TO A CORPORATION OR ASSOCIATION

A personal representative is required to send a written notice, within three months of the grant of letters, to each corporation or association named as a beneficiary in the decedent's will. The notice must state the date of the decedent's death, the county where the will has been probated and the fact that the corporation or association has been named a beneficiary: PEF 3330. This notice requirement may be fulfilled by sending the notice required by Supreme Court Orphans' Court Rule 5.6.

## § 6.26 NOTICE TO BENEFICIARIES AND INTESTATE HEIRS

Effective for decedents dying on or after January 1, 1999, Supreme Court Orphans' Court Rule 5.6 was amended as set forth hereafter. Prior Rule 5.6 remains effective for decedents dying on or after July 1, 1992 to December 31, 1998.

Rule 5.6. Notice to Beneficiaries and Intestate Heirs.

(a) *Requirement of Notice*. Within three (3) months after the grant of letters, the personal representative to whom original letters have been granted, or the personal representative's counsel, shall send a written notice of estate administration in the form approved by the Supreme Court to:

(1) every person, corporation, association, entity or other party named in the decedent's will as an outright beneficiary whether individually or as a class member;

(2) the decedent's spouse and children, whether or not they are named in, or have interest under, the will;

(3) where there is an intestacy in whole or in part, to every person entitled to inherit as an intestate heir

under Chapter 21 of the Probate, Estate and Fiduciaries Code;

(4) the appointed guardian of the estate, parent or legal custodian of any beneficiary who is a minor child under the age of eighteen (18) years;

(5) the appointed guardian of the estate, or, in the absence of such appointment, the institution or person with custody of any beneficiary who is an adjudicated incapacitated person;

(6) the Attorney General on behalf of any charitable beneficiary whose interest exceeds $25,000 or which will not be paid in full;

(7) the Attorney General on behalf of any governmental beneficiary;

(8) the trustee of any trust which is a beneficiary; and

(9) such other persons and in such manner as may be required by any local rule of court.

(b) *Definition of Beneficiary*. "Beneficiary" shall be deemed to include any person who may have an interest by virtue of the Pennsylvania anti-lapse statute, 20 Pa. C.S. § 2514.

(c) *Manner of Notice*. Notice shall be given by personal service or by first class, prepaid mail to each person and entity entitled to notice under subdivision (a) (1)-(9) whose address is known or reasonably available to the personal representative.

(d) *Certification of Notice*. Within (10) days after giving notice required by subdivision (a) of this Rule, the personal representative or the personal representative's counsel shall file with the Register or clerk a certification that notice has been given as required by this Rule. No fee shall be charged by the Register of Wills for filing the certification required by this subdivision.

(e) *Failure to File Certification*. Upon the failure by the personal representative, or the personal representative's counsel, to file the certification on a timely basis, the Register shall, after ten (10) days prior written notice to the delinquent personal representative and his counsel, notify the Court of such delinquency.

(f) *Effect of Notice*. This rule shall not alter or diminish existing rights or confer new rights.

(g) *Copies of Rule*. The Register shall deliver a copy of Rule 5.6 and the forms of notice and certification approved by the Supreme Court to each personal representative and counsel at the time letters are granted.

*Official Note*: It is not the intention of the Rule to require notice beyond the degree of consanguinity entitling a person to inherit under Chapter 21 of the Probate, Estates and Fiduciaries Code.

The form of notice and certification of notice required by Rule 5.6 were revised in 2006. See Appendixes 10 and 11 for forms.

Failure to give the notice required by Rule 5.6 was in part the basis, in addition to a finding, of fraud by procuring a disclaimer from her father without disclosing the size of the estate of which he was sole beneficiary, for setting aside the disclaimer. *Hydock Est.*, 26 Fiduc. Rep. 2d 209, annotated *Fiduc. Rev.*, Sept. 2006, p. 4.

## § 6.27 COMPENSATION OF THE PERSONAL REPRESENTATIVE AND ATTORNEY

The personal representative is allowed compensation or commissions for carrying out the administration of the decedent's estate. Compensation allowed for the administration of realty is discussed in Section 9.7. PEF 3537 provides that "The Court shall allow such compensation to the personal representative as shall in the circumstances be reasonable and just, and may calculate such compensation on a graduated basis."

It has been said that the court has "both the power and the duty *on its own motion* to pass upon the reasonableness of the compensation claimed. An executor or a trustee is an officer of the orphans' court and accountable to such court for all his actions of commission and omission in the performance of his fiduciary duties; such duty to account embraces all payments made from estate or trust funds by way of compensation to himself or his counsel": *Thompson Est.*, 426 Pa. 270, aff'g 16 Fiduc. Rep. 279. For compensation with respect to the collection and preparation of personal effects for sale, see *Miller Est.*, 15 Fiduc. Rep. 581. It should be noted that an executor who acts in good faith is entitled to "expenses of administration, costs, fees and commissions" for so acting even though the will is set aside: *Navitsky Est.*, 57 Berks 206. Compensation may include travelling expenses of the personal representative: *Hall Est.*, 16 Bucks 48. See *Seidel Est.*, 22 Fiduc. Rep. 343, allowing slightly more compensation than "the normal" in a large estate for "extraordinary services," particularly in view of the appreciation in value of the gross estate by reason of "investments and timely disposal of decedent's assets."

The allowance of compensation to personal representatives and their counsel is elastic and necessarily dependent on the circumstances of each case including any contract in regard thereto. Examples of the application of the broad standard stated in PEF 3537 are found in 1 Hunter, O.C. Commonplace Bk. (2d Ed.), Commissions, and in annotations of cases in *Fiduciary Review*, including Aug. 1965, p. 2, March 1981, p. 3, May 1982, p. 4, Dec. 2001, p. 1, June 2004, p. 1, July 2004, p. 4, Mar. 2006, p. 4, Nov. 2007, p. 1, Jul. 2008, p. 1, Oct. 2009, p. 1, Sept. 2010, p. 1, Apr. 11, p. 4.

See also *Johnson Est.*, 4 Fiduc. Rep. 6, in which schedules for compensation of personal representatives and attorneys are included. The schedules are stated to have been approved by the Attorney General who has since denied such approval. Many factors impact on the appropriate fees. See *LaRocca Est.*, 431 Pa. 542, for factors relating to attorney fees. See § 14.11 concerning possible inclusion of personal representatives' commissions as self employment income reportable on Form 1040, Schedule SE.

In *Burke Est.*, 2 Fiduc. Rep. 2d 259, commission on real estate was not limited to 3% and in *Crawford Est.*, 2 Fiduc. Rep. 2d 229, additional counsel fees and expenses were allowed for successful defense against claimed surcharge. See also *Fiduc. Rev.* July 1981, p. 3.

In practical operation, the personal representative includes the claimed compensation as one of the last items in his principal and income disbursements and usually withholds payment thereof until his account has been approved. In the event of objection thereto by a party in interest, the issue comes before the court at audit and the suggested disbursement must be supported by evidence of the services rendered and responsibility assumed. For an instance when the claimed compensation for extraordinary services was reduced, see *Farley Est.*, 130 Pitts. 116. For an instance where claimed compensation was approved, see *Menzer Est.*, 30 Fiduc. Rep. 495.

The long standing rule of *Williamson Est.*, 368 Pa. 343, that a trustee who had received compensation as an executor could not receive compensation from principal was overturned by the Supreme Court which affirmed the Superior Court's reversal of the lower court which denied compensation: *Estate of Freidenberg v. Comm.*, 33 A.3d 581 (2011). The principle of *stare decisis* did not require continued support of the *Williamson* rule. Legislative changes permitted application of new rules concerning compensation from principal.

For division of compensation between personal representatives in event of dispute, see *Baum Est.*, 30 Fiduc. Rep. 574, aff'd per cur. 298 Pa. Super. 593, annot. *Fiduc. Rev.* May 1982, p. 4, and *Paller Est.*, 2 Fiduc. Rep. 3d 322, annot. Fiduc. Rev., Sept. 2012, p. 1.

## § 6.28 DISCLAIMERS AND RENUNCIATIONS

As suggested in Section 1.6, a disclaimer authorized under Chapter 62 of the PEF Code is an important subject for early consideration and disposition. The requirements for the filing, delivery and recording thereof, as set forth in PEF 6204, should be followed. See generally *Fiduc. Rev.* July 1967, p. 3, Oct. 1976, Oct. 1976 and Mar. 2005, p. 4; cf. *Dickey Trust*, 1 Fiduc. Rep. 2d 144. If the advantages of disclaimers, renunciations or spouse's election in reducing or avoiding Pennsylvania inheritance tax are to be realized, the time periods of § 1716(c) of the Inheritance and Estate Tax Act must be met. See Section 13.1. The time requirement of Section 2055 of the Internal Revenue Code also must be followed if a disclaimer is to be employed to obtain a charitable deduction for federal estate tax purposes. Of paramount consideration is the impact of disclaimers on the distributive shares of those disclaiming. As stated in PEF 6201, "The right to disclaim shall exist notwithstanding any limitation on the interest in the nature of a spendthrift provision or similar restriction."

For situations where disclaimers have been set aside, see *Gallagher v. Riddle*, 850 A.2d 748, annot. *Fiduc. Rev.* Sept. 2004, p. 3 (fraudulent conveyance) and *Hydock Est.*, 26 Fiduc. Rep. 2d 209, annot. *Fiduc. Rev.* Sept. 2006, p. 4 (fraud and failure to give 5.6 notice).

For disclaimer within nine months after minor reaches age eighteen, see annotation *Fiduc. Rev.* July 2005, p. 1.

## § 6.29 MISCELLANEOUS

A number of miscellaneous but important duties devolve upon a personal representative. He should, for example, consider whether guardians for minors should be appointed. With respect to the possible appointment of a guardian ad litem, see *Clement Trust*, 18 Fiduc. Rep. 135, dispensing with such appointment where the interests of the minors were identical with the interests of adult children. See also *Calantzis v. Collins*, 440 Pa. 354, annot. *Fiduc. Rev.* March 1971; *Smith Trust*, 21 Fiduc. Rep. 312. He should determine whether ancillary administration will be required. See Sections 3.16, 5.8. If the decedent was himself an executor or a trustee, steps should be taken to secure his discharge and, if necessary, to have a successor appointed. See "Suc-

## Principal Duties of an Efficient Executor or Administrator in Administering an Estate

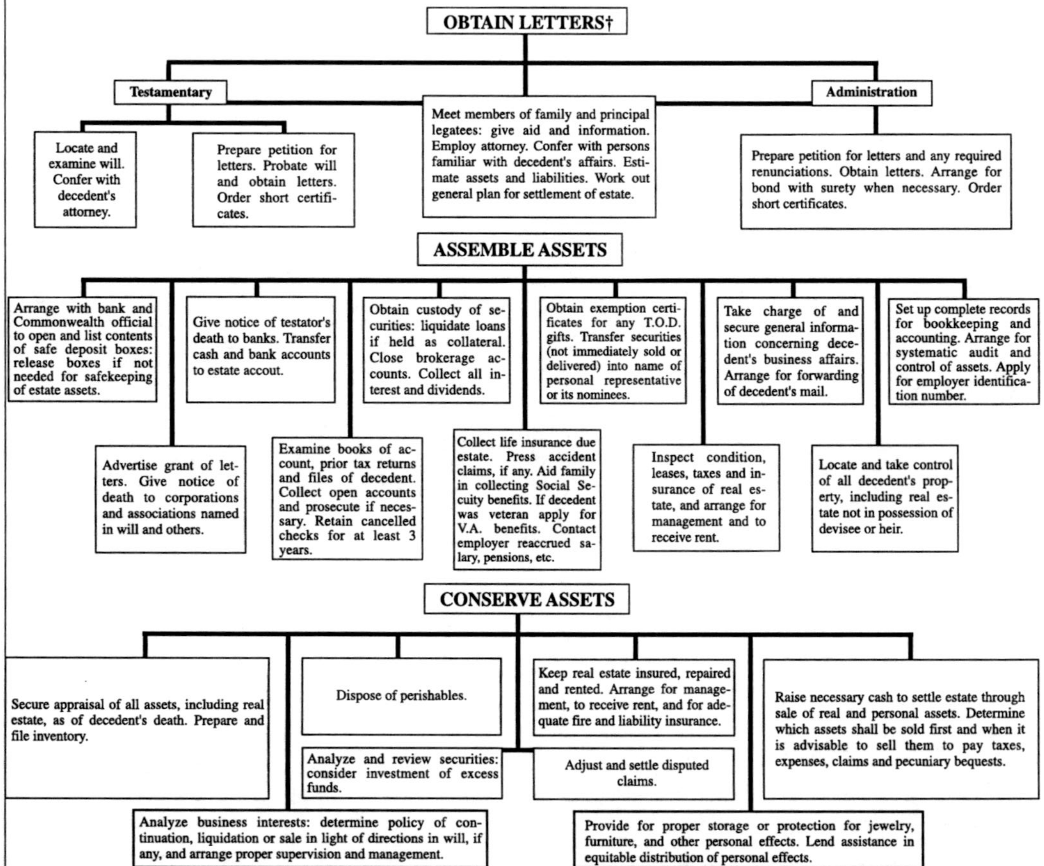

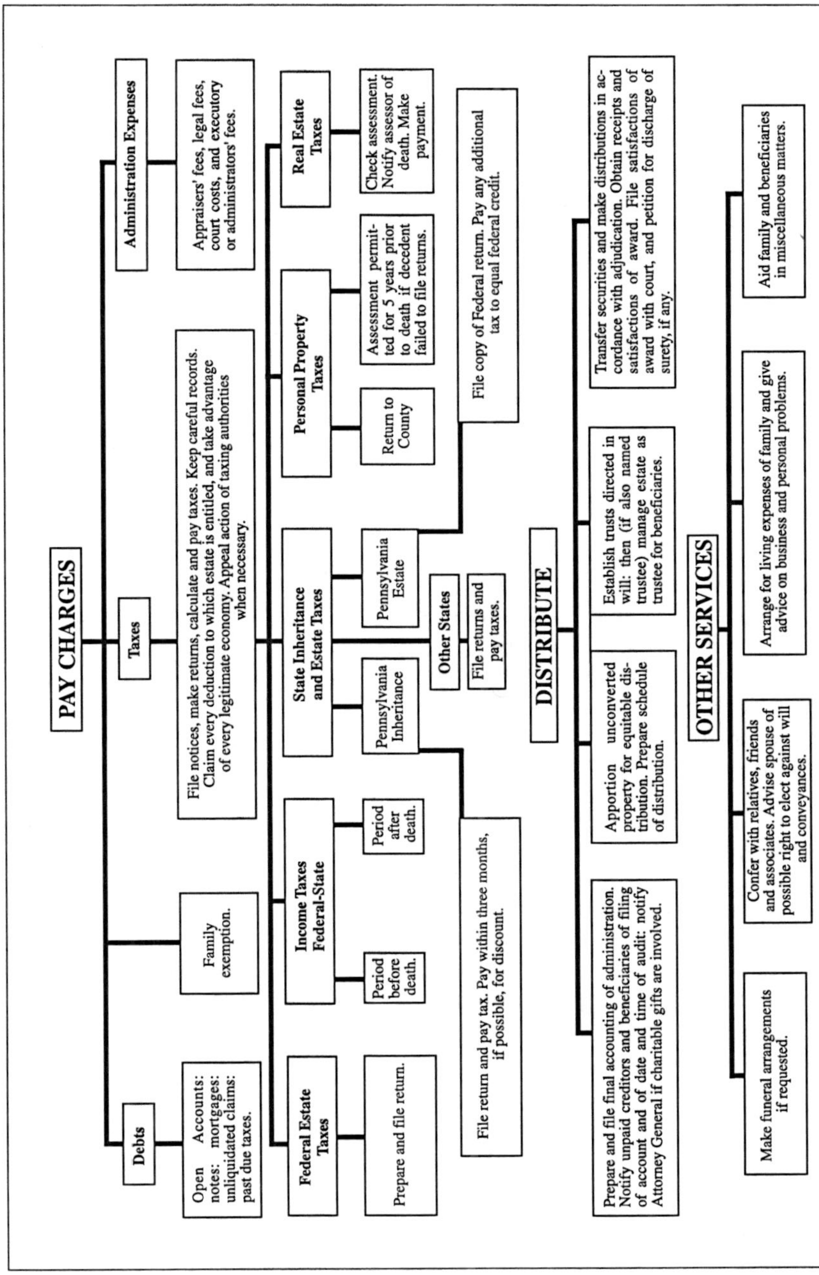


† **If personalty in estate is less than $25,000, consider settlement under PEF 3102. In all cases, consider possibility of settlement by family agreement: *Pa. Fiduciary Guide*, § 2.5**

cessor Fiduciaries—Liability for Predecessor's Administration," *Fiduc. Rev.* March 1964, p. 3. For designation of a successor fiduciary, see *Fiduc. Rev.* May 1975, p. 3; *Bailey Trust*, 25 Fiduc. Rep. 388.

The personal representative should ascertain whether the decedent was a party to any pending litigation and take appropriate steps with respect thereto. See Chapter 11. See *Maurice Est.*, 21 Fiduc. Rep. 368, annot. *Fiduc. Rev.* Sept. 1971, finding that executor in the circumstances there involved should not have employed a tax consultant. The annotation discusses the employment of consultants and specialists.

If more than one personal representative is appointed, they will have individual as well as joint responsibilities. See discussion in *Fiduc. Rev.* Sept. 1945. In the case of co-executors, PEF 3328(a) provides that the decision of the majority is to be controlling where the will does not direct otherwise; a dissenter to some extent may avoid liability for consequences of such majority action. If there is no agreement of a majority of the co-executors, application may be made to the court for a direction as to the exercise or non-exercise of the power in dispute: PEF 3328(b). See *Floyd Est.*, 1 Fiduc. Rep. 283, annot. *Fiduc. Rev.* June 1951. Regarding the voting of stock by co-executors, and delegation of nondiscretionary powers, see PEF 3319, 3320.

For possible contemptuous conduct of the personal representative, see *Ingaglio Est.*, 492 Pa. 270.

The Liquor Code, 47 P.S. §4-491, since amendment in 1984, permits the personal representative to sell publicly or privately liquor which was an asset of the decedent. Sales will be subject to regulations of the Pennsylvania Liquor Control Board to ensure that state taxes will be paid from the proceeds of the sale.

Chapter 7

# FAMILY EXEMPTION



## § 7.1 IN GENERAL

The surviving spouse or members of the decedent's family are entitled to a "family exemption" of $3,500. The foundation of the right is the family relationship. It accrues to the spouse or children of a decedent who dies domiciled in Pennsylvania. In the absence of a spouse or child entitled to the exemption, the "parent or parents of the decedent who are members of the same household as the decedent" are entitled thereto. Statutory provisions with respect to this exemption are found in PEF 3121–3126.[1]

The exemption is a right to *retain* as well as to *claim* either real or personal property of the decedent to the value of $3,500, and it is, in a sense, an interest in the property rather than a mere preference in distribution. It does not de-

**§ 7.1**

**1.** The right to an exemption, measured by dollar value, has existed in Pennsylvania since the Act of 1851, P.L. 612: see *Fiduc. Rev.* Dec. 1966; 43 Dick. L. Rev. 31, 32; 12 Pa. Bar Assn. Q. 313. Although later extended to surviving husbands, and parents, the exemption was originally justified and inspired by consideration of the welfare of the family, that it might not be wholly deprived of support after the death of the head of the family: *Henkel Est.*, 13 Pa. Super. 337. It was a benefit similar to the debtor's exemption given the decedent in his lifetime: see *Neff Ap.*, 21 Pa. 243, 247.

pend on the poverty or necessities of those entitled thereto (*Calhoun Est.*, 1 Fiduc. Rep. 162;[2] *Palethorp Est.*, 14 C.C. 286), and it is payable whether the decedent has died testate or intestate. It exists regardless of testamentary provision to the contrary (*Peebles Est.*, 157 Pa. 605) or whether there is an election to take under or against the will (*Farrell Est.*, 4 W.N.C. 383; *Vasil Est.*, 2 Fiduc. Rep. 615). It may not be waived by nuptial agreement or family settlement which makes no specific reference to it: *Fishel Est.*, 24 Fiduc. Rep. 387; *Tofini Est.,* 17 Fiduc. Rep. 545. The exemption should be claimed as soon as possible after the death of the decedent, as it may be lost if not claimed within a reasonable time. See Section 7.5. It may be obtained by retaining possession of particular property, or by demand from the personal representative, or by special application to the court (see Section 7.4), whether or not letters have been granted (PEF 3122), or as a distributive share of the estate at the time of distribution. The exemption may not be claimed in property theretofore sold by the personal representative. See Section 9.5; PEF 3121, 3126(b); cf. *Miller Est.,* 27 D. & C. 2d 460, disallowing claim for exemption where real estate was sold at judicial sale, and awarding proceeds to judgment creditor. Payment of the family exemption will not be deemed an income distribution for purposes of federal income taxation: Cf. IRC §§ 661, 662; Reg. § 1.661(a)–2(e). With respect to the disallowance of the family exemption as an inheritance tax deduction where there are no probate assets against which it may be claimed, see *Stevens Est.*, 434 Pa. 259, annot. *Fiduc. Rev.* June 1969, p. 3.

## § 7.2 PERSONS ENTITLED TO THE EXEMPTION

Since January 1, 1950, the surviving husband as well as the surviving wife has been entitled to claim the exemption: *Williams Est.*, 2 Fiduc. Rep. 46. The surviving spouse is

---

§ **7.1**

**2.** The words "as a reasonable requirement for support during the settlement of the estate," first included in the 1949 act (so that the exemption would qualify as a then existing deduction for federal estate tax purposes), were deleted by the Act of 1956, P.L. 1084.

first entitled to *retain* or *claim* the entire exemption, and "if there be no spouse, or if he [or she] has forfeited his [or her] rights, then such children as are members of the same household as the decedent" are entitled to the exemption. In absence of a spouse or child entitled to the exemption the "parent or parents . . . who are members of the same household as the decedent" have been entitled to the exemption since Sept. 1, 1963: PEF 3121. See Section 7.6. The son of a common law husband of decedent has been held entitled to the family exemption: *Wawrzyniak Est.* 28 Fiduc. Rep. 654, annot. *Fiduc. Rev.* Feb. 1979. An illegitimate daughter forming part of the decedent's household has been held not entitled to family exemption: *Clark Est.*, 26 Fiduc. Rep. 427. However, it would appear that under more recent developments an illegitimate child forming a part of decedent's household would be entitled to the exemption. See *Fiduc. Rev.* Jan. 1979. If the surviving spouse is not capable of claiming, the children may claim the exemption in his or her stead (*Bell Est.*, 139 Pa. Super. 11, annot. *Fiduc. Rev.* March 1940, p. 3; *Otteni Est.*, 486 Pa. 631) unless failure of the spouse to claim the exemption constitutes a waiver (*Lentz Est.*, 11 Fiduc. Rep. 399; *Griffith Est.*, 11 Fiduc. Rep. 182). No distinction is made between children who are minors and those who are adults (*Gehringer Est.*, 10 D. & C. 279; *Fiduc. Rev.* March 1940, p. 3), between natural and adopted children (*Bryan Est.*, 22 D. & C. 713), nor whether the decedent was the father or mother (cf. *Fiduc. Rev.* Oct. 1944, p. 3). The exemption is not allowed to a stepchild: *Wheeler Est.*, 13 Fiduc. Rep. 360.

When a person entitled to the exemption is a minor, his guardian, or in the absence thereof the personal representative, must claim the exemption on his behalf: PEF 3122(b); *Kreppenneck Est.*, 29 Fiduc. Rep. 497. Claim on behalf of an incapacitated person should be made by the guardian: *Cacciatore Est.*, 61 D. & C. 266.

For assignment of right to receive the exemption, see *Allen Est.*, 488 Pa. 415; *Bracken Est.*, 9 Fiduc. Rep. 49 and *Gramacki Est.*, 15 Fiduc. Rep. 365.

## § 7.3 PRIORITY OF THE EXEMPTION

Prior to May 5, 1970, persons entitled to the family exemption were not limited in the choice of property which they could retain or claim.[1] Since that date assets "specifically devised or bequeathed by the decedent, or otherwise specifically disposed of by him, may not be so retained or claimed if other assets are available for the exemption": PEF 3121. Subject only to that limitation, those entitled to the exemption are not limited in the choice of property which they may retain or claim: *Sipler Est.*, 16 Fiduc. Rep. 615, annot. *Fiduc. Rev.* Dec. 1966; cf. *Prutsman Est.*, 10 Fiduc. Rep. 532. "While the claimant has the right to select whatever real estate she desires, she cannot select various parcels when one parcel chosen will satisfy her claim": *Skonieczki Est.*, 12 Fiduc. Rep. 57, 62.

The exemption is in the nature of a property right passing to those entitled when retained or claimed and is preferred to all claims against the estate other than administration expenses. See Section 10.2; PEF 3392. It takes precedence over the rights of all creditors (including funeral expenses, *Fiduc. Rev.* April 1940) and judgment creditors (*Graves Est.*, 134 Pa. 377), distributees, heirs, claims of the Commonwealth and claims of the United States (see Sections 10.2, 10.4; *Hildebrand Est.*, 262 Pa. 112; *Jones Est.*, 84 Pa. Super. 170). However, although the exemption is broadly interpreted to favor those entitled thereto, it is subordinated to property interests established before the decedent's death and identified with particular property. For example, it is subordinate to mortgages upon the lands which secure them (*Kauffman Ap.*, 112 Pa. 645) and to liens (including judgments) for purchase money of real estate (PEF 3126(a)).

---

**§ 7.3**

**1.** Before May 5, 1970, the unlimited choice of property available to the exemption included property specifically devised or bequeathed by the decedent: *Stachnick Est.*, 376 Pa. 592; *Fiduc. Rev.* June 1953, p. 3; *DiMaio Est.*, 6 Fiduc. Rep. 188. In such circumstances, it had been held the disappointed legatee was not entitled to be made whole out of the residue under the theory that the spouse's selection has the effect of an ademption: *Pratt Est.*, 60 York 41.

## § 7.4 PROCEDURE FOR OBTAINING THE EXEMPTION

(1) *Personal property*. When the exemption is claimed from the decedent's personal estate, the procedure may be very simple. If the claimant has possession of tangible property, he or she can retain it. However, when possession is in another, or when the property is intangible and requires a transfer of title papers, assistance of the personal representative, or of the court, to transfer title may be essential. If the estate is small and no administration is contemplated, the exemption can be acquired by application to the court under PEF 3122(c), or it can be acquired in connection with application to the court under PEF 3102. See Section 2.4; *William Est.*, 12 Fiduc. Rep. 284; Aker PEF Code Annot. § 3102. The right to the exemption is personal and may not be claimed by the personal representative of the person entitled: *Hartman Est.*, 20 Fiduc. Rep. 308. The right to claim particular property for the exemption may be lost if not claimed before the property is sold by the personal representative (PEF 3121, 3126) or it may be waived by delay in asserting the right thereto (*Jenks Est.*, 18 Fiduc. Rep. 209, annot. *Fiduc. Rev.* June 1968, p. 4).

The requisite formality for claiming the exemption depends upon the circumstances: *Fiduc. Rev.* July 1970. A mere listing of the claim by a widow-administratrix in her inheritance tax return and affidavit has been held to be insufficient (*Wraught Est.*, 347 Pa. 165; *Schwartz Est.*, 166 Pa. Super, 459, annot. *Fiduc. Rev.* May 1950, p. 4; cf. *Beck Est.*, 20 Fiduc. Rep. 268), whereas an *oral* claim by a widow awaiting an operation was held to be sufficient (*Cochran Est.*, 28 Dist. 654). Cf. *Friedrich Est.*, 11 Fiduc. Rep. 558, holding that a letter from a widow's attorney to the executor's attorney was sufficient. In all cases, the position of the claimant should be indicated promptly and in writing in order clearly to provide evidence that the "claim" has been made. The same is true even when the person entitled to the exemption is the personal representative; a written demand addressed to himself, together with credit thereof in the account, would seem to suffice: see *Fiduc. Rev.* Nov. 1944, p. 3; cf. *Racik Est.*, 78 D. & C. 602.

If letters testamentary or of administration have been granted to a personal representative, he can transfer property claimed for the exemption with a minimum of risk without insisting upon a prior court approval of his act. The risks are those involved in the following questions:

(a) Is the person making claim entitled to the exemption?

(b) Are there sufficient other assets to pay administration expenses?

(c) Is it clear that there are no property rights in others existing prior to the death of the decedent in the property claimed?

(d) Is the value of the property $3,500 or less?

If all such questions can be answered affirmatively, the exemption can be paid or distributed without risk and without the need of court action. However, if any of the answers to these questions is uncertain, distribution of the claim may be delayed, pending application of the claimant to the court under PEF 3122(c), or pending audit of the account, when the exemption may be distributed along with other distributive shares of the estate: *McCarter Est.*, 36 D. & C. 625; cf. *Fiduc. Rev.* June 1968, p. 4. If application for the exemption is made to the court prior to audit of the account, care must be exercised to comply with rules of the Supreme Court (O.C. Rule 12.1), as well as of the local court. As heretofore stated, special provisions are made for claim of the exemption on behalf of minors and incapacitated persons: PEF 3122(b).

(2) *Real estate.* The exemption may be claimed from real estate, whether or not the real estate exceeds in value the exemption claimed: cf. *Skonieczki Est.*, 12 Fiduc. Rep. 57. The procedure in connection therewith is outlined in PEF 3123. In addition to the procedure there outlined, it is clear

that real estate may be awarded by the court at audit in the same manner as any other distributive share of the estate. See Section 9.8. Cf. *Fuller Est.*, 6 Fiduc. Rep. 2d 181.

If the real estate claimed is appraised in excess of the exemption and it cannot be divided so as to set apart the amount claimed without prejudice to or spoiling the whole or any parcel of the real estate, the claimant may choose to take the real estate and pay the surplus within six months from the court's confirmation of the appraisement: PEF 3123(b).

In most situations, at least when there is no dispute, it would seem preferable to claim personal property for the exemption, or else to wait until audit to claim the real estate rather than to incur the expense of a separate petition. Retention of an exemption, as contrasted with a claim therefor, is practical only when personal property, which can be readily appropriated, is involved. When real estate is involved, or securities requiring formal evidence of ownership, the claimant must make a "claim" for exemption to perfect title in himself. Until a claim is allowed, or until credit in an accounting is approved, the claimant's title to the assets retained is in suspense. If real estate is set aside for the exemption, it may be lost to a subsequent bona fide purchaser or lien holder if the decree setting aside the real estate is not duly recorded: PEF 3126.

(3) *Valuation—Income*. When there is no dispute as to the right to the exemption, and when the claim therefor is not delayed, personal property may be delivered to the claimant at values fixed by the inventory. When a dispute arises over the valuation, the claimant may petition the court to fix the valuation: PEF 3122(c). Inventory values probably will not be conclusive in the event of dispute or delay in claiming the exemption: PEF 3122(c); cf. *Stokes Est.*, 167 Pa. Super. 128, annot. *Fiduc. Rev.* Sept. 1950, p. 4. However, whenever real estate is involved, and is not to be awarded at the time of audit based on its then value, petition for the appointment of two appraisers must be made to the court, and the valuation to be taken is as of the date of the petition for such appointment: PEF 3123(a).

When the court has appointed appraisers to value real estate, its only choice is to accept the valuation so fixed, except when it is shown that it is too low or that a "palpable wrong has been inflicted by stealth, fraud or other unfair means": *Williams Est.*, 2 Fiduc. Rep. 46, 50. In that event, the court can set aside the appraisement and appoint new appraisers, but it has no authority to alter the appraisement made.

Although the exemption right does not carry with it interest as such (*Brusstar Est.*, 27 Berks 242, annot. *Fiduc. Rev.* Jan. 1936), the claimant nevertheless may be entitled to a portion of the income earned by the estate pending satisfaction of the exemption claim: PEF 3124.

(4) *Challenge of the exemption*. At any time before a decree of confirmation, a "party in interest" may subject the exemption allowance and/or the appraisement of the property claimed to the control of the court: PEF 3122(c). Once a decree of confirmation of allowance or appraisement has been entered, it may not be attacked collaterally (*Merion Title & Trust Co. v. Stadelman*, 12 Dist. 641), nor in answer to a petition for sale (*Greenawalt Est.*, 16 Pa. Super. 263), nor at audit of the personal representative's account (*Scott Est.*, 18 Pa. Super. 375; *Pratt Est.*, 60 York 41); cf. *Heckman Est.*, 17 D. & C. 761, where confirmation of appraisement was unnecessary. The decree of confirmation, however, may be attacked directly when the petition to vacate alleges facts sufficient to show the claimant was not entitled to the exemption allowed: *Kerns Ap.*, 120 Pa. 523; *Somers Est.*, 14 Phila. 261; *Walters Est.*, 12 Dist. 122.

## § 7.5 WAIVER AND FORFEITURE OF RIGHTS

Prima facie, a surviving spouse, child or parent is entitled to the exemption, and those objecting thereto must satisfactorily prove, by clear and convincing testimony, a state of circumstances from which it can be found that the right has been forfeited or waived. It is not lost by a levy in the decedent's lifetime under a confessed judgment containing waiver of exemption: *Beetem & Co. v. Getz*, 5 Pa. Super. 71; cf. *First National Bank v. Jackson*, 36 D. & C. 295. The surviving spouse is competent to testify when forfeiture is alleged: PEF 3121.

Persons otherwise entitled to the exemption have been held to have waived or forfeited it under one or more of the following circumstances:

(1) Failure to demand within a reasonable time: *Cram Est.*, 114 Pa. Super. 463, citing *Davis Ap.*, 34 Pa. 256. What constitutes laches in a particular case depends on the circumstances, and the question will usually turn upon whether the delay has been prejudicial to others: *Davies Est.*, 146 Pa. Super. 7; cf. *Prutsman Est.*, 10 Fiduc. Rep. 532, *Fiduc. Rev.* June 1968, p. 4. It should be noted that the claim must be made before the death of the person entitled and may not be made by his personal representative: *Matheny Est.*, 164 Pa. Super. 18; *Kornman Est.*, 6 Fiduc. Rep. 666. In *Tofini Est.*, 17 Fiduc. Rep. 545, it was held that neither a family settlement agreement nor laches barred the claim by a daughter for family exemption when she claimed it more than three years after the decedent's death but did so promptly upon being advised of her right to do so, not having theretofore been advised of her rights, because the claim was not prejudicial to others, and the delay did not result from her own lack of diligence. "There is no specific statutory time limit within which a family exemption claim must be filed. Laches is available only if the delay has caused detriment": *Wilson Est.*, 22 Fiduc. Rep. 126. The claim has been denied to a widow represented by counsel when filed more than one year after probate: *Wilson Est.*, 25 Fiduc. Rep. 278 and to a son who claimed to have first learned about the exemption three years after death although he was represented by counsel: *Rohrbaugh Est.*, 8 Fiduc. Rep. 2d 201. However, a family exemption claimed more than one year after death has been allowed where no one was prejudiced by the delay: *Klein Est.*, 26 Fiduc. Rep. 37, aff'd 474 Pa. 416.

(2) Intentional relinquishment: *Bell Est.*, 139 Pa. Super. 11.

(3) Antenuptial and post nuptial agreements (*Tiernan v. Binns*, 92 Pa. 248; *Haendler Est.*, 81 Pa. Super. 168), provided they met the standards required for such contracts to be effective: *Fiduc. Rev.* Jan. 1954, p. 3; *Jackson Est.*, 14 Fiduc. Rep. 391; *Dekarski Est.*, 15 Fiduc. Rep. 576; cf. *Harrison Est.*, 456 Pa. 356. Such an agreement must expressly waive the right to the exemption. Thus, a postnuptial agreement which waived all rights "to elect to take against the will of the other or to enter any proceeding against the estate of the other contrary to the expressed provisions of their respective wills" did not waive the right to the family exemption: *Hughes Est.*, 17 Fiduc. Rep. 114. Cf. *Hines Est.* 30 Fiduc. Rep. 363, annot. *Fiduc. Rev.*, June 2006, p. 4. In August, 1968, the Supreme Court restated "clearly and more definitely the applicable standards and principles" in the field of antenuptial agreements in its decisions in *Hillegas Est.*, 431 Pa. 144; *Harris Est.*, 431 Pa. 293; *Lock Est.*, 431 Pa. 251 and *Vallish Est.*, 431 Pa. 88. These decisions are discussed in *Fiduc. Rev.* Sept. 1968. See *Leonard Est.*, 435 Pa. 641, where the widow was not barred by a contemplated nuptial agreement, because ". . . the parties had agreed to substantially all the terms of the proposed family settlement agreement [but] the agreement contemplated a writing . . ." which was never signed.

(4) Voluntary separation: *Crawford Est.*, 81 Pa. Super. 222; cf. *Auch Est.*, 174 Pa. Super. 406; *Arnout Est.*, 283 Pa. 49. Where the break in the family relationship is the fault of the decedent, his widow does not lose her right to claim the exemption: *Lean Est.*, 16 Fiduc. Rep. 602. See *Jenkins Est.*, 50 Wash. 72, where the widow who had lived separately from the testator for more than one year prior to death was nevertheless entitled to elect against the will because the "separation was by mutual consent and lacked the elements of a willful and malicious desertion." *Marinkov Est.*, 12 Leb. 50, holds that the family relationship continues where a husband had "ordered his wife to leave the matrimonial domicile and he had consented in her staying away until his death."

(5) Desertion, in the sense of actual abandonment of matrimonial cohabitation with an intent to desert: *Braum Est.*, 86 Pa. Super. 245; *Stambaugh Est.*, 11 Fiduc. Rep. 622.

See *Marinkov Est.*, 12 Leb. 50, holding that the record of proceedings in which the husband was ordered to pay support to his wife was admissible in order to support an inference that the wife was not guilty of desertion.

(6) Divorce: (*Limber Est.*, 284 Pa. 346).

(7) Adultery: *Dauscher Est.*, 21 Lehigh 240; cf. *Trostle Est.*, 61 York 90, for condonement of adultery.

(8) Invalid marriage: *Tighe Est.*, 15 D. & C. 474.

(9) Remarriage: Prior to 1950 remarriage was sufficient to bar a "widow" of her right to exemption if not claimed before the remarriage: *Clark Est.*, 275 Pa. 506; *Kerns Ap.*, 120 Pa. 523; see Gest, Drawing Wills and Settlement of Estates 122 (1909). The present statute employs the term "spouse"; therefore it is not clear whether remarriage will cause a forfeiture. Cases under prior law reasoned that a "widow" can only be an unremarried spouse. Since this reasoning might be extended to cover "spouse of any decedent," it seems only prudent for a surviving spouse firmly to establish his or her right to the exemption before remarriage: see *Fiduc. Rev.* April 1964, p. 3.

(10) Any action which would bar the spouse from receiving an intestate share of the decedent's estate or from electing to take against a will: PEF 2106, 2208. Act 135 of 1976 amended PEF 2106 and 2509 to eliminate any distinction between a surviving husband and a surviving wife in the forfeiture of intestate shares or elective rights because of failure to support the decedent-spouse. See *Fiduc. Rev*. July 1975 and Feb. 1976, re the "Equal Rights Amendment" to the Pa. Constitution, Art. 1, Section 28, as it applies to the duty, if any, of one spouse to support the other. Act 23 of 1978 repealed PEF 2509, and added new Chapter 22, and specifically PEF 2208.

Slaying the spouse (*Pinder Est.*, 61 D. & C. 193) and failure of a husband to support his wife would operate to forfeit the exemption.

## § 7.6 HOUSEHOLD

It should be noted that a temporary or even extended absence from home does not necessarily result in forfeiture of the exemption: *Sadowski Est.*, 158 Pa. Super. 119; *Piskorick Est.*, 29 Fiduc. Rep. 58; *Gress Est.*, 25 Fiduc. Rep. 81; *Skonieczki Est.*, 12 Fiduc. Rep. 57; *Stambaugh Est.*, 11 Fiduc. Rep. 622. See, however *Bitler Est.*, 68 D. & C. 2d 485; *Hines Est.*, 28 Fiduc. Rep. 476; *Seyler Est.*, 27 Fiduc. Rep. 242. When the separation from or disruption of the household is caused by the decedent, the courts generally construct a household relationship in order not to deprive the surviving spouse of the exemption because of acts over which he or she had no control: *Auch Est.*, 174 Pa. Super. 406; *Celenza Est.*, 308 Pa. 186. The exemption has been allowed to a son with whom the decedent resided for many years despite the fact that the decedent resided in another home where he could receive better care for a short time before his death: *Henicle Est.*, 15 Fiduc. Rep. 353. See also *Torkos Est.*, 2 Fiduc. Rep. 3d 127, annot. *Fiduc. Rev.* May 2012, p. 1, where mother lived in a nursing home for two years after a stroke and son who resided with her for many years was entitled to family exemption. The family exemption was refused to daughter with whom decedent resided for four days after hospitalization where he had lived with another daughter prior thereto for seven years: *Gallagher Est.*, 19 Fiduc. Rep. 2d 243, annot. *Fiduc. Rev.* July 1999, p. 2. It was there said that "The courts ought not to favor removal of a fatally ill person from one child's home to another in a degrading race for family status so as to establish a claim to the . . . exemption."

The family relationship and residence with the decedent, not dependence upon him, is the criterion for claiming the exemption. Prior to the Act of 1956, P.L. 1084, the right of a child to the family exemption depended in some counties upon whether the child formed a part of the *decedent's* household or whether the decedent formed part of the child's household: *Lerew Estate*, 7 Fiduc. Rep. 481. Under present law it is sufficient if they formed part of the same household: *Otteni Est.*, 486 Pa. 631. However, difficulties still remain in determining when persons form part of the same household: *Shank*

*Est.*, 399 Pa. 656, rev'g 10 Fiduc. Rep. 177; *Caprioli Est.*, 9 Fiduc. Rep. 434, annot. *Fiduc. Rev.* Sept. 1959. In *Einsig Est.*, 21 Fiduc. Rep. 481, no "household" existed in a situation involving a trailer. The burden of proof on the claimant to establish a household relationship is not as great as that of a claimant generally, and the tests of domicile and residence are not applicable: *Shuman Est.*, 55 Berks 90.

Even though the parent took turns living with various children so that it was "fortuitous" that he was a member of a particular household at death, nevertheless, the child in whose home he then resided is entitled to the exemption: *Gana Est.*, 14 Fiduc. Rep. 1. *Zappardino Est.*, 14 Fiduc. Rep. 212, ruled that "a decedent cannot maintain more than one household at a time" under PEF 3121, and denied the exemption to a son with whom decedent sometimes stayed overnight, where she never abandoned her own home. However, where decedent resided in a daughter's home, the daughter was entitled to the exemption even though decedent paid for services rendered: *Hunter Est.*, 56 Berks 143. An attempted surcharge of an administrator for failing to claim the family exemption as an inheritance tax deduction has been dismissed where it was averred that the exemption was available to a child who was entitled to the entire estate, where the child was living with her mother from whom the decedent was separated. The court noted that the right to the exemption was debatable, and therefore surcharge was not proper: *Buck Est.*, 16 Fiduc. Rep. 389.

# Chapter 8

# ELECTIVE SHARE OF SURVIVING SPOUSE

---



---

## § 8.1 IN GENERAL

In addition to the family exemption, the surviving spouse has the right to an elective share in certain property identified with the decedent. This elective right is set forth in Chapter 22 of the PEF Code, effective June 18, 1978. For the origin and inspiration of Chapter 22 of the PEF Code from Section 11 of the Estates Act of 1947, the Uniform Probate Code and sections of earlier Wills Acts, see *Fiduc. Rev.* April 1972, June 1978. See chart at Section 8.8 for an overview of the elective share of a surviving spouse.

Act No. 144 of 2004, 23 Pa. C.S. § 1103, provides that no common law marriage contracted after January 1, 2005 shall be valid, but any common law marriage otherwise lawful and contracted on or before January 1, 2005 is not affected. Prior to this legislation the Commonwealth Court in *PNC Bank Corp. v. Workers' Compensation Appeal Board*, 831 A.2d 1269, decided September 13, 2003, had abolished common law marriage, with the decision to be given "purely prospective effect." Until the Superior Court and the Supreme Court deal with this issue, the status of common law marriage contracted between September 13, 2003 and January 22, 2005 is unclear. See *Fiduc. Rev.* June 2004, p. 3 and March 2005, p. 3.

*Precautions*—An initial concern of the personal representative and legal counsel is a possible conflict between a duty to carry out the provisions of the will, and a duty to inform the spouse of such elective rights: *Taylor Est.* (*No. 1*), 24 D. & C. 512; *Freer Est.*, 353 Pa. 351; *Morrison Est.*, 275 Pa. 180; cf. *Amon Est.*, 27 Fiduc. Rep. 1. See *Rowe Est.*, 17 Fiduc. Rep. 107, annot. *Fiduc. Rev.* March 1967, where a petition to vacate the widow's election against the will was denied because she was not specifically informed of the relevant factors by the executor and had no counsel of her own. See Section 6.3. The advisable course for the personal representative is to establish a record that the surviving spouse has been advised of his or her elective rights. If the fact situation is such that there could be doubt as to whether the surviving spouse would benefit financially by the exercise of elective rights, separate legal counsel should be recommended. Until a substantial body of case law develops more exact guidelines, those counselling the surviving spouse must be exceptionally vigilant in assembling all relevant information concerning property subject to elective rights and the tax consequences of an election and possible post-death estate planning including the possible use of disclaimers and family agreements.

In circumstances where the valuation of assets for death tax purposes created a conflict of interest between the widow-executrix who had elected against the will and other beneficiaries, the court appointed an administrator pro tem under PEF 4301(2) to negotiate liability of the estate for federal estate and state death taxes: *Smith Est.*, 29 Fiduc. Rep. 175.

Regarding the election generally, see Hunter, O.C. Commonplace Book (2d ed.), Election by Spouse; Brégy, Intestate, Wills and Estates Acts of 1947, *Fiduc. Rev.* June 1962; Elective Share—Augmented Estate Concept Under the Uniform Probate Code, 62 Iowa L.R. 981; Elective Share, 12 Real Property, Probate and Trust J. 323. For form for electing against will and conveyances see Aker, PEF Code Annot. § 2210.

Orphans' Court Division has jurisdiction over spouse's elective share where husband moved to Arizona seven months before death for health reasons after living in Pennsylvania for more than thirty years where assets were owned jointly with sons.

*Amendments*—Concurrently with the addition of Chapter 22 to the PEF Code, PEF 2105 was amended and PEF 2508-2513 and 6111 were repealed. In place of the repealed sections the new Chapter 22 was added to the PEF Code as was a new PEF 6111.1 dealing with the effect of a divorce on inter vivos transfers. These new provisions, effective only as to the estates of decedents dying after June 17, 1978, are discussed in the May and June 1978 issues of *Fiduciary Review*.

Consistent with the enhanced authority granted attorneys-in-fact (now agent) in Chapter 56, PEF 2206 now reads:

"*Right of election personal to surviving spouse*. The right of election of the surviving spouse may be exercised in whole or in part only during his lifetime by him or by his attorney-in-fact in accordance with section 5603(d) (relating to implementation of power of attorney). In the case of a minor spouse, the right of election may be exercised in whole or in part only by the spouse's guardian; in the case of an incapacitated spouse, the right of election may be exercised in whole or in part only by the spouse's guardian or by his attorney-in-fact in accordance with section 5603(d) if the power of attorney qualifies as a durable power of attorney under section 5604 (relating to durable powers of attorney); provided, that, in each case, the election shall be exercised only upon order of the court having jurisdiction of the minor's or the incapacitated person's estate, after finding that exercise of the right is advisable."

Subsection (c) was added to PEF 2210 to supply what was inadvertently omitted when Chapter 22 was added to the

PEF Code and the former PEF 2510 was replaced by PEF 2210. Subsection (c) reads:

"(c) *Costs.*—The costs of filing and recording the election shall be reimbursed out of the estate as a part of the administration expenses."

## § 8.2 EARLIER DECISIONS

While the cases hereinafter noted apply (except as indicated otherwise) to the law as it existed prior to June 17, 1978, they should be of assistance in the interpretation of the current statutory language.

Like PEF 2206, the right to elect under prior law was personal and could not be exercised by the personal representative of a decedent. However, where the surviving spouse was incompetent, an election against the will or inter vivos transfers (as now in PEF 2206) could be made by the guardian only with approval of the court. See *Peden Est.*, 409 Pa. 194; 2 Hunter O.C. Commonplace Book (2d ed.), Election by Spouse § 12; 15 Ala. L.R. 338. See *Grappy Est.*, 21 Fiduc. Rep. 504, annot. *Fiduc. Rev.* Dec. 1971, p. 3, as to computation of the elective share. The computation is similar under PEF 2203: *Massey Est.*, 3 Fiduc. Rep. 2d 26, annot. *Fiduc. Rev.* March 1983, p. 4. See also *Gentle Est.*, 22 Fiduc Rep. 352, for the method of allocating by reason of valuation changes during administration in which partial distributions had been made. And see *Ruck Est.*, 22 Fiduc. Rep. 462, concerning effect of election upon specific devise and payment of sewer assessment after death.

(*a*) *Assets subject to election*

In determining the size of the decedent's estate, the surviving spouse was entitled to treat property transferred during the decedent's lifetime as part of the testamentary estate when it had been conveyed without his or her joinder (*Fiduc. Rev.* June 1962; Sept. 1965; Oct. 1965; p. 4; Oct. 1966; March 1968, p. 3), or in fraud of marital rights (*Montague Est.*, 403 Pa. 558), or the decedent had retained a "power of appointment by will, or a power of revocation or consumption over the principal thereof" (*Fiduc. Rev*. July 1953; March 1954; Feb. 1955; March 1955, p. 3; June 1962, p. 3). For the applicability of this provision to particular types of property and transfers, see *Henderson Est*., 8 Fiduc. Rep. 409, annot. *Fiduc. Rev*. Sept. 1958 aff'd, 395 Pa. 215 (proceeds of life insurance); *Behan Est*., 399 Pa. 314, annot. *Fiduc. Rev*. May 1960 (trust over which settlor retained power of appointment); *Huested Est*., 403 Pa. 185, and *Hunt Est*., 10 Fiduc. Rep. 33 (inter vivos trust); *Shlit Est*., 26 Fiduc. Rep. 505, annot. *Fiduc. Rev*. Jan. 1977, p. 3, *Krasney Est*., 7 Fiduc. Rep. 403, and *Vache Est*., 9 Fiduc. Rep. 465 (tentative trust); *Hershey Est*., 10 Fiduc. Rep. 390 and *Voell Est*., 26 Fiduc Rep. 109 (joint bank accounts); *Cost v. Caletri*, 483 Pa. 11 (certificates of deposit); *Ross Est*., 12 Fiduc. Rep. 63 and *Saylor Est*., 2 Fiduc. Rep. 2d 1 (profit-sharing plan); *Brown Est*., 446 Pa. 401, annot. *Fiduc. Rev*. May 1972 (stock subject to buy-sell agreement); *Snyder Est*., 15 Fiduc. Rep. 608, and *Maley Est*., 21 Fiduc. Rep. 618 (Public School Employees Retirement Fund Annuity); *Killion Trust*, 13 Fiduc. Rep. 397 (irrevocable trust, taxes on which are charged to residuary estate passing under will); *Fiduc. Rev*. July 1967, regarding United States savings bonds in the name of the decedent "or" another; *Fiduc. Rev. Sept*. 1967, p. 3, re employment benefits; *Schwartz Est*., 449 Pa. 112, re Gift to Minors Act assets. No elective rights existed in property irrevocably transferred regardless of intention of avoiding elective rights: *Hahn Est*., 28 Fiduc. Rep. 406; *Biernacki Est*., 2 Fiduc. Rep. 2d 174, annot. *Fiduc. Rev*. July 1982.

It is to be noted that a spouse electing against a will, consistent with Chapter 22, was required to elect against all inter vivos conveyances of which such spouse was a beneficiary, and that a spouse electing against such inter vivos conveyances was required to elect against the will if such spouse were a beneficiary thereunder. However, a surviving spouse electing against inter vivos transfers did not forfeit the spouse's allowance in an intestate estate: *Hershey Est. (No. 2)*, 11 Fiduc. Rep. 122. An election against the will also could result in forfeiture of the benefit of a provision therein that the electing spouse's funeral expenses be paid: cf. *Brachman Est*., 11 Fiduc. Rep. 310. But there was no forfeiture of the right to the family exemption: *Vasil Est*., 2 Fiduc. Rep. 615, or the direction to pay death taxes: *Neamand Est.*, 456 Pa. 22, annot. *Fiduc. Rev.* June 1974, p. 3.[1]

Application of PEF 6111 was limited to conveyances during marriage and did not apply to real estate placed in joint ownership of decedent and his sister eight years prior to marriage: *Kotz Est.*, 486 Pa. 444, annot. *Fiduc. Rev.* Nov. 1979. See also *Leary Est.*, 30 Fiduc. Rep. 197; cf. *Durant v. Durant*, 294 Pa. Super. 202.

As to whether one may elect against conveyance of real estate in trust with reservation in grantor of a life interest, see *Fiduc. Rev.* Feb. 1976, p. 4.

(*b*) *Elective share*

Regarding the interest which the surviving spouse obtained in assets of the estate, see *Fiduc. Rev.* July 1950, July 1960, p. 3, Aug. 1966, Aug. 1967, March 1969, Dec. 1971, p. 3. For a summary of the elective rights under the then existing law in comparison with the Uniform Probate Code provisions, see *Fiduc. Rev.* April 1972.

(c) *Nuptial agreement—Waiver of elective rights*

The elective rights of a surviving spouse can be waived by antenuptial or postnuptial agreement: *Fiduc. Rev.* Sept. 1968; *Cummings Est.*, 493 Pa. 11; *Kester Est.*, 27 Fiduc. Rep. 644, annot. *Fiduc. Rev.* Nov. 1977, p. 3, aff'd, 486 Pa. 349; cf. *Harrison Est.*, 456 Pa. 356. This is now incorporated in PEF 2207. However, a widow will not be barred where there was no provision for her in the postnuptial agreement or disclosure of assets: *Hahn Est.*, 28 Fiduc. Rep. 406. And, the waiver was not all inclusive when it referred only to an interest in real property: *Jackson Est.*, 29 Fiduc. Rep. 538. See *Hoffman Est.*, 73 Luz. 17, as to burden of proof.

(*d*) *Forfeiture of right of election*

---

**§ 8.2**

**1.** The direction concerning death taxes has been changed by PEF 2204(d) and 3702(e); cf. *Bertolet Est.*, 27 Fiduc. Rep. 441, annot. *Fiduc. Rev.* Oct. 1977, p. 3; *Sable Est.*, 27 Fiduc. Rep. 539, annot. *Fiduc. Rev.* Oct. 1977, p. 4; *Faulkner Est.*, 30 Fiduc. Rep. 433, annot. *Fiduc. Rev.* Oct. 1980.

As now provided in PEF 2208, the earlier case law also recognized that elective rights could be lost by desertion or failure to meet support obligations: *Powell Est.*, 28 Fiduc. Rep. 522. Cases finding no forfeiture include *Schleid Est.*, 27 Fiduc. Rep. 469 and *Marianelli Est.*, 28 Fiduc. Rep. 579.

(*e*) *Marriage*

The surviving spouse is entitled to an elective share in the estate regardless of the automatic share provided in PEF 2507(3) for an after-married spouse: *Hagy Est.*, 15 Fiduc. Rep. 456, annot. *Fiduc. Rev.* Sept. 1965. For proof of marriage in Russia, see *Loik Est.*, 493 Pa. 512, and for the burden of proof in establishing status under a common law marriage, see *Gavula Est.*, 490 Pa. 535 and *Riley Est.*, 2 Fiduc. Rep. 2d 219, annot. *Fiduc. Rev.* Sept. 1982. A relationship which began when the decedent was incompetent to marry can change into a valid common law marriage after the impediment is removed: *Jacobs Est.*, 2 Fiduc. Rep. 2d 68, aff'd, 494 Pa. 133, annot. *Fiduc. Rev.* April 1982, p. 3; cf. *Interest of Miller*, 301 Pa. Super. 511; *Rees Est.*, 3 Fiduc. Rep. 2d 113.

(*f*) *Time for making election*

In proper circumstances, the court on petition (as now in PEF 2210) could grant an extension of time for making the election or could grant leave to make the election nunc pro tunc. See *DiMarco Est.*, 435 Pa. 428, annot. *Fiduc. Rev.* Nov. 1969. The election could be made prior to probate: *Levin Est.*, 13 Fiduc. Rep. 392. In *Dudek Est.*, 30 Fiduc. Rep. 359, annot. *Fiduc. Rev.* Oct. 1980, the court permitted the surviving spouse to withdraw an election earlier made because of the "complicated piece of legislation" involved.

For form to elect against will and conveyances, see Aker, PEF Code Annot. § 2210.

## § 8.3 EVIDENCE

In accord with PEF 2209 as amended, earlier case law barred the survivor from testifying as to the existence of a common law marriage (*Zeigler Est.*, 30 Cumb. 90; *Comer*

*Est.*, 3 Fiduc. Rep. 2d 117) but allowed the survivor to testify as to the other matters regarding his or her elective rights. A person claiming the right to elect against a will is not a competent witness as to the creation of her status as the surviving spouse. *Stauffer Est.* (Pa. Supreme), 476 A.2d 354, annot. *Fiduc. Rev.*, Oct. 1984, p. 3. Compare *Kester Est.*, 486 Pa. 349, annot. *Fiduc. Rev.* Nov. 1977, p. 3, with *McClain Est.*, 481 Pa. 435, annot. *Fiduc. Rev.* March 1979. Two persons of the same sex cannot validly contract a common law marriage: *DeSanto v. Barnsley*, 70 Dela. 1.

## § 8.4 EFFECT OF DIVORCE

The earlier rule that a divorced spouse-named beneficiary is entitled to the proceeds of life insurance on the life of his or her deceased spouse remains intact despite the provisions of PEF 6111.1; *Equitable Life Assur. Soc. v. Stitzel*, 1 Fiduc. Rep. 2d 315, aff'd, 299 Pa. Super. 199; cf. *Simpkins v. Dodolak*, 1 Fiduc. Rep. 2d 120, annot. *Fiduc. Rev.* May 1981.

In 1994, PEF 6111.2 was amended to make it clear that upon divorce all beneficiary designations of employee benefits and life insurance shall be "construed as if such former spouse had predeceased" the deceased spouse. Although the amendment was stated to apply to beneficiary designations whenever made, it was held by the Pennsylvania Supreme Court that it cannot be applied retroactively to a beneficiary designation made prior to its effective date. The designation of decedent's former wife as beneficiary was not altered by their divorce: *Parsonese v. Midland Nat'l Ins. Co.,* 550 Pa. 423.

The Pennsylvania Law Journal Reporter of January 18, 1982, includes an interesting and informative article by Hon. Lawrence W. Kaplan entitled *The Impact of Death on a Pending Divorce*. It concludes with the observation that "We are on the fringes of the frontier. Undoubtedly, the surface has only been scratched [by the questions raised in the article] and the variety of questions which will be presented will be limited only by the limitless vagaries of human endeavor and the unlimited imaginations of the Pennsylvania Bar."

## § 8.5 LIVE-IN PARTNER

The claim of a live-in partner for his or her alleged contributions or for unjust enrichment must be carefully pleaded to support a contract or claim for unjust enrichment: *Beros v. Haberman*, 40 Som. 265. However, claims in a decedent's estate for specific items of tangible personal property and for a dog have been sustained: *Toloczko Est.*, 2 Fiduc. Rep. 2d 418, annot. *Fiduc. Rev.* Dec. 1982. See *Banko v. Malanecki*, (Pa. Supreme), 451 A.2d 1008, annot. *Fiduc. Rev.* March 1983, for adjustment of claims regarding household furnishings, joint bank accounts, car loan, and house mortgage when live-in partners separate.

Legislation adopted in Act 124 of 1996 amends the Marriage Law of 1990, 23 Pa. C.S. § 1102 to limit the marital status to "one man and one woman" and to deny recognition of other unions entered into in other jurisdictions. See annotation in *Fiduc. Rev.* Nov. 1997, p. 3.

## § 8.6 FOREIGN DECEDENT—FOREIGN REAL ESTATE

For a discussion of the conflict of laws problem where the decedent died domiciled in one state leaving assets located in another state and the surviving spouse's elective rights differ under the laws of such states, see *In re Clark*, 288 N.Y.S. 2d 993, annot. *Fiduc. Rev.* July 1968, p. 4. See *Mayor Est.*, 20 Fiduc. Rep. 284, annot. *Fiduc. Rev.* May 1970, p. 3, regarding conflicts of laws questions raised by a spouse's elective rights. Regarding problems of abatement caused by an election, see *Whitworth Est.*, 20 Fiduc. Rep. 196.

Where decedent-wife died in Ohio and her surviving husband elected against her will, the surviving husband was entitled to receive the statutory allowance of $5,000 and an automobile under Ohio law independent of his elective share.

He also was entitled to reimbursement for funds advanced to pay estate obligations: *Fiedler Est.*, 18 Mercer 177.

## § 8.7 EQUITABLE DISTRIBUTION

PEF 2211(b) states the "effect of election" in language consistent with prior case law (see *Fiduc. Rev*. Nov. 1944) and in clause (4) thereof provides:

> "*Windfalls.*—If the election and disclaimers, releases and conveyances by a surviving spouse in connection therewith result in an increase in the value of the interest of a beneficiary, the court may require contributions from such a beneficiary, directly or by sequestering the disclaimed, released or conveyed interests, in relief of other beneficiaries, so that no beneficiary will receive more value than he would have received in the absence of the election."

It has been held that: a provision in a will regarding the effect of election caused a future interest to be defeated: *Morrison Est.*, 463 Pa. 163; a provision in a will requiring the spouse to receive her elective share in trust is ineffective and remainder of such share is not accelerated: *Guy Est.*, 28 Chester 237; decrees of the lower court disposing of assets of charitable remainders cy pres were affirmed where widow, who died in 1972, had elected against the will and trust of a 1956 decedent: *Behan Est.*, 491 Pa. 421 (see *Behan Est.*, 399 Pa. 314); upon widow's election against the will, the balance of the estate after deduction of widow's one-third share was distributed equitably so that the loss was apportioned "in such a way that no beneficiary receives a windfall at the expense of another beneficiary." *Buryj Est.*, 30 Fiduc. Rep. 194.

## § 8.8 OVERVIEW OF GENERAL PLAN OF PEF CHAPTER 22

The following is based on a chart appearing in *Fiduc. Rev*. Mar. 1993.

The elective share is one-third which must be asserted within six months of the decedent's death or probate: 2210. This presents only the general plan of PEF Chapter 22 applicable in estates of decedents domiciled in Pa.: 2202.

*Assets Subject to Election (2203(a)).*

*One-third of:*

1. Property in excess of $3,000 conveyed during the marriage by decedent to any one donee without adequate consideration within one year of death.

2. Probate property.

3. Property conveyed[1] during marriage without adequate consideration by decedent where he retained:

(a) income or use

(b) power of revocation, consumption, invasion or disposal[2]

(c) joint ownership with power of severance or conveyance

(d) annuity

*Assets Not Subject to Election (2203(b)).*

Property conveyed with consent of spouse.

Life insurance on life of decedent.

Employee benefits.

---

§ 8.8

**1.** "Conveyance" means "an act by which it is intended to create an interest in real or personal property whether the Act is intended to have inter vivos or testamentary operation": 2201. The beneficiary designation on a deferred compensation plan does not constitute a conveyance: *Korn Est.*, 322 Pa. Super. 154, annot. *Fiduc. Rev.* Oct. 1984.

**2.** The time of the conveyance is not limited in this clause (b) to "during marriage." Power in non-adverse party to distribute to decedent is treated as a power of invasion.

Property passing by decedent's exercise or non-exercise of any power of appointment given by someone other than decedent.

Property transferred by decedent to extent decedent received adequate consideration (2205).

*Loss of Elective Share (2207–8).*

Divorce: 2507(2); 6111.1.

Desertion: 2106(a).

Nonsupport: 2106(a).

Slaying: 2106(c); 8803.

Waiver: 2207.

Laches: 2210.

Nuptial agreement and/or joinder in conveyance: 2207.

*Offsets Against Elective Share (2204).*

The election by the surviving spouse constitutes a disclaimer of the interest obtained by the surviving spouse from decedent in the following (but see footnote 3 as to limited right of retention):

Probate property.

Property passing to surviving spouse by decedent's exercise or non-exercise of power of appointment.

Inter vivos trust created by decedent.

Life insurance on life of decedent if premiums paid by decedent, his employer, partner or creditor.

Annuity contract purchased by decedent, his employer, partner or creditor.

---

**§ 8.8**

**3.** The surviving spouse has an election to accept as an advancement on account of the value of the one-third share in assets subject to election any interest acquired outright or in fee simple, from the decedent. All other assets which may be offset against the election must be disclaimed, released or conveyed so that equitable adjustments can be made among disappointed beneficiaries in assets subject to the election.

Employee benefits originating from services or disabilities of decedent.

Joint, entireties or community property to extent of decedent's contribution.

Property given by decedent during lifetime to spouse or proceeds thereof owned by spouse at decedent's death.

## § 8.9 DECISIONS UNDER CHAPTER 22

An article by Philip A. Brégy, Esquire, in the June 1978 of Fiduciary Review, summarized the then recently enacted provisions of Chapter 22 of the PEF Code and referred to earlier articles in *Fiduciary Review* and to the Uniform Probate Code. This was followed by a chart on page four of the August 1978 issue of *Fiduciary Review* which gave a "birdseye" picture of the then existing statutory and case law relating to the elective share. See § 8.8.

*(a) Property subject to election*

PEF 2203(a) sets forth the property subject to election. See section 8.8, infra. Accounts in husband's name in trust for his mother were revocable conveyances, subject to election. *Inter Est* (Pa. Super.), 664 A.2d 142, annot. *Fiduc. Rev*. Feb. 1996. A widow also has elective rights against property conveyed to her husband and a person described as his "wife" with whom he had entered into a ceremonial marriage even though not divored. *Bruce Est.* (Pa. Super.), 538 A.2d 293, rev'g 7 Fiduc. Rep. 2d 246, annot. *Fiduc. Rev*. Aug. 1987.

Although decedent had the right under PEF 6303 to consume the entire account during his lifetime (he being the sole contributor), the widow's elective share was only one-third of one-half of a joint survivorship account, PEF 6303 being ineffective with regard to election. *Ortmann Est.*, 5 Fiduc. Rep. 2d 243, annot. *Fiduc. Rev*. Aug. 1985.

Under PEF 2203(a) (4) property conveyed with right of survivorship is subject to election only if conveyed during marriage, this subsection being an exception to PEF 2203(a)(3). *Lazewski Est.*, 18 Fiduc. Rep. 2d 439; *Ciocco Est.*, 18 Fiduc. Rep. 2d 87; *Hart Est.*, 801 A.2d 599.

Real estate conveyed for one dollar within one year of death is also subject to election to the extent value exceeds three thousand dollars. *Esters v. Jackson (No. 2)*, 14 Fiduc. Rep. 2d 29.

Under PEF 2211 (b) (1) the elective share must be apportioned against the entire estate to which the election applies, including non-probate assets. *Fox Est.*, 26 Fiduc. Rep. 2d 243. See annotation in *Fiduc. Rev.* Dec. 2006, p. 3 regarding the status of IRA accounts when the spouse elects against the will.

*(b) Property not subject to election*

Deferred compensation under plan of decedent's employer is not subject to elective rights because the beneficiary designation is not a "conveyance" as defined by PEF 2203(a)(3). *Korn Est.* (Pa. Super.), 480 A.2d 1233, reversing in part 3 Fiduc. Rep. 2d 138, annot *Fiduc. Rev.* Oct. 1984. An IRA account is not a conveyance, so it is not subject to election. *Zebe Est.*, 20 Fiduc. Rep. 2d 39, annot. *Fiduc. Rev.* Feb. 2001, p. 1 and Mar. 2001, p. 3.

The Retirement Equity Act of 1984 requires that a surviving spouse receive certain minimum rights to retirement plan benefits as a matter of federal law. The impact upon the surviving spouse's elective share generally remains to be determined as a matter of state law, but it does seem clear that the surviving spouse (who would not under PEF 2203(b)(3) have a right to reach a broad-based plan benefit payable to others) will participate as a matter of federal law in such benefits. The general PEF scheme is therefore modified by the federal law. Election is permitted where the spouse breached the post-nuptial agreement. *In re O'Brien*, 898 A.2d 1075.

*(c) Disclaimers*

Contribution to entireties property by wife who was a homemaker was not established by the evidence and therefore her surviving husband who elected against her will was not required to disclaim entireties property. *Sowers Est.* (O.C. Div. Bucks), 6 Fiduc. Rep. 2d 251, annot. *Fiduc. Rev.* Sept. 1986, p. 1. See PEF 2204.

*(d) Property transferred for value*

A widow-sole beneficiary of her decedent-husband's will may not pursue her dower rights in property conveyed without her consent without also electing against husband's will and relying on her interest in his augmented estate as provided in PEF 2201 et seq. *Bialczak v. Moniak* (Pa. Super.), 540 A.2d 962. See PEF 2205.

*(e) Election personal to spouse*

A spouse may file an appeal from probate asserting undue influence after she filed an election against the will under PEF 2203. *Hollabaugh Est.*, 13 Fiduc. Rep. 2d 133, annot. *Fiduc. Rev.* May 1993.

See *Reifsneider Est.* (Pa.), 610 A.2d 958 annot *Fiduc. Rev.* Dec. 1992, where attorneys in fact acting under a durable power of attorney filed an election against deceased husband's will within six months after his death. More than six months after his death, they filed a petition for approval of the election, which the lower court denied and the Superior Court agreed with this action. The Supreme Court concluded that the election was timely, but did not indicate how long thereafter the petition for approval may be filed.

*(f) Waiver*

In accordance with prior law, PEF 2207 sets forth the principle that a spouse may waive the right of election, either before or after marriage or before or after the decedent's death. There is no per se requirement that parties have separate legal counsel to enter into an antenuptial agreement. *Simeone v. Simeone* (Pa.), 581 A.2d 162. However, separate counsel would tend to insulate the agreement against subsequent claims that disclosures were not made or that information was concealed. See *Martin Est.*, 3 Fiduc. Rep. 2d 356, annot. *Fiduc. Rev.* Dec. 1983. Compare *Stoner v. Stoner*, 819

A.2d 529 where the Court required full disclosure of resources, but no "extra requirement that the parties be advised of their statutory rights." A provison in the agreement that full disclosure has been made is presumptively valid. *Cooper v. Oakes, Adm.*, 427 Pa. Super. 430. Wife's waiver was effective even though information about the estate size was fifty percent greater than the estimate set forth in the waiver since there was no active fraud. *Pantages Est.*, 2 Fiduc. Rep. 3d 329, annot. *Fiduc. Rev.* Aug. 2012, p. 1.

*(g) Forfeiture*

Under PEF 2208, the right of election is lost if the spouse has, for one year or more prior to death of the other spouse, failed to support or deserted or is a slayer. The heavy burden on those asserting desertion is illustrated by *Massey Est.*, 3 Fiduc. Rep. 2d 20, annot. *Fiduc. Rev.* March 1983, aff'd (Pa. Super.), 476 A.2d 65. Statements made in a will concerning a wife's alleged desertion have no evidentiary value as proof of desertion. *Kostick Est.*, (Pa.), 526 A.2d 746, annot. *Fiduc. Rev.* Oct. 1987. Protection from abuse order removing husband for more than one year constituted desertion and forfeited elective right. *Cochran Est.* (Pa. Super.), 738 A.2d 1029.

But election will not be permitted where the spouse engages in post-separation marital misconduct. *Reason Est.*, 21 Fiduc. Rep. 2d 173.

*(h) Procedure for Election*

An election to elect or not to elect must be in a signed writing filed with the clerk of the orphans' court division and notice must be given to the personal representative. PEF 2210(a). Filing must be before expiration of six months from death or probate, whichever is later. Even though a widow consulted with an attorney who failed to advise her of the right to elect, filing after the six month period is not permitted. *Dengler Est.*, 5 Fiduc. Rep. 2d 233, annot. *Fiduc. Rev.* Aug. 1985. Absent proof of actual fraud, filing after six months is time barred. *Winkler Est.*, 17 Fiduc. Rep. 2d 106.

## Chapter 9

# ADMINISTRATION OF REAL ESTATE

---



---

## § 9.1 IN GENERAL

Prior to the Fiduciaries Act of 1949, a clear distinction existed between the administration of real and personal property. This distinction was historical rather than logical in origin: see *Fiduc. Rev.* June 1948. With the enactment of the Fiduciaries Act of 1949, almost all needless distinctions in the administration of real and personal property were obliterated. However, some have been continued to ensure the ready marketability of real estate and in some instances to avoid expenses of an administration.

Unlike personal property, title to which passes to the personal representative at death (PEF 301(a)), the legal title to real estate passes at death to the decedent's "heirs or devisees, subject, however, to all the powers granted to the personal representative by [the PEF Code] and lawfully by the will and to all orders of the court" (PEF 301(b)). The powers granted to the personal representative and the duties imposed on him are so substantial as to make administration of real estate comparable to administration of personalty. For a summary, see Eckert, The Pennsylvania Fiduciaries Act of 1949,

11 U. of Pitts. L. Rev. 194, *Fiduc. Rev.* July 1964. These powers may be enlarged or curtailed by provisions in the decedent's will: cf. PEF 3354.

For a deed to a deceased grantee, see *Moore v. Bailey*, 14 D. & C. 3d 417, annot. *Fiduc. Rev.* April 1981, p. 2. For a deed without joinder of spouse, see *Weaver v. Eidemiller Enterprises, Inc. & Crouse*, 1 Fiduc. Rep. 2d 8, annot. *Fiduc. Rev.* April 1981, p. 3. See *Griffith v. Kirsch*, 886 A.2d 249 where owner of one-half interest prohibited sale, severance, subdivision, and division without written consent of co-owner brother.

## § 9.2 POSSESSION

Of immediate concern to those interested in the decedent's real property is the question of who is entitled to its possession.[1] The personal representative has the right and obligation, subject to exceptions mentioned below, to take possession of and administer the decedent's real property until it is awarded in distribution: PEF 3311. Until the personal representative qualifies as such, the right to possession is in the decedent's heirs or devisees. In *Dame Est.*, 27 Fiduc. Rep. 461, the duty to take possession of and sell the property was directed by the will to be undertaken following the death of the life tenant. Since, during the administration of the decedent's estate, the personal representative may maintain any action with respect to it (PEF 3311), he is empowered to obtain possession by ejectment or other appropriate action (*Cryder v. Garrison*, 387 Pa. 571; *Coble v. Arnold*, 13 Fiduc. Rep. 281). However, in the absence of a court order,[2] the personal representative is not entitled to possession or administration (see *Ladley Est.*, 1 Fiduc. Rep. 281) of real estate occupied by an heir or devisee: (PEF 3311); *Fleischut Est.*, 2 Fiduc. Rep. 2d 17. This means an heir or devisee in possession at the decedent's death, including a surviving spouse who lived with decedent and elects against his will (*Lehman Est.*, 43 Som. 372), and not one who acquires posses-

---

**§ 9.2**

**1.** Problems relating to lapse because of death of devisee are discussed in § 16.5.

**2.** Court orders are granted when the court decides this procedure is necessary to protect the rights of claimants or other parties: PEF 3311.

sion between the date of death and grant of letters to the personal representative: PEF 3311; see *Fiduc. Rev.* Oct. 1964. An heir or devisee in possession need not pay rent for his occupancy (*Groff Est.*, 37 Som. 145; *Smith Est.*, 5 Fiduc. Rep. 2d 360, annot. *Fiduc. Rev.*, Jan. 1986; cf. *Dykes Est.*, 26 Fiduc. Rep. 2d 429) but is responsible for utility charges from the date of death (*Sanders Est.*, 12 D. & C. 3d 204) and may convey his rights to a grantee: *Brown v. Bailey*, 2 Fiduc. Rep. 342. Where the heir in possession is entitled to only a fractional interest in the property and is using it for business purposes he is accountable to the estate for its use: *Carr Est.*, 2 Fiduc. Rep. 2d 98.

In instances in which the personal representative's possession of real estate is not required for the protection of claimants and distributees, the court, upon application of a party in interest, may direct that possession of real estate be delivered to a distributee prior to the decree of distribution: PEF 3535. Although the personal representative and parties in interest in most instances achieve the same results without a court decree, the possibility of a surcharge will be avoided by proceeding under this section. Application to the court is unnecessary, and will not be acted upon by the court, when the distributee is already in possession: *Ladley Est.*, 1 Fiduc. Rep. 281. The orphans' court division of the court of common pleas has exclusive jurisdiction to determine the right of possession during the period of estate administration: *Pres. Church of Lewistown v. Ulsh*, 12 Fiduc. Rep. 562.

## § 9.3 CONTRACTS OF DECEDENT

The real estate administered in a decedent's estate is the decedent's interest therein. Thus the decedent's title is subject to outstanding mortgages, liens, leases and contracts with respect thereto. These outstanding rights must be taken into consideration in valuing and describing the decedent's real property in the inventory and tax returns. See Section 12.9.

A personal representative may consummate contracts made by the decedent to sell his property without the necessity of prior court approval, and if he fails to do so voluntarily, the court may compel him to do so: PEF 711(13), 3390; cf. *Fiduc. Rev*. Aug. 1948; March 1949, p. 3. For form of petition, see Partridge-Remick, O.C. Practice § 15.09, Form 15. The orphans' court division has exclusive jurisdiction to enforce the contract of either the decedent or his personal representative: *Chernow v. Manieri Est.*, 410 Pa. 658; *Walcott v. Boyle*, 1 Fiduc. Rep. 465; *Ferguson v. Hildebrand*, 2 Fiduc. Rep. 1.

Real estate subject to an agreement of sale should be listed in the inventory and tax returns, as in the case of other real estate, with a notation of the outstanding agreement and of payment made on account of the purchase price. Such real estate should be valued in the inventory and tax returns at the balance payable under the contract. See Section 12.9. There would seem to be no reason, in ordinary circumstances, to make a similar notation of outstanding leases or other rights relating to real estate.

To ensure good title in the purchaser under contract with the decedent, a personal representative who has been required to give bond should apply to the court for an order excusing him from giving additional bond; if the court requires additional bond with respect to such real estate, he should enter this additional security: PEF 3351, 3357. See Section 9.5.

## § 9.4 DUTY TO RENT, INSURE, REPAIR AND PAY TAXES

With the personal representative's right to possession goes the corresponding duty to make the property productive by rental[1] (PEF 3352) or other appropriate action, and to preserve it by insurance (see *Fiduc. Rev*. Dec. 1941), repair and

§ 9.4

**1.** But rents are not to be collected from real estate occupied by an heir or devisee unless needed for payment of claims: PEF 3311.

In *Malinowski Est.*, 9 Fiduc. Rep. 44, the executrix-devisee, who was in possession of realty at the decedent's death, was required to account for its net rental value where the decedent's assets were insufficient to pay his debts. See also *Reese Est.*, 22 Fay. 109.

In *Wisotzkey Est.*, 1 Adams 43, the rental due from the personal representative under a lease with decedent was increased.

the payment of taxes (see Section 6.21; PEF 3311). The personal representative should immediately notify all tenants of his appointment and request that rentals be paid to him or his agent: *Fiduc. Rev.* Feb. 1958. He should continue to collect such income until the real estate has been sold or distributed: PEF 3311; cf. *Shelleman Est.*, 7 Fiduc. Rep. 207.

If there is any property owned by the decedent which is vacant but rentable, the personal representative should attempt to rent it. However, unless the will provides greater flexibility, his leases are limited to a term "expiring not more than one year after the decedent's death" unless "terminable by the personal representative at any later time on thirty days' notice, or unless a longer term is approved by the court": PEF 3352.

*Maintenance.* The personal representative should inspect all real estate of the decedent, especially improved real estate. He has the duty to make arrangements for any repairs or maintenance which appear to be reasonable or necessary in order to safeguard and preserve any property not in the possession of devisees: PEF 3311. The cost of surveying has been allowed: *Bosico Est.*, 2 Fiduc. Rep. 2d 416. See *Weber Est.*, 22 Fiduc. Rep. 331, annot. *Fiduc. Rev.* July 1972, p. 4, regarding maintenance and repair of real estate forming part of the residuary estate, and *White Est.*, 22 Fiduc. Rep. 457, for real estate specifically devised but used for estate purposes.

*Fire and public liability insurance.* The personal representative should examine all insurance policies carried by the decedent on his properties and assure himself that such insurance is adequate in kind and amount in the event of fire or other casualty and furnishes adequate protection against liability to third persons for injuries. See Section 6.16; PEF 3313. See *Estate of Higgins v. Washington Mutual Fire Insurance Company*, 838 A.2d 778, annot. *Fiduc. Rev.* April 2004, p. 1, where vacancy provision in insurance policy precluded recovery for fire loss.

*Real estate taxes.* The personal representative should ascertain the amount of real estate taxes, whether due or owing, and notify the tax collector of the death of the owner. He should advise the tax collector to mark his records accordingly and to send all future notices to him or to the specific devisee.

## § 9.5 SALE OR MORTGAGE BY THE PERSONAL REPRESENTATIVE

PEF 3351 gives the personal representative authority to sell real estate at a public or private sale without application to the court, unless the will specifically devises it (in which case the devisee's joinder will be necessary) or denies the power to sell: *Biddle Est.*, 1 Fiduc. Rep. 1; *Schroyer Est.*, 28 Fiduc. Rep. 452. However, when the personal representative is required to give bond (see Sections 3.10, 5.4), no proceeds of such sale or an involuntary conversion may be paid to him until the court excuses him from entering additional security or he enters the additional security required (PEF 3351): see Section 9.3. Thus, if the real estate is not specifically devised and sale thereof is not prohibited, the personal representative may sell the real estate immediately upon obtaining letters.[1] If security is required, it seems that receipt of the proceeds need be delayed only for a period sufficient to allow the personal representative to enter such security.[2] See *Fiduc. Rev.*, Oct. 1996, for discussion of impact on fiduciaries of disclosure requirements for sales of one to four family residential dwelling properties.

In instances in which the real estate is specifically devised and the devisee will not join in the sale, or in which there is a prohibition against sale but it is nevertheless advisable to sell, or when good title cannot be given because of liens, application can be made to the court for authority to

§ 9.5

**1.** See *Quality Lumber Co. v. Andrus and Zupancic*, 414 Pa. 411, 201 Pa. Super. 189, 13 Fiduc. Rep. 353, annot. *Fiduc. Rev.* July 1963, p. 2, and July 1964, 69 Dick. L. Rev. 161, holding mortgage given by sole heir in possession after appointment of administratrix is ineffective against purchasers from administratrix. Regarding sale by administrator, see "Real Estate—Sale by Fiduciary—Court Approval" in *Fiduc. Rev.* June 1972, p. 3, annot. *Stewart Est.*, 22 Fiduc. Rep. 257, and *Pozoici Est.*, 22 Fiduc. Rep. 203. See *Mellott Est. v. Hayden*, 22 Fiduc. Rep. 594.

**2.** But the sale may be restrained, under PEF 3355, as described below.

sell; if sale is authorized in such instances, the sale will have the effect of a judicial sale: PEF 3353, 3357.[3] In some circumstances the court will refuse to authorize sale, and direct a mortgage or lease as an alternative: *Klingerman Est.*, 2 Fiduc. Rep. 425; *Johnson Trust*, 9 Fiduc. Rep. 57. An executor acting in good faith in absence of gross negligence is not liable for sale at less than its original appraised value: *Strong Est.*, 460 Pa. 419. Rejection of an earlier offer is no occasion for a surcharge for loss of income on funds which could have been invested or for its rental value: *May Est.*, 2 Fiduc. Rep. 2d 232.

(1) *Public or private sale.* The sale may be made publicly or privately in the discretion of the personal representative (PEF 3351) or as directed by the court (PEF 3353); for form of petition, see Partridge-Remick, O.C. Practice § 15.09, Forms 3 and 11; see also Aker, PEF Code Annot. § 3353. Sale under court order cannot be set aside by collateral attack: *Bochniowich Est.*, 26 Fiduc. Rep. 584. In *Tscheschlog Est.*, 2 Fiduc. Rep. 2d 291, sale at public auction was approved where the agreement was ambiguous as to whether or not court approval was required.

The personal representative must use his best judgment as to whether the sale should be public or private, but there is less opportunity for criticism if the sale is made publicly and is adequately advertised. If there is to be a public sale, the personal representative must determine whether there should be an absolute auction or a reservation of a bid.[4] If there is to be a private sale, consideration should be given to reservation of a right to sell to a higher bidder if such a person appears before final settlement is made: *Penrose Est.*, 486 Pa. 9, annot. *Fiduc. Rev.* Sept. 1979, p. 3. When a per-

---

§ **9.5**

**3.** *Quality Lumber and Millwork Company v. Andrus*, 414 Pa. 411, annot. *Fiduc. Rev.* July 1964 and *DiLoretto v. Marsidell Inc.*, 414 Pa. 572, annot. *Fiduc. Rev.* July 1964, p. 3.

**4.** Unless such a reservation is made, the personal representative cannot change his mind and refuse to complete his contract: cf. *Diamandas Est.*, 1 Fiduc. Rep. 165. It should be noted that Uniform Commercial Code § 2328 is not applicable to the sale of realty. See definition of "goods" in § 2105(a) [13 Pa. C.S.].

sonal representative desires to become the purchaser, no sale can be consummated, whether the sale is public or private, without prior court approval: PEF 3356; see *Gabell Est.*, 4 Fiduc. Rep. 184, annot. *Fiduc. Rev.* April 1954; *Catanese Est.* 13 Fiduc. Rep. 534. Cf. *Lynch v. Hook*, 298 Pa. Super. 27, re the responsibility of fair dealing by the estate attorney in attorney–client transactions. For form of petition, see Partridge-Remick, O.C. Practice § 15.09, Form 7. A personal representative selling real estate through a broker should insist that checks for deposit money be made out to him as fiduciary or to the estate of the decedent. If the check is drawn to the broker, he would be prohibited by the Act of 1980, P.L. 15, § 604, as amended, 63 P.S. § 455.604(5), from turning it over to the fiduciary before settlement: see *Fiduc. Rev.* Sept. 1957, p. 4; *Trott v. Hild*, 190 Pa. Super. 85, annot. *Fiduc. Rev.* Aug. 1959, p. 3.

The personal representative should accept the highest net offer without regard to a broker's lost commission: *Warfel Est.*, 417 Pa. 458; *Fiduc. Rev.* Feb. 1972, p. 3, June 1972, p. 3.

(2) *Restraint of sale.* Unless sale is made under authority granted by a will,[5] a sale made by a personal representative may be restrained by the court on its own motion or upon application of any party in interest. For form of petition, see Partridge-Remick, O.C. Practice § 15.09, Form 12. The order restraining sale may be conditioned on the applicant giving bond. The order is void against a bona fide grantee or lien holder unless the decree restraining the sale, or a duplicate original or certified copy thereof, is recorded in the county where the real estate lies: PEF 3355; see 99 U. of Pa. L. Rev. 1164, 1181 (1951). Sale under the statutory power will be restrained when a distributee wishes to receive the prop-

---

**§ 9.5**

**5.** A fiduciary with a testamentary power to sell can sell irrespective of the wishes of the heirs: cf. PEF 3355. Their only legal sanctions to prevent abuse of this power are the possibility of surcharge for negligence or bad faith, or to petition the court to set aside the contract for fraud, accident or mistake: PEF 3360; *Curtis Trust*, 437 Pa. 123.

erty in kind and when there is no necessity to sell for payment of debts: *Polanco Est.* (*No. 1*), 2 Fiduc. Rep. 124, annot. *Fiduc. Rev.* March 1952; *Friedman Est.*, 11 Fiduc. Rep. 174. However, sale may be authorized for purposes of distribution when this is the wish of those having a majority interest: *Hageter Est.*, 426 Pa. 619; *Brodoski Est.*, 16 Fiduc. Rep. 506.

Sale also will be restrained when there is fraud by the executor or on the executor (*Elliott Est.*, 66 York 173) or, self-dealing (*Skalski Est.*, 420 Pa. 385), or confidential relationship of real estate appraiser (*Evasew Est.* (Pa. Supreme), 584 A.2d 910), and possibly when there is a later substantially higher offer. See *Fiduc. Rev.* Oct. 1968, p. 3; Feb. 1972, pp. 3 & 4; June 1972, p. 3; *Curtis Trust*, 437 Pa. 123; *Watt Est.*, 23 Fiduc. Rep. 557.

(3) *Specifically devised property.* In the absence of a court order (PEF 3353), specifically devised property may be sold by the personal representative only when the devisee joins in the conveyance (PEF 3351). In such circumstances, the purchaser obtains good title, but the personal representative should account for the proceeds and, if he desires, make advance distribution to the devisee. In *Dobrosielski Est.*, 6 Fiduc. Rep. 2d 9, annot. *Fiduc. Rev.*, Feb. 1986, sale without joinder of devisees or prior court approval was confirmed where sale was necessary to discharge estate obligations. However, petition for prior approval would have been preferable.

(4) *Mortgages.* Under authorization of the orphans' court division of the county where letters were granted, the personal representative may mortgage or exchange any of the decedent's realty, including property specifically devised, or may grant an option for the sale or exchange of such property, upon such terms with such security as the court may direct: PEF 3353. A power to sell, given in the decedent's will, includes the power to mortgage and pledge but does not include the power to grant an option without court approval. Provisions governing the effect of testamentary powers are found in PEF 3354. See Judicial Code, § 8152 "Judicial sale as affecting lien of mortgage."

(5) *Effect of appeal from probate or change of circumstances.* Questions may arise as to the effect of occurrences subsequent to the execution of the will or the probate thereof on the personal representative's powers and duties with regard to real property. Neither the decedent's divorce or marriage, the birth or adoption of children, slaying of the decedent (*Ulatoski Est.*, 29 Fiduc. Rep. 27, annot. *Fiduc. Rev.* Mar. 1979), election to take against his will or appeal from the will's probate, nor subsequent revocation of letters restricts the power which the personal representative has to deal with real estate: PEF 793, 908(c), 3329, 3357. For the effect of the death of a devisee before the decedent, see Section 16.13.

Anyone who deals in good faith with a duly qualified personal representative can rely upon his authority. This is so regardless of the good or bad faith of the personal representative, or the subsequent revocation of his letters, or the subsequent probate of a later will or codicil: PEF 3329. Cf. Section 17.3. It should be noted that the right of the personal representative to dispose of and administer particular real property is cut off when it is claimed for the family exemption. See Section 7.1. However, the exemption cannot be claimed in property theretofore sold by the personal representative (PEF 3121), and a decree setting apart the exemption is void as against a bona fide grantee unless recorded as provided in PEF 3126(b).

## § 9.6 INVENTORY AND ACCOUNTING

All of the decedent's real estate must be included in the inventory and in the account regardless of whether or not the personal representative is entitled to its possession. See Chapters 12 and 15; *Bennicas Est.*, 1 Fiduc. Rep. 643; *Brooks Est.*, 2 Fiduc. Rep. 57, 62, annot. *Fiduc. Rev.* Feb. 1952, p. 3; PEF 3301(a). See also Section 9.3 and 9.4 with respect to outstanding leases and agreements of the decedent. Real estate outside of the Commonwealth is included only as a memorandum item in the inventory: *Barnash Est.*, 56 Wash. 172.

See Section 12.1; PEF 3301(b). The description of the property should be sufficient to identify the property, but not by metes and bounds. See Section 12.9 for form of entry. In some instances fuel oil (cf. *Hilt Est.*, 1 Fiduc. Rep. 2d 426, annot. *Fiduc. Rev.* Dec. 1981, p. 4), right to apply for a liquor license, contents of a motel and the motel business itself should be inventoried as an adjunct of the decedent's real estate: *Fleischut Est.*, 2 Fiduc. Rep. 2d 17.

There is no statutory or Supreme Court rule requiring that real estate be listed or accounted for separately from personal property. See Supreme Court O.C. Rule 6.1(b) and approved form of account, 24 Fiduc. Rep. 113. However, good practice dictates that all property be classified as stocks, bonds, mortgages, real estate or miscellaneous, for the purpose of orderly presentation. In addition, there are instances when it is advisable to block or separately treat items of accounting relating to a particular asset, as when there are apportionment problems of unproductive property, as in *Crozer Est.*, 346 Pa. 446, or when there is real estate specifically devised: PEF 3543(b). Some local rules of orphans' courts require that there be an entirely separate inventory and accounting of real estate.

The most serious accounting difficulty with respect to real estate is in properly apportioning items between income and principal. Chapter 81 of the PEF Code is relevant to this problem, but it should be noted that that Chapter is applicable only when the intention of the testator as to what shall be considered principal and what shall be considered income is not expressed: *Sheen Est.*, 65 Montg. 306.

Some of the more important items to be apportioned are as follows:

(1) *Receipts*. Rentals due and unpaid at death are principal and included in the inventory, even though they are intended to cover a period after death. Special treatment may be required if rental for an extended period has been paid in advance. See Section 12.9, note 3.

(2) *Disbursements*. (a) Real estate taxes assessed before the decedent's death are debts of the estate and payable from principal: *Austin Est.*, 52 D. & C. 681; *Cope Est.*, 3 Fiduc. Rep. 299; Goeltz Est., 1 Fiduc. Rep. 552.

(b) Public liability insurance for at least one year is payable from principal: PEF 3313; *Anderson Est.*, 1 Fiduc. Rep. 449.

(c) The cost of recording decrees awarding real estate is an administration expense payable from principal: PEF 3536.

(d) Real estate taxes following the year of death, current repairs (*Brooks Est.*, 2 Fiduc. Rep. 57), fire insurance (*Anderson Est.*, 1 Fiduc. Rep. 449), and other property insurance are payable from income. In the absence of income from which to pay these items, they are payable by the specific devisee or from principal: see PEF 8111, 8112; *Schott Est.*, 11 D. & C. 373.

## § 9.7 COMPENSATION OF THE PERSONAL REPRESENTATIVE

Prior to the Fiduciaries Act of 1949, the generally accepted rule was that the personal representative was entitled to compensation with respect to real estate only when he had effected an authorized sale of real property in the estate: see *Harrison Est.*, 217 Pa. 207. Thus, although the personal representative may have reported the real estate in his tax returns and frequently rendered other services in connection with it, he received no fees therefor: *Lehman Est.*, 54 Dauph. 99. Extra compensation for services in rental collections may be appropriate: cf. *Klein Est.*, 26 Fiduc. Rep. 559.

Since the Fiduciaries Act of 1949, placing many additional duties and responsibilities on the personal representatives with respect to administration of real estate, there would seem to be no reason why the personal representative's compensation should be any less with respect to real estate than with respect to other types of property. See Section 6.27. Under PEF 3537 the personal representative, without any apparent distinction between real and personal property, is now entitled to such compensation "as shall in the circumstances be reasonable and just, and may calculate such compensation on a graduated percentage." The personal representative's compensation may be in addition to the commission paid a real estate broker: *Miller Est.*, 3 Fiduc. Rep. 379. In *Geary Est.*, 26 Fiduc. Rep. 477, a corporate executor was allowed a 7% broker's commission as well as compensation as executor. The compensation of the personal representative for administering real property is a general administration expense (see Section 10.2(1)) and is not charged against specific property, whether or not it is specifically devised (*Anderson Est.*, 1 Fiduc. Rep. 449). For discussion of executor's compensation for administration and conversion of realty, see *Shelleman Est.*, 7 Fiduc. Rep. 207 (3%) and *Purdy Est.* (*No. 2*), 14 Bucks 115 (5%).

It would appear that commissions on realty are to be based upon the appraised value thereof in the first instance unless exceptional circumstances require an increase or decrease in the base upon which they are calculated: *Gardner Est.*, 323 Pa. 229; *Miller Est.*, 132 Pa. Super. 437; *Smith Est.*, 35 D. & C. 383; *Reynold Est.*, 60 D. & C. 90. References may be found in the cases both to the use of sale price (*Smith Est.*, 2 Fiduc. Rep. 169; *Anderson Est.*, 1 Fiduc. Rep. 449; *Rosenthal Est.*, 41 D. & C. 292; *Lutz Est.*, 40 D. & C. 611) and of appraised value (*Flores Est.*, 2 Fiduc. Rep. 412; *Peck Est.*, 42 D. & C. 47; *Smith Est.*, 35 D. & C. 383) as the base for calculating commissions. See *Zezenski Est.*, 12 Fiduc. Rep. 28. Thus, in the case of realty sold for either more or less than its appraised value, the determination of the proper base for commissions is apparently dependent on whether the court believes the situation is so exceptional that appraised values are to be departed from. If the parties in interest agree to commissions, that would seem to conclude the matter (*Lilly Est.*, 181 Pa. 478; *Eberle Est.*, 25 Dist. 625; cf. *Schoonover Est.*, 250 Pa. 353), even insofar as inheritance tax deduction therefor is concerned (*Shafar Est.*, 1 Fiduc. Rep. 321, annot. *Fiduc. Rev*. June 1951). For detailed discussion, see Note, 100 U. of Pa. L. Rev. 545. See especially, 1 Hunter O.C. Commonplace Bk. (2d ed.), Commissions.

## § 9.8 DISTRIBUTION

When there is a formal accounting (see Chapter 15), and real estate is awarded in distribution, the distributee is assured of having acquired the decedent's title therein: cf. PEF 3521. A copy of the decree awarding real estate should be recorded as provided in PEF 3536. Section 1752 of the Inheritance and Estate Tax Act provides that when a tax is paid on realty located in another county, the register to whom the tax is paid shall forward a certificate of payment to the register of the county where the real estate is located. The attorney should request the register to forward such certificate. The personal representative is relieved of liability with respect to both real and personal estate distributed in conformity with a decree of court or in accordance with a rule of court after confirmation of an account: PEF 3533.[1] These provisions represent a substantial improvement over the prior law, particularly when there are a number of heirs or devisees.

Where daughter recorded deeds from her mother more than seven years after certificate of award to son pursuant to when will was recorded, quiet title action was decided in her favor because son was not a bona fide purchaser. *Rau v. Rau*, 22 Fiduc. Rep. 2d 323, annot. *Fiduc. Rev.* Sept. 2002, p. 1.

(1) *Distribution pursuant to an agreement of parties.* When all parties in interest are sui juris and agree to the distribution to be made, and distribution can be accomplished with a minimum of difficulty, either by submitting to the court at the time of audit (or otherwise in accordance with local rules) a suggested schedule of distribution, in which the real estate is described by metes and bounds, or by submitting the schedule after audit if directed by the court's adjudication. In either event, the schedule should carry the written approval of the parties in interest or their counsel. Signatures of spouses to the schedule are unnecessary. A certified copy of the schedule of distribution or a certified excerpt therefrom should then be recorded in the office of the recorder of deeds

**§ 9.8**

**1.** The distribution decree may include the proceeds of the sale of out of state real estate. Cf. *Janney Est.*, 498 Pa. 398, annot. *Fiduc. Rev.* Oct. 1982.

in the county where the real estate is located: PEF 3536. Thus, there appears in the office of the recorder of deeds a record, indexed in the name of the decedent as grantor and in the name of the distributee as grantee, which evidences the passing of title from the decedent to the distributee. The award should be of all the right, title and interest of the decedent and should include a recital of title referring to the last recorded deed, and indicating the interests acquired by the distributee similar to the following:

(a) When the estate is in fee simple: To A, his heirs and assigns. See *Morgan Est.*, 1 Fiduc. Rep. 91.

(b) When there is but one trust under the will: To A Trust Company, its successors and assigns, trustee for B under the will of D.

(c) When there are several trusts under the will: To A, his successors and assigns, trustee for B under Item IX of the will of D.

(d) When there is a life and remainder interest: To Joseph Doe, for life, and remainder to Mary Doe, her heirs and assigns.

(e) When there is uncertainty concerning disposition of the remainder, or when the remainder is contingent or may be divested: To A for life or until remarriage. Cf. *Garnet Est.*, 9 Chest. 206.

(f) When the devise is to man and wife: To H and W, their heirs and assigns as tenants by the entireties.

(g) When a devisee who survived testator has since died: To the heirs and devisees of A, subject to the powers and duties of his personal representative and to all orders of the court: *Possen Est.*, 5 Fiduc. Rep. 23.

(h) When two devisees receive title as joint tenants with right of survivorship: To A and B as joint tenants, to the survivor of them and to the heirs and assigns of the survivor.

(i) When two of the heirs or devisees receive title as tenants in common: To A and B, their heirs and assigns each a one-half undivided interest as tenants in common.

(2) *Conveyance by heirs or devisees.* Conveyances by heirs or devisees of their interest in real estate pending its award to them can be confirmed by the orphans' court by making an award directly to the grantee. Cf. *Brown v. Bailey*, 2 Fiduc. Rep. 342, 349. However, an award to someone other than the distributee can be accomplished only by submission to the court of a properly executed instrument of assignment or conveyance, not merely a stipulation of the devisee or heir: *Zook Est.*, 4 Fiduc. Rep. 488.

(3) *Award of the family exemption.* Real estate chosen in satisfaction or partial satisfaction of the family exemption or spouse's allowance may be awarded in distribution in the same manner as other distributive shares unless it has been earlier set aside. See Section 7.4; Supreme Court O.C. Rule 12.2(c).

(4) *Disagreement of heirs or devisees.* Ample power is given the court to resolve the difficulties which arise when distributees are unable to agree upon the distribution of real estate. By PEF 3534, the court is empowered to award undivided interests in real estate. This is not a satisfactory form of ownership when distributees are not in agreement, and in most instances it will merely delay partition proceedings. The further authority granted by PEF 3534 to "fairly divide, partition and allot" the properties or to "direct the personal representative to sell at a sale confined to the distributees, or at a private or public sale not so confined" empowers the court to employ the method for distribution best suited to the particular circumstances. Power is given the court to protect the distributee who is not in a position to bid against other distributees and to ensure that each distributee receives his full share with a minimum of delay and expense. See *Dougherty Est.*, 1 Fiduc. Rep. 169, for a partition proceeding in distribution.

(5) *Creditors of heirs and devisees.* A creditor of an heir or devisee can have no greater rights in the estate of the

decedent than his debtor-heir or debtor-devisee: *Frey v. Stetson*, 370 Pa. 132; *Fiduc. Rev.* Aug. 1952; July 1963, p. 4; July 1964. However, a creditor is entitled to recognition when he has taken the proper steps to ensure his position. See *Farrell Est.*, 7 Fiduc. Rep. 549, annot. *Fiduc. Rev.* Oct. 1957; *Staller Est.*, 7 Fiduc. Rep. 129; *Adamo Est.*, 2 Fiduc. Rep. 618; *Fiduc. Rev.* Dec. 1952; cf. *Hoy Est.*, 25 Fiduc. Rep. 623. Since the real estate may be sold during administration free of his claims (cf. PEF 3357) and may be awarded to someone other than his debtor, a creditor cannot rely upon his entry or revival of his judgment after the decedent's death as an assurance that his claim will be recognized in distribution (cf. *McCormick Est.*, 1 Fiduc. Rep. 225). However, if he secures an assignment, presents his claim at audit (PEF 3386) or issues an attachment execution against his debtors' interest in the estate, it would seem that his rights will be recognized. See *Fiduc. Rev.* April 1955; March 1957; Nov. 1967, p. 4.

(6) *Voluntary distribution.*[2] As in the case of personal property, the personal representative may make a voluntary distribution of real property or its proceeds. See Section 16.2; PEF 3532. Any such distribution is at the risk of the possible probate of a will or later will within one year, but the personal representative will be free of the claims of creditors (except those having liens of record at death) who have not given or do not give notice of their claims within a year after the first complete advertisement of the grant of letters or before the distribution. See Section 10.1.

The personal representative's recorded deed, pursuant to a family agreement, is sufficient evidence of distributee's title, in the absence of positive proof of its nondelivery: *Claar v. Burket*, 390 Pa. 576.

(7) *Spouse's allowance.* After real estate was brought into administration by the Fiduciaries Act of 1949, the in-

---

§ 9.8

2. In *McCrea Est.*, 475 Pa. 383, the executors were surcharged for failure to distribute property for over 12 years despite its increase in value from an estimated $39,000 to an estimated $218,000.

volved procedure prescribed by Section 10 of the Intestate Act of 1947 for the setting aside of the spouse's allowance from real estate became unnecessary, and a new Section 10 was enacted (effective April 1, 1956). It is now PEF 2110. Consistent with the treatment of personal property, the surviving spouse now has no right to choose particular real estate, which can be awarded in distribution: Pa. Supreme Ct. O.C. Rules 12.2(c). See *Bireley Est.*, 10 Fiduc. Rep. 158, where the entire balance of the estate, including real estate, was awarded, upon the administratrix' accounting, to the administratrix individually on account of the spouse's allowance.

## Chapter 10

# DEBTS AND CLAIMS AGAINST THE ESTATE



## § 10.1 IN GENERAL

A primary responsibility of the personal representative is to claimants for debts owed by the estate. See generally 2 Hunter, O.C. Commonplace Book (2d ed.), Debts of Decedents. These will have been discovered in the course of the initial steps of administration (see Chapter 6) or will have been formally presented as a result of advertising the grant of letters. However, before any creditor is paid, the personal representative should satisfy himself that the estate is solvent. If the estate is not solvent, and a creditor is paid more than he is entitled to receive, the personal representative will be responsible to the extent of the overpayment.

The personal representative also may be liable if he distributes estate property without having given proper notice to those having claims against the estate. See Section 16.2. The initial notice required of the personal representative is proper notice of the grant of letters. See Section 6.2.[1] Thereafter, the burden is upon creditors to give written notice, or the equivalent thereof, as set forth in PEF 3384: 4 Hunter, O.C. Commonplace Book (2d ed.), Limitations of Actions, § 3(b). A secured creditor[2] need not give notice unless the amount of his claim exceeds the value of his security. See Section 10.3.

If a claimant (other than the Commonwealth in respect to a claim for maintenance in a state-owned institution) fails to give written or equivalent notice of his claim within one year of the date of the first complete advertisement of the grant of letters, the personal representative thereafter may distribute estate property without liability for that claim (PEF 3532). Cf. *Hawkins Est.*, 416 Pa. 180, annot. *Fiduc. Rev.* Jan. 1965; *Mowrey Est.*, 19 Fiduc. Rep. 582. All claims except those of the United States must be perfected at or before audit. See Sections 10.4, 15.5. However, the obligation of a creditor to give notice of his claim after the grant of letters has been properly advertised does not apply to the lien of a secured creditor: PEF 3381. See Section 10.2.

When the estate is plainly solvent, it is sound practice for the personal representative to begin to pay clearly established obligations of the estate as soon as funds are available to do so. Since the payment of an improper claim may result in a surcharge against the personal representative, he should delay payment of doubtful claims until directed by the court to pay them following audit. See Section 16.29.

---

**§ 10.1**

**1.** Additional notice to the Commonwealth or political subdivision which has a claim for maintaining the decedent in an institution is required to be given within three months of death if the decedent died in such an institution: PEF 3393.

**2.** The secured creditor of an heir or devisee cannot rely similarly on his lien: see Section 9.8.

Although the orphans' court division has exclusive jurisdiction of the administration and distribution of a decedent's estate (PEF 711(1); *Trout v. Lukey*, 402 Pa. 123), claims against a decedent's estate may be established by suit in the trial division or other appropriate court, as well as by proof thereof in the orphan's court division (*Commonwealth v. Easton Trust Co.*, 347 Pa. 162; *Ohio v. Union Trust Co. of Pittsburgh*, 137 Pa. Super. 75; *Perkasie Vulcanizing Co. v. Mundorf*, 24 Fiduc. Rep. 475; *Fiduc. Rev.* Aug. 1948). In some circumstances claims of creditors may be determined in the federal courts: *Fiduc. Rev.* Dec. 1962. For refusal of federal district court to assume jurisdiction of claim, see *Hollander Est.*, 27 Fiduc. Rep. 567. In all cases the judgment obtained must be presented to the orphans' court division when enforcement of the claim against the decedent's estate is sought: *Biglin Est.*, 14 Fiduc. Rep. 109. PEF 3389 authorizes the orphans' court division to make such provision "as shall be equitable" for claims being litigated in other courts at the time of audit: *Ferrar Est.*, 388 Pa. 105. See Section 10.7. It is settled that all tort claims must be reduced to judgment in another court: *Gilbert Est.*, 350 Pa. 13; *Hornsey v. Jacono*, 12 D. & C. 2d 291, 294; *Fiduc. Rev.* Oct. 1964, p. 2; cf. *Harley Est.*, 12 Fiduc. Rep. 194; *Glace Est.*, 36 Northumb. 178.

See *Scholl Est.* (*No. 2*), 7 Leb. 46, regarding the burden of costs of an unsuccessful claim. In *Graham Est.*, 15 D. & C. 3d 466, the claimant was required to deposit $1,000 with the prothonotary to reimburse bank for its necessary and reasonable expenses of complying with subpoena duces tecum in regard to records of its commercial department of possible relevancy in a claim against an estate of which the bank was the executor. Regarding the admissibility of business records in support of claims, see *Fiduc. Rev.* Oct. 1959, July 1963; *Murdough Est.*, 14 Fiduc. Rep. 131. Claims against the estate of a deceased incompetent are to be presented to his personal representative, not at the audit of the guardian's account: *Bruch Est.*, 7 Fiduc. Rep. 69. For claims of a former spouse under a separation agreement, see *Fiduc. Rev.* Aug. 1966; May 1965, p. 2, but see *Cammarota Est. No. 2*, 24 Fiduc. Rep. 2d 389, annot. *Fiduc. Rev.* Jan. 2005, p. 1, where the agreement was held to be a settlement agreement rather than a separation agreement. *Camp-*

*bell Est.* (No. 2), 2 Fiduc. Rep. 3d 369, annot. *Fiduc. Rev.* Oct. 2012, p. 1 where widow was awarded attorney fees incurred to enforce contractual provision in prenuptial agreement.

For punitive damages, see *G.J.D. v. Johnson* (Pa. Supreme), 713 A.2d 1127, annot. *Fiduc. Rev.* Dec. 1998 and *Weimer Est.*, 11 Fiduc. Rep. 2d 311, annot. *Fiduc. Rev.* Jan. 1992.

## § 10.2 ORDER OF PAYMENT

The order in which claims against a decedent's estate must be paid is set forth in PEF 3392. This order of priorities is, however, subject to claims due the United States and to the claims of secured creditors who have liens or charges on the decedent's real or personal property. See Sections 10.3, 10.4; PEF 3381.

The order of payment is specified in PEF 3392 as follows:

> *Classification and order of payment*— If the applicable assets of the estate are insufficient to pay all proper charges and claims in full, the personal representative, subject to any preference given by law to claims due the United States, shall pay them in the following order, without priority as between claims of the same class:

(1) The costs of administration;

(2) The family exemption;

(3) The costs of the decedent's funeral and burial, and the costs of medicines furnished to him within six months of his death, of medical or nursing services performed for him within that time, of hospital services including maintenance provided him within that time, of services provided under the medical assistance program provided within that time, and of services performed for him by any of his employees within that time;

(4) The cost of a gravemarker;

(5) Rents for the occupancy of the decedent's residence for six months immediately prior to his death;

(5.1) Claims by the Commonwealth and the political subdivisions of the Commonwealth;

(6) All other claims.

(1) *Administration expenses.* Administration expenses are given first priority because they are incurred in the course of ascertaining and reducing to a distributable form the assets of the estate. Administration expenses may include, in addition to court costs and compensation of the personal representative, attorney fees (*Imblum Est.*, 26 Dist. 852), accounting aid (*Zavelle Est.*, 7 Fiduc. Rep. 638; *Geary Est.*, 26 Fiduc. Rep. 477; cf. *Hahl Trust*, 4 Fiduc. Rep. 351, 358), expenses of litigation (*Gulick Est.*, 63 Pitts. 68; *Arnold Est.*, 64 Pitts. 784), including witness fees and mileage (*Dunn Est.*, 26 Fiduc. Rep. 33), the cost of preserving property, for example, for services of carpenters and painters (*Marberger Est.*, 56 Montg. 30), maintenance of the decedent's home until it is sold (*Tofini Est.*, 17 Fiduc. Rep. 545), and insurance of household and personal effects (PEF 3313; *Bell Est.*, 7 Fiduc. Rep. 1, aff'd, 393 Pa. 623), storage, insurance, packing and delivery of tangible personal property to a beneficiary (PEF § 3534.1). For investment aid as an administration expense, see *Fiduc. Rev.* Sept. 1975, p. 3.

Travel, telephone and miscellaneous personal expenses have been disallowed: *Bell Est.*, supra. Administration expenses of a wife's separate estate are not chargeable to her surviving husband (*Geer Est.*, 20 Erie 397), nor are expenses chargeable against property belonging to a claimant (*Pierce Est.*, 398 Pa. 505). See *Fiduc. Rev.* March 1940. Counsel fees of attorney in successful defense against attempted surcharge are allowed: *Lavino Est.*, 30 Fiduc. Rep. 176. Administrator's travel expenses and attorney fees in regard to unsuccessful objection to a claim have been allowed: *Yetter Est.*, 30 Fiduc. Rep. 124, aff'd per cur., 487 Pa. 452.

(2) *The family exemption.* Except for secured claims, the right of the surviving spouse, children or parents to retain or claim a family exemption is preferred to all claims

against the estate other than administration expenses. See Section 7.3. The family exemption is subordinate to mortgages, whether or not for purchase money (*Miller Ap.*, 122 Pa. 95; *Rowe Est.*, 22 Pa. Super. 597), to outstanding leases (*Titus Est.*, 18 D. & C. 344), and to chattel mortgages (*Branhill Est.*, 28 D. & C. 409). The family exemption is superior to lien of judgments, even if the decedent had waived his debtor's exemption (*Spencer Ap.*, 27 Pa. 218; *Graves Est.*, 134 Pa. 377), to real estate taxes (*Allentown Ap.*, 109 Pa. 75), to mechanics' liens (*Hildebrand Ap.*, 39 Pa. 133) and to federal tax liens (see § 10.4). However, judgments which are purchase money liens have priority over family exemption rights (*Jackson Est.*, 1 Chest. 309; *Engel Est.*, 4 Northamp. 198; *Mayhugh v. Washington*, 25 Lanc. 197), but a judgment creditor who lent the purchase money gains no such priority (*Badders Estate*, 30 Lanc. 270; see *Fiduc. Rev.* April 1940, p. 3; Sept. 1941).

(3) *Cost of funeral and burial, of medicines furnished within six months and for medical and employees' service performed within that time.* The priority given to funeral and burial expenses also includes a moderate sum for mourning (*Wood Est.*, 1 Ashm. 314), food for mourners (*Mensch Est.*, 74 Montg. 263), and costs of transportation of the decedent's remains (*Carpenter Est.*, 16 Phila. 290; cf. *Gallagher v. State Farm Auto Ins. Co.*, 27 D. & C. 2d 611; *Tofini Est.*, 17 Fiduc. Rep. 545). If the estate is insolvent, the court will reduce an excessive claim for funeral expenses (*Steen Est.*, 11 Fiduc. Rep. 330), even on its own motion (*Hughes Est.*, 56 Montg. 81; see *Fiduc. Rev.* April 1940, p. 4). For reduction of funeral expense in a solvent estate, see *Sobolak Est.*, 10 Fiduc. Rep. 161; cf. *Liversidge Est.*, 14 Fiduc. Rep. 464, 489. For a burial reserve in insolvent incapacitated person's estate, see PEF 5537. For authority to order funeral, cf. *Scott Est.*, 17 Fiduc. Rep. 372. Under the equal rights amendment of the Pennsylvania Constitution the primary obligation of a husband to support his wife no longer exists and, consequently, the wife's medical and funeral expenses are deductible without considering the surviving husband's ability to pay them: *Rush Est.*, 26 Fiduc. Rep. 212; *Albert Einstein Medical Center v. Nathans*, 27 Fiduc. Rep. 561; cf. *LeVan Est.*, 28 Fiduc. Rep. 480.

The word "medicines" includes everything to be applied for the purpose of healing, whether externally or internally: *Baker Est.*, 11 Northamp. 9. "Nursing" does not include menial labor (*Larer Est.*, 11 Dist. 72), but only such immediate attendance on the sick as is directed to an alleviation or a recovery (*Silvius Est.*, 3 Lack. L.N. 84), even when rendered by a nonprofessional (*Baker Est.*, 11 Northamp. 9). Services and materials of a dentist fall within the category of medicines and medical or nursing services: *Feld Est.*, 6 Fiduc. Rep. 613.

The word "employees" is used in the statute rather than "servants" so as not to restrict services to those of house servants: cf. *Gilbert Est.*, 6 Fiduc. Rep. 124; *Ex parte Meason*, 5 Binn. 167; see generally *Fiduc. Rev.* Aug. 1940, p. 3; Sept. 1941.

(4) *The cost of a gravemarker*. The cost of a tombstone or gravemarker is included as a separate item so that it will not be given priority as an administration or funeral expense and yet will not be omitted entirely from the preferential list: cf. *Krewson Est.*, 37 D. & C. 555. A marker ordered by the decedent prior to his death will be accorded no different treatment: *Strayer Est.*, 33 Lanc. 57. The court will reduce an excessive claim for a gravemarker if the estate is insolvent (*Bracken Est.*, 9 Fiduc. Rep. 49; *Wienandt Est.*, 2 Fiduc. Rep. 441) and will charge the administratrix with the portion of a double memorial purchased for herself: *May Est.*, 2 Fiduc. Rep. 2d 232. It should be noted that a surviving husband, in absence of contract, is not liable for a marker on his wife's grave: *Mitchell Est.*, 79 Pa. Super. 208; *Fiduc. Rev.* Dec. 1954, p. 3.

(5) *Unpaid rent*. Unpaid rent for the decedent's residence is given priority only for the six-month period immediately preceding the date of death; rents prior to that period or rents due after death (unless a proper administration expense) constitute general claims: *Rainow Est.*, 2 Montg. 167. Provisions in the lease making rent payable in advance on the first of the month, or acceleration clauses advancing subsequent rental, do not advance the landlord's right to preference: *Hughes Est.*, 56 Montg. 81; *Wacker Est.*, 29 Del. 144. Rent entitled to priority does not include costs of collection (*Scott Est.*, 35 Pitts. L.J. 443) nor interest thereon (*Vandegriff Est.*, 3 Dist. 421).

The statute expressly requires "occupancy of the decedent's residence," so that if the decedent did not actually occupy the premises as his residence, except for temporary travel or hospitalization, there would be no priority. Earlier cases (*Dawson Est.*, 35 Pitts. L.J. 63; *Rinck Est.*, 49 Montg. 378) held under the prior law that the landlord's priority was not dependent on whether the decedent lived in or had property on the premises (see generally *Fiduc. Rev.* Sept. 1940, p. 3).

(5.1) *Claims by the Commonwealth and the political subdivisions of the Commonwealth.* This provision was added by amendment effective February 21, 2006 and applies to "the estate of a decedent who dies on or after the effective date of this act." Act No. 2006-17. The provision with respect to debts due the Commonwealth relates to all claims, including those for taxes. *Mathe Est.*, 34 D. & C. 647.[1] See 2 Hunter, O.C. Commonplace Book (2d ed.), Debts of Decedent, § 8(h).

(6) *All other claims.* The last class specified in the statutory order of payment is all other creditors.

Secured creditors claiming a deficiency are also in this class of general creditors. Creditors, only part of whose claims are preferred, may claim the deficiency as general creditors. A landlord in making claim as a general creditor for the rent for the balance of the term of the lease has no duty to re-let vacated premises: *Adams Est.*, 20 Fiduc. Rep. 88. In *Friedlin Est.*, 26 Fiduc. Rep. 442, a widow who remained in apartment was entitled to reimbursement for one-half the rent until termination of the lease. Cf. *Korn Est.*, 3 Fiduc. Rep. 2d 138. The fact that a secured creditor could have been paid in full had he realized upon his collateral promptly after the decedent's death and before it depreciated does not bar him from sharing with the general creditors as to the deficiency: *Miller Est.*, 132 Pa. Super. 437; cf. *In re Salmon Weed & Co.*, 53 F.2d 335 (2d Cir.); *Fiduc. Rev.* May 1941.

---

§ **10.2**

**1.** It is not clear that this provision applies to claims for inheritance taxes. For a survey of legislation prior to the Fiduciaries Act of 1949 dealing with the priority of claims of the Commonwealth against a decedent's estate, see *Fiduc. Rev.* July 1946, p. 3.

It will be noted that the order of payment established in PEF 3392 is expressly "subject to any preference given by law to claims due the United States." The position of federal claims is discussed in Section 10.4, but, generally speaking, claims due the United States are paid after administration expenses, the family exemption and funeral and burial expenses: *Black Est.*, 2 Fiduc. Rep. 2d 267.

Employee benefits under a federally qualified profit-sharing, pension or stock bonus plan are not available for payment of obligations of the decedent or of his estate: PEF 2514(19), 6114(7).

## § 10.3 SECURED CREDITORS

The assets included in the decedent's estate are subject to the prior rights of bailees, pledgees, execution creditors, mortgagees and lien creditors. Thus liens or charges on real or personal property are not impaired by the death of the decedent: PEF 3381; *Fiduc. Rev.* Sept. 1941. Bailees, pledgees and lien creditors have property rights which are not forfeited on the owner's death (*Kittera Est.*, 17 Pa. 416; *Schroeter Est.*, 50 Pitts. L. J. 431); in fact, the lien of a bailee must be paid before the personal representative is entitled to possession of the goods (*Steinman v. Wilkins*, 7 W. & S. 466; *Rodgers v. Grothe*, 58 Pa. 414). Neither the preferences listed in PEF 3392 nor the priority of the United States (*United States v. Hahn*, 37 Mo. App. 580) supersedes record liens (*Romani Est.* (Pa. Supreme), 688 A.2d 703, annot. *Fiduc. Rev.* July 1997, aff'd U.S. Supreme Court, April 29, 1998; *Schofield Est.*, 10 Fiduc. Rep. 224; *DePeio Est.*, 13 Fiduc. Rep. 88; *Hoch Est.*, 2 Fiduc. Rep. 193). It should, however, be noted that the provision in PEF 3381 with respect to secured creditors is qualified in some respects by the rights of a surviving spouse, children or parents to claim a family exemption in property not subject to a purchase money lien: PEF 3126(a). See generally Chapter 7.

An additional lien against real property for overdue support obligations was created by Act 58 of 1997, amending 23 Pa. C.S. § 4352(d). Among other provisions, the lien attaches automatically to after-acquired property, retains its priority without revival, continues after a sale or transfer, is not divested by judicial sale or execution on a lien with less priority, and expires 20 years after due date of the last unsatisfied overdue support payment. Provision is made for the domestic relations section to issue a certification of the overdue amount. Note that the estate of a deceased parent is not obligated to provide post-death support for a minor child under a pre-death court order for support. *Benson v. Patterson*, 782 A.2d 553, annot. *Fiduc. Rev.* Feb. 2002, p. 4, aff'd, 574 Pa. 346.

A creditor (including the corporate executor: *Geary Est.*, 26 Fiduc. Rep. 477) holding shares of the decedent's stock as security may retain the same until the debt is paid (*Evans Est.*, 86 Pitts. 545), and if not paid can compel the personal representative to endorse the stock certificates so that they can be sold (*Novinger v. Barnhart*, 29 D. & C. 469). If there is no equity to be preserved for the estate, the personal representative may abandon property pledged or subject to assessment (see Section 12.10; *Reynolds v. Cridge*, 131 Pa. 189; cf. PEF 3312), or he may pay the debt and receive back the collateral (*Thomas v. Waters*, 342 Pa. 125). Expenses of the sale of collateral are properly chargeable only against the fund realized from the sale: *Ruff v. Barclay-Westmoreland Trust Co.*, 79 Pa. Super. 370. However, the funds realized from the sale may not be used for general administration expenses of the personal representative, but must be applied first to the secured debt: *Phillips Est.*, 21 D. & C. 464; *Gulick Est.*, 63 Pitts. 68.

The rights of all creditors are fixed at the death of the decedent, and no one can obtain preference over others by proceedings commenced thereafter: *Strouse v. Lawrence*, 160 Pa. 421. Attachment after death is futile (*Godley Est.*, 25 D. & C. 555); for example, a mechanic's lien filed after death gives no priority even if the repairs were made in the decedent's lifetime (*Watts v. Vezin*, 12 W.N.C. 250; cf. *Hershey v. Shenk*, 58 Pa. 382; contra: *Baker Est.*, 47 D. & C. 444). As explained in Section 11.6, if a creditor of the decedent has obtained judgment against the decedent in his lifetime, or against the personal representative subsequently, the creditor is forbidden to levy on any real or personal property of the estate in execution on the judgment unless the personal representative agrees thereto in writing or unless the execution is approved by the court. The rule is inapplicable to proceedings to enforce mortgages,[1] ground rents, pledges or conditional sales: PEF 3377(b). For form of petition to stay execution, see Partridge-Remick, O.C. Practice § 16.07, Form 4. If property is improperly sold on execution after a debtor's death, the proceeds should be paid to the executor or administrator and distributed by the orphans' court division: *Patane v. Fulton*, 46 Montg. 213.

Although secured creditors of an insolvent decedent are privileged in that they can enforce collection from collateral, their advantage ends there. Their claims against other property of the decedent are limited to the deficiency: *Miller Est.*, 122 Pa. Super. 51; *Fiduc. Rev.* May 1941. Judgments which are not liens at death are treated as ordinary debts not of record: *Henry Est.*, 34 Pa. Super. 597; *Stahlnecker v. Stahlnecker*, 1 D. & C. 745.

The priority of lien creditors does not extend to rentals on the property subject to the liens which have accrued in the hands of the personal representative; such rentals are distributed as other personal property: *Downes Est.*, 27 Del. 319; *Baker Est.*, 46 Lanc. 21.

Employees, in addition to priority rights granted them by PEF 3392, may be in the position of secured creditors if they are entitled to a lien for wages for a period not exceeding six months prior to death and not in excess of $200: see 43 P.S. §§ 221 et seq.; *Fiduc. Rev.* Aug. 1940, p. 3; *Marberger Est.*, 6 Montg. 30; *Allam Est.*, 199 Pa. 573. If an employee's lien attaches to property, it takes precedence over all debts listed in PEF 3392; cf. Scott, Intestate System of Pennsylvania 440; *Patane v. Fulton*, 46 Montg. 213.

Judgments which are liens on the decedent's real estate at the time of death remain such for five years from their inception or last revival, or for one year from the decedent's death, whichever shall be longer: PEF 3382. For form of scire

**§ 10.3**

**1.** Foreclosure should not be instituted by entering judgment on the bond: *Polish Beneficial Assn. v. Dungan*, 12 Fiduc. Rep. 243.

facias to revive or extend lien, see Partridge-Remick, O.C. Practice § 16.07, Form 2; Pa. RCP 3025 et seq.

## § 10.4 CLAIMS OF THE UNITED STATES

If the estate of the deceased is not sufficient to pay all of his debts, claims owing to the United States must be paid first: 31 U.S.C. § 191. In these circumstances, the personal representative is himself answerable for the decedent's obligations due the United States to the extent that he pays first any other claims not entitled to a preference: 31 U.S.C. § 3713. This right of the United States to priority is statutory (*United States v. Fidelity & Deposit Co. of Maryland*, 214 F.2d 565 (5th Cir.)), and it cannot be impaired or superseded by state law (*United States v. Oklahoma*, 261 U.S. 253; *Kuhn Est.*, 146 Pa. Super. 1). Similarly, state statutes regulating the procedure for establishing claims do not bind the United States in the collection of its debts: *United States v. Backus*, 24 Fed. Cas. 932 (No. 14491). Thus, the federal government is the one exception to the requirement that claims must be perfected at or before audit: *LaMont Est.*, 30 Fiduc. Rep. 71.

The priority of the claims of the United States extends to all of the decedent's property, but it does not prevail over lien creditors, administration expenses, family exemption, funeral expenses or secured debts. See Section 10.2; *United States v. Fidelity & Deposit Co. of Maryland*, 214 F.2d 565 (5th Cir.); *Liversidge Est.*, 14 Fiduc. Rep. 464; *Black Est.*, 2 Fiduc. Rep. 2d 267; *White Est.*, 27 Fiduc. Rep. 2d 289. However, the problem of when a creditor's lien is perfected (13 Tax L. Rev. 247, 459; Proc. A.B.A., Section of Real Property, Probate and Trust Law 76 (1961); Digest of Tax Articles 34 (Oct. 1960)) so as to have priority over a federal claim is a federal question, and a state court's finding may be re-examined in the federal courts (*Gordon v. Campbell*, 329 U.S. 362)

The lien for federal income taxes against a husband attached to Michigan entireties property. The Supreme Court ruled that each tenant possesses individual rights in the entireties estate sufficient to constitute property or rights to property for the purposes of the lien. *United States v. Craft*, 535 U.S. 274, annot. *Fiduc. Rev.* July 2002, p. 1. Since Michigan's law governing entireties property is similar to Pennsylvania law, this important decision apparently would apply to Pennsylvania. However, there is no reason to believe that protection against other claimants afforded by entireties ownership would be affected.

Special provisions creating a general lien for any unpaid tax are contained in Sections 6321 through 6323 of the Internal Revenue Code of 1954. See *Fiduc. Rev.* Oct. 1958, p. 3; *Bracken Est.*, 9 Fiduc. Rep. 49; *Catena Est.*, 19 Fiduc. Rep. 82; 35 Taxes 684. In dealing with a bankrupt estate, any priority established in 31 U.S.C. § 3713 would be controlled by 11 U.S.C. § 507 (*In re Jacobson*, 263 Fed. 83 (7th Cir.); *Reese v. United States*, 75 F.2d 9 (5th Cir.)); the procedure for proof and allowance of claims of creditors of bankrupts is found in 11 U.S.C. §§ 501 and 502.

For claims of the United States against a deceased veteran, see Section 16.8. A Veterans' Administration claim is not a debt due the United States entitled to a preference: *Karlavage Est.*, 15 Fiduc. Rep. 289.

General discussion of the claims of the United States may be found in *Fiduc. Rev.* July 1940, p. 3; March 1943, p. 3; June 1955.

## § 10.5 CLAIMS OF COUNTY AND COMMONWEALTH

In the absence of judgments obtained by the Commonwealth in the lifetime of the decedent which have priority in real estate upon which they are liens (PEF 3381), the status of the Commonwealth as a claimant must be evaluated carefully. This is especially true if the assets of the decedent's estate originated from veterans' benefits (*Jones Est.*, 15 Fiduc. Rep. 397; *Grcich Est.*, 492 Pa. 210, annot. *Fiduc. Rev.* Feb. 1979, p. 2, Aug. 1979; *Pierce Est.*, 492 Pa. 10) or social security benefits: *Kauffeld Est.*, 20 Fiduc. Rep. 612; *Christinis Est.*, 1 Fiduc. Rep. 2d 131.

The county is a frequent claimant for unpaid personal property tax which is collectible for five years as well as the year of death: See *Fiduc. Rev.* Jan. 1946; *Peter Est.*, 25 D. & C. 3d 301. Following the decision dealing with the North Carolina intangibles tax in *Fulton Corp. v. Faulkner*, 116 S. Ct. 848, that such a tax is unconstitutional as a violation of the Commerce Clause, litigation attacking the personal property tax levied by counties on all corporate stock owned by Pennsylvania residents not otherwise exempted or excluded led the counties to discontinue imposition of the tax.

While criminal fines abate at death (*Stauch Est.*, 451 Pa. 288), the Commonwealth's status as a general creditor is not relegated to last position as it was under the 1917 Fiduciaries Act (see *Fiduc. Rev.* Nov. 1940, p. 4) and it frequently is not barred by laches: *Munchel Est.*, 75 York 117.

A new lien was created in 1994 by addition of Section 1412 to the Public Welfare Code. The estate recovery program provides for repayment of medical assistance paid for individuals fifty-five years of age or older to the Commonwealth from the probate estate. The claim has priority as a medical expense, incurred within six months of death in part and as a claim under PEF 3392 (5.1) as to any excess. See Appendix 12 for a suggested form of notice. Pennsylvania Department of Public Welfare regulations under the Medical Assistance Estate Recovery law are set forth at 31 Pa. Bulletin 6034, annot. 73 Pa. Bar Assoc. Q. 112. See 23 Pa. C.S. 4601–4606 for provision of support for the indigent, added by Act No. 2005-43.

## § 10.6 INTEREST ON CLAIMS

Whether or not a claim bears interest depends on the contract of the parties, the due date of the obligations, general business usage and whether or not the estate is solvent. Interest should be claimed at audit, but it may be allowed without being claimed: *Carey Est.*, 15 Dist. 527; cf. *Fendrich Est.*, 21 Lanc. 233. In the absence of express agreement, interest on claims for personal services is calculated from the date the last services were rendered (*Reck Est.*, 56 Montg. 312; *Stuard Est.*, 24 D. & C. 468), interest on goods sold runs from the date of sale (*Daus Est.*, 8 Dist. 326), and interest on a compromised debt runs from the date of compromise: *Wallace Est.*, 13 Dist. 155 (O.C. Phila.); cf. *Elverson Est.*, 16 D. & C. 731; *Hoff Est.*, 14 Fiduc. Rep. 119; *Rowland Est.*, 13 Fiduc. Rep. 196.

In solvent estates, both secured and unsecured creditors are entitled to interest to the time the debt is paid: *Yeatman Ap.*, 102 Pa. 297; *Bebout Est.*, 50 Pitts. 279; cf. *Hartzog Est.*, 17 Northamp. 188. With respect to insolvent estates, the amount due—both principal and interest—at the date of the death of the debtor is the amount due unsecured creditors, since that is the time the estate passes in trust for creditors: *Lamb Est.*, 11 Dist. 243; *Daus Est.*, 8 Dist. 326; *Dickinson Est.*, 14 Dist. 4; *Schumann Est.*, 28 Fiduc. Rep. 433. There is some question as to whether, in the case of an insolvent estate, interest will be allowed on preferred claims: cf. *Shultz Ap.*, 11 S. & R. 182; *Vandegriff Est.*, 3 Dist. 421. However, interest on Nursing Home claim at six per cent has been allowed in insolvent estate. *Longo Est.*, 1 Fiduc. Rep. 3d 266. Interest bill unpaid for several years on a funeral has been disallowed in an insolvent estate: *Mickey Est.*, 68 D. & C. 2d 473. When allowed, as against the fund produced by sale of collateral, interest may be charged to the date of the sale of the pledge (*Moreland Est.*, 349 Pa. 374; *Peterson v. Guarantee Trust & Safe Deposit Co.*, 4 Walk. 430), but not thereafter: *Fulton Est.*, 65 Pa. Super. 437; *Keebler Est.*, 4 Dist. 346. Interest has been disallowed where its allowance "would be highly unfair and inequitable": *Boyd Est.*, 398 Pa. 421; *Dougherty Est.*, 7 Fiduc. Rep. 138; cf. *Keener Est.*, 413 Pa. 267; *Pellegrino Est.*, 2 Fiduc. Rep. 2d 355, annot. *Fiduc. Rev.* Dec. 1982, p. 3.

See generally *Fiduc. Rev.* June 1941, p. 3, June 1963, p. 2; *Riehl Est.*, 23 Fiduc. Rep. 540.

## § 10.7 CONTINGENT AND UNMATURED CLAIMS; CLAIMS SUBJECT TO LITIGATION IN OTHER COURTS

If a claim is contingent or is not yet due, the court may provide for payment upon satisfactory proof or admission thereof: *Ferrar Est.*, 388 Pa. 105; *Duval Est.*, 11 Bucks

266, 13 Bucks 492; cf. *Martin Est.*, 87 Montg. 151; *Wasserman Trust*, 19 Fiduc. Rep. 404. The methods provided may include immediate payments or ordering the personal representative to retain sufficient assets to pay the claim when it becomes due or becomes absolute, as the case may be: *Fiduc. Rev.* June 1944, p. 3.

When the claim is being litigated in another court, the orphans' court division may make such provision for the distribution or satisfaction of the claim as it deems equitable (*Mellon Est.*, 455 Pa. 294, annot. *Fiduc. Rev.* Feb. 1974) including suspending distribution (*Zimmerman Est. (No. 2)*, 32 D. & C. 2d 391; *Franks Est.*, 25 Fiduc. Rep. 646) or allowing distribution of income alone (*Apfelbaum Est.*, 21 Fiduc. Rep. 300): PEF 3389. Distribution will not be delayed because of an unliquidated claim against a distributee: *Rupert Est.*, 26 Fiduc. Rep. 535. A compromise approved in another court is not subject to collateral attack: PEF 3323; *Pellegrino Est.*, 2 Fiduc. Rep. 2d 355.

Pa. R.C.P. 2355 provides a form of notice to be filed with the Prothonotary when a party to a pending action dies.

## § 10.8 TAX CLAIMS

In the course of the initial steps outlined in Chapter 6, the personal representative should have ascertained the existence of taxes due from or owed by the decedent. These may include federal and Pennsylvania income tax, federal gift tax and Pennsylvania personal and real property taxes,[1] wage and similar taxes. Such taxes are debts of the estate. There may also be tax claims of other states: *Ritz Est.*, 8 D. & C. 2d 115; 96 Trusts & Estates 444. When ascertained, they should be paid promptly to avoid interest charges: cf. *Martin Est.*, 16 Fiduc. Rep. 664. Federal law imposes personal liability upon an executor who pays debts not entitled to a preference be-

§ 10.8

1. Real estate taxes on unseated lands, in regard to which no personal liability attaches to the legal owner, are not a claim against his estate: *Hoverter Est.*, 50 Berks 171.

fore satisfying claims of the United States: 31 U.S.C. § 192. See Section 10.4. For priority of federal liens and tax claims, see *Fiduc. Rev.* June 1955.

## § 10.9 CLAIMS FOR HOUSEHOLD SERVICES

Claims for household services are given separate attention because they arise frequently, and they usually depend on parol testimony for proof and the claimant is barred from testifying in support of the claim by the Dead Man's Act: *Skelly Est.*, 27 Fiduc. Rep. 426; cf. *Edinger Est.*, 28 Fiduc. Rep. 297. Definite and precise proof is required: *Sanders Est.*, 370 Pa. 208; *Greeby Est.*, 13 Fiduc. Rep. 148. Cf. *Greaves Est.*, 1 Fiduc. Rep. 2d 139; *Lorah Est.*, 2 Fiduc. Rep. 2d 34.

There is a presumption of periodic current payment for personal services performed in a household (*Sanders Est.*, 370 Pa. 208; *Dart Est.*, 426 Pa. 296) or for board bills and nursing: *Consentino v. Vittoria*, 394 Pa. 538; *Mooney Est.*, 328 Pa. 273. The presumption does not apply to a physician's services (*Morris Est.*, 76 Pa. Super. 50), to services rendered in decedent's business (*Petro v. Secary Est.*, 403 Pa. 540; *Istocin Est.*, 126 Pa. Super. 158), nor to services performed under a contract calling for payment at one specified time: *Manone v. Culp*, 350 Pa. 319; *Fondelier v. Riddle*, 152 Pa. Super. 586. See *Hammer Est.*, 28 Cambria 231, for services of a registered nurse.

A family relationship may serve to rebut the implied contract to pay for services: *Gadola Est.*, 410 Pa. 250. The presumption of payment may, of course, be rebutted by competent evidence: *Irvine Est.*, 372 Pa. 110; *Seiler Est.*, 169 Pa. Super. 359. When the claimant has received some payment for services rendered, it will be presumed that the payment was in full satisfaction of the debt: *Hoefner v. Franklin Tr. Co.*, 147 Pa. Super. 404; *Calvert v. Eberly*, 302 Pa. 152. A claim based upon notes under seal allegedly given for money loaned and services rendered has been disallowed as to decedent's widow but allowed as to other distributees. *Wendt Est.*, 7 Fiduc. Rep. 693; cf. *Rynier Est.*, 347 Pa. 471, annot. *Fiduc. Rev.* Oct. 1943.

## § 10.10 CLAIMS FOR BREACH OF CONTRACT TO MAKE A WILL

Claims arising from a breach of contract to make a will are commonly based either on the allegation that a legacy was promised in exchange for present services or on the allegation that mutual wills constituted a contract.

(1) *Promised legacy or devise in exchange for present services.* Courts view with distaste alleged contracts which come to light after the death of one of the parties: *Vajentic Est.*, 453 Pa. 1. In the absence of a written contract, the claimant may be required to overcome a presumption that the services were rendered gratuitously (*Burgess v. Burgess*, 109 Pa. 312) or that payments were made periodically as the services were rendered (*Gilbraith Est.*, 270 Pa. 288). Furthermore, the survivor is incompetent to testify in support of his claim (*Nakoneczny Est.*, 456 Pa. 320), and when real estate is involved the requirements of the statute of frauds must be satisfied: *Stafford v. Reed*, 363 Pa. 405; *Pulli v. Henry Est.*, 470 Pa. 158; cf. *Beeruk Est.*, 429 Pa. 415, annot. *Fiduc. Rev.* May 1968; *Pinney Est.*, 411 Pa. 230. Exclusive possession and improvements by the claimant may satisfy the statute of frauds (*Byrne Est.*, 122 Pa. Super. 413), as may a will making reference to the contract (*Smith v. Tuit*, 127 Pa. 341), but a devise making no reference to the contract does not: *Cramer v. McKinney*, 355 Pa. 202.

Services rendered in the mere expectation of a legacy do not constitute a contract, and no recovery will be allowed thereon: *Miller Est.*, 136 Pa. 239, 248; *Cadola Est.*, 410 Pa. 250; cf. *Cummiskey Est.*, 224 Pa. 509, 513. Reliance during the testator's lifetime on the terms of a will may or may not create a contract (*Smith v. Tuit*, 127 Pa. 341; *Rowan Ap.*, 25 Pa. 292), and while reliance on statements made by the testator to third persons does not create a contract (*Shaffer Est.*, 205 Pa. 145), it may do so where the statement is that decedent and claimant actually met and formulated a contract: *Tetlow Est.*, 321 Pa. 305, 310.

Although the statute of frauds prevents specific performance of an oral contract to devise real estate, the person who rendered the services may recover the value of the services rendered or the consideration put forth in reliance on the contract: *Snyder v. McGill*, 265 Pa. 122; *Hertzog v. Hertzog*, 34 Pa. 418; *Klotz Est.*, 4 Fiduc. Rep. 594.

If it can be shown that there was a valid contract to leave a legacy of a definite sum to a promisee, he is entitled to the amount promised and may sue the personal representative for damages for the breach of the agreement: *Nusbaum Est.*, 101 Pa. Super. 17, 21; cf. *Fahringer v. Strine*, 420 Pa. 48, annot. *Fiduc. Rev.* Feb. 1966, p. 3. However, if the promise is to give the entire estate, the claimant may be limited to recovery of the value of his services: *Fiduc. Rev.* Feb. 1953, p. 3. But see *Pavlinko Est.*, 399 Pa. 536. The promisee may also have the alternate remedy of suing for the value of the services or other consideration furnished by the promisee. For the advantage of making the claim in the alternative, see *Visco Est.*, 2 Fiduc. Rep. 2d 327, annot. *Fiduc. Rev.* Nov. 1982.

(2) *Contract to make a will.* A contract to make a will cannot be probated unless executed with the formalities required of a will. However, if the agreement is valid by the law of contracts, it may be enforced against the estate of the promisor: *Burkett Est.*, 426 Pa. 617; *Musselman Est.*, 494 Pa. 571; *Fiduc. Rev.* Nov. 1966, p. 3. See also *Thompson Est.* (Pa. Super.), 481 A.2d 655, where the court held that a distribution question exists where a later will revoked provisions of the earlier will made pursuant to the contract. Concerning a contract to devise and rights of a subsequent spouse, see 44 Iowa L. Rev. 800; 57 Mich. L. Rev. 1254; *Beeruk Est.*, 429 Pa. 415, annot. *Fiduc. Rev.* May 1968. For failure of unsigned will to alter antenuptial agreement see *Friedman Est.,* 483 Pa. 614, annot. *Fiduc. Rev.* March 1979, p. 3. An instrument may be both a contract and a will, and this is frequently contended when a joint or mutual will is involved.[1] Often such a will is accompanied by a contract not to revoke, and in the absence thereof one can be implied when the circumstances clearly warrant

**§ 10.10**

**1.** A joint will is the will of two or more persons embodied in the same words contained in one instrument; a mutual or reciprocal will is an expression of the will of two or more persons in separate instruments, but each substantially identical with the other or others: Aker, Law of Wills in Pennsylvania § 1.3; 32 Pa. Bar Assn. Q. 291; *Fiduc. Rev.* Jan. 1972.

such implication. Breach of the contract, if one exists, is a claim which may be asserted against the decedent's estate. There may be an anticipatory breach of such contract: *Wertman v. Gilmore*, 8 Fiduc. Rep. 125. Contractual arrangements relating to succession, effective as to contracts made on or after January 1, 1993, must be in writing as set forth in PEF 2701.

The fact that wills are written at the same time and contain reciprocal provisions does not, or itself, constitute a contract, even when written as a single joint or double instrument: *Rhodes Est.*, 277 Pa. 450; *Cawley Est.*, 136 Pa. 628; *Hoffert Est.*, 65 Pa. Super. 515; *Imbruglia Est.*, 479 Pa. 95; *Kester Est.*, 477 Pa. 243, annot. *Fiduc. Rev.* April 1968. However, extrinsic evidence is admissible to prove the contract; *Swenk Est.*, 176 Pa. Super. 513; *Haines Est.*, 22 Fiduc. Rep. 619. For a more extended discussion, see *Fiduc. Rev.* Feb. 1953, p. 3, Jan. 1955, July 1968, p. 3; 53 Mich. L. Rev. 1; Aker, Law of Wills in Pennsylvania § 1.6. For perpetuation of testimony to support future claim of alleged oral contract, see *Flum v. Lichtenfeld*, 2 Fiduc. Rep. 2d 158. For rights of a third party beneficiary, see *Cheplic Est.*, 28 Fiduc. Rep. 380, annot. *Fiduc. Rev.* Sept. 1978.

## § 10.11 CLAIMS TO SPECIFIC PROPERTY

Frequently a dispute arises in the settlement of a decedent's estate as to whether property was owned by the decedent and consequently whether it formed a part of his estate at his death. The question is often complicated because jurisdiction of the orphans' court division to settle the dispute depends upon whether the property claimed was in the actual or "constructive" possession of the decedent: see *Fiduc. Rev.* April 1952, p. 2; *Bee Est.*, 29 Fiduc. Rep. 63. However, it is clear that the orphans' court division may determine the title to personal property in the possession of the personal representative, or registered in the name of the decedent or his nominee, or when the personal representative alleges the property was in possession of the decedent when he died: PEF 711(17); *Soupcoff Est.*, 1 Fiduc. Rep. 2d 399. The orphans' court division also has exclusive jurisdiction to partition (*Van Wie v. Headings*, 25 Fiduc. Rep. 657; PEF 3534) and distribute the decedent's real estate (PEF 711(1)) and, in addition, may determine at any time the persons to whom title has passed by devise or descent from a decedent: PEF 712(1); *Tallarico v. Bellotti*, 414 Pa. 535; *Fiduc. Rev*. March 1964; *Pope v. Dascher*, 429 Pa. 576.

Jurisdiction of the orphans' court division includes disputes regarding rentals collected by decedent's agents after his death (*Webb Est*., 7 Fiduc. Rep. 169, 391 Pa. 584, annot. *Fiduc. Rev*. Feb. 1958); specific performance of decedent's contract (*Chernow v. Monieri Est*., 410 Pa. 658); a bank account changed from decedent's name to the names of himself and another, two weeks before death (*Rogan Est*., 394 Pa. 137; see also *Balfour Est. v. Seitz*, 392 Pa. 300; *Hallman v. Carr*, 404 Pa. 216); certificate of deposit in the name of decedent "in trust" for another (*Powell Est*., 1 Fiduc. Rep. 2d 347); automobile titled in decedent's name but in possession of one alleging a gift causa mortis (*Jennings Est*., 8 Fiduc. Rep. 31); joint savings account where decedent had given temporary custody of bankbook to claimant (*Amour Est*., 397 Pa. 262); ring delivered by A to decedent's personal representative forty-five minutes prior to the filing of a writ of replevin against A (*Remaly v. Martin*, 35 Northamp. 31); furniture alleged to have been in decedent's possession at death (*Test's Executrix v. Test*, 9 Fiduc. Rep. 548); stock certificates in decedent's possession (*Schofield Est*., 10 Fiduc. Rep. 224); and insurance payable to a named beneficiary where the policies were found among decedent's effects and thereafter held by counsel for the co-executor: *Henderson Est*., 8 Fiduc. Rep. 409, annot. *Fiduc. Rev*. Sept. 1958, aff'd 395 Pa. 215. Regarding the contents of a safe-deposit box, the lease of which provides for survivorship in the ownership of the contents, see *Rodenheiser Est*., 76 Montg. 78; *Fiduc. Rev*. May 1962; *Stevenson v. Economy Bank of Ambridge*, 413 Pa. 442. Jurisdiction is conferred by PEF Chapter 22 in the case of conveyances by the decedent when the surviving spouse elects against them: *Henderson Est*., supra; *Johnson v. Tr., Church of the Lord Jesus Christ*, 408 Pa. 31; *Ross Est*., 12 Fiduc. Rep. 63; *Cutone Est*., 89 Montg. 93; *Fiduc. Rev*. May 1960, March 1968.

There is no jurisdiction of stock (and dividend checks thereon) registered in the name of the decedent, with claimant as "beneficiary," where the shares have been in claimant's possession (*Orndorff Est.*, 8 Fiduc. Rep. 531; cf. *Kaeb v. Kaeb*, 58 Lack. 209), or of realty prima facie in the name of another: *Cogan v. Cogan*, 10 Fiduc. Rep. 269. An action may be brought in equity regarding property placed in the name of others prior to decedent's death: *Rossi v. Palino*, 25 D. & C. 2d 340. The orphans' court division has no jurisdiction over a partnership where the executor of a deceased partner seeks an accounting: *Volpe Est.*, 10 Fiduc. Rep 262, annot. *Fiduc. Rev.* Nov. 1960, p. 4. See, however, *Eberhart v. Ovens*, 436 Pa. 320, annot. *Fiduc. Rev.* March 1970, where registered ownership was in a deceased partner; cf. *Fiduc. Rev.* Feb. 1964, p. 4. A citation to the executor to show cause why assets should not be delivered to the alleged donee should be dismissed, the claim being deferred to audit: *Weber v. Stroudsburg Security Trust Co.*, 18 D. & C. 2d 348; cf. *Horstman Est.*, 398 Pa. 506, dismissing a rule to show cause why United States savings bonds should not be included in the inventory.

Regarding claims by beneficiaries of life insurance policies subject to loans, by way of subrogation or for reimbursement, see *Miller Est.*, 402 Pa. 140, annot. *Fiduc. Rev.* Jan. 1961; *Cohen Est.*, 469 Pa. 29. For claims of live-in partners, see *Toloczko Est.*, 2 Fiduc. Rep. 2d 418, annot. *Fiduc. Rev.* Dec. 1982; *Brown Est.*, 28 Fiduc. Rep. 623.

When the ownership of property is in dispute, the personal representative should include the item "short" in the inventory. See Section 12.8. A party in interest dissatisfied with the position taken by the personal representative as to the ownership of the property in dispute may object to the inventory (see Section 12.4) and may compel the filing of the inventory if one has not been filed: see Section 12.3.

Disputes as to whether a claimant or the decedent owned certain property involve questions of the admissibility of evidence under the "dead man's" rule: see Section 10.16. The testimony of an alleged donee is admissible after a prima facie gift is established by the testimony of independent witnesses: *Roos Est.*, 109 Montg. 346.

See generally *Miller Est.*, 11 Fiduc. Rep. 115, annot. *Fiduc. Rev.* March 1961, p. 3; *Duffy v. Nolan*, 51 Luz. 29.

## § 10.12 CLAIMS AGAINST REAL ESTATE AND THEIR PRESERVATION

(1) *When a personal representative has been appointed.* All unsecured creditors who wish to preserve their rights against real estate until it is sold or awarded in distribution as against persons later dealing with the real estate must file, within one year of the decedent's death, written notice of their claim with the clerk of the orphans' court division where letters were granted: PEF 3532(b)(2); see *Fiduc. Rev.* April 1956.[1] The claim so filed expires at the end of five years from the decedent's death, unless (a) the personal representative files an account, or (b) the claimant files a petition to compel such an accounting: PEF 3532(b)(2). If no such claim is filed within the one-year period, or if no account or petition therefor is filed within the five-year period, distributees or persons claiming through them may rely upon the personal representative's deed in distribution as passing the decedent's title to them, free of creditors' claims.

The personal representative remains personally accountable to claimants who give notice of their claims before real property is voluntarily distributed, regardless of whether the claim has been filed with the clerk within the allotted time. Claimants whose claims are not admitted must prove them at the audit of the personal representative's account: PEF 3386. See Section 16.4. Sale or award in distribution will free real estate of all claims whether or not notice thereof has been filed: PEF 3357, 3386. For a successful claim by the grantee, under an unacknowledged and unrecorded deed to property sold by the executor without notice to the claimant, see *Hahn Est.*, 20 D. & C. 2d 240, aff'd, 402 Pa. 376. Collection of mortgage given more than twenty years before death is barred by presumption of payment under PEF 3554. *Snyder Est.*, 1 Fiduc. Rep. 3d 173.

Even though a judgment lien has not been revived within five years before death, claimant may give notice be-

**§ 10.12**

1. For rights of secured creditors, see Section 10.3.

fore distribution to request payment. *Kowalczyk Est.*, 2 Fiduc. Rep. 3d 295, annot. *Fiduc. Rev.* July 2012, p. 4.

(2) *When no personal representative has been appointed.* If no personal representative has been appointed, claimants who wish to preserve their rights in real estate until it is sold or awarded in distribution should also file, within one year of the decedent's death, written notice of their claims with the clerk of the orphans' court division having jurisdiction: PEF 3532(b)(2); cf. PEF 3385; *Fiduc. Rev.* July 1964. Since there is sometimes doubt as to which court has jurisdiction, it is generally advisable for the claimant to enforce appointment of a personal representative if the decedent had residences in more than one county or if he was a nonresident of the Commonwealth. See Sections 3.7, 5.2.

If letters have not been taken out, or if there is a vacancy in administration, and if no claim has been filed with the clerk within a year of the decedent's death, a claimant's rights against real estate (regardless of any rights he may have against the heirs or devisees) may be lost through sale or encumbrance by the heirs or devisees: PEF 3385. In any event, steps should be taken to enforce an accounting within five years of the decedent's death so that a claimant's rights to follow the real estate will not be entirely lost. The procedure to enforce an accounting is discussed in Section 15.1.

(3) *Suggested form of notice of claim.*

ESTATE OF T., DECEASED

To the clerk of the Orphans' Court Division:

Take notice of the claim of the undersigned in the amount of $ . . . . . . . . against the estate of the above decedent and make the proper entry thereof in your official records.

. . . . . . . . . . . . . . .
*Claimant*

A more comprehensive form of notice is provided by Allegheny County Orphans' Court Rule 40, which includes the following form:

IN THE COURT OF COMMON PLEAS OF ALLEGHENY COUNTY, PENNSYLVANIA
Orphans' Court Division

*In re Estate of*

No. . . . . . of 20 . . .

. . . . . . . . . . . . . . . , Deceased

CLAIM

To the Clerk of the Orphans' Court Division:
Index and make proper entry in your official records of the claim of . . . . . . . . . . . . . . . . . . . . . . . . . . . . . . . . in the amount of
(Claimant)
$ . . . . . . . . against the estate of the above-named decedent. This claim is filed under Section 3532(b)(2) PEF Code, 20 Pa. C.S. § 3532(b)(2).
The said decedent, whose last known residence was at . . . . . . . . .
(Address)
died on . . . . . . . . . ., 20 . . .
Written notice of this claim was given to . . . . . . . . . . . . . . . . . . . . . . . . . . . . . . . . . . . . . . . . . . . . . . on . . . . . . . . . . . . . . . . . . , 20 . . .
(Personal representative, if any, or his counsel)

. . . . . . . . . . . . . . . . . . . . .
(Claimant)

. . . . . . . . . . . . . . . . . . . . .
(Claimant's Address)

## § 10.13 ORDER OF AVAILABILITY—MARSHALING

The order of availability of decedent's property for the payment of his debts is fully set forth in PEF Code 3541:

> Section 3541. Order of Abatement.—
> (a) *General Rules.* Except as otherwise provided by the will, if the assets are insufficient to pay all claimants and distributees in full, the shares of distributees, without distinction between real and personal estate, shall have priority of distribution in the following order:

(1) Property specifically devised or bequeathed to or for the benefit of the surviving spouse;

(2) Property specifically devised or bequeathed to or for the benefit of the decedent's issue;[1]

(3) Property specifically devised or bequeathed to or for the benefit of other distributees;

(4) Property disposed of by will in the form of a general bequest of cash, stocks or bonds;

(5) Property disposed of by general devise or bequest and not included in a residuary clause;

(6) Property devised or bequeathed in a residuary clause;

(7) Property not disposed of by the will.

(b) *Demonstrative Legacies.* Property out of which a demonstrative legacy is primarily to be paid shall be deemed to be specifically devised or bequeathed to the extent of such demonstrative legacy.

It should be noted that the foregoing abolishes any distinction of availability based on whether the property is real or personal: *Fiduc. Rev.* Mar. 1950, p. 4; *Diesing Est.*, 11 Fiduc. Rep. 45; *Comins Est.*, 14 Fiduc. Rep. 88.

For a graphic illustration of the working of both PEF 3541 (order of availability of property) and PEF 3392 (priority of claims), see chart "Distribution of Decedent's Assets" in *Fiduciary Review* April 1969 and at the beginning of Chapter 16. The order of availability prior to the 1949 act is discussed in *Fiduc. Rev.* Sept. 1941, p. 3.

Where other assets of the estate are insufficient to meet the debts of the decedent's estate as well as administrative costs, the amounts contained in tentative trusts may

---

**§ 10.13**

**1.** "Issue" includes all lineal descendants, not only those who would take by intestacy: *Thornton Est.*, 420 Pa. 521, annot. *Fiduc. Rev.* April 1966, p. 3.

be reached for satisfaction of these claims. *Stevenson Est.* (Pa. Super.), 648 A.2d 559, annot. *Fiduc. Rev.* Dec. 1994.

Act 135 of 1976 added PEF 2514(19) and 6114(7) which provides a rule of presumed intention for wills and inter vivos trusts, reading:

"Benefits received by a trust under a federally qualified profit sharing, pension or stock bonus plan shall not be available for the payment of obligations of the decedent or of his estate."

## § 10.14 LIMITATIONS UPON CLAIMS

PEF 3383 provides that the decedent's death does not stop the running of the statute of limitations applicable to a claim against him, but that a claim which would otherwise be barred within one year of his death is not barred until one year after his death. See *Fiduc. Rev.* Jan. 1965, Sept. 1967, p. 4, Nov. 1967; 4 Hunter, O. C. Commonplace Book (2d ed.), Limitation of Actions, § 3. Written notice of any claim or its equivalent, given to the personal representative (including an administrator pendente lite: *Pellegrino Est.*, 2 Fiduc. Rep. 2d 355) or his attorney will toll the statute of limitations: PEF 3384.

## § 10.15 CLAIMS IN ANCILLARY ADMINISTRATION

When the estate is solvent, the Pennsylvania ancillary personal representative may pay Pennsylvania creditors and legatees as well as nonresident creditors and legatees before transmitting funds to the domiciliary personal representative (cf. *Barry Ap.*, 88 Pa. 131, and *Middleby Est.*, 249 Pa. 203, 254 Pa. 328, with *Bertin Est.*, 245 Pa. 256, *Mamato Est.*, 43 D. & C. 331, *Parkhurst Est.*, 8 Fiduc. Rep. 442, *Reck Est.*, 56 Montg. 312, and *Warrington Est.*, 7 Dist. 712), but may not discriminate in favor of Pennsylvania residents in an insolvent estate (see *Blake v. McClung*, 172 U.S. 239; *Fox Est.*,

15 Dist. 470). However, the court has discretion to refuse to make an award to anyone but the domiciliary personal representative: *Hazel Est.*, 11 Fiduc. Rep. 169, annot. *Fiduc. Rev.* April 1961. A creditor who received partial payment in another jurisdiction may receive payment from the ancillary administrator in Pennsylvania until he receives the full amount of his claim, but in an insolvent estate his total shares wherever received cannot exceed his appropriate pro rata share: see *Fox Est.*, 15 Dist. 470; *Warrington Est.*, 7 Dist. 712; Restatement of Conflict of Laws §§ 500, 501. See also *Parkhurst Est., (No. 2)*, 10 Fiduc. Rep. 475, which refused to pass on the claim of distributee domiciled at decedent's domicile, and passed on a claim of a distributee domiciled in Pennsylvania.

## § 10.16 DEAD MAN'S STATUTE

The Dead Man's Statute of 1887, as restated in the Judicial Code, 42 Pa. C.S. § 5930, so far as relevant provides:

". . . where any party to a thing or contract in action is dead, or has been adjudged a lunatic and his right thereto or therein has passed, either by his own act or by the act of the law, to a party on the record who represents his interest in the subject in controversy, neither any surviving or remaining party to such thing or contract, nor any other person whose interest shall be adverse to the said right of such deceased or lunatic party, shall be a competent witness to any matter occurring before the death of said party or the adjudication of his lunacy . . . unless the issue or inquiry be devisavit vel non, or be any other issue or inquiry respecting the property of a deceased owner, and the controversy is between parties respectively claiming such property by devolution on the death of such owner, in which case all persons shall be fully competent witnesses."

In evaluating the merit of debts and claims against a decedent's estate, it is well for personal representatives to be aware of the effect of the Dead Man's Act on the ability of the claimant to establish his claim if forced to a proof of it by litigation. Consequently, it is important that nothing be done to waive the bar of the statute if the claim is to be contested. The personal representative's duty to pay all just debts of the decedent must be balanced with his obligation toward those entitled to distributive shares. And, in the case of an insolvent estate, consideration must be given to creditors whose rights are established as against creditors whose claims may be barred by adherence to the bar of the statute. The estate's request that the claimant supply an itemized statement in support of a claim will not of itself constitute a waiver of the statutory bar: *Lorah Est.*, 2 Fiduc. Rep. 2d 34, annot. *Fiduc. Rev.* Feb. 1982; cf. *Bolinger Est.*, 3 Fiduc. Rep. 2d 274, nor did failure of the executrix to appear at discovery depositions to assert the bar of the Dead Man's Rule constitute a waiver in a medical malpractice action. *Schroeder v. Jaquiss*, 813 A.2d 916, annot. *Fiduc. Rev.* Nov. 2003, p. 2. On the other hand, the cross-examination of the claimant (*Fiduc. Rev.* March 1961, p. 3) or the taking of depositions (*Fiduc. Rev.* Feb. 1962); *Rosenthal v. Kramer*, 40 D. & C. 3d 291; *G.J.D. v. Johnson* (Pa. Super.), 669 A.2d 378. may constitute a waiver of the statutory bar. See generally *Fiduc. Rev.* Oct. 1955, July 1963, March 1966, March 1979, Dec. 1979, p. 4, March 1980, April 1982, p. 3; 52 Pa. Bar Ass'n Q. 84; 2 Hunter O.C. Commonplace Book (2d ed.), Evidence, 1(a); The Dead Man's Rule, 23 Fiduc. Rep. 2d 177.

For consideration of whether the attorney-client privilege should be asserted or waived by the personal representative, see *Fiduc. Rev.* April 1983.

## Chapter 11

# SURVIVAL, ABATEMENT AND CONTROL OF ACTIONS



## § 11.1 SURVIVAL ACTIONS

No action may be brought or continued (*Volk Est.*, 16 Fiduc. Rep. 156) against a dead man, but all causes of action or proceedings, real and personal[1] survive the decedent, and they may be brought by or against his personal representative as though the decedent were alive: PEF 3371, 3373; 42 Pa. C.S. § 8302. The former exception of actions for libel and slander has been changed by amendment to PEF 3371 and by the provisions of Section 8302 of the Judicial Code. See *Moyer v. Phillips*, 462 Pa. 395, annot. 80 Dick. L. Rev. 342. For action on libelous testamentary statements, see *Schell Will*, 10 Fiduc. Rep. 123, annot. *Fiduc. Rev.* Feb. 1960; cf. *Menefee v. CBS*, 458 Pa. 46. See also *Becker v. Knecht*, 67 Schuyl. 90, where it was held that an action for invasion of privacy abates due to plaintiff's death before trial.

Tort actions must be brought in the trial division: *Gilbert Est.*, 350 Pa. 13; *Franks Est.*, 25 Fiduc. Rep. 646; see *Fiduc. Rev.* March 1962; cf. *Harley Est.*, 12 Fiduc. Rep. 194; *Zimmerman Est.*, (*No. 2*), 32 D. & C. 2d 391. Conviction of

**§ 11.1**

1. Contracts for personal services do not survive: *Sorber v. Masters*, 264 Pa. 582.

murder is conclusive proof of liability of defendant in a wrongful death and survival action: *Allison Est. v. Sharp*, 96 York 1. Estate of victim of homicide is "in the shoes of the victim" eligible to benefit from restitution directed as part of a criminal sentencing under 18 Pa. C.S. § 1106. *Comm. v. Lebarre*, 961 A.2d 176. Included among the personal representative's powers is the power to consummate legally binding contracts of the decedent to purchase or sell real or personal estate. If he fails to do so, the court, upon the application of any party in interest, may order specific performance of the agreement if it would have been enforced specifically in the decedent's lifetime: PEF 3390; *American Bank v. Lied Est.*, 25 Fiduc. Rep. 633, aff'd, 487 Pa. 333, annot. *Fiduc. Rev.* March 1980, p. 3. The administrator of the estate of an unborn child, or stillborn viable fetus, cannot bring a survival or wrongful death action: *Carroll v. Skloff*, 415 Pa. 47; *Marko v. P.T.C.*, 420 Pa. 124; *Scott v. Kopp*, 494 Pa. 487; cf. *Speck v. Finegold*, 497 Pa. 77.

If an action is pending at the time of the decedent's death, his personal representative may become a party thereto by filing of record a statement setting forth the facts on which the right of substitution is based: Pa. Rules of Civil Procedure 2352(a).[2] Failure of the personal representative to substitute himself voluntarily gives an adverse party the right to obtain compulsory substitution: Pa. Rules of Civil Procedure 2352(b). However, the personal representative of a decedent who died prior to being served as defendant in a trespass action cannot be substituted as a defendant under such rule: *Love v. Vincent*, 27 Fay. 131.

Any proceeding may be brought against a personal representative in the county where his letters have been granted. (The personal representative, not the "estate," is the proper party: *Alesczyk v. Glen Alden Corp.*, 29 D. & C. 2d 138). Thus, a suit against the "estate" of a decedent—not naming the personal representative—cannot be amended to include

§ **11.1**

**2.** When a fiduciary who is a party to an action or proceeding dies, resigns or has his powers annulled or revoked, the action or proceeding does not abate. The successor of the fiduciary may be substituted in the same way that a personal representative is substituted for a deceased party: Pa. Rules of Civil Procedure 2352.

the personal representative after the statute of limitations has expired: *Oswald v. Heimback*, 23 Fiduc. Rep. 107; *Myers v. Estate of Wilks*, 440 Pa. Super. 176, 665 A.2d 176, annot. *Fiduc. Rev*. June 1995. If he is not a resident of that county, procedures are established for the service of process upon him elsewhere: PEF 3157, 3391. Provision is made for securing appointment of a personal representative against whom suit can be brought when the decedent was a nonresident and left no property in the state: PEF 3151. This is especially helpful in cases of deceased nonresident operators of aircraft and motor vehicles: see *Fiduc. Rev*. April 1956, p. 4. See also *Brandt v. Daniel Est.*, 7 Fiduc. Rep. 473; *Hoover Est.*, 7 Fiduc. Rep. 476; *Paton Est.*, 7 Fiduc. Rep. 684; 44 Iowa L. Rev. 402; 44 id. 268; 57 Mich. L. Rev. 406; 25 Mo. L. Rev. 83.

## § 11.2 WRONGFUL DEATH ACTIONS

Frequently confused with survival actions are so-called "death actions," which may arise at, but not prior to, the decedent's death. If the decedent's death resulted from the tortious act of another, there are two separate causes of action—a tort action which survives him and a "death action" which accrues for the benefit of certain of his relatives and is free from the claims of creditors and death taxes: 42 Pa. C.S. §§ 8301, 8302. Although the terms "survival action" and "death action" are sometimes used interchangeably, they are entirely distinct: cf. *Burns v. Goldberg*, 210 F.2d 646 (3d Cir.). See *Fiduc. Rev*. March 1962, June 1958, p. 3; *Johnson v. Peoples First National Bank and Trust Co.*, 394 Pa. 116; *Gortva v. Feldman*, 12 D. & C. 2d 188; *Borzik v. Greene County Motor Co.*, 22 Fay. 5; 62 W. Va. L. Rev. 101. The table on page 218 (from *Fiduc. Rev*. Feb. 1972, p. 2, as revised) illustrates the principal differences.

The proper venue for suit is the county in which the injury occurred, not the county in which death occurred. *Sunderland v. R. A. Barlow Home Builders*, 791 A.2d 1026.

Concerning measure of damages in both types of actions, see *Incollingo v. Ewing*, 444 Pa. 299, annot. *Fiduc. Rev*. Feb. 1972; 17 Villa. L. Rev. 723. The following discussion (as revised) appeared in the *Fiduciary Review* annotation:

*Action begun before death*: Damages may be recovered for pain and suffering, medical, nursing and hospital (but not funeral) expenses, and "loss of gross earning power from the date of injury until death, and loss of earning power less personal maintenance expenses from the time of death through decedent's estimated working lifespan": *Incollingo v. Ewing*, 444 Pa. 299, 309. Six percent simple interest has been used in reducing damages to present value: *Brodie v. P.T.C.*, 415 Pa. 296. However, the Supreme Court in *Kaczkowski Admr. v. Bolubasz*, 491 Pa. 561, annot. 87 Dick. L. Rev. 1, said ". . . today, in light of clear scientific evidence of the fact that inflation and productivity have become an established part of our economy, it becomes necessary that these factors be considered" in making award with respect to personal injury action damages for lost future earnings. ". . .we find as a matter of law that future inflation shall be presumed equal to future interest rates with these factors offsetting. Thus, the courts of this Commonwealth are instructed to abandon the practice of discounting lost future earnings."

In the case of a minor plaintiff, the portion of the damages based upon economic loss compensates the estate "only for economic loss from the age of majority": *Incollingo v. Ewing*, supra, at p. 307.

*Survival action*: The measure of damages is the same as stated above, as a result of the *Incollingo* decision. Where death results from a cause not related to the cause of action, the measuring period for future earnings is from injury to date of death: *Mohler v. Worley*, 179 Pa. Super. 56.

*Wrongful death action*: Damages may be recovered for medical, nursing and hospital expenses, funeral expense, and the present worth of decedent's probable future contributions to his family (i.e., earnings, less cost of his maintenance, less any amounts the family may have contributed to decedent's support): *Skoda v. W. Penn Power Co.,* 411 Pa. 323, 334–335; *Gaydos v. Domabyl,* 301 Pa. 523. Damages may include such intangible benefits as the guidance and service of a mother to a child: *Gaydos v. Domabyl*, supra; *Lynch v. Letterman*, 29 Erie 52; *Boyle v. Lehigh Valley Trans. Co.*, 19 Leh. 309; cf. *Rodney v. Staman*, 371 Pa. 1, 9.

The rules regarding survival and death actions are designed to avoid duplication of damages in those companion actions. The allocation of damages in the death of a six year old was 80% to the wrongful death action payable to father because of mother's negligence in the automobile action which resulted in the child's death and 20% to the survival action. *Coleman Est.*, 772 A.2d 384. A potential claimant against a decedent's estate has no standing to object to the allocation of proceeds of 90% to wrongful death and 10% to survival. *Webb Est.*, 21 Fiduc. Rep. 2d 101.

A cause of action for the wrongful death of a decedent and a survival action for his injuries may be enforced in one action; but if independent actions are begun, they must be consolidated for trial. Pa. Rules of Civil Procedure 213(e); *Fiduc. Rev.* July 1968, p. 3. although the actions are cumulative and not alternative, they must not result in a duplication of damages and thereby compel the tort-feasor to pay more than the maximum damage caused by his negligent act: *Pezzulli v. D'Ambrosia,* 344 Pa. 643, 647–648. Act 46 of 1995 amends 42 Pa. C.S. § 8301(a) to permit commencement of wrongful death actions even though suit was commenced during decedent's lifetime if no recovery was obtained and the pending suit is consolidated with the new action, effective for causes of action accruing on or after September 4, 1995. If diversity of citizenship is involved, the federal courts also have jurisdiction, and separate actions can be maintained since the Pennsylvania rules of procedure cannot oust the jurisdiction of the federal court: *Hopkins v. Pennsylvania Power & Light Co.,* 112 F. Supp. 136 (E.D. Pa.); *Wertz Est.*, 6 Fiduc. Rep. 252.

Diversity jurisdiction exists even though all who benefit by the recovery reside in the same state as defendant, and only the administrator resides in another state: *Borror v. Sharon Steel Co.,* 327 F.2d 165 (3rd Cir.).

See *McSparran v. Weist*, 18 Fiduc. Rep. 538 (3rd Cir.), annot. *Fiduc. Rev.* Nov. 1968, p. 4, prohibiting "manufactured" diversity jurisdiction: *Groh v. Brooks & Shallway Outdoor Adv. Co.*, 421 F. 2d 589; *Butler, gdn. v. Cofelt*, 313 F. Supp. 527, aff'd, 439 F. 2d 882; *Joyce v. Seigel*, 429 F.2d 128.

| | SURVIVAL ACTION | DEATH ACTION |
|---|---|---|
| 1. Who may bring the action? | The personal representative of the decedent. PEF 3371, 3373. | The personal representative of the decedent or if no action is brought within six months, then also the surviving spouse, parents or children. Pa. Rules of Civil Proc. 2202; 42 Pa. C.S.A. § 8301. |
| 2. For whose benefit may the action be brought? | Decedent's estate. PEF 3371, 3373. See *Edelman v. Flyte*, 35 Northamp. 102. | Surviving spouse, children or parents, according to intestate shares. see *Fiduciary Rev*. June 1968, p. 3, and *Seymour v. Rossman*, 449 Pa. 515 (1972) regarding possible exclusion of some statutory beneficiaries.** See *Hughes Est.*, 14 Adams 106, holding Pa. law not applicable in action arising from death at sea. |
| 3. Rights of decedent's creditors. | Amount recovered becomes part of decedent's estate and may be reached by creditors. *Patton v. Baltimore & Ohio Ry. Co.*, 197 F. 2d 732 (3rd Cir.). | No rights to any part of amount recovered. 42 Pa. C.S.A. § 8301; *Lucabaugh Estate*, 74 D. & C. 68, 75 (O. C. York); Cf. *Chapman Est.*, 16 Fiduc. Rep. 459. |
| 4. Statute of limitations. | Two years from the time of injury. *Stegner v. Fenton*, 351 Pa. 292. See *Cates v. Gimbel Bros.*, Inc., 105 Pitts. L. J. 314. | Two years from date of death. 42 Pa. C.S.A. § 5524(2); *Skoda v. W. Penn Power Co.*, 411 Pa. 323. |
| 5. Pa. inheritance tax. | Subject to tax. *Olson Estate*, 12 Fiduc. Rep. 36 (O. C. Phila.) annotated in *Fiduciary Review* (March 1962). | Not subject to tax. *Hoover Estate*, 7 Fiduc. Rep. 476; *Chapman Estate*, 16 Fiduc. Rep. 459. |
| 6. Federal estate tax. | Subject to tax. Cf. *Estate of McGlue*, 41 B.T.A 1199, 1202. See Rev. Ruls 75-126 and 75-127 for nontaxability where decedent died instantaneousy. | Not subject to tax. Rev. Rul. 54-19, 1954-1 C.B. 179. |

**If none of those entitled survives the decedent, the personal representative may recover reasonable hospital, nursing, medical and funeral expenses and expenses of administration necessitated by reason of injuries causing death. 42 Pa. C.S.A. § 8301.

The Supreme Court has held that the orphans' court division has no jurisdiction to deal with disputes arising over counsel fees, and the disposition of the net recovery obtained in a wrongful death action: *Pozzuolo Est.*, 433 Pa. 185.

Regarding conflicts of laws questions involved in the measure of damages for wrongful death, see 65 W. Va. L. Rev. 146. In the wake of *Griffith v. United Airlines*, 416 Pa. 1, it is becoming apparent that the law applicable to a particular survival or wrongful death action is not necessarily the law of the place of the accident. See, for example, *Kuchinic v. McCrory*, 422 Pa. 620, where such actions were held to be governed by Pennsylvania law where only Pennsylvania residents were involved in a Georgia airplane accident.

## § 11.3 COMPROMISE OF ACTIONS

(1) *Wrongful death actions.* Settlement or compromise of a wrongful death action does not require court approval, unless the interest of a minor is involved: *Wexler v. Philadelphia Transit Co.*, 5 Fiduc. Rep. 269. The personal representative may not settle a wrongful death action without the consent of the beneficiaries: *Zielinski v. McGovern*, 28 Chester 381. The discontinuance or settlement of an action in which a minor has an interest must be approved by the court as being fair and equitable: Pa. Rules of Civil Procedure 2206(a); *Fiduc. Rev.* Nov. 1956; cf. *Eby Est.*, 25 Fiduc. Rep. 602, annot. *Fiduc. Rev.* Nov. 1975, p. 3. When the recovery is insufficient to pay all claims in full, the policy of the law is to favor the wrongful death claim and to give it full priority over the survival claim: *Ringler Est.*, 29 Fiduc. Rep. 499. In *Manning v. Capelli*, 270 Pa. Super. 207, the direction in the Wrongful Death Act that the sum recovered shall go to the husband, widow, children or parents of the deceased "in the proportion they would take his or her personal estate in case of intestacy," was not controlling and a daughter who was living apart from decedent's home and not dependent on the decedent was not entitled to share in the settlement of the wrongful death action with the surviving spouse and dependent children.

(2) *Actions that survive*. Although PEF 3323 gives to a personal representative broad powers to compromise or settle without court approval any claim by or against the estate of a decedent, the orphans' court division appears to have power to pass upon the propriety of a compromise when no action has been started in any court: *Fiduc. Rev*. May 1955, p. 3, Nov. 1956. However, it has been held that if an action was started in the decedent's lifetime, the orphans' court division has no such jurisdiction: *Muenker Est*., 5 Fiduc. Rep. 274. Caution dictates that the personal representative consult legal counsel before any compromise or settlement is consummated on behalf of the decedent's estate.

## § 11.4 ABATEMENT OF ACTIONS

If the personal representative dies or resigns, or his authority is terminated, an action or proceeding to which he is a party is not abated, and his successor may be substituted therein: PEF 3374, as modified by Pa. Rules of Civil Procedure 2375(8). However, if the decedent was a plaintiff in any pending action, and if no personal representative is appointed within a year, the defendant may petition the court to abate the action: PEF 3375. The purpose of this requirement is to ensure the prompt prosecution of all pending claims and proceedings.

Application for expenses for litigation of wrongful death and survival action in behalf of minors where motions to set aside substantial verdict were pending, was denied in *Roland Minors' Estates*, 2 Fiduc. Rep. 2d 295.

## § 11.5 STATUTES OF LIMITATIONS

The decedent's death does not stop for more than one year the running of the statute of limitations applicable to any claim or cause of action of the decedent which survives his death: PEF 3376. Steps should be taken promptly to prosecute such claims on behalf of the estate before the particular statute has run. Failure or delay to take out letters testamentary or of administration does not affect the operation of any statute applicable to a debt or liability owed the estate.

Claims against the decedent also will be barred by the applicable statute of limitations when the specified period has run, but that period will not be less than one year after decedent's death: PEF 3383. See *Fiduc. Rev.* March 1951; *Stephenson v. Wildasin Est.*, 20 Fiduc. Rep. 100. Statute of limitations begins to run on date of death and not date of discovery of cause of death. *Gravinese v. Johns-Manville Corp.* (Pa. Super.), 471 A.2d 1233.

The statute of limitations is now two years for both the wrongful death and survival actions: Judicial Code, § 5524.

Letters of administration may be obtained to create a party defendant: *Johnston, Admx. v. Johnston Executrix*, 71 D. & C. 2d 745. And, in special circumstances, the doctrine of relation back may protect the claimant from the bar of the statute: *D'Orazio v. Locust Lake Village*, 267 Pa. Super. 124; *Wilkes-Barre General Hospital v. Lesho*, 62 Comm. Ct. 222, annot. *Fiduc. Rev.* Feb. 1982; *Campbell v. Shadyside Hospital*, 21 Fiduc. Rep. 2d 291.

The printed word "Seal" or "L.S." on a printed form document cannot be relied on as conclusive that the document is under seal: *Associates Consumer Discount v. Gabriel*, 72 D. & C. 2d 687; *Investors Loan Corp. v. Perez*, D. & C. 2d 149.

## § 11.6 EXECUTION ON JUDGMENTS

If a creditor of the decedent has obtained judgment against the decedent in his lifetime or against his personal representative subsequently, the creditor is forbidden to levy on any real or personal property of the estate in execution on the judgment unless the personal representative agrees thereto in a writing filed in the execution proceeding, or the execution is approved by the court after the giving of notice as directed: *Pfeffer v. Mills*, 13 Fiduc. Rep. 500. The foregoing is inapplicable to proceedings to enforce mortgages, ground rents, pledges or conditional sales: PEF 3377; see Section 10.3. For procedure to execute, see PEF 784 (personal property) and PEF 786 (real property).

# Chapter 12

# INVENTORY

---



---

## § 12.1 WHEN AND WHERE TO FILE INVENTORY

An inventory of all the decedent's real and personal estate must be filed with the register of wills by every personal representative no later than the date he files his account or the due date, including any extension, for the filing of the inheritance tax return, whichever is earlier: PEF 3301(c). The inventory is the basis of the account which the personal representative will later file. See Chapter 15. It should be prepared with great care not only for this reason but as a protection to the personal representative himself. Compliance with the steps outlined in Chapters 6 through 11 will have furnished most of the information required. "The function and object of an inventory and appraisement in a decedent's estate is to fix *presumptively* the existence of property in the possession of the fiduciary and the value thereof. This is only *prima facie* evidence of ownership and value. Such listing does not affect the true ownership and value." *Donsavage Est.*, 420 Pa. 587.

The inventory must be filed in duplicate and be verified by the affidavit of the personal representative:[1] PEF 3301(a). The verified original remains with the register of wills and is indexed and recorded: PEF 922. The other copy is forwarded to the county board of assessment for purposes of the county personal property tax and for a determination of whether the estate owes any such tax:[2] Act of 1947, P.L. 1249, § 3, 72 P.S. § 4844.2. Even though personal property tax is not payable, duplicate copies of the inventory are filed. See *Fiduc. Rev.*, Apr. 2010, p. 1 re Register of Wills requirement that inventory be filed with inheritance tax return.

The personal estate includes not only tangible assets but securities, notes, debts and claims due the estate, unpaid rents, wages or salary due and life insurance payable to the estate. Even worthless assets may be listed. See Section 12.10. For a discussion of what personal property should be included in the inventory, see Section 12.9; Partridge-Remick, O.C. Practice § 13.04; *Dobbins Est.*, 24 Erie 92; *Moyer Est.*, 2 Leb. 188. Partnership assets passing to the surviving partner under 15 Pa. C.S. §§ 8813 and 8342 should not be included in the inventory. *Beeson Est.*, 22 Fiduc. Rep. 2d 20, annot. *Fiduc. Rev*. Feb. 2002, p. 3. Valuation is discussed in Sections 12.5 and 12.9.

All of the decedent's real estate must be included in the inventory. See Section 9.6. Real estate outside of Pennsylvania including real estate in foreign countries (*Barnash Est.*, 56 Wash. 172) should be listed in memorandum form only, and the value, if the personal representative elects to indicate it, should not be extended into the totals of the inventory or included as real estate in subsequent accountings:

---

**§ 12.1**

**1.** Filing of separate personal property affidavits is no longer required. The inventory still must be verified by affidavit since PEF 761 applies only to applications to the court.

**2.** It may be advisable to indicate the date of acquisition of taxable assets to ensure that tax thereon will not be included in any assessment for prior years. When the decedent has not paid personal property taxes prior to death, the tax may be assessed for five years prior to year of death and 6% interest may be added. However, the county is not entitled to collect a 5% penalty as well: *Martin Est.*, 16 Fiduc. Rep. 664; *Peter Est.*, 25 D. & C. 3d 301.

PEF 3301(b). The purpose of including realty outside Pennsylvania in the inventory is to supply essential information to creditors and others interested in the estate.

An ancillary personal representative is required to include in the inventory only those assets for which he is responsible: PEF 3301(a).

## § 12.2 SUPPLEMENTAL INVENTORY

If, after the original inventory is filed, additional property is found, the personal representative must file with the register of wills a supplemental inventory listing and valuing such property. A supplemental inventory must be filed within thirty days of the discovery of the additional property: PEF 3303.

Frequently, assets of an inconsequential nature are discovered after the personal representative has prepared and filed his inventory. In such circumstances it is approved practice to include such assets in a subsequent accounting without going to the expense and trouble of filing a supplemental inventory.

## § 12.3 COMPELLING THE FILING OF AN INVENTORY

If a personal representative refuses or neglects to file the required or supplemental inventory, he may be compelled to do so upon petition to the orphans' court division filed by any party in interest. While PEF 3301(c) permits an interested person to request earlier filing of an inventory, it is usual to allow at least six months to elapse from the time letters are granted and then petition for a citation on the personal representative to file the inventory and also an account. If sufficient cause is shown, an order will be made compelling the fiduciary to file a true and accurate inventory or supplemental inventory, as the case may be: *Kauffman Est.*, 9 Fiduc. Rep. 670; cf. *Brose Est.*, 423 Pa. 420; *Hammer Est.*, 389 Pa.

78. Lack of significant assets is no excuse for failure to file a requested inventory: *Drummond Est.*, 29 Fiduc. Rep. 372, annot. *Fiduc. Rev.* Jan. 1980, p. 3. No separate inventory is required when an estate is settled pursuant to a small estate petition under PEF 3301. *Estates of Kruth, Kelly and Adams,* 19 Fiduc. Rep. 2d 313, annot. *Fiduc. Rev.* Nov. 1999.

If a personal representative persists in his failure to file an inventory, he may be required to give bond or increase the amount of the bond already given or may be removed by petition on behalf of interested parties, or even be summarily removed by the court on its own motion: PEF 3171–3175. Other means available to the court to enforce its decrees probably would not be utilized in this situation: PEF 781–786. For procedure and forms, see Aker, PEF Code Annot. § 3501.1: Partridge-Remick, O.C. Practice §§ 13.07, 13.08.

## § 12.4 OBJECTIONS TO INVENTORY

When assets which should be included in the inventory are omitted, or conversely, when assets are inventoried which should be excluded, parties in interest may object immediately to their exclusion or inclusion, as the case may be: *Horstman Est.*, 398 Pa. 506. See Aker, PEF Code Annot. § 3305 for form for objections to inventory. The court's decision is not appealable until after audit of the account: *Nunnamaker Est.*, 452 Pa. 467 and *Strunk Est.*, 453 Pa. 19, annot. *Fiduc. Rev.* Aug. 1973. Objections may be delayed until the account is filed (see Section 15.10) and then be made in the form of objections to the account. When objections are filed prior to the accounting, hearing thereon in the discretion of the court may be delayed until the audit of the account: PEF 3305.[1] See *Hoopes Est.*, 25 Fiduc. Rep. 110; Section 14.8; *Schoonover Est.*, 28 Fiduc. Rep. 219.

---

§ 12.4

1. Prior to enactment of the wording now embodied in PEF 3305 on February 23, 1956, there was considerable confusion as to how questions about the inventory could be raised, and it had been decided that objections should be delayed until an accounting: *Rogers Est.*, 379 Pa. 494, annot. *Fiduc. Rev.* Dec. 1954, Jan. 1956.

When a personal representative includes property as an item in the inventory submitted, a presumption arises that the decedent was the owner of that property, and a party claiming that the decedent did not own the property has the burden of rebutting the presumption: *Hendrickson Est.*, 388 Pa. 39; *Cobb Est.*, 21 Fiduc. Rep. 161, aff'd 444 Pa. 612; *Conway Est.*, 12 Fiduc. Rep. 283.

## § 12.5 VALUATION

A personal representative is under a duty to determine and state for each asset listed in the inventory its fair value as of the date of the decedent's death: PEF 3302. The values used in the inventory no longer need be based upon figures supplied by two or more sworn appraisers. The responsibility is now solely with the personal representative to establish correct figures, and he should secure information and assistance in each estate according to its peculiarities. In many instances the assistance of persons qualified to appraise particular assets is required. See Section 6.7. In these circumstances, the expense of their services is a justified charge against the estate, and a fee which bears a fair relation to the work and responsibility involved will be approved. The appraisals of paid experts should be submitted in written form signed by the appraisers and retained in the estate files.

Values listed in the inventory are not conclusive but are *prima facie* evidence of value: cf. *Seidman Est.*, 261 Pa. 540; *Yetzer Est.*, 3 Fiduc. Rep. 469.

Discussion of valuation of particular kinds of assets will be found in Section 12.9. See also Partridge-Remick, O.C. Practice § 13.05.

## § 12.6 EFFECT OF INVENTORY

As stated in Section 12.4, when assets have been listed in the inventory there is a presumption that the decedent was the owner thereof. The list of assets and their values also sets forth the extent of *prima facie* liability of the personal representative and is regarded as an admission on his part that the property embraced in it came into his possession as legal representative of the decedent and that no part of it is owned individually by him: *Haire Est.*, 28 West. 1; *Deist Est.*, 15 Som. 325. Items which he claims individually can be listed "short." See Section 12.8. A subsequent denial of estate ownership, without substantial support, will not overcome the presumption. However, the court may initiate an investigation to the extent necessary to inform itself whether the denial is made in good faith and a substantial dispute exists: *Hermann Est.*, 226 Pa. 543. For effect of omission from inventory, see *Searight Est.*, 8 Fiduc. Rep. 174. When a substantial dispute as to ownership exists, a jury trial must be granted if requested by any party in interest: PEF 777(a).

## § 12.7 CLAIMS AGAINST PERSONAL REPRESENTATIVE

When the personal representative is indebted to the decedent, or the decedent had a claim against the personal representative, the personal representative's appointment does not operate as a discharge of the debt or claim. See Section 6.23. Such debt or claim must be included in the inventory by the personal representative: PEF 3304; see Section 12.8 re short entry. However, the personal representative is not precluded thereby from interposing any valid defenses to its collection or enforcement.[1] If litigation is required to collect a debt or enforce a claim against the personal representative, one of the interested parties may be appointed trustee ad litem for the estate for the purpose of the suit (*Flick Est.*, 24 Fiduc. Rep. 376) or objection can be filed to the inventory: *Warner Est.*, 3 Fiduc. Rep. 2d 13, annot. *Fiduc. Rev.* March

---

**§ 12.7**

**1.** The inclusion of the debt or claim in the inventory is not regarded as an acknowledgment which will stop the running of the statute of limitations in his favor: *Bell Est.*, 25 Pa. 92.

1983, p. 3. In *Lux Est.*, 480 Pa. 256, attorney fees were allowed to attorneys responsible for forcing executrix to include in the inventory assets claimed by her individually.

If the decedent held a judgment which is a lien on the real estate of the personal representative, any party in interest may suggest his interest in the judgment upon the record thereof and bring an appropriate action to revive it and to continue its lien: PEF 3318.

## § 12.8 SHORT OR MEMORANDUM ENTRIES IN INVENTORY

Aside from real estate outside of Pennsylvania (§ 12.1), there are several situations in which it may be advisable for a personal representative to list assets "short" in his inventory for the purpose of disclosing information to interested parties: see *Fiduc. Rev.* April 1952, p. 2. These include:

(1) Property which is in the possession of the personal representative but title to which is disputed either because it is claimed by the personal representative as an individual or by a third person: *Karr Est.*, 11 Fiduc. Rep. 91; *Penny Est.*, 4 Fiduc. Rep. 615.

A suggested form of the inventory entry for such property might be:

1969 Ford Coupe $75.00
(Claimed by A under assignment dated . . . . . .)

(2) Property which is in the name of the decedent or his nominee but which belongs to another because it was given or sold in the decedent's lifetime.[1] Also, property which the decedent apparently owned jointly with another (*Keeney Est.*,

§ 12.8
1. It also would be appropriate to include a liquor license which despite its value is not an estate asset: see *Kauffman Est.*, 29 Fiduc. Rep. 229, annot. *Fiduc. Rev.* Jan. 1980, p. 3.

465 Pa. 45; *Fiduc. Rev*. Feb. 1976, p. 3) or in a trust capacity where it is not entirely clear that title thereto passed to the other by right of survivorship: cf. Sections 6.9, 6.11; *Karr Est.*, 11 Fiduc. Rep. 91.

(3) Assets which are in the possession of and claimed by a third person but which are also claimed by the personal representative as belonging to the decedent's estate. A suggested form of the inventory entry for such property might be:

100 shares, common, Erie Steamer Co. $2,124.00
(In possession of and claimed by A)

(4) Assets *retained* by a surviving spouse, children or parents for or on account of the family exemption. See Chapter 7.

(5) Any asset which is subject to administration in another jurisdiction should be disclosed in the inventory but not carried into the totals: *Fulginiti Est.*, 12 Fiduc. Rep. 137.

## § 12.9 ASSETS WHICH SHOULD BE INCLUDED IN INVENTORY: FORM OF INVENTORY ENTRY

Although PEF 3301 does not contain a detailed list of property which should be included in the inventory, it is clear that all real[1] and personal assets of the decedent must be included therein, even assets of questionable or of nominal value. See Section 12.10. The principal purpose of the inventory is to supply information to parties in interest in the estate, and they are entitled to complete information. The following is a typical list, together with a suggested form of entry to aid in the actual preparation: see *Fiduc. Rev*. May 1953; Partridge-Remick, O.C. Practice § 13.06. It is assumed that the decedent died on March 10, 1973.

---

**§ 12.9**

**1.** Real estate outside the Commonwealth is listed in a memorandum at the end of the inventory: see Section 12.1. It is not an asset which should be carried into accounting totals: see *Fulginiti Est.*, 12 Fiduc. Rep. 137.

*Real Estate and Interests Therein*[2]

| | |
|---|---|
| 1811 Willow St., Norristown, Pa., as described in deed of Robert Halladay to Richard Dare, dated 11/1/60, recorded in Montg. County D.B. 213, p. 54 (subject to mortgage of $5000 given by Richard Dare to Home Trust Company dated 11/1/60 recorded in Mortgage Book 100, p. 55, interest, 5%) | $10,000.00 |
| Rent due 3/1/73 | 60.00[3] |
| Oil in tank | 75.00[4] |
| 1011 Main St., Norristown, Pa., as described in deed of Isaac Norris to Richard Dare, dated 12/24/60, recorded in Montg. County D.B. 214, p. 294 (subject to agreement of sale made 2/14/73 to C. Valentine for $50,000, of which $5000 has been paid on account—rent due 3/1/73 paid in advance)[3] | 45,000.00 |
| 1709 Pine St., Norristown, Pa., as described in deed of John Barry to Richard Dare, dated 5/2/38, recorded in Montg. County D.B. 132, p. 42 (occupied by devisee) | 5,000.00 |

*Memorandum of Real Estate Outside of Pennsylvania*

| | |
|---|---|
| 98 acres of woodland, Raleigh County, South Carolina, as described in deed of S. Jackson to U. Grant, dated July 1, 1866, and recorded in Raleigh County D.B. 13, p. 1 | $500.00 |

---

§ **12.9**

**2.** Property insurance has a cancellation value and theoretically should be listed, but as a matter of practice it is seldom included in the inventory, since it is considered an accessory of real estate. Although not required, it is suggested that a notation be made of encumbrances on property included in the inventory, especially mortgages and judgments on real estate. Such encumbrances do not affect the listed value, however.

**3.** Rent due prior to the decedent's death is included without apportionment. When it was paid in advance it is theoretically considered part of the value of the real estate. See Section 9.6. Real property subject to an executory contract of sale made by the decedent, in some circumstances, will be regarded as having been converted into personalty.

**4.** Oil in tank on property is personal property and might be so listed in appropriate circumstances: see *Hilt Est.*, 1 Fiduc. Rep. 2d 426, annot. *Fiduc. Rev.* Dec. 1981, p. 4.

*Stocks*

| | |
|---|---|
| 30 shares National Steel Corp., capital ($10) at 35 | $1,050.00 |
| Dividend payable 3/15/73 to stockholders of record 3/1/73 | 67.50[5] |
| 45 shares Common Burgoon Utility Co. at 52 (pledged as collateral for $1000 note of Richard Dare to Penn-Phila. Trust Co., dated 12/24/72) | 2,340.00 |
| 100 shares Common Erie Steamer Co. at 26.60 (*in possession of and claimed by Mary Dare*) | |
| | $2660.00 |

When securities owned by the decedent are traded on the stock exchanges, it is relatively easy to ascertain the value of shares as of the decedent's death. In addition to newspapers, several well-known services can be consulted to determine stock market quotations of shares on a given date. See Section 13.11 for method of using quotations for tax return and inventory purposes.

(1) *Close corporations*. When the shares of the decedent are in a close or family corporation and are not traded on the stock exchanges, the personal representative is confronted with the difficult problem of fairly and accurately valuing or appraising such shares of stock: see *Fiduc. Rev*. July 1975, p. 3. In some circumstances the court may accept the book value of the stock as the most convincing evidence. Occasionally, the decedent's will may place a value on such shares. Although such a statement does not control the tax appraisal by the state, it constitutes a factor which must be taken into account. A buy-and-sell agreement may establish the value for inventory and tax purposes: Inh. & Tax Act, § 1721(f); cf. *Moyer Est*., 23 Fiduc. Rep. 583, annot. *Fiduc. Rev*. Dec. 1973, p. 2.

§ **12.9**

**5.** The date when a dividend accrues to the person who is entitled to it is the date specified by the corporation as the one on which the stockholders entitled thereto are determined (record date) or, if no record date is specified, then the date the dividend is declared: PEF 8105(f). It is important to check decedent's dividend records to be certain that shares for small stock dividends and shares in dividend reinvestment programs are not overlooked.

The independent opinion of disinterested investment security dealers may also be sought, but the value of the stock is a question of fact, generally to be determined by analyzing the past earnings and financial policy of the corporation as well as the book value of the stock: *Moffett Est.*, 369 Pa. 159.

*Bonds*

| | |
|---|---|
| $1000 U.S. Savings Bond, Series E, due 5/1/76 | $ 860.00[6] |
| $5000 U.S. Savings Bonds, Series G, 2 1/2% due 3/1/75 (registered in the name of decedent "p.o.d." Richard Dare, Jr.) | $5000.00[7] |
| $5000 U.S. Treas. Bond 2 1/2% due 12/15/77-72 (claimed by Richard Dare, Jr., by gift inter vivos) | $5100.00[8] |
| Accrued interest from 12/15/72 to 3/10/73 $31.25[9] | |

*Miscellaneous*

| | |
|---|---|
| Cash on hand | $ 71.85 |
| Savings Account No. 4532 Penn-Phila. Trust Co. | 658.90 |
| Accrued interest to 3/10/73 | 18.40 |
| Merchandise and Equipment of Norristown Restaurant & Bar | 4,578.00[10] |
| Liquor License | 10,000.00[11] |

---

**§ 12.9**

**6.** Redemption value: *Doherty Est.*, 12 Fiduc. Rep. 185.

**7.** See Grossman & Smith, *Pa. Inheritance and Estate Tax* (1993 Rev. Ed.) § 9102(26.9) § 102(24)-4.5 concerning various types of U.S. savings bonds and aspects of inheritance tax valuation.

**8.** See § 12.8; *Fiduc. Rev.* April 1952, p. 2.

**9.** On all interest-bearing securities such as bonds and mortgages, interest must be calculated to the date of the decedent's death.

**10.** Although it is good practice to make a complete inventory of the items on hand, it seems inadvisable to list them in the estate inventory; cf., however, *Schwartz Est.*, 68 D. & C. 154.

**11.** Although the liquor license is a personal privilege and terminates upon the death of the license, it may have substantial value: *Feitz Est.*, 402 Pa. 437; cf. Inh. & Est. Tax Act § 1702(v). However, it might be more appropriate to list it as a short entry: see Section 12.8.

| | |
|---|---|
| Lease on Premises 11 East Main St., Norristown, Pa., expiring Dec. 1, 1973; rental $300 a month including option to purchase at $150,000 | 1.00[12] |
| Note of John General | 1,000.00[13] |
| Accrued interest from 3/1/73 to 3/10/73 | 1.70 |
| Note ($500) of John Brown, deceased (estate insolvent) | $1.00[14] |
| Salary, Mont-Sears Co. from 3/1/73 to 3/10/73 | 248.72[15] |
| Interest in estate of Harvey Maxwell, deceased | 1,000.00[16] |
| 1969 Ford Coupe (claimed by John General under assignment executed the day before decedent died) | $75.00[17] |
| Jewelry as follows: gold wrist watch, $10; pocket watch, $25; diamond stock pin, $175; lady's engagement ring, $150 | 360.00 |
| Furniture for apartment 11 East Main St., Norristown, Pa., as follows: bed, $5.00; bureau, $3.50; safe, $30.00; stand, $.50; chair, $3.00; phonograph, $.50 | 42.50 |
| *Mortgage* | |
| B. E. Sharpe Mortgage ($2000) dated July 1, 1968, interest at 5 1/2%, recorded in Montg. County M.B. 99, p. 5, on dwelling 306 Main St., Norristown, Pa., reduced by amortization payments to | $1,840.00 |
| Accrued interest from 3/1/73 to 3/10/73 | 2.81 |

(2) *Items to be omitted from the inventory*. As stated in Section 2.2, there are certain types of property which, be-

§ **12.9**

**12.** Leasehold should be inventoried: *Wartanian Est.*, 305 Pa. 333.

**13.** This is a debt of the personal representative; cf. PEF 3304. See Section 12.7.

**14.** It is advisable to carry notes and other forms of debt owed at their full amount, unless there are genuine doubts as to their collectibility. If there are such doubts, a discount should be applied.

**15.** This should be stated without deduction for federal withholding tax on any salary due and payable after death, since the executor cannot receive credit for such payments by the decedent's employer.

**16.** Cf. *Reed Est.* (*No. 2*), 236 Pa. 578.

**17.** For special problems concerning the decedent's automobile, see *Fiduc. Rev.* Feb. 1956, p. 3; Jan. 1957.

cause of their nature or because of statutory provisions relating thereto, are not part of the decedent's estate (except for tax purposes), and since they pass without administration need not be included in the inventory. However, they can be carried as a short entry for information purposes, if such action seems feasible in the circumstances of the particular estate. See Section 12.8.

(a) Entireties property and other property, including bank account, owned jointly with right of survivorship, provided that the right of the survivor is clear: cf. *Fiduc. Rev.* Jan. 1953, p. 3; *Rapkin v. Israel*, 4 Fiduc. Rep. 57; *Waltersdorff Est.*, 69 York 101; *Toucheloskie Est.*, 4 Fiduc. Rep. 511. In *Klein Est.*, 17 Fiduc. Rep. 212, aff'd 429 Pa. 27, it was held that cash on his person and personal effects in his household presumptively belonged to the deceased husband.

(b) Cemetery lots. See PEF 2514(14); *Fiduc. Rev.* July 1953, p. 4; *Parento Est.*, 22 Fiduc. Rep. 179. However, a burial lot in which no one is buried should be included and the placing of a stone monument on the lot is not the equivalent of a burial: *Klein Est.*, 429 Pa. 27.

(c) Life insurance payable to a named beneficiary who survives the decedent. Insurance payable to the estate[18] because the designated beneficiary is dead must, however, be included. If pledged as collateral, it may be entered "short" for information purposes: see *Fiduc. Rev.* Feb. 1950, p. 4; April 1952; Jan. 1961.

(d) Property over which the decedent had a power of appointment.

(e) United States bonds which were registered "p.o.d." or in two names where the beneficiary or co-owner has survived: see *Fiduc. Rev.* July 1952.

---

**§ 12.9**

**18.** That paid under a facility of payment provision to an individual is normally not a part of the estate: *Witcofskie Est.*, 57 Schuyl. 177

(3) *When decedent was an incapacitated person or minor.* When the decedent was an incapacitated person for whom a guardian had been appointed, the personal representative should list the assets held in the hands of the guardian as of the day of death, rather than the balance shown in the guardian's account. The duties of the guardian, except to file his account and pay necessary administration expenses of the guardianship, terminate at the date of death.

Claims against the estate of a deceased incapacitated person are to be presented to his personal representative, not at the audit of his guardian's account: *Bruch Est.*, 7 Fiduc. Rep. 69; *Hartzell Est.*, 16 Fiduc. Rep. 325. However, in *Bliem Est.*, 8 Fiduc. Rep. 131, a balance of $339.56 in the account of a guardian of a deceased incompetent's estate was awarded to the undertaker under PEF 3102, and in *Simmons Est.*, 13 Fiduc. Rep. 41, the estate was awarded to heirs upon the guardian's accounting. See also *Leedom Est.*, 17 Fiduc. Rep. 28. See PEF 3501.2 and *Ayers Est.*, 7 Fiduc. Rep. 669, for procedure whereby duplicate accounting may be avoided upon an incapacitated person's death. In *Ayers Estate* the guardian's account was attached as an exhibit to the inventory of the personal representative: see also *Carter Est.*, 12 Fiduc. Rep. 23.

Regarding a claim for reimbursement by a life insurance beneficiary where the guardian of an incompetent insured borrowed on the policy, see *Miller Est.*, 402 Pa. 140, annot. *Fiduc. Rev.* Jan. 1961.

Act No. 37 of 1978, effective June 27, 1978, amended PEF 5161 (for minors) and PEF 5531 (for incapacitated persons) so that an accounting at the termination of the guardianship is optional with the guardian, unless the court directs otherwise. As amended, guardians of minors (PEF 5163) and of incapacitated persons (PEF 5533) now have the privilege theretofore limited to personal representatives and trustees (PEF 7183(13)) to file receipts, releases and refunding agreements with the clerk of the orphan's court division following a risk distribution.

## § 12.10 WORTHLESS ASSETS—RENUNCIATION

Worthless assets may be listed and so appraised. When any item of property is of no value to the estate, the court may, if requested, authorize the personal representative to renounce his right to administer it: PEF 3312. In *Leichner Est.*, 2 Fiduc. Rep. 361, the personal representative was authorized to abandon seven mortgages which appeared to be worthless. Cf. *Pearlman Trust*, 348 Pa. 488. In *Miller Est.*, 3 Fiduc. Rep. 379, the personal representative was authorized to dispose of a revolver to the City of Philadelphia Detective Bureau or an authorized dealer. In that case the personal representative filed an affidavit of record describing the disposition of the revolver and her compliance with the order of court. Abandonment of a claim for death does not preclude action against the attorney whose alleged malpractice caused the claim to be unenforceable: *Cooperman Est. and Tr.*, 3 Fiduc. Rep. 2d 327. For form of petition to abandon property, see Partridge-Remick, O.C. Practice § 14.03.

# Chapter 13

# PENNSYLVANIA INHERITANCE, ESTATE AND INCOME TAXES



## § 13.1 IN GENERAL[1]; TIMETABLE

One of the important duties of an executor or administrator is to file a return and pay the inheritance and estate taxes due on the estate. The Pennsylvania taxes are dealt

§ **13.1**

**1.** All citations of authority in this Chapter 13 which state numbers not otherwise identified are to sections of the Inheritance and Estate Tax Act effective October 3, 1991 using Pa. Consolidated Statutes Annotated numbering. References to Grossman and Smith, Pennsylvania Inheritance and Estate Tax are to the 2nd Revised Edition of 2002 dealing with the 1991 Act as amended.

with in this chapter, and the federal taxes in Chapter 14. These matters are dealt with in broad outline only, since the questions involved are frequently complex. The Inheritance and Estate Tax Act is applicable to estates of decedents dying on or after October 3, 1991, and to inter vivos transfers, whenever made, by such decedents, and the discussion in this chapter is confined to that Act as amended. Extensive discussion of the law prior to October 3, 1991, may be found at various points in Grossman and Smith, Pennsylvania Inheritance and Estate Tax (2nd Rev. Ed. 2002). See also comparative statute table for old and new section numbers.

The following Timetable gives an overall view of estate administration aspects which involve the Pennsylvania death taxes:

## Pennsylvania Inheritance and Estate Tax Timetable

### for Immediate Attention

Arrange for entry into safe deposit box and preparation of inventory, with personal representative, when there is no surviving spouse entitled to access: § 9191 et seq. (Entry without preparation of inventory may be made to obtain will and cemetery deed: § 9192.) For comprehensive regulations, see Pa. Inheritance and Estate Tax (Bisel Co. 2nd Rev. Ed 2002). See also 12 Fiduc. Rep. 470 (deposit box of attorneys); 13 Fiduc. Rep. 633 (power of attorney over deposit box of husband and wife); 14 Fiduc. Rep. 569 (deposit box of business firm); *Fiduc. Rev.* Nov. 1998, p. 4. *See* Section 6.6 for procedure for entry into safe deposit boxes after May 11, 2011.

### Within three months of death

Make payment on account of tax, to obtain the 5% discount: § 9142.

Where decedent had a life estate, the fiduciary should pay tax on remainder interest (or succeeding life estates) unless such tax has earlier been paid: Inheritance & Estate Tax Act of 1961, §§ 506, 712 (1982 Act § 1721(e)). For prepayment of tax on future interests where all persons having vested interests do not wish to prepay the tax, see 61 Pa. Code § 93.121.

## For early attention

Consider renunciation of distributive shares, within nine months from death: § 9146(c). See *Fiduc. Rev.* July 1967, p. 3; Oct. 1976.

## Within nine months of death

File inheritance tax return, or apply to Secretary of Revenue for six-month extension of time for filing (§ 9136(d)) to avoid penalty: § 9153. Extension does *not* stop running of interest: § 9143. Extension is obtainble by e-mail to RA–InheritanceTaxExt@state.pa.us. Since Inheritance Tax Division does not respond to extension request unless it is refused, it is important to retain proof of requesting the extension.

Pay balance of inheritance tax (§ 9142) to avoid interest charge: § 9143.[2]

Pay Pennsylvania estate tax: § 9145(c) for decedents dying on or before December 31, 2004.

## Subsequent to nine months after death

File copy of federal estate tax return with Register, within one month after filing: § 9145(b). (Also file copy of any changes made by federal government.) Since Pennsylvania estate tax is no longer in effect for decedents dying after December 31, 2004, no additional estate tax will be due.

File certificate of payment of tax in counties where real estate is located; §§ 9152, 9169, 9175.

## With reference to contested tax

*Appeals.* Within sixty days of receipt of notice of appraisement, of disallowance of deductions, or of assessment of tax, either:

---

§ **13.1**

**2.** See *Fiduc. Rev.* June 1982, for calculation of interest under Section 806 of the Fiscal Code.

A) file protest with Department of Revenue (§ 9186(a)(1)),

B) notify Register to postpone matter to audit (§ 9186(a)(2)), or

C) appeal to orphans' court division (§ 9186(a) (3)).

If proceeding was by protest to Department of Revenue, appeal to orphans' court division, from department's decision, within sixty days of receipt of notice thereof: § 9188. If department has not acted on protest within thirty days from its filing, consider filing petition with orphans' court division for transmittal of record to court: § 9188.

*Refunds*. Apply for refund of tax to which Commonwealth is not rightfully or equitably entitled (§ 9181(a)) within three years after date of payment, date of the notice of the assessment or delinquency, whichever is later (§ 9181(d)(5)), unless special provisions allow greater time. Interest on refundable tax is payable at the same rate as the interest rate on deficiencies of tax provided in Section 9143: § 9181(b); *Fiduc. Rev*. June 1982.

## § 13.2 NATURE OF THE INHERITANCE TAX AND PERSONS LIABLE

The Pennsylvania transfer inheritance tax is a tax on the privilege of inheritance; it is not a tax on property or persons: *Denniston Est*., 325 Pa. 453. Although it is not assessed against the decedent or his estate, but against the distributee or transferee (*Schaeffer Est*., 62 York 113), the tax bill is rendered to the personal representative. The personal representative is responsible not only for the payment of tax on the property passing through administration, but also on other property which he is "in charge of or in possession of": § 9146. See Sections 9167–9175 regarding sale and distribution of real estate. The personal representative is obligated to report all taxable property "which is or may be subject to inheritance tax of which he shall have or acquire knowledge": § 9136(a)(1). However, he is not liable for the payment of tax on any property which he is not in charge of or in possession of (*Truszkowski Est.*, 35 Beaver 134) such as a joint bank account: *Baker Est.*, 30 Fiduc. Rep. 302. Note, however, that the tax clause of a will may direct payment by the personal representative on property not in his control.

## § 13.3 SAFE-DEPOSIT BOX "FREEZE"

Part XII of the Inheritance and Estate Tax Act imposes certain restrictions upon entry into a "safe-deposit box of the decedent" by persons who have actual knowledge of his death: § 9191. A safe-deposit box of a decedent includes:

(1) a box registered in decedent's name;

(2) a box registered jointly in the names of the decedent and one or more others, excluding boxes in the joint names of husband and wife;

(3) a box registered in a partnership, fictitious or trade name, where the decedent had access thereto as principal, agent or deputy; and

(4) a box registered in an assumed or maiden name where decedent had access thereto other than as deputy or agent.[1]

It does not include a box registered in the name of a corporation, church, lodge, eleemosynary corporation or association or fiduciary.

*Methods of entry*. Reference has already been made to the right to search for, and remove, decedent's will and cemetery deed from a safe-deposit box. See Section 1.2. However, the entry subsequent to an entry for such purpose is subject to the restrictions of Part XII of the Inheritance and Estate Tax Act. The other means for accomplishing entry into the safe-deposit box are described in Section 6.6. It is the duty

---

**§ 13.3**

**1.** Where the right to access was solely as agent or deputy, there is no "freeze," for the decedent was required during his lifetime to refrain from use of the principal's deposit box for the decedent's personal business.

of the bank employee to certify under § 9192(e) that only the will or cemetery deed has been removed.

## § 13.4 WHEN AND WHERE TAX IS PAID

Inheritance tax is payable at death and becomes delinquent nine months thereafter: § 9142. Payment of tax on future interests is not to be postponed except by special arrangement with the Department of Revenue: § 9150.

The taxable estate is reportable to the register[1] within nine months after decedent's death, unless an extension of the time for filing has been granted: § 9136. A 5% discount is allowed on any tax paid within three months of the death of the decedent: § 9142.[2] If the tax is not paid by the delinquent date, interest will accrue thereon in most cases at the rate established pursuant to section 806 of the Fiscal Code: § 9143; see *Fiduc. Rev.* June 1982. It is to be noted that an extension of the due date for filing the return does not prevent the running of interest on delinquent tax.

According to guidelines issued by the Pennsylvania Department of Revenue, as to estates of decedents dying on or after December 13, 1982, in absence of a request for a compromise tax amount, all contingent future interests will be assessed at the highest rate at all the points of uncertainty in the chain of distribution.

A request for a compromise amount may be made for the estate at the time the return is filed or prior thereto. In the latter case, the determination can be made by using a hypothetical valuation for the assets. Calculations, if any, submitted by the estate will be subject to review by the Department of Revenue. According to the Department of Revenue:

---

**§ 13.4**

**1.** Unless the decedent was a nonresident in whose estate no letters have been granted in Pennsylvania, in which case nearly all tax transactions are with the Department of Revenue in Harrisburg.

**2.** A personal representative cannot be surcharged automatically for failure to secure a discount for payment of the tax within the discount period: *Lux Est.*, 26 Fiduc. Rep. 544; *Schultheis Est.* (Pa. Super.), 747 A.2d 918.

"The proposed compromise amount is not subject to negotiation, once issued by the Department. The Department will advise the estate of the proposed compromise tax through written communication. This Notice will act as the agreement between the Department and the Estate concerning the amount of future interest tax when it is returned to the Department within thirty (30) days of receipt by the Estate.

"The communication will be structured in such a way as to constitute a final agreement between the Department and the Estate as to the amount of future interest tax. The agreement is consummated through:

"1). Signing and returning the proposal to the Department within thirty (30) days of receipt.

"2). Payment of tax to the Register within sixty (60) days of signing. A copy of the signed agreement must accompany payment. Regardless of date of compromise agreement, interest will continue to be imposed from the delinquency date.

"3). Allocation of the prepayments to the future interest tax must be identified on the agreement form returned to the Department and on the copy filed with the Register. Failure to specifically allocate prepayments to the future interest tax renders the agreement null and void."

## § 13.5 RATE OF TAX

Recent changes have established or expanded inheritance tax rates. Since 1995 transfers to husbands and wives have been taxed at 0%: § 9116 (a)(1). Parties to a New Jersey civil union moved to Pennsylvania. The surviving party is not entitled to the family exemption or the 0% spousal tax rate. *Warnock Est.*, 1 Fiduc. Rep. 3d 437, annot. *Fiduc. Rev.* Dec. 2011, p. 3. Effective for decedents dying after June 30, 2000 transfers from a child twenty-one years of age or younger to or for the use of a natural parent, an adoptive parent or a step-parent of the child are also taxed at 0%. Act 23 of 2000.

The 6% rate prior to July 1, 2000, now $4^1/_2$%, for property passing to or for the use of grandfather, grandmother, father, mother, children, lineal descendants and the "wife or widow and husband or widower of a child": § 9116(a). "Lineal descendants" are defined in Section 9102 as "All children of the natural parents and their descendants, adopted descendants and their descendants, stepchildren and their descendants and children and their descendants of the natural parent who are adopted by his spouse. Lineal descendants include illegitimate issue of the natural father": *Minarich Est.*, 28 Fiduc. Rep. 288. *Carlson Est.*, 479 Pa. 421, held that an adopted person takes as a lineal descendant of his natural paternal grandmother despite his adoption by his mother's second husband.

Effective July 1, 2000, transfers to siblings are subject to a 12% tax rate.

The 15% tax is imposed on property passing to or for the use of any other persons with the following exceptions:

(1) Transfers to or for the use of the United States, Pennsylvania or a political subdivision of Pennsylvania are exempt: § 9111(b).

(2) Transfers to or for the use of charities and fraternal organizations are exempt: § 9111(c).

(3) Transfers to or for the use of a husband and wife with right of survivorship are wholly taxable at $4^1/_2$% where either one of the transferees is taxable at the $4^1/_2$% rate regardless of whether transfer to other spouse alone is taxable at the 15% rate: § 9116(a)(3).

(4) Awards to the Commonwealth as statutory heir, by escheat (except as custodian for a known distributee, when tax is deducted from the award) are exempt: § 9111(b).

(5) The ultimate results of certain compromises and renunciations may control the rate of tax to be applied: § 9116(c) and (d).

(6) Historically inheritance tax may not be deducted from residue in calculating tax, even where the tax on pre-residuary gifts results in nothing passing to residuary beneficiaries. However, in *Ross Est.*, 815 A.2d 30, annot. *Fiduc. Rev.* March 2003, p. 3, the Court concluded that residue used to pay tax for 6% [now 4½%] transferees should be taxed at a rate of 6% rather than 15%.

The rates applicable were 2% and 15% from December 21, 1951, to December 29, 1967 (with some variations in the persons taxable in each category), while the rate applicable to Class B (collateral) transferees was 10% for some time prior to December 21, 1951. The 2% rate became 6% on Dec. 29, 1967. These earlier rates of tax are of practical importance if a remainder interest in property is involved, for the tax on remainders created by earlier decedents is not due until "the person liable for the same shall come into actual possession" (see Grossman and Smith, Pennsylvania Inheritance and Estate Tax (Rev. Ed. 1993), § 9142-3.1), and is then taxed at the rate applicable at the death of the original decedent, in the estate of such decedent.

As set forth in *Fiduc. Rev.* August 1995, p. 1, Act 21 of 1995 "[amends] Section 2116 of the Inheritance and Estate Tax provisions of the Tax Reform Code of 1971 by reducing the rate on spousal transfers to zero, retroactive to estates of decedents dying on or after January 1, 1995. The retroactive effective date similarly applies to Section 2113 transfers in a trust or similar arrangement for the exclusive benefit of the surviving spouse. Application of Section 2113 will not be automatic. Instead, the decedent's personal representative may elect not to have Section 2113 apply to an otherwise eligible trust or similar arrangement."

After the decision in *Goldman Est.*, 21 Fiduc. Rep. 2d 333, 781 A.2d 259, which included a provision giving the surviving spouse the unlimited right during her life to withdraw or appoint principal and gave the remainder to charity, held that the trust qualified as a sole use trust with a zero tax rate, the definition of sole use trust was amended by Act. No. 89 of 2002, effective July 1, 2002 to reverse this result. See annotation in *Fiduc. Rev.*, Aug. 2002, p. 3.

Spousal transfers are therefore taxable as follows:
Decedents dying on or before June 30, 1994—6%
July 1 to December 31, 1994—3%
thereafter—0%

This zero rate applies also to transfers in trust (or similar arrangement) for the sole use of the surviving spouse during the spouse's entire lifetime unless the transferor's personal representative elects to pay tax in the first to die spouse's estate, or as stated, not to have §2113 apply. This election can be all or a portion of a trust. See discussion in *Fiduc. Rev.* August 1995, p. 1, concerning post-death planning opportunities presented by this election right.

See *Pa. Inheritance and Estate Tax*, Grossman and Smith (Bisel Co.—Fifth Ed. 2002) for more detailed discussion of changes in rates.

The chart on the following pages sets out rates for Pennsylvania inheritance tax and updates a similar chart from *Fiduc. Rev.* Nov. 1995. Step-grandchildren and step great grandchildren remain step-descendants entitled to the $4^1/_2$% rate even if the step-ancestor remarried after the death of the spouse. *Hartenstein Weaver Est.*, 1 Fiduc. Rep. 3d 309.

## Pennsylvania Inheritance Tax—Rates

### Transfers Subject to Tax

The tax is applicable to transfers of all present and future interests of any nature in property to or for the benefit of the transferee "without valuable and adequate consideration" (9107(c)(1)), including the right of surviviorship (9108(a)) and property passing from a presumed decedent (9107(b)). It applies to fractional as well as whole interests in property (9107(c)(2)) and transfers wihtin one year prior to death to the extent the value thereof exceeds $3,000 as to each transferee in each calendar year (9107(c)(3)).

The rates of tax are applicable in estates of decedents dying on or after January 1, 1995. For rates applicable in prior years, see charts in the November 1952, August 1956, and January 1962 issues of *Fiduciary Review*. For discussion of the zero rate and of 2113 trusts, see *Fiduciary Review*, August 1995. For spousal transfers July 1 to December 31, 1994, rate is 3%.

| **Relationship to Decedent (Valid renunciations and and compromises will control rate: see 9116(c) and (d))** | **Tax Rate*** | **Authority; Comment** |
|---|---|---|
| husband or wife | 0% | 9111(m) including property passing by survivorship from deceased spouse 9108(b); 9116(a)(3) and life interest in trust which qualifies under 9113. The personal representative of the decedent may make a timely election to prepay tax on remainder interests in 9113 trusts. Marital claims under agreement with former spouse are not deductible: 9130(2). |
| natural or adoptive parent or step-parent | 0% | transfer by child twenty-one year age or younger. Decedent dying after June 30, 2000. |
| "grandfather, grandmother father, mother" | $4^1/_2$ | 9116(a)(1)(i)—There is no reduction of the 15% rate to $4^1/_2$% for interests passing to *great* grandparents. |
| children; adopted children stepchildren; wife or widow of a child; husband or widower of a child; lineal descendants children, adopted children or stepchildren | $4^1/_2$ | The preferred tax relationship continues to exist regardless of adoption by others. The tax rate is $4^1/_2$% to the husband or wife of a transferee entitled to the $4^1/_2$% rate: 9116(b.1) *Englund Est.,* 25 Fiduc. Rep. 341, annot. *Fiduc. Rev.* July 1975. Formerly 6%, reduced to $4^1/_2$% as of 7-1-2000 |

| Relationship to Decedent (Valid renunciations and and compromises will control rate: see 9116(c) and (d)) | Tax Rate* | Authority; Comment |
|---|---|---|
| brothers or sisters | 12% | Decedents dying after June 30, 2000 |
| heirs, next of kin and relatives not listed above and entities not listed below as not subject to tax | 15% | The 15% rate is applicable to all present and future interests. |

*When calculating compromised value of remainder interests, rights of withdrawal by the surviving spouse not exercised within nine months of the transferor's death shall be ignored: 9116(e).

## Transfers Not Subject to Tax (9111)

| Transferee | |
|---|---|
| United States of America<br>Commonwealth of Pennsylvania | Includes property awarded to Commonwealth as statutory heir, by escheat or as and its political subdivisions custodian (9111(1)) |
| Charities | entities "organized and operated exclusively for religious, charitable, scientific, literary or educational purposes, including the encouragement of art and the prevention of cruelty to children or animals" (9111(c)(1)) |
| Fraternal Organizations | for its charitable purposes (9111(c)(2)) |
| Veterans Organizations | "no part of the net earnings of which inures to the benefit of any private shareholder or individual" (9111(c)(3)) |

Reversionary interest retained by the decedent the value of which immediately before decedent's death does not exceed 5% of the value of the property transferred: 9107(c)(4).

**Exempt Property (9111)**

Life insurance on life of decedent including refunds of unearned premiums and post mortem dividends (9111(d)), governmental insurance (9111(e)), armed service pay and allowances (9111(f) and (j)).

Social Security, railroad retirement or county veterans death benefit (9111(p) and (q)).

Property transferred inter vivios to a charity or governmental body (9111(g)).

Intangible personal property of a nonresident decedent (9111(h))

Advancements and similar transfers (9111(i)) if not included under 9107(c)(3).

Appointed property in estate of donee (9111(k)).

Nominal ownership (9111(n)).

Employee benefits meeting the test of 9111(r).

Real estate and tangible personal property located outside Pennsylvania unless under decedent's agreement of sale: *Wolfe v. Lewisburg Trust & Safe Deposit Co.*, 305 Pa. 583, 589; *McGeorge Est.*, 25 Fiduc. Rep. 7.

Agricultural property—see § 13.9(10)

---

## § 13.6 RENUNCIATIONS—DISCLAIMERS—COMPROMISES

As in the 1961 Act (§§ 406, 407), and 1982 Act (§1716(c) and (d)), Section 9116(c) and (d) of the 1991 Act enables parties in interest, with the cooperation of the personal representative, to engage in post-death planning under which the burden of inheritance tax may be reduced. In addition to recognizing the effect of the exercise of elective rights of a spouse, and the authority to renounce and compromise set forth in Section 9116 of the Inheritance Tax Act, the PEF Code outlines the statutory right of a spouse to alter distributive shares of the estate by exercise of elective rights under Chapter 22 thereof, and the right of all distributees to disclaim their interests in Chapter 62 and to compromise disputes among parties in interest (PEF 5521) or with creditors (PEF 3323). In all such instances the personal representative must exercise caution so that there is no assignment (*Zindel*

*Est.*, 3 Fiduc. Rep. 2d 29), the statutory time requirements are met (cf. *Fiduc. Rev*. Aug. 1981, p. 2) and court approval is obtained when required.

After the decison in *Bernecker Est.*, 13 Fiduc. Rep. 2d 347, annot. *Fiduc. Rev*. Dec. 1993, permitting disclaimers of probate and non-probate assets, the Pennsylavania Department of Revenue adopted a statement of policy regarding disclaimers of nonprobate assets for inheritance tax purposes. 27 Pa. Bulletin 4115.

## § 13.7 PROPERTY TAXABLE

The personal representative is required to list all property subject to tax, whether or not passing through administration: § 9136. The return should include the following property,[1] if it is the subject of a taxable transfer.[2] "Property" or "estate" is defined in Section 9102 as follows:

(1) Real estate located in Pennsylvania: § 9102 (1) and (4). Realty located outside Pennsylvania is not taxable, unless the owner is a Pennsylvania resident who had contracted for its sale prior to his death and the state of its situs does not impose a death tax thereon: § 9102 (3). It includes a nonresident decedent's interest in Pennsylvania real estate under agreement of sale at his death: *Highberger Est.*, 468 Pa. 120. *See Fiduc. Rev.*, Aug. 2012, p. 4 concerning taxation of mineral rights and natural gas rights.

(2) Tangible personal property located in Pennsylvania: § 9102 (1) and (4). Such property outside Pennsylvania, if owned by a resident of Pennsylvania, may be taxable under the same rule described above as to real estate: § 9102 (3).

---

**§ 13.7**

**1.** For more detailed information on what property is taxable, see discussion at § 9102(18) of Grossman and Smith, *Pennsylvania Inheritance and Estate Tax* (Fifth Ed. 2002).

**2.** Regarding taxable transfers, see Section 13.8.

(3) Intangible personal property of a resident of Pennsylvania: § 9102 (2). Such property, if owned by a nonresident, is exempt from inheritance tax: § 9111(h).

(4) A Pennsylvania liquor license: § 9102 (5); *Kauffman Est.*, 29 Fiduc. Rep. 229.

## § 13.8 TRANSFERS TAXABLE

The inheritance tax is a tax on transfers of property: § 9106. Thus the tax accrues only when the subject of the transfer is "property" *and* the transfer[1] is in a form rendered taxable by the statute. Taxable transfers include the following:

(1) Transfers by will or intestacy from a resident or nonresident:[2] § 9106(b).

(2) Accrual of ownership by right of survivorship as a result of a joint tenancy (except a tenancy by the entireties not created in more than $3,000 within one year of death): *Brown Est.*, 489 Pa. 199. The taxable portion of the transfer is determined by dividing the value of the whole property by the number of joint tenants immediately prior to the decedent's death, irrespective of amounts contributed by each: § 9108. But cf. Grossman and Smith, *Pennsylvania Inheritance and Estate Tax* (2nd Rev. Ed. 2002) § 9108(c)(1.5). Convenience bank accounts composed of funds of survivor are subject to inheritance tax on one-half of their value: *Olson Est.*, 447 Pa. 483, annot. *Fiduc. Rev.* July 1972; *Gillespie Est. and Wingerter Est.*, 462 Pa. 455, annot. *Fiduc. Rev.* Sept. 1975; *Brant Est.*, 463 Pa. 230; *Munro Est.* (Comwlth. Ct.), 516 A.2d 289; *Imrisik Est.*, 2 Fiduc. Rep. 2d 406. If created in consideration of decedent being given a home it may not be taxable: *DiCarlo Est.*, 2 Fiduc. Rep. 2d 346. Compare *Pettenati Est.*, 760 A.2d 1229 where brother alone deposited funds in account in names of

**§ 13.8**

1. For more detailed information on what transfers are taxable, see Grossman and Smith, *Pennsylvania Inheritance and Estate Tax* (2nd Rev. Ed. 2002) §§ 9106-9108.
2. For transfers from a presumed decedent, see § 9107(b).

brother and sister with no designation of the type of account. On sister's death the court admitted parol evidence that brother intended an account in his name payable on death to sister. The account was not subject to inheritance tax.

(3) Transfers made by the decedent within one year of death. If such transfer is made "without valuable and adequate consideration in money or money's worth" within one year prior to death, it is taxable to the extent it "exceeds $3,000 in any calendar year": § 9107(c)(3).

(4) Transfers "without valuable and adequate consideration in money or money's worth" if (a) the transfer takes effect in possession or enjoyment at or after death and the transferor has retained a reversionary interest worth, immediately prior to his death, more than 5% of the value of the property transferred (§ 9107(c)(4)), or (b) the transferor reserved the possession or enjoyment or income from the property, or the power (alone or with one not having an adverse interest[3]) to designate those who shall enjoy the property or income therefrom, for his life or a period not in fact ending before his death (§ 9107(c)(5)), or (c) the transferee has promised to make payments to, or to support, the transferor for the remainder of the transferor's life (§ 9107(c)(6)), or (d) the transferor has the power (alone or with one not having an adverse interest[4]) to alter, amend or revoke the interest of the beneficiary (§ 9107(c)(7)).

## § 13.9 PROPERTY AND TRANSFERS NOT TAXABLE

Even where the transfer is of property otherwise subject to inheritance tax (see Section 13.7), it may be exempt because of the identity of the transferee, and of course the transfer may be of property expressly exempted. Prominent among such exempt property and transfers are:

---

§ **13.8**

**3.** *Id.*

**4.** *Id.*

(1) Intangible personal property of nonresidents: § 9111(h); *Lucas Est.*, 3 Fiduc. Rep. 2d 54, annot. *Fiduc. Rev.* April 1983, p. 3.

(2) Real estate and tangible personal property, located outside Pennsylvania and owned by residents. It is taxable if the decedent had contracted for its sale prior to his death and the state of its situs imposes no death tax thereon: § 9102 "Property".

(3) Transfers to the United States, Pennsylvania or a political subdivision of Pennsylvania: § 9111(b).

(4) Transfers to charities and fraternal organization: § 9111(c).

(5) Life insurance and war risk insurance proceeds including unearned premiums and post mortem dividends: § 9111(d) and (e). Contracts issued by life insurance companies to a trust to pay annuity benefits at maturity where owner would have been 111 years of age or older are exempt as life insurance and not taxable as annuities. *Ewing Est.*, 26 Fiduc. Rep. 2d 151.

(6) Appointed property in the estate of the donee of the power of appointment. Such property is taxed only in the donor's estate at the rates applicable to the donor-appointee relationship: § 9111(k).

(7) Property owned jointly by husband and wife, in the estate of the first of the tenants to die, so long as the ownership was not created within one year of death (§ 9111(m)) and in that event only to the extent it exceeds $3,000 during any calendar year: § 9107(c)(3). Note that the tax rate would be 0%.

(8) Social security and similar death benefits: § 9111(p) and (q), including Veterans Administration and county lump sum death benefits expressly excluded by Act 22 of 1991.

(9) Pension, stock-bonus or profit-sharing benefits which were not vested in decedent and/or which are exempt from federal estate tax and life insurance proceeds payable under such benefit plans regardless of vesting: § 1711(r);

*Ravdin Est.*, 484 Pa. 562, aff'g 25 Fiduc. Rep. 640, annot. *Fiduc. Rev*. Nov. 1978; *Rankin Est.*, 487 Pa. 70, rev'g 27 Fiduc. Rep. 576, annot. *Fiduc. Rev*. April 1978, p. 2. Regulations concerning taxation of payments from employment benefit plans and life insurance contracts (61 Pa. Code §93.131) were adopted on October 11, 1986.

A more comprehensive list of exempt transfers may be found in Section 9111, which is similar to Article III of the 1961 Act and § 1711 of the 1982 Act. For a more detailed discussion, see Grossman and Smith, *Pennsylvania Inheritance and Estate Tax* (Fifth Ed. 2002), §§ 9111.

(10) Transfers of real estate devoted to the business of agriculture to member of the same family effective for estates of decedents dying after June 30, 2012: 9111(s). See *Fiduc. Rev*. Aug. 2012, p. 3.

## § 13.10 DEDUCTIONS

Part VI of the Act of 1991 contains a comprehensive list of allowable deductions, all of which are discussed in detail in Grossman and Smith, Pennsylvania Inheritance and Estate Tax. The items specified in the Act are deductible regardless of whether or not they are paid from assets subject to tax, except that a transferee of an inter vivos transfer may claim them against the value of such transfer only if he has actually paid them and either he was legally obligated to do so or the estate subject to administration was insufficient to do so:[1] See § 9126.

*Deductible*. Among the deductions authorized by the Act are:

(1) Reasonable administration expenses: See § 9127(1). Bequests to a personal representative or his attorney are de-

**§ 13.10**

**1.** As in the 1961 and 1982 Acts, this changes the rule of *Kritz Estate*, 387 Pa. 223, annot. *Fiduc. Rev*. Feb. 1957, that one-half the mortgage debt on entireties property was deductible from the value of property owned by decedent and her sister with right of survivorship, although there was no probate estate and the surviving spouse paid the mortgage debt: see Grossman and Smith, *Pennsylvania Inheritance and Estate Tax* (Fifth Ed. 2002), § 9126-1.2.

ductible to the extent they do not exceed reasonable compensation: § 9127(2).

(2) The family exemption: § 9127(3); cf. *Stevens Est.*, 434 Pa. 259, annot. *Fiduc. Rev.* June 1969, p. 3; see Chapter 7.

(3) Funeral expenses, cost of burial lot, cost of monuments or gravestones on decedent's burial lot, bequests or amounts expended for care of the lot in which decedent is buried (*Crouthamel Est.*, 25 Fiduc. Rep. 113), and bequests for masses or other religious observances. All such expenses are deductible only to the extent they are reasonable: § 9127 (4, 5, & 6); Grossman and Smith, *Pennsylvania Inheritance and Estate Tax* (Fifth Ed. 2002), §§ 9127(4)(5) and (6).

(4) Taxes, such as property or income taxes, owing at decedent's death: § 9128(1). Federal income tax on decedent's final life period return paid from the estate on the accumulated interest on U.S. savings bonds was allowed as a deduction. *Estates of Stewart and Krasner*, 21 Fiduc. Rep. 2d 199, annot. *Fiduc. Rev.* July 2001, p. 1.

(5) Death taxes (excluding federal estate tax and Pennsylvania inheritance tax) in certain limited situations: § 9128(2). Cf. paragraph (7) infra.

(6) Decedent's liabilities, generally to the extent contracted "bona fide and for an adequate and full consideration in money or money's worth": § 9129; cf. *Polizotto Est.*, 28 Fiduc. Rep. 145.

Subparagraphs (c) et seq. of Section 9129 state in detail the rules for deductions in certain specific circumstances; perhaps of greatest general interest are the rules that decedent's liability on a secured loan or on a joint obligation is deductible whether or not the property securing its payment is taxable and that a married person's obligations are deductible in the estate regardless of the surviving spouse's primary liability for their payment.

(7) Tax on future interests—Decedent's death prior to 12/13/82. Federal estate tax and Pennsylvania inheritance tax are "deductible" in the following limited circumstances: where, following payment of inheritance tax on life or other

limited estates, federal estate tax is paid out of property supporting the limited estate, and the Pennsylvania inheritance tax on remainder interests was *not* prepaid, the appraisement of the remainder interest at the time it comes into possession and enjoyment is of the then-value thereof without any addition back of such taxes (or additional administration expenses) paid theretofore: Inh. & Est. Tax Act of 1961, § 651. The result is the same even in the case of a prepayment: *Miller Est.*, 467 Pa. 193, annot. *Fiduc. Rev.* May 1976. See, generally, Grossman and Smith, *Pennsylvania Inheritance and Estate Tax* (Rev. Ed. 1993), § 9129(k)E.

*Not deductible*. Section 9130 states that the following shall not be deductible:

(1) The spouse's allowance under PEF 2102(3).

(2) Claims by any persons under the provisions of an agreement between spouses, to the extent they arise in consideration of relinquishment of marital or support rights: see Grossman and Smith, *Pennsylvania Inheritance and Estate Tax* (Rev. Ed. 1993), § 9130(a).

(3) Beneficiary's litigation expenses.

(4) Debts secured by real estate or tangible personal property outside Pennsylvania, except to the extent they exceed the value of such property.

The foregoing do not constitute all disallowable items, and are only illustrative. The deductions listed as deductible in Subchapter F are stated in Section 9126 to be "the only deductions from the value of the property transferred."

Among the obligations not deductible are decedent's medical expenses to the extent the decedent's estate will be exonerated or reimbursed for such expenses from another source. This changes the rule in *Goldberg Est.*, 29 Fiduc. Rep. 561, aff'd 486 Pa. 507, annot. *Fiduc. Rev.* Dec. 1979, July 1981, p. 3. Federal income tax attributable to accrued interest on U.S. bonds is not deductible: *Veway Est.*, 30 Fiduc. Rep. 256, *Scott Est.* (Comwlth. Ct.), 544 A.2d 544, even if income tax thereon is actually paid upon redemption after death. *Dembroski Est.*, 12 Fiduc. Rep. 2d 380. Contra, *Estates of Stewart and Krasner,* 21 Fiduc. Rep. 199, annot. *Fiduc. Rev.* July 2001, p. 1. Cf. Chapter 14 § 5(2)(a) concerning deductibility for federal estate tax purposes.

## § 13.11 VALUATION, COMPUTATION AND PAYMENT OF TAX

(1) *Valuation.* The inheritance tax return must include a valuation of each item listed thereon, which is generally its market value at the date of death: § 9102(26). There is no "alternate valuation date" such as that for federal estate tax purposes. Where the decedent owned only a part interest, the valuation will be the appropriate fractional share of the total market value, perhaps reduced by a discount because the interest was an undivided one: *Brone Est.*, 6 Fiduc. Rep. 411; cf. *McConnell Est.*, 73 Montg. 475; *Hacker Est.*, 9 Fiduc. Rep. 581; *Berry Est.* 27 Fiduc. Rep. 2d 219, annot. *Fiduc. Rev.* July 2007, p. 3. where discount of limited partnership interest value was disallowed even though granted for Federal estate tax purposes. If real estate is sold shortly after death, the actual sale price should be reported, since the appraiser may use that as the basis of the appraisement.

Stocks and bonds should be valued as of the market quotation on the date of death, by taking the mean between the high and low prices; if death occurred on a weekend, the mean of the immediately preceding Friday and following Monday quotations should be employed: see Grossman and Smith, Pennsylvania Inheritance and Estate Tax (Fifth Ed. 2002). Securities in closely held corporations can often be valued on the basis of a statement of the corporate assets and liabilities: see Section 12.9. However, it is advisable to submit some type of statement to substantiate the valuation, although as a practical matter the appraiser checks the corporate returns at Harrisburg: see Grossman and Smith, *Pennsylvania Inheritance and Estate Tax* (Fifth Ed. 2002), § 9102(26.7); *Gudebrod Est.*, 24 D. & C. 2d 517. Statements of a business conducted as a partnership or sole proprietorship should be filed with the return.

Anticipated income and other taxes thereon are no longer available as an offset in valuing receivables owned by decedent: § 9102. See *Rose Est.*, 465 Pa. 53, annot. *Fiduc. Rev*. Jan. 1976, p. 3, for the rule applicable under the 1961 Act.

Buy-and-sell agreements, if they meet the requirements of Section 9121(f), may conclusively establish tax value, although prior to the 1961 Act they did not. See *Fiduc. Rev*. Nov. 1971, p. 3; *Moyer Est*., 23 Fiduc. Rep. 583, annot. *Fiduc. Rev*. Dec. 1973, p. 2; 24 Fiduc. Rep. 103.

Life interests, interests for terms certain and future interests are to be valued "in accordance with rules and regulations promulgated by" the Department of Revenue. Until so determined "the regulations in effect for federal estate tax purposes shall apply": § 9121. In the situation where the limited estate terminates within nine months of the decedent's death the actuarial determination gives way to the actual facts: § 9121(d). Section 9122 includes the provisions of the 1961 Act (added by Act 207 of 1980) for valuing farmland, including amendment regarding valuation of interests in land which is part of an agricultural easement at fifty percent of the value otherwise determined.

Based on expert testimony, the survival action was determined to have a date of death value of $1,120,887 even though the settlement five years thereafter produced $4,076,023 allocated to the survival action. *Pearlstein Est.*, 23 Fiduc. Rep. 2nd 301, annot. *Fiduc. Rev*. Sept. 2003, p. 1.

The Department of Revenue will permit an estate to suspend valuation of real estate for up to fifteen months after the date of death, recognizing that sale may be difficult to complete. Also, if the property is sold in an arms-length sale for less than the amount reported, a refund may be requested on a timely filed refund petition. If a sale is not completed, the date of death value can be established by appraisal or use of common level ratio. *See Fiduc. Rev*. Jan. 2012, p. 4. See discussion re leasehold interests for oil and gas in Pa. Inheritance and Estate Tax, Grossman & Smith (Fifth Ed.—2002) Supplement § 9102 [26.3].

(2) *Computation.* The net taxable estate is computed by subtracting the allowable deductions from the gross values of the taxable transfers: § 9139.[1] Deductions are not apportioned pro rata against legacies (*Camp Est.*, 298 Pa. 405), except that a mortgage on specifically devised real estate is deductible, not from the total taxable estate, but only from the value of the devise passing to the specific devisee: *Inheritance Taxes: Appraisement of Mortgaged Real Estate*, 11 Fiduc. Rep. 444.

(3) *Payment.* Payment of the tax should be made to the register; if the decedent was a nonresident in whose estate no letters have been granted in Pennsylvania, payment is made to the Department of Revenue in Harrisburg: § 9145(g). Usually the full tax is paid[2] when the return is filed, so that interest will not accrue (see Section 13.4, supra). Remainder tax in estates of decedents who died before December 13, 1982 may be prepaid by an election filed with the register at date of election values:[3] Inh. & Est. Tax Act of 1961, §§ 713–715. The Commonwealth may require a bond to secure payment of future interest tax (other than on a future interest in realty) or of delinquent tax: Inh. & Est. Tax Act of 1961, §§ 761, 771. For remainder tax for those dying after December 13, 1982, see Sections 9150, 9151.

Query whether the Judicial Code § 5527 (b) limitation period of six years applies to inheritance tax collection. See *Estate of Trowbridge*, 920 A.2d 901, annot. *Fiduc. Rev.* Aug. 2007, p. 1.

## § 13.12 ALLOCATION

In a departure from the earlier law, Section 718 of the Inheritance and Estate Tax Act of 1961 (and PEF Code 2514(15) and 6114(6)) altered the rule that each legatee nor-

---

§ **13.11**

**1.** For alternate computation in the estates of nonresidents, see § 9116(b)(2).

**2.** A 5% discount will have been allowed on tax paid within three months after the decedent's death: § 9142.

**3.** Under the 1961 Act, prepayment of tax could be made at date of death values if the election was filed within nine months of decedent's death.

mally bears the burden of tax on his legacy. It is now provided in Section 9144, as in the 1961 and 1982 Acts, that:

(1) Unless the testator expresses a contrary intent in the will, inheritance tax on outright pre-residuary bequests and devises is payable from the residuary estate. Cf. *Skeffington Est.*, 3 Fiduc. Rep. 2d 80.

(2) Unless a contrary intent appears in the instrument of transfer, inheritance tax on estates for years, for life or for other limited periods, created by will or inter vivos transfer, is payable out of the principal of the property supporting such estate.

(3) In all other cases, the transferee bears the burden of the inheritance tax, unless the will or other instrument of transfer directs otherwise. It is to be noted that the duty imposed by Section 9146 to collect the tax from the legatee, and the power to sell the property of a recalcitrant legatee, is subject to the provisions of Section 9144.

"Frequent disputes arise concerning allocation of taxes where a broad "pay tax" clause is used without careful consideration of the impact of the clause, resulting in charities paying a portion of the tax on non-charitable transfers and sometimes increasing taxes where the federal estate tax circuity calculations are involved. See *Benham Est.*, 4 Fiduc. Rep. 2d 202, annot. *Fiduc. Rev*. July 1984, and *Stackhous Est.*, 433 Pa. Super. 641, affirming 12 Fiduc. Rep. 2d 311 and 331, annot. *Fiduc. Rev*. Sept. 1992; *Berkey Est.*, 26 Fiduc. Rep. 2d 265, annot. *Fiduc. Rev*. July 2006, p. 1. See cases collected at 2 *Hunter's Orphans' Court Commonplace Book*, Estate Tax 12 and Volume 3A, Inheritance Tax 14(o).

If property passes to a transferee other than through administration by the personal representative (e.g., United States savings bonds), the personal representative will be responsible for collecting tax thereon *if* such property was in, or has come into, his possession, and he should therefore not deliver such property to the person entitled until provision has been made for payment of tax thereon: § 9146. For apportionment of federal and Pennsylvania estate taxes, see Section 13.16. Death taxes payable to jurisdictions other than Pennsylvania and the United States on legacies and devises are not payable from the residue in the absence of a clause so directing; see *Felger Est.*, 15 Fiduc. Rep. 172, regarding Canadian Succession tax.

Act 21 of 1995 provides for postponement of payment of inheritance tax on a qualified trust until the death of the surviving spouse. Code Section 2113. The source of payment of tax on a trust which is taxed at the surviving spouse's death would be the trust itself, unless the surviving spouse by "express reference" to the trust directs some other source. The "express reference" requirement is made so that a broad tax clause will not inadvertently impose tax on the surviving spouse's probate estate.

## § 13.13 APPRAISEMENT, ALLOWANCE OR DISALLOWANCE OF DEDUCTIONS AND ASSESSMENT

The Inheritance and Estate Tax Act, in Sections 9136 through 9154, states the procedures leading to a determination of the inheritance tax. Following the filing of the tax return (no later than nine months from the decedent's death, unless an extension has been granted: § 9150) the Department is required to file an appraisement, and to pass upon claimed deductions, within six months[1] from the filing of the return or request for allowance of the deductions. Notice of the action is given to the personal representative or to his attorney. In addition, the court has authority to allow "last minute" deductions at audit, with the proviso that such deductions aggregating more than $100 may not be allowed unless the register has had thirty days' prior notice thereof or the Commonwealth is represented at audit: § 9137.

**§ 13.13**

1. If the appraisement or determination of deductions is not forthcoming within such time, the court may be requested to order filing thereof: §§ 9137, 9138.

Within one month of the later of filing of the appraisement or determination of deductions, the tax is assessed and notice is given to the personal representative or his attorney: § 9140. (In the case of a nonresident in whose estate no letters have been granted in Pennsylvania, the foregoing actions are performed by the Department of Revenue.) Each of the three procedures of appraisement, determination of deductions and assessment is appealable separately: (§ 9186), and each may be postponed until audit of the personal representative's account. See generally Grossman and Smith, *Pennsylvania Inheritance and Estate Tax* (Fifth Ed. 2002), § 9126-1.2.

## § 13.14 APPEALS

As noted in Section 13.13, the appraisement, determination of deductions and assessment of tax are each appealable to the court. Any party in interest[1] not satisfied with any one of those determinations may have the determination suspended until audit of the personal representative's account by so notifying the register (§ 9186(a)(2)), or may file a written protest with the Department of Revenue (sending a copy thereof to the Office of the Attorney General) in Harrisburg (§ 9186(a)(1)), or may appeal directly to the court (§ 9186(a)(3)). Any such action must be taken within sixty days of receipt by the party of notice of the action complained of, and the notification, protest or appeal must specify all objections thereto. The decision of the Department of Revenue upon a protest may be appealed, within sixty days of receipt of notice of its decision, to the court, and if the Department of Revenue has not acted upon the protest within thirty days after its filing the party may petition the court to have the record removed from the Department of Revenue and transmitted to the court: § 9188(a). No appeal bond is required for any stage of the appellate or protest procedure: § 9187. The decision of the court in any of the foregoing proceedings may be appealed to the Superior Court.

---

**§ 13.14**

1. Including the Commonwealth and the personal representative.

It would seem that disputes concerning valuation, or the inclusion of property or transfers, are to be resolved by notification of postponement until audit, protest or appeal regarding the appraisement, while those involving the appropriate rate of tax are to be resolved by disputing the assessment. Prompt action regarding disputed items of inclusion of property and transfers following filing of the appraisement should be taken, for it may be too late to challenge them upon an appeal from an assessment. Similarly, disputes regarding deductions should be pursued within sixty days from the determination of deductions, without awaiting the assessment. Of course, the protective action to be taken need be no more than a notification of election to postpone the dispute until audit, where all disputes regarding any one or more of the appraisement, determination of deductions or assessment may be consolidated for hearing.

## § 13.15 PENNSYLVANIA ESTATE TAX

With changes in the Federal Estate Tax provisions, the credit for state death taxes has been eliminated and replaced by a deduction for state death taxes, including inheritance tax for decedents dying on or after January 1, 2005.

Pennsylvania lawmakers first attempted to de-couple the estate tax from changing federal law by declaring a "freeze" to the federal estate tax as it existed in 2001 and then, faced with possible constitutionality challenges, retroactively eliminated the decoupling. Act 46 of 2003, discussed in *Fiduc. Rev.* April 2004, p. 4.

## § 13.16 ESTATE TAX APPORTIONMENT

Chapter 37 of the PEF Code, "*Apportionment of Death Taxes*," prescribes equitable apportionment rules for the federal and Pennsylvania estate taxes. See also Section 9145(b). Thus, directions to pay estate tax, like the Pennsylvania inheritance tax (see Section 13.12, supra), from the residuary estate or any other source specified in an instrument of transfer, including tax on property not passing through administration can be made. In the absence of such direction, the Act provides that the tax be apportioned among the beneficiaries of the gross estate property in proportion of the value of such property to the net estate before exemption, except that property allowable as a deduction bears no tax. Act No. 50 of 2002 amended PEF 3701 and 3702 to calculate apportionment of taxes at the top marginal rate rather than the average rate where qualified terminable interest trusts and qualified domestic trusts are involved. Act 85 of 2010 amended PEF 3706 to require payment by the party liable on due dates for payment rather than upon final federal estate tax determination. For apportionment of tax as directed by will, see *Fischer Est.*, 30 Fiduc. Rep. 476, aff'd (Pa. Super.), 450 A.2d 1055, annot. *Fiduc. Rev.* Jan. 1981, p. 3. See *Smith Est.*, 3 Fiduc. Rep. 1, where an administrator pro tem was appointed to settle the estate's liability for taxes where the personal interest of the executrix was to obtain a high basis for stock.

Since the personal representative is primarily responsible for the payment of the entire federal estate tax (IRC § 2002), he must pay the tax, but may then, under the PEF Code, enforce contribution from property not passing under his control. Claim for contribution of tax under PEF Chapter 37 must be asserted before expiration of six years after the due date for payment of the tax (nine months after death). The cause of action accrues on the date the tax return was due, not when the tax return is filed and the tax finally assessed. *Nixon Est.*, 8 Fiduc. Rep. 2d 110, annot. *Fiduc. Rev.* June 1988.

## § 13.17 REFUNDS

Cash refunds of Pennsylvania inheritance and estate taxes erroneously paid may be obtained by application to the Department of Revenue in Harrisburg. Interest is allowed on refunds at the same rate as is charged on delinquent tax payments in accord with Section 806 of the Fiscal Code: § 9181(b). Application must be made within three years of the occurrence of the events specified in Section 9181(d). A refund can also be requested by checking the block "Refund Requested" on the inheritance tax return, in which case a separate application for refund is not required.

The Board of Finance and Revenue has suggested forms for requests for refunds, and provides a memorandum of instructions to assist in preparation thereof. The petition for refund must be signed under oath, set forth the essential facts and have attached to it certified copies of the tax determination and receipt for payment. If deductions were disputed, a certified copy of the final adjudication or decree allowing the deduction must be attached.

## § 13.18 PENNSYLVANIA INCOME TAX

The personal income tax applies to estates as well as to individuals. Generally speaking, the tax applies to Pennsylvania residents (the personal representative's residence being irrelevant), and the tax on income which is currently distributable or in fact distributed is paid by the beneficiary; remaining income is taxed in the estate. Administration expenses are not deductible. The return requirements are much like the federal ones, as to time and payment dates: see *Fiduc. Rev*. Oct. 1971.

Trusts and estates are required to pay estimated taxes for Pennsylvania income tax purposes if estimated income will be $8,000 or more for the year. Instructions for estimated income tax returns require estimated tax payments beginning with taxable years ending two or more years after the decedent's death. See *Fiduc. Rev.* Nov. 1991, Jan. 1992 and May 1992. Safe harbor rules protect from penalties in circumstances set forth in the instructions.

# Chapter 14

# FEDERAL ESTATE AND INCOME TAXES

---



---

## A. FEDERAL ESTATE TAX

## § 14.1 NATURE OF TAX AND PERSONS LIABLE

The federal estate tax, unlike the Pennsylvania inheritance tax (see § 13.1) is a tax on the transfer of the decedent's "taxable estate" as defined in IRC § 2051.[1] The tax is due upon the death of any citizen or resident of the United States who leaves a "taxable estate": IRC § 2001. Special rules are applicable to nonresidents who are not citizens but who own property in the United States at the time of death: IRC §§ 2101 et seq. The rate of the tax is determined by the size of the taxable

---

**§ 14.1**

**1.** All IRC references are to the 1986 Internal Revenue Code as amended.

estate, and neither the identity of the beneficiary nor his relationship to the decedent is relevant except to the extent that property passing to a particular beneficiary may be deductible in determining the taxable estate, as for example, a charitable gift or a gift to the surviving spouse (see § 14.5).

The primary responsibility for the payment of the tax is on the personal representative (IRC § 2002), and he may become personally liable to the extent that he pays debts or distributes the estate without having paid the tax (IRC § 2204). Legatees, beneficiaries, transferees and trustees of property includible in the decedent's gross estate, whether or not passing under the personal representative's control, may also become personally liable for tax to the extent of the value of the asset received: IRC §§ 6324(a)(2), 6901(a)(1)(A)(ii). If the tax is paid out of the share of a particular legatee, and this tax is more than should be imposed on the particular share, the legatee is entitled to reimbursement out of any part of the estate still undistributed, or by an equitable contribution by the persons whose interests were benefited by this "additional" payment: IRC § 2205. See also Section 13.16 for discussion of the estate tax apportionment provisions of the PEF Code. Beneficiaries of life insurance, of appointed property and of qualified terminable interest property may also become personally liable: IRC §§ 2206, 2207, 2207A.

A lien for the taxes attaches to the entire gross estate, except that part of the estate which a court having jurisdiction thereof allows to be used as a payment of charges against the estate and expenses of its administration, for ten years or until the tax is paid: IRC § 6324(a)(1).[2] See also *Fiduc. Rev.* March 1943, p. 3; June 1955.

The consent of the District Director of Internal Revenue should be secured when property is to be disposed of prior to final settlement of the tax. As to personal property, see Reg. § 20.2031-6(c); as to real estate, see Reg. § 301.6325-1(b)(4).

---

**§ 14.1**

**2.** See IRC § 6324A for lien of tax deferred under IRC § 6166, and IRC § 6324B for lien of additional estate tax attributable to farm etc. valuation.

The Tax Relief, Unemployment Insurance Reauthorization and Job Creation Act of 2010 permits executors of persons who died in 2010 to apply estate tax and carryover basis rules as if the 2010 Act had not been adopted or apply the estate tax reinstated by the 2010 Act and deferred until 2013 the return to an exemption amount of one million dollars and 2001 rates of taxation, along with other changes.

## § 14.2 WHEN AND WHERE PAID

The taxable estate is reportable and the taxes are payable to the District Director of Internal Revenue in whose district the decedent was domiciled at the time of his death: IRC § 6091(b)(3). It is the duty of the executor or administrator to file the return within nine months after the date of death in every case in which the gross taxable assets are in excess of a certain value: IRC §§ 6075(a), 6018(a)(1).[1] An extension for filing not exceeding six months may be obtained upon application to the Secretary of the Treasury: IRC § 6081(a). An extension for a shorter period sometimes may be obtained upon application to the local District Director of Internal Revenue. The return is filed on Form 706, which is obtainable from the Internal Revenue Service, and only the original of the return need be filed: Reg. § 20.6018-1(a). The return should be accompanied by a certified copy of the will, if the decedent died testate.

The tax must be paid at the place fixed for filing the return within nine months after the date of death (IRC § 6151(a)), but extensions may be granted (IRC § 6163). After nine months, interest is assessable (IRC § 6601). Unlike the Pennsylvania inheritance tax, no discount is given for early payment of the tax.

For a discussion of the use of certain Treasury bonds issued before March 4, 1971, P.L. 92-5, in payment of the fed-

**§ 14.2**

**1.** In the case of decedents dying prior to January 1, 1987, the return must be filed if the gross estate exceeds: 1983—$275,000; 1984—$325,000; 1985—$400,000 and in 1986—$500,000. See § 14.5(1) for exclusion amount for 1998 and thereafter.

eral estate tax at their par value, regardless of lower market values, see *Fiduc. Rev.* March 1969, p. 4.[2]

Provision is made for installment payments of the estate tax attributable to the value of a closely held business, over a period of ten years with interest on the unpaid tax: IRC § 6166.

Regarding the redemption of stock in a closely held corporation, free of income tax, in an amount not exceeding the sum of death taxes (with interest), and funeral and administration expenses, see IRC § 303.

## § 14.3 RATE OF TAX

The tax rate for taxable values in excess of the exclusion amount for years 2010 through 2012 is 35%. For 2010 decedents, an election can be made to accept no estate tax and use carryover basis. Although this usually would be used only for estates exceeding five million dollars, assets of each estate should be reviewed. If no legislative change is made, the 2013 rates will range from 18% to 55% in accordance with pre-2002 rates.

## § 14.4 PROPERTY TAXABLE

The personal representative is required to report all property (except real estate situated outside of the United States) in which the decedent had an interest: IRC §§ 2031, 2033. The tax is based on the taxable estate, which is the gross estate, as defined in IRC § 2031, minus specified deductions and exemptions. See Section 14.5. The report must include the following:

(1) Real estate in the United States.

(2) Personal property of all kinds regardless of location (IRC §§ 2031, 2033), except mortgages and leases of for-

---

**§ 14.2**

**2.** This discussion is of historical interest only since all such bonds have matured.

eign real estate which are characterized as realty by the law of the situs.

(3) Interests held as dower or curtesy or a statutory share in lieu thereof: IRC § 2034.

(4) All transfers made whereby the decedent has retained, for life or for any period which does not in fact end before his death, either the possession or enjoyment of the income from the property transferred or the power to designate the persons who should enjoy or possess the property or income therefrom: IRC § 2036. Also included are certain transfers of property subject at the date of the decedent's death to the power of the decedent to alter, amend, revoke or terminate the enjoyment of the property transferred: IRC § 2038. In addition, there should be included certain transfers intended to take effect at the decedent's death: IRC § 2037. See *Fiduc. Rev*. April 1978, p. 2, regarding employee trusts. Transfers in contemplation of death are no longer taxable, except in limited circumstances: IRC § 2035. Present interest gifts not exceeding $13,000 to a donee in a calendar year are not taxable and is scheduled to increase to $14,000 for 2013.

(5) Annuities with certain exceptions: IRC § 2039. See *Fiduc. Rev*. Sept. 1954.

(6) Jointly owned property, with survivorship rights (unless owned by husband and wife) to the extent of the decedent's interest therein: IRC § 2040. Such jointly held property is presumed to belong 100% to the owner who dies first, and the burden is on the taxpayer to prove the survivor's contribution. However, entireties property is treated as if owned one-half by each regardless of which spouse furnished the consideration.

(7) Property over which the decedent had a power of appointment, but depending on three factors: (a) the time of creation of the power, (b) whether or not exercised by the decedent and (c) the character of the power: IRC § 2041.

(8) Life insurance on the decedent's life and payable to his estate, or payable to others if the decedent retained any of the incidents of ownership: IRC § 2042. Form 712 should

be obtained from the insurance company and filed with the return. See *Fiduc. Rev*. Sept. 1954; Nov. 1954, p. 2.

## § 14.5 DEDUCTIONS AND CREDITS

The taxable estate is calculated by subtracting the allowable deductions from the gross estate: IRC § 2051. Credits against the tax for certain specifically enumerated items may be allowed (IRC §§ 2010-2016), but some credits cannot be taken until the taxable estate is computed because the size of the taxable estate determines whether certain credits are allowable and, if so, the amount thereof.

(1) *Unified credit*. Until 1997, credit of $192,800 was allowed to the estate of every decedent dying after 1986. In the case of decedents dying in 1998 and thereafter, the credit and amount excluded are:

| For Decedent Dying | Credit Amount | Exclusion Amount |
|---|---|---|
| 1998 | $202,050 | $625,000 |
| 1999 | 211,300 | 650,000 |
| 2000–2001 | 220,550 | 675,000 |
| 2002–2003 | 345,800 | 1,000,000 |
| 2004–2005 | 555,800 | 1,500,000 |
| 2006–2008 | 780,800 | 2,000,000 |
| 2009 | 1,455,800 | 3,500,000 |
| 2010 | estate tax repealed or | |
| 2010 | 35% on excess | 5,000,000 |
| 2011 | 35% on excess | 5,000,000 |
| 2012 | 35% on excess | 5,120,000 |
| 2013 | See § 14.3 | 1,000,000 |

For estates of persons dying in 2011 and 2012 the exclusion amount of a spouse not used in the estate of the first to die may be used by the surviving spouse's estate, provided that an election to do so is made by the estate of the first to die. This portability provision would not apply after 2012 unless legislation is passed.

(2) *Deductions*. The allowable deductions are set forth in IRC §§ 2053-2056 and include the following:

(a) Funeral expenses, administration expenses,[1] claims against the estate and unpaid mortgages on, or any indebtedness in respect of, property when the value of the decedent's interest is included in the value of the gross estate: IRC § 2053(a). Taxes accrued before death, including income tax on Series HH bond accrued interest includible by executrix election on decedent's final income tax return (Technical Advice Memorandum 9232006), are also deductible: see IRC § 2053(c)(1)(B). This group of deductions has been enlarged so as to permit the deduction of any items expended or owed by the decedent with respect to property includible in the gross estate even though not subject to creditor's claims, provided that they are paid before the end of the period of limitation for assessment: IRC § 2053(b). Thus, expenses incurred with respect to an inter vivos trust are deductible if the trust is subject to an estate tax and the expenses are paid within three years after the return was filed: see *Fiduc. Rev.* Sept. 1954.

Amendments to IRS Reg. § 20.2051 and § 20.2053 allow consideration for post-death events—i.e., amounts paid on claims after death, as opposed to estimated amounts viewed as of date of death. Also addressed is the issue of protective claims for refund. T.D. 9468, CCH Fed. Est. & Gift Tax Rep. ¶ 43.127.

I.R.S. Revenue Procedure 2011-48 (CCH Fed. Estate & Gift Tax Rep. ¶ 30,689) explains rules for filing protective claims for refund, based on Section 2053, where amounts are not deductible in the filed return because not yet paid or adjudicated in contested matters.

(b) Losses[2] which are attributable during the administration of the estate to fire, storms, shipwrecks or other casu-

---

**§ 14.5**

**1.** The administration expenses allowable as a deduction are similar to those allowable under the Pennsylvania inheritance tax. see also note 2.

**2.** For election to deduct administration expenses and losses in estate income tax return, see § 14.10.

alties and losses from theft, to the extent that such losses are not compensated for by insurance or otherwise: IRC § 2054.

(c) Charitable deductions. Deductions are allowed for the full value of all property passing to the use or benefit of a charitable, religious, scientific, educational or similar organization, provided that the amount of the deduction does not exceed the value of the transferred property required to be included in the gross estate:[3] IRC § 2055; as to charitable remainders, see *Fiduc. Rev.* Oct. 1970, p. 3; July 1971; Oct. 1971, p. 3; March 1975 and Aug. 2007, p. 4 concerning split interest trusts. The deduction is not applicable to a residuary bequest to an individual member of a religious order who has taken a vow of poverty, even though the assets were transferred to the order. *Technical Advice Memorandum* 200437032.

(d) Marital deduction. A deduction is allowed for the full value of property which passes or has passed to the surviving spouse (IRC § 2056(a)), to the extent that such property is included in the gross estate. Further limitations are set forth in IRC § 2056(b). Property subject to both a life estate and a power of appointment in the surviving spouse exercisable in favor of such surviving spouse or in favor of his or her estate falls within the marital deduction: IRC § 2056(b)(5). See *Fiduc. Rev.* Sept. 1954; 62 Dick L. Rev. 111. The deduction is allowed also for gifts to the surviving spouse for life with no power of appointment or other control over principal: IRC § 2056(b)(7) and (8).

(e) The amount of any estate, inheritance, legacy or succession taxes actually paid to any state or territory, or the District of Columbia, or any possession of the United States is deductible beginning in 2005 pursuant to provisions of the Economic Growth and Tax Relief Act of 2001. This deduction will change to a credit after 2012 unless legislation is enacted to change this result.

It should be noted that amounts allowable as deductions for estate tax purposes, as well as for income tax pur-

---

**§ 14.5**

**3.** IRC § 2055 also recognizes as an irrevocable disclaimer for purposes of this section a termination of a power to consume, invade or appropriate property if the termination should occur before the power is exercised.

poses, are not allowed as income tax deductions on the return of the estate unless a waiver is filed of the right to have such amounts allowed as estate tax deductions: IRC § 642(g). An exception to the disallowance of double deductions is contained in the last sentence of IRC § 642(g) with respect to income of a decedent dealt with in IRC § 691. See Section 14.10.

(3) *Credits*. The tax imposed (IRC § 2001) is reducible by the amount of certain other credits (IRC §§ 2011-2016), which include the following:

(a) The former credit for state death taxes paid was phased out from 2002 to 2004 by reducing it 25% each year. As set forth in paragraph 2(e) above, there is now a deduction for state death taxes. The credit would return in 2013 unless legislation is enacted.

(b) Gift taxes paid on any gift made by the decedent in his lifetime, which gift is required to be included within his estate for estate tax purposes. The limitations on this credit are set forth in the relevant code section with adjustment for gifts considered made one-half by a spouse: IRC § 2012(c).

(c) All or part of the federal estate tax paid with respect to the transfer of property to the decedent by a person who died within ten years before, or within two years after, the decedent's death: IRC § 2013. See *Fiduc. Rev.* Sept. 1954.

(d) Additional credit may be allowed for nonfederal death taxes when federal estate tax payments on certain remainders or reversions are postponed: IRC § 2015.

(e) Up to certain limits there is a credit for death taxes paid to any foreign country: IRC § 2014.

If any tax claimed as a credit for state death taxes under prior law (IRC § 2011) or a foreign death tax (IRC § 2014) is recovered from any state or foreign country, the "executor"[4] is required to give notice to the Secretary of the

§ 14.5

4. IRC § 2203 defines the term "executor" to mean an executor or administrator of the decedent, or if no executor or administrator is appointed, then any person in actual or constructive possession of any property of the decedent.

Treasury and the Secretary will then redetermine the amount of tax. Upon notice and demand, the executor must pay the tax due on redetermination: IRC § 2016.

In the settlement of any estate in which the applicability of the laws of any foreign country may be involved, a standard tax publication should be consulted to ascertain whether or not the foreign country in question has entered into a tax treaty with the United States, and if so whether the provisions of such treaty deal with the problems in question.

## § 14.6 VALUATION, COMPUTATION AND PAYMENT OF TAX

The estate tax return must include a valuation of each item listed therein. The general rule is to use the market value as of the date of death: IRC § 2031(a). However, the personal representative may elect on the tax return to value the property as of six months after the death: IRC § 2032. See *Fiduc. Rev.* Sept. 1959, p. 2. This alternate date permits a lower tax only when values shrink from conditions other than mere passage of time: IRC § 2032(a)(3). If this election is made, any property that is sold, distributed, exchanged or otherwise disposed of, within that six month period, must be valued as of the date of sale, distribution, exchange or other disposal, and not the alternative date. The election is effective only if it results in a reduction of value of the gross estate and a smaller estate tax liability. The rules for methods of valuation generally are similar to those for the Pennsylvania tax (see Section 13.11), but the federal regulations should be consulted for details.

The valuation of listed stock is the mean between the highest and lowest quoted selling prices on the valuation date. The valuation of stocks and securities which are listed is controlled by Reg. § 20.2031-2(b). (See also Grossman and Smith, Pennsylvania Inheritance and Estate Tax (Rev. Ed. 1993) § 9102[26]) It is there provided that if there were no sales on the valuation date, the value is determined by taking a weighted average of the means between the highest and lowest sales on the nearest dates before and after the valuation date (within reasonable limits); the average is weighted inversely by the number of trading days between the sale dates and the valuation date. Where death occurs on a weekend and there are Friday and Monday sales, a simple average is taken for the mean prices on those days. Mutual fund shares are valued at the redemption (bid) price: *Cartwright Est.*, 411 U.S. 546. Stocks and securities which are not listed and are not actively sold should have a valuation based on the company's net worth, earning capacity, dividend rate of payment and the value of listed stocks or securities in companies engaged in the same or a similar line of business: IRC § 2031(b). For effect of buy-and-sell agreements upon valuation, see *Fiduc. Rev.* Dec. 1960; Nov. 1971, p. 3.

The value of a life interest in a charitable remainder unitrust is determined under actuarial tables unless facts known at decedent's death indicate that the life beneficiary is afflicted with an incurable condition rendering death imminent. The actual period of survival for a beneficiary whose terminal condition was diagnosed five months after decedent's death is not relevant. *Burchell Est.*, 2001-1 U.S.T.C. ¶ 60,410.

The tax is computed by subtracting the deductions and exemptions from the gross estate as described in Sections 14.4 and 14.5. The actual computation of the amount of the tax owed is made from the tables in IRC §§ 2001 and 2010. See Section 14.3. The credits against the tax are computed as limited by the taxable estate, and are then subtracted.

The full tax is to be paid at the time of filing the return (IRC § 6151(a)), except that the tax on certain remainders and reversions may, at the election of the executor, be postponed until six months after the precedent interest terminates (IRC § 6163), in which case interest will be assessed beginning with the date the tax payment first became due (IRC § 6601). In case of undue hardship, the time for payment of the estate tax may be extended by the Secretary of the Treasury for a period not to exceed ten years (IRC § 6161(a)(2)), in which case a bond may be required (IRC § 6165). Tax attributable to closely held business interests may be postponed: IRC § 6166. See Section 14.2.

## § 14.7 APPORTIONMENT

The Pennsylvania estate tax apportionment provisions of Chapter 37 of the PEF Code are discussed in Section 13.16. See IRC §§ 2206, 2207 regarding liability for payment of tax on life insurance or appointed property. See IRC § 2207A for payment of tax on qualified terminable interest property (QTIP).

## § 14.8 ASSESSMENT AND APPEAL

After the personal representative files the return and pays the tax due thereon, he should consider whether it is advisable to write to the District Director of Internal Revenue and request an audit of the return and a determination of the tax liability within one year from the date of the letter: IRC § 2204. The initial audit is performed by the Audit Division of the District Director's office. Any agreement reached by the agent and the personal representative is subject to confirmation by the District Director. When the tax has been finally determined and has been paid in full, the personal representative should consider requesting from the District Director a certificate releasing him from personal liability for payment of the federal estate tax, if he had earlier filed notice of the fiduciary relationship: IRC § 6903; Reg. § 301.6903-1(b).

If there is an assessment, the personal representative will receive notice of the determination of tax by the Internal Revenue Service. The assessment must be made within three years after the return is filed: IRC § 6501. However, there is no time limit if a false or fraudulent return is filed or if there is a willful attempt to evade the tax, or if no return is filed at all: IRC § 6501(c). If the Service's determination is the same as that of the taxpayer, the matter is closed. If the Service determines that additional tax is due, the taxpayer receives a deficiency notice. Deficiency procedures for estate taxes are covered in IRC §§ 6211–6215. Formal notice of a deficiency by certified or registered mail (IRC §§ 6212(a), 6212(b)(3)) is required before any assessment can be made (IRC § 6213(a)). Within ninety days (150 days in special circumstances) after the notice of deficiency has been mailed, the taxpayer must file a petition with the tax court for a redetermination of the deficiency: IRC § 6213(a). If no petition is filed (IRC §§ 6213(c), 7481) or, if filed after the tax court decision becomes final (IRC § 6214(c)), the deficiency will be assessed (see IRC § 6303).

Failure to pay the amount assessed will be met with enforcement action entered in a federal district court (IRC § 7403), and interest will be assessed (IRC § 6601(a)). The usual procedure in the case of a deficiency is for the taxpayer to file a protest with the Revenue Service, after which a hearing will be arranged to discuss the merits of the deficiency claim. If the Service fails to agree, a formal deficiency assessment will then be made.

The taxpayer may elect to pay the tax deficiencies and then sue for a refund. Payment under protest or duress is not a prerequisite to a refund action: IRC § 7422(b). There must be a claim for refund filed with the Secretary of the Treasury or his delegate before suit will be entertained: IRC § 7422. In the case of overpayment, interest will be allowed on the refund. IRC § 6611(a).

## B. FEDERAL INCOME TAX

### § 14.9 DECEDENT'S INCOME TAX

It is the duty of the personal representative (or if none, of one "charged" with the property of the decedent, such as the surviving spouse) to file an income tax return on decedent's behalf for the part of his taxable year during which he was alive, if the decedent would have been required to do so: IRC § 6012(b)(1). Even if the decedent's income was insufficient to require him to file a return, one may be necessary to obtain a refund of tax withheld or estimated tax paid. The return may be a joint one with the surviving spouse: IRC § 6013(a)(3). The return is due on the same date that it would have been due had the decedent lived to the end of his taxable year (i.e., April

15 of the year following death for a decedent who was on a calendar year basis; see IRC § 6072(a)) and will include income actually or constructively received up to the date of decedent's death (or accruable to that date in the case of an accrual basis taxpayer). Deductions are to be claimed only for items actually paid[1] up to the time of decedent's death (or accrued thereto in the case of an accrual basis taxpayer), but the decedent's personal exemption or exemptions need not be prorated because of his death. In preparing the decedent's final income tax return, the personal representative should consider the advisability of electing to accrue interest on United States Savings Bonds therein: IRC § 454(a); *Fiduc. Rev.* March 1960, p. 3; *Doherty Est.*, 12 Fiduc. Rep. 185.

No declaration of estimated tax, or payment of estimated tax, is required on decedent's behalf after his death: Reg. §§ 1.6015(g)-1, 1.6153-1(a)(4); cf. Reg. § 1.6015(b)-1(c)(2). See IRS Letter Ruling 9102010.

Regarding the personal representative's responsibilities where the decedent had failed to file proper income tax returns during his lifetime, see *Fiduc. Rev.* Oct. 1958, p. 3.

Intestate heirs, as part of an effort to locate assets, may obtain a copy of decedent's income tax return for the year prior to death upon written request to the IRS with documentation of their relationship. *Revenue Ruling* 2004-68.

## § 14.10 ESTATE'S INCOME TAX

An estate is a taxable entity during the period of administration, and if its gross income exceeds $600, a return must be filed on Form 1041: IRC § 6012(a)(3). For permissible length of administration for tax purposes, see *Fiduc. Rev.* Oct. 1961, p. 3. The estate may choose either a calendar year,

---

**§ 14.9**

**1.** However, decedent's medical expenses are deductible in his final return if paid from his estate within one year after death and if not claimed as a federal estate tax deduction. If paid by a surviving spouse, they will be deductible in the spouse's income tax return: IRC § 213.

in which case its first return will be for the period from decedent's death to the end of that year, or a fiscal year ending on the last day of any month other than December, in which case the first return will be for the period from decedent's death to the end of the chosen fiscal year: IRC § 441. The estate's $600 exemption (IRC § 642(b)) is not reduced by reason of any of its taxable years being less than twelve months (IRC § 443(c)). The estate's income tax return is due on the fifteenth day of the fourth month following the close of its taxable year, and is filed with the District Director at the personal representative's residence: IRC §§ 6072(a), 6091(b)(1). See 22 Journal of Taxation 220 for a helpful article on preparing the return in a small estate.

The estate's first income tax return will include items received from the time of decedent's death to the end of the taxable year. Among such items may be "income in respect of a decedent"—items not includible in decedent's final return because of his method of accounting—such as a cash basis decedent's accrued income, income accrued solely by reason of death in the case of an accrual basis decedent, and income to which decedent had a contingent claim at death: see IRC § 691. Such income is includible by the estate in the year it is received if the estate has acquired the right thereto from the decedent, and has the same quality (e.g., capital gain, interest, etc.) as it would have had if received by the decedent. The estate tax attributable to inclusion of "income in respect of a decedent" in his gross estate is an allowable income tax deduction: IRC § 691(c).

The estate income tax return also will include deductions for allowable items paid during the period it covers. It is to be noted that all or part of the estate administration expenses, including executor's[1] and attorney's compensation,

---

**§ 14.10**

**1.** Where the executor is also a beneficiary, he should consider a written waiver of his right to commissions prior to undertaking his duties (Rev. Rul. 56-472) to save personal income taxes, as opposed to taking commissions which will be deductible in either the estate tax or the income tax return. The waiver must be timely to avoid gift tax consequences: Rev. Rul. 64-225, annot. in *Fiduc. Rev.* Oct. 1964, p. 4; Rev. Rul. 66-167, annot. *Fiduc. Rev.* Aug. 1966, p. 4.

may be claimed either as income tax or as estate tax deductions: IRC § 642(g); Reg. § 1.642(g)-2. (Certain items are deductible for both federal estate and income tax purposes—e.g., interest, taxes and business expenses: see IRC §§ 642(g), 691; Reg. § 1.642(g)-2.) The method of so electing and the ramifications of the choice thereby given the personal representative are discussed in *Fiduc. Rev.* Nov. 1958. The personal representative should consider not only the over-all tax savings which may result from electing to claim such expenses as income tax deductions rather than for federal estate tax purposes, but also the effects thereof on a marital deduction gift, and the possibility that adjustments among the distributees of the estate may be required where those who bear the increased estate tax do not receive the benefit of reduced income tax: see *Fiduc. Rev.* Nov. 1958.

Consideration also should be given to payment of administration expenses just prior to termination of the estate administration, and treatment thereof as income tax deductions, so that such deductions where they exceed estate income may be carried over into the beneficiaries' individual income tax returns: IRC § 642(h).

The timing of distributions during administration may also produce substantial tax savings (cf. *Emmers Est.*, 22 Fiduc. Rep. 498), and the personal representative therefore should consider distribution of sufficient income to equalize the resulting income tax rates applicable to the estate and to the distributees,[2] particularly in view of compression of income tax brackets for estates and trusts in the Tax Reform Act of 1986. Distributions from estates may be made within 65 days after the end of a fiscal period. Distributions to a surviving spouse in the year of decedent's death may be especially advantageous where the spouse and the personal representative are filing a joint tax return for such year. Distributions of principal may be treated for federal income tax purposes as if they were distributions of income to the ex-

**§ 14.10**

**2.** Surcharge of the executor has been refused where it was alleged the beneficiaries would have paid the tax at a lower rate if distributions had been made: *Burke Est.*, 2 Fiduc. Rep. 2d 259.

tent that the estate has taxable income (see Internal Revenue Code of 1954, § 661 et seq.) and the possibility of equitable adjustment between various distributees also must be considered in such situations: *Salesky Est.*, 15 Fiduc. Rep. 213.

However, the separate share rule applicable to trusts was made applicable to estates pursuant to the Taxpayer Relief Act of 1997 amendment of IRC § 663(c). Reg § 1.663(c) details the effect of this change on estates. Previously, income of the estate was allocated to a person receiving distribution during the fiscal period, even though that person was not ultimately entitled to all income. With this change, only the proportionate share of the income would be allocated to the recipient. For problems as to income tax effect of advance distributions, see *Fiduc. Rev.* March 1971, p. 3. If a charity is a residuary beneficiary, consideration should be given to distributions during administration. See generally Post-Death Tax Planning Checklist, Appendix 4.

Estimated tax payments must be made by estates for taxable year commencing more than two years after decedent's death and by trusts. Some exceptions apply, including waiver of estimated tax payments where the tax for the fiscal period is less than an amount set by regulations which changes from time to time. See *Fiduc. Rev.*, June 1987, p. 3, for a discussion of estimated tax payment requirements.

## § 14.11 FIDUCIARY'S INCOME

Fees of non-professional fiduciaries who serve in isolated instances will not be treated as self employment income unless estate assets include a trade or business, the fiduciary actively participates in the operation of the trade or business and the fees are related to the operation of the trade or business. However, extensive management activities for an estate over a long period of time may alter this conclusion. See Rev. Rul. 58-5 1958-1 CB 322 and Internal Revenue Code. Regs. 1.1402(c)-7. Although such a personal representative's commissions are taxable income, in usual circumstances inclusion on Form 1040, Schedule SE, is not required.

# Chapter 15

# ACCOUNTING



## § 15.1 DUTY TO ACCOUNT

One of the most important duties of a personal representative in the settlement of an estate is the accounting of his administration of the assets of the decedent.[1] The account may be filed any time after four months from the first complete advertisement of the grant of letters. The filing of an account may be enforced after six months from the first com-

**§ 15.1**

**1.** If the personal representative dies before he has filed an account, then his personal representative must file the account for him (PEF 3324), but he is responsible only for that which he actually received from his decedent (*Pittsburgh Coal v. Newcomer*, 365 Pa. 462). Where the personal representative died after signing the account but before audit, his personal representative may be given authority to make distribution of the original estate: PEF 3324; *Weihenmayer Est.*, 7 Fiduc. Rep. 185. The same is true of the guardian of an incapacitated personal representative: PEF 3324; see *Rosenstein Est.*, 7 Fiduc. Rep. 181.

The accounts of a deceased executor and of an administrator d.b.n.c.t.a. should not be combined: cf. *Hipple Est.*, 10 Fiduc. Rep. 206; *Schmucker Est.*, 10 Fiduc. Rep. 348.

plete advertisement of the grant of letters, except in the circumstances outlined in Section 15.4, and may be directed to be filed by the court at any time (PEF 3501.1), regardless of whether there has been prior application for it: *Rose Est.*, 25 Fiduc. Rep. 428. There can be no order to pay a legacy unless an accounting has preceded the order and there has been an award of the legacy: *Vassilakis v. Vassilakis*, 371 Pa. 268; *Kreiders Est.*, 21 Erie 114; *Plogstert Est.*, 350 Pa. 474. Any distribution made prior to the accounting will be at the risk of the personal representative. See Section 15.3.

The accounting is for the benefit of creditors and distributees so that they may know what the fiduciary has received and what disbursements he has made during the period of his administration.

If the personal representative neglects or refuses to file his account, any person having a direct interest in the estate—as heir, beneficiary or creditor[2]—may file a petition with the court requesting the delinquent personal representative to file an accurate account of his administration. A divorced spouse has standing under a post-nuptial agreement to petition for an accounting. *Wedler Est.*, 22 Fiduc. Rep. 2d 7. The personal representative may be cited to account even though he has not taken out formal letters of administration, provided that he was named in the decedent's will and has performed duties of administration: *Hart Est.*, 48 D. & C. 101. If a personal representative delays in filing his account, he is liable for any damage caused by delay: *Stephen Est.*, 320 Pa. 97. If the personal representative states that he is unable to file an accurate account because of the complexities of the estate, the court may appoint an auditor to state an account for him: PEF 751(3); *Griffith Est.*, 2 Fiduc. Rep. 487; *Smith Est.*, 324 Pa. 575; *Fiduc. Rev.* Nov. 1972. Should the personal representative refuse to comply with a mandate of the court to file an accurate account, he may be removed. See Section 3.15; PEF 3182. His person may also be attached, in which case

§ **15.1**

**2.** A petitioning creditor must make out a prima facie claim to be entitled to an accounting: *Lightner Est.*, 144 Pa. 273; *Centrella Est.*, 10 Fiduc. Rep. 344; cf. *Cohen Est.*, 16 Fiduc. Rep. 322.

the constitutional privilege against self-incrimination does not extend to him as a representative of an artificial entity. *Baehr Est.*, 10 Fiduc. Rep. 2d 393, annot. *Fiduc. Rev.* Feb. 1991, aff'd in part, 408 Pa. Super. 172. The interested parties, however, may lose their right to cite a personal representative to file an account when they have been guilty of prejudicial delay: *McGrann v. Allen*, 291 Pa. 574; *Mulligan Est.*, 16 Fiduc. Rep. 657, aff'd, 426 Pa. 374.

The filing of an account may be compelled by a co-executor. See *Best Est.*, 8 Fiduc. Rep. 235, where the widow co-executor had all the files and the attorney co-executor desired to present his claim for services. And a beneficiary may compel an accounting even though his interest will not materialize until the executor sells property which the will allows the executor to use as long as he desires: *Logan Est.*, 56 Lanc. 53. For filing of objections where the person who forced filing of the account dies prior to audit, see *Bernard Trust*, 8 Fiduc. Rep. 525.

For forms to compel accounting, see Aker, PEF Code Annot., § 3501.1; 8 Dunlap-Hanna, Pennsylvania Forms § 76.02.

## § 15.2 TIME AND PLACE OF FILING

The personal representative may be cited to file an account with the clerk of orphans' court (PEF 745 and 3502) at the expiration of six months from the first complete advertisement of the original grant of letters: PEF 3501.1; Sup. Ct. O.C. Rule 6.4. See Section 6.2. While an interested party or creditor can demand an accounting anytime after six months (PEF 3501.1; *Mane Est.*, 12 Fiduc. Rep. 522; *Lightner Est.*, 144 Pa. 273), in practice the accounting frequently is delayed until the completion of administration. The personal representative may not file the account within four months unless directed by the court. The court may direct an accounting within six months when an administration pendente lite has been raised and a will contest or litigation involving the estate was settled within six months: see *Fiduc. Rev.* Aug. 1959, p. 4. An administrator de bonis non may file his account at any time provided four months have expired since the original grant of letters: PEF 3501.1; cf. Sup. Ct. O.C. Rule 6.4. For accounting in a federal court, see *Fiduc. Rev*. Dec. 1962; cf. *Hamilton Est*., 17 Fiduc. Rep. 96.

Once the account has been filed, audit and confirmation by the orphans' court division take place on dates fixed by local rules of court: PEF 910. The clerk of the orphans' court division is required to advertise the accounts at least once a week during the two weeks immediately preceding the time for presentation: PEF 745.

If the decedent was an inmate of a state-owned mental hospital or other institution where he was maintained in part by the Commonwealth, a copy of the account of the fiduciary must be filed also with the Department of Revenue: Sup. Ct. O.C. Rule 6.7; cf. PEF 3393.

If the decedent was a veteran of any war, or was the minor child of such veteran, and if such veteran or his minor child had been receiving benefits of compensation or insurance or other gratuity from the United States Government, a copy of the account of the fiduciary must be filed also with the United States Veterans' Administration or its successor: Sup. Ct. O.C. Rule 6.8.

## § 15.3 DISTRIBUTION BEFORE ACCOUNTING

A personal representative may distribute assets of the decedent's estate before he files his account, but he does so at his own risk. See Section 16.2; PEF 3532; *Adamo Est*., 2 Fiduc. Rep. 618. Such distribution should not be made unless the estate is solvent and the distribution involved is either a specific bequest or made with the assent of the next of kin and residuary legatees. Distribution is also at the risk of the personal representative if the account is prematurely filed: *Hayden Est*., 28 Dist. 39. However, the personal representative who makes a premature distribution is not liable to any claimant against the decedent who has not given to him written notice of his claim within one year after the first complete advertisement of the grant of letters or thereafter but prior to such distribution: PEF 3532. As to the necessity for written notice, see PEF 3384(a); *Fiduc. Rev.* Sept. 1967, p. 4. An executor who makes distribution before audit in reliance upon a distributee's assignment risks a surcharge if the assignment is later attacked: *Coffey Est.*, 8 Fiduc. Rep. 192, annot. *Fiduc. Rev.* May 1958, p. 3. See Section 16.18. In *Weber v. Stroudsburg Security Trust Co.*, 18 D. & C. 2d 348, a citation to enforce delivery of assets was dismissed, the matter being deferred until audit. Special care must be exercised with regard to distribution of stock and dividends therefrom during the period of administration, especially when the will has made a general bequest of stock: *Watson Est.*, 15 Fiduc. Rep. 120, annot. *Fiduc. Rev.* Feb. 1965, p. 3.

## § 15.4 WHEN ACCOUNTING IS NOT REQUIRED

There are several situations in which an accounting is not required:

(1) *Family settlement.* If a family settlement has been made (see Chapter 2), a party to the settlement cannot later compel an accounting: *Edelman Est.*, 336 Pa. 4; *Eisenbach Est.*, 4 Fiduc. Rep. 51. But unpaid creditors not a party to the settlement are still entitled to an accounting: *Stein Est.*, 42 Lanc. 441, 45 York 73; *Becker Est.*, 55 Lanc. 115; *Bennicas Est.*, 1 Fiduc. Rep. 643.

(2) *Family settlement presumed.* If the demand for an accounting is delayed unreasonably and without valid explanation, a family settlement will be presumed: *Cannon Est.*, 330 Pa. 513; *Kondraskas Est.*, 1 Fiduc. Rep. 318. Clearly, however, this is no reason for failure to file an account at the proper time. Note that the Attorney General is entitled to notice of *all* proceedings involving pecuniary charitable gifts, except those of $25,000 or less, paid in full: *Pruner Est.*, 390 Pa. 529; *Garrison Est.*, 391 Pa. 234; *Fiduc. Rev.* April 1958; Sup Ct. O.C. Rule 5.5. Presumably this includes notice of a family agreement where the will involves charitable gifts, even

though the charity may be in existence and a party to the agreement: see *Little Est.*, 403 Pa. 534.

(3) *If the entire estate goes to a beneficiary who is also the sole personal representative, and if there are no unpaid creditors and taxes have been paid.*

(4) *If formal proceedings for the settlement of the estate are waived by the agreement of all parties in interest.* If such an agreement is contemplated, it is good practice for the personal representative to exhibit his account and let all parties in interest append their approval. In addition, Act 135 of 1976 amended PEF 3532 to add:

"(c) *Record of risk distributions.*—The personal representative may file with the clerk receipts, releases and refunding agreements which he may have received from persons to whom he has made a risk distribution, or from other parties in interest. Receipts, releases and refunding agreements so filed shall be indexed under the name of the estate. Their acceptance shall not be construed as court approval of any act of administration or distribution therein reflected."

(5) *Small estates.* If the estate of decedent does not exceed $25,000, exclusive of real estate and wages, salary or employee benefits paid under PEF 3101, the court on petition of any party in interest may direct distribution of the property to the persons entitled to it. See generally Chapter 2. However, this statutory form of distribution does not become final for a year, and a petition to revoke may be filed by any party in interest in the meantime: PEF 3102; *Trusky Est.*, 52 Lanc. 31. See Aker, PEF Code Annot. § 3102, for form of petition. Note that this procedure is available whether or not there has been a grant of letters to a personal representative.

If the gross estate *real and personal* does not exceed $25,000, the court, on petition of the personal representative with an annexed account and after the expiration of one year from the first complete advertisement of the grant of letters, may approve the distribution theretofore made, order distribution of assets not theretofore distributed and discharge the personal representative from future liability without the expense of a formal accounting, provided that there is satisfactory proof of notice to all known parties in interest: PEF 3531; *Goldberg Est.*, 4 Fiduc. Rep. 264. For form of petition with attached account, see Partridge-Remick, O.C. Practice § 15.09, Form 9.

## § 15.5 NOTICE TO PARTIES IN INTEREST

The personal representative is required to send written notice that he has filed his account to the following:[1]

(1) Every unpaid claimant who has given written notice of his claim to the personal representative or to the personal representative's attorney,[2]

(2) Every person known to the personal representative to have an interest in the estate as a beneficiary, heir or next of kin.[3]

The personal representative should give at least ten days' notice prior to the date fixed for the audit of the account:

---

**§ 15.5**

**1.** The notice may be sent by mail. If such notice is properly addressed and stamped, it is presumed to have been received and the presumption is not overcome by mere denial: *Wagman v. Paradise Fire Ins. Co.*, 65 York 109; cf. *Fiduc. Rev.* Oct. 1974, p. 3; for a suggested form of notice, see Appendix 6, infra.

**2.** PEF 3503. If the personal representative did not receive such notice, then the public advertisement of the filing of the account by the clerk of the orphans' court division constitutes constructive notice to the claimant and the account will not be reopened on petition of such a claimant at a later date: *Mack Est.*, 111 Pa. Super 20. For acts which are the equivalent of the giving of written notice, see PEF 3384(b). Oral notice is not adequate: cf. *Byer Est.*, 17 Fiduc. Rep. 472, annot. *Fiduc. Rev.* Sept. 1967, p. 4.

**3.** PEF 3503; Sup. Ct. O.C. Rule 6.3. Note that the beneficiaries need not give written notice of their interests. In at least one county the notice must include a statement of any material questions to be passed upon by the court and copies of material instruments involved: *Draper Est.*, 6 Fiduc. Rep. 105. For adequacy of notice to persons in military service outside of continental United States, see *Steingrabe, Minor*, 26 Fiduc. Rep. 540. Notice should be given to known creditors even though they have not given written notice of their claims.

Sup. Ct. O.C. Rule 5.3. By local rules, 15 or 20 days advance notice of audit may be required. Special circumstances may alter the requirements. In *Kelsey Est.*, 1 Fiduc. Rep. 267, ten day's notice was held to be insufficient for notice where the recipient was an employee of the army in Berlin. It is usually required by local rule that a report be made to the court of the method, manner and date of giving such notice.

The Attorney General must be given notice of proceedings involving charitable trusts: Sup. Ct. O.C. Rule 5.5. In the absence of a local rule to the contrary, no notice is required with respect to pecuniary legacies to charities of $25,000 or less which have been or will be paid in full. Although such notice would appear to be surplusage where a charitable beneficiary is in existence and represented, it will be of greater importance where a present distribution is to be made to unnamed charities or to a charitable corporation to be formed: see *Fiduc. Rev.* April 1958. However, possible distributees of charitable funds are not parties in interest entitled to special notice of audit: *Nevil Est.*, 414 Pa. 122.

The Commonwealth should be notified if it may have an interest as statutory heir: *Landell Est.*, 7 Fiduc. Rep. 273.

If a beneficiary's whereabouts are unknown, or if there is doubt as to his existence, then notice should be given in the manner directed by the court: PEF 751(6); Sup. Ct. O.C. Rule 13.1. In such a situation, notice by public advertisement will probably be sufficient: *Barry Est.*, 1 Fiduc. Rep. 327.

When a personal representative has failed to comply with the mandatory rules of notice set forth above, his account should not be confirmed (Sup. Ct. O.C. Rule 6.3) and, if confirmed, may be opened on petition of any party in interest when it appears that such party has been prejudiced by the absence of proper notice: *Dukinas Est.*, 61 D. & C. 24; cf. *Liggett Trust*, 19 Fiduc. Rep. 510, annot. *Fiduc. Rev.* Sept. 1969. Note, however, that other parties in interest who received proper notice may not participate in the reopening of the account: *Kelsey Est.*, 1 Fiduc. Rep. 267.

Minors and other parties in interest who are legally incompetent and are not represented by a fiduciary may be represented in the accounting proceedings by a guardian or trustee ad litem if the court deems it necessary: PEF 751(6); *Blatz Trust*, 10 Fiduc. Rep. 416. When not so represented the adjudication may not be binding: *Sautter Est.*, 26 Fiduc. Rep. 569.

## § 15.6 PARTIAL ACCOUNTS

The personal representative usually files only one account—"the first and final account"; but if some assets remain for future accounting, then the first account is only partial and the "first and partial account" may be followed by a "second and partial account" or a "second and final" account.[1] Partial accounts of the entire administration to date, or of a controversial transaction only, are advisable if final accounts will be delayed because of the complexities of an estate or because lengthy administration is required: PEF 762; *Cassatt Est.*, 105 Pa. Super. 14. The device of a so-called "brief account" has been approved by the courts as a "practical and economical way" to decide particular questions such as matters of apportionment of receipts from shares of stock: *Spear Trust*, 15 Fiduc. Rep. 94, annot. *Fiduc. Rev.* April 1965, p. 3. Confirmation of partial accounts by the court is conclusive only as to what they contain. See 25 Temple L.Q. 314, 318; *McLellan Ap.*, 76 Pa. 231. For problems which can arise in regard to partial and supplemental accounts, see *Grote Trust (No. 2)*, 2 Fiduc. Rep. 2d 360, annot. *Fiduc. Rev.* Dec. 1982, p. 4. The court's direction to file a supplemental account is interlocutory and not appealable: *LaRocca Trust*, 485 Pa. 236.

If a disagreement arises among co-fiduciaries, it sometimes is advisable to file a partial account and have the court resolve the dispute: cf. PEF 3328.

---

**§ 15.6**

**1.** Subsequent accountings can be avoided in many cases by setting aside a fund to meet anticipated claims and taxes. See Section 16.33.

## § 15.7 FORM OF ACCOUNTING

The form of an account of a personal representative is a matter usually regulated by local rules of court. Such rules therefore must be consulted and complied with. This section sets forth the Supreme Court rules of general applicability and a form that may serve as a model: see *Fiduc. Rev.* Dec. 1973.

The account should be prepared on letter-size paper, typewritten, signed by all those accounting and sworn to by at least one of them. If a co-executor disapproves of any item or items, he should make a note of it; if he fails to do so, his signature and affidavit on the account may estop him from filing objections: *Steen Est.*, 2 Fiduc. Rep. 495; *Waltersdorff Est.*, 70 York 85; cf. *Johnson Est.*, 8 Fiduc. Rep. 353. The account should not be signed by the attorney for the accountants.

The following is Rule 6.1 of the Supreme Court Orphans' Court Rules and Uniform Fiduciary Accounting Principles and Model Account Formats 1983:

> "Accounts shall conform to the following rules:
>
> (a) The dates of all receipts and disbursements, the sources of the receipts, and the persons to whom disbursements are made and the purpose thereof shall be stated except that where a number of payments have been received from the same source or disbursed to the same recipient for the same purpose over a period of time, such receipts or disbursements need not be itemized but may be stated in total amounts only with dates of beginning and ending of the period covered.
>
> (b) Except where otherwise provided by a special order of the local Court in a particular case, items of administration, distribution, receipts, disbursements, principal, and income shall be separately stated.
>
> (c) Assets held by the accountant on the date of filing the account shall be separately itemized.

(d) Testamentary assets shall be segregated from appointive assets.

(e) Each local Court may adopt further rules not inconsistent with the foregoing regulating the form of accounts.

(f) Accounts may be prepared and filed in substantial conformity with either (i) the rules prescribed or forms approved by the local Court or (ii) any form approved by the Supreme Court of this Commonwealth—whichever the accountant may elect."[2]

(g) The Uniform Fiduciary Accounting Principles and accompanying commentaries and illustrations recommended by the Committee on National Fiduciary Accounting Standards in collaboration with the National Center for State Courts are approved as an elaboration of the requirements of this rule. Reference may be made to them for determination of the adequacy of a particular account. The model Account formats attached thereto are the approved forms for purposes of paragraph (f)(ii) of this Rule in lieu of all forms heretofore approved. [Added January 1, 1984].

## UNIFORM FIDUCIARY ACCOUNTING PRINCIPLES AND MODEL ACCOUNT FORMATS 1983

Report of Fiduciary Accounting Standards Committee

Scope of the Project

"Fiduciary Accounting" does not have one commonly understood meaning. In a broad sense, it can mean the entire process whereby a fiduciary—normally a personal representative, trustee or guardian—communicates information on an ongoing basis regarding his administration of a fund and periodically justifies his administration to the parties in interest and, perhaps, to a court. In another sense, it may be

---

§ **15.7**

**2.** *Grote Trust*, 1 Fiduc. Rep. 2d 173, 179, dismissed objection to account conforming to local rules.

the process whereby a fiduciary—here more often a trustee—periodically keeps parties in interest currently informed of transactions and investment policies being followed.

In a narrower sense, to which this report is directed, a fiduciary accounting may refer to the statement prepared by a fiduciary at the close of his administration of a fund (or at some appropriate intermediate stage) to reflect transactions that have occurred and to be presented to the parties in interest as part of a process whereby the fiduciary seeks discharge from liability for the events disclosed.

There is undoubtedly much that can be accomplished to improve the general administration of estates and trusts. A broad study of our basic fiduciary accounting models could lead to dramatic change in the future. But such a study as well as general questions regarding what constitutes fair and adequate procedures in a large variety of circumstances remain beyond the scope of this project.

*Advantages to Be Gained from Uniformity*

The manner in which a fiduciary records receipts and disbursements and gains and losses from investment during the course of administration is commonly dictated by local practice, court rule or statute. In many jurisdictions there is a lack of clarity or consistency regarding the form and content of such an accounting. A uniform form of account and the creation of guiding principles of accounting would be a most helpful development.

Through the development of a uniform form of account the forms that are now in use can be improved. It would not be expected that immediate change to a model account format would be required of corporate fiduciaries with substantial investments in computer programs but ultimately, standardization of forms will permit more effective utilization of machine record keeping techniques and significant cost savings. Standards for acceptable accounting practices will provide needed guidelines.

Since proposed standards can be illustrated by example, we have focused on form and content of a statement of transactions, recognizing that a proper form of account is important whether the account is to be presented in court or employed as part of an informal settlement process between a fiduciary and beneficiaries.

*Performance Accounting Distinguished*

No effort has been made to standardize that kind of fiduciary accounting which is directed toward an analysis of the investment performance of a fund. Accounts of this type are often distributed to beneficiaries by corporate fiduciaries at regular intervals, generally one year or less, and contain statements of receipts, disbursements and assets on hand at the close of the period. The statement of assets customarily discloses additional information such as cost or tax basis, current market value, current yield expressed sometimes both in dollars and as a percentage of cost or market, and may show the distribution of investments among various categories such as bonds and stocks with subdivision of stocks by industry. These statements can be immensely valuable, both as an aid to the fiduciary in analyzing the structure of the portfolio, and for the information of beneficiaries. Indeed, because this form of report reflects and analyzes current investment policy, it may be described as more positive and forward looking than an unrationalized account of past transactions which is commonly used as a basis for discharge from responsibility for past acts. However, accountings of this type are fundamentally different in purpose from the traditional concept of discharge accounting by a fiduciary. There are inherent limitations that tend to restrict their use to professional institutionalized fiduciaries, and the need for establishment of standards appears to be less pressing than in the conventional area of discharge accounting.

Basic Objectives and General Standards of Fiduciary Accounting

The fundamental objective of an account should be to provide essential and useful information in a meaningful form to the parties interested in the accounting process. It is also important that the account should be sufficiently simple to enable its preparation without unreasonable expense to the fund, or undue distraction from the on-going administration of the estate. Finally, although the parties should understand the nature of the accounting process and the need to protect their interests, the relationship of trust and confidence existing between the fiduciary and beneficiaries is itself important and the account should not be presented in an adversary format that will unnecessarily impair this relationship.

*Competing Goals*

Maximum clarity, full disclosure and complete description and explanation of all events to be disclosed appear to be standards that all would accept. But, in combination, they may present many difficulties. For example, clarity may be obscured by the detail that is required for a disclosure that omits nothing. Full explanation of all investment decisions might produce a massive document that few beneficiaries would read. On balance, a set of flexible principles keyed to the standard of good faith supports the utmost protection of the parties and permits accounting standards to change and mature as circumstances require.

Fiduciary accounts rarely will be identical. In addition to the predictable variables of the size and composition of the assets, the period covered and the position of those interested, the significance of particular issues in a controversy may be illuminated by special accounting treatment of some portion of a fund. This suggests that a fiduciary should have enough flexibility to state an account in the manner best adapted to the particular circumstances and discourages any effort to prescribe a totally rigid format. Accordingly, the following principles are suggested as general standards for fiduciary accounting.

*Model Accounts*

Sample Executor's and Trustee's accounts are attached to illustrate the application of the suggested standards for fiduciary accounting.

Fiduciary Accounting Principles

I. ACCOUNTS SHOULD BE STATED IN A MANNER THAT IS UNDERSTANDABLE BY PERSONS WHO ARE NOT FAMILIAR WITH PRACTICES AND TERMINOLOGY PECULIAR TO THE ADMINISTRATION OF ESTATES AND TRUSTS.

*Commentary:* In order for an account to fulfill its basic function of communication, it is essential that it be stated in a manner that recognizes that the interested parties are not usually familiar with fiduciary accounts. It is neither practical nor desirable to require that accounts be tailored to meet individual disabilities of particular parties but any account should be capable of being understood by a person of average intelligence, literate in English, and familiar with basic financial terms who has read it with care and attention.

Problems arising from terminology or style are usually a reflection of the fact that people who become versed in a particular form of practice tend to forget that terms which are familiar and useful to them may convey nothing to someone else or may even be affirmatively misleading. For example, the terms "debit" and "credit" are generally incomprehensible to people with no knowledge of bookkeeping and many people who are familiar with them in other contexts would assume that in the context of fiduciary accounting, the receipt of an item is a "credit" to the fund rather than a "debit" to the fiduciary.

While the need for concise presentation makes a certain amount of abbreviation both acceptable and necessary, uncommon abbreviation of matters essential to an understanding of the account should be avoided or explained.

No position is taken for or against the use of direct print-outs from machine accounting systems. The quality of the accounts produced by these systems varies widely in the extent to which they can be understood by persons who are not familiar with them. To endorse or object to a direct print-out because it is produced by machine from previously stored data would miss the essential point by focusing attention upon the manner of preparation rather than the product.

II. A FIDUCIARY ACCOUNT SHALL BEGIN WITH A CONCISE SUMMARY OF ITS PURPOSE AND CONTENT.

*Commentary:* Very few people can be expected to pay much attention to a document unless they have some understanding of its general purpose and its significance to them. Even with such an understanding, impressions derived from the first page or two will often determine whether the rest is read. The use that is made of these pages is therefore of particular significance.

The cover page should disclose the nature and function of the account. While a complete explanation of the significance of the account and the effect of its presentation upon the rights of the parties is obviously impractical for inclusion at this point, there should be at least a brief statement identifying the fiduciary and the subject matter, noting the importance of examining the account and giving an address where more information can be obtained.

It is assumed that the parties would also have enough information from other sources to understand the nature of their relationship to the fund (e.g., residuary legatee, life tenant, remainderman), the function of the account, and the obligation of the fiduciary to supply further relevant information upon request. It is also assumed that *notice* will be given of any significant procedural considerations such as limitation on the time within which objections must be presented. This would normally be provided by prior or contemporaneous memoranda, correspondence or discussions.

A summary of the account shall also be presented at the outset. This summary, organized as a table of contents, shall indicate the order of the details presented in the account and shall show separate totals for the aggregate of the assets on hand at the beginning of the accounting period; transactions during the period; and the assets remaining on hand at the end of the period. Each entry in the summary shall be supported by a schedule in the account that provides the details on which the summary is based.

III. A FIDUCIARY ACCOUNT SHALL CONTAIN SUFFICIENT INFORMATION TO PUT THE INTERESTED PARTIES ON NOTICE AS TO ALL SIGNIFICANT TRANSACTIONS AFFECTING ADMINISTRATION DURING THE ACCOUNTING PERIOD.

*Commentary:* The presentation of the information in an account shall allow an interested party to follow the progress of the fiduciary's administration of assets during the accounting period without reference to an inventory or earlier accounting that is not included in the current account.

An account is not complete if it does not itemize assets on hand at the beginning of the accounting period.

*Illustrations:*

3.1 The first account for a decedent's estate or a trust should detail the items received by the fiduciary and for which he is responsible. It should not simply refer to the total amount of an inventory filed elsewhere or assets described in a schedule attached to a deed of trust.

3.2 In later accounts for an estate or trust, the opening balance should not simply refer to the total value of principal on hand as shown in detail in the prior account, but should list each item separately.

Instead of retyping the complete list of assets in the opening balance, the accountant may prefer to attach as an exhibit a copy of the inventory, closing balance from last account, etc., as appropriate.

Transactions shall be described in sufficient detail to give interested parties notice of their purpose and effect. It should be recognized that too much detail may be counterproductive to making the account understandable. In accounts covering long periods or dealing with extensive assets, it is usually desirable to consolidate information. For instance, where income from a number of securities is being accounted for over a long period of time, a statement of the total dividends received on each is more readily understandable and easier to check for completeness than a chronological listing of all dividends received.

Although detail should generally be avoided for routine transactions, it will often be necessary to a proper understanding of an event that is somewhat out of the ordinary.

*Illustrations:*

3.3 Extraordinary appraisal costs should be shown separately and explained.

3.4 Interest and penalties in connection with late filing of tax returns should be shown separately and explained.

3.5 An extraordinary allocation between principal and income such as apportionment of proceeds of property acquired on foreclosure should be separately stated and explained.

3.6 Computation of a formula marital deduction gift involving non-probate assets should be explained.

IV. A FIDUCIARY ACCOUNT SHALL INCLUDE BOTH CARRYING VALUES—REPRESENTING THE VALUE OF ASSETS AT ACQUISITION BY THE FIDUCIARY—AND CURRENT VALUES AT THE BEGINNING AND END OF THE ACCOUNTING PERIOD.

*Commentary:* In order for transactions to be reported on a consistent basis, an appropriate carrying value for assets must be chosen and employed consistently.

The carrying value of an asset should reflect its value at the time it is acquired by the fiduciary (or a predecessor fiduciary). When such a value is not precisely determinable, the figure used should reflect a thoughtful decision by the fiduciary. For assets owned by a decedent, inventory values or estate tax values—generally reflective of date of death values—would be appropriate. Assets received in kind by a trustee from a settlor or an inter-vivos trust should be carried at their value at the time of receipt. For assets purchased during the administration of the fund, cost would normally be used. Use of Federal income tax bases for carrying value is acceptable when basis is reasonably representative of real values at the time of acquisition. Use of tax basis as a carrying value under other circumstances could be affirmatively misleading to beneficiaries and therefore is not appropriate.

In the Model Account, carrying value is referred to as "fiduciary acquisition value." The Model Account establishes the initial carrying value of assets as their value at date of death for inventoried assets, date of receipt for subsequent receipts and cost for investments.

Carrying value would not normally be adjusted for depreciation.

Except for adjustments that occur normally under the accounting system in use, carrying values should generally be continued unchanged through successive accounts and assets should not be arbitrarily "written up" or "written down." In some circumstances, however, with proper disclosure and explanation, carrying value may be adjusted.

*Illustrations:*

4.1 Carrying values based on date of death may be adjusted to reflect changes on audit of estate or inheritance tax returns.

4.2 Where appropriate under applicable local law, a successor fiduciary may adjust the carrying value of assets to reflect values at the start of his administration.

4.3 Assets received in kind in satisfaction of a pecuniary legacy should be carried at the value used for purposes of distribution.

Though essential for accounting purposes, carrying values are commonly misunderstood by laymen as being a representation of actual values. To avoid this, the account should include both current values and carrying values.

The value of assets at the beginning and ending of each accounting period is necessary information for the evaluation of investment performance. Therefore, the account should show current values at the start of the period for all assets whose carrying values were established in a prior accounting period.

*Illustrations:*

4.4 The opening balance of the first account of a testamentary trustee will usually contain assets received in kind from the executor. Unless the carrying value was written up at the time of distribution (e.g., 4.2 or 4.3 supra) these assets will be carried at a value established during the executor's administration. The current value at the beginning of the accounting period should also be shown.

4.5 An executor's first account will normally carry assets at inventory (date of death) values or cost. No separate listing of current values at the beginning of the accounting period is necessary.

Current values should also be shown for all assets on hand at the close of the accounting period. The date on which current values are determined shall be stated and shall be the last day of the accounting period, or a date as close thereto as reasonably possible.

Current values should be shown in a column parallel to the column of carrying values. Both columns should be totalled.

In determining current values for assets for which there is no readily ascertainable current value, the source of the value stated in the account shall be explained. The fiduciary shall make a good faith effort to determine realistic values but should not be expected to incur expenses for appraisals or similar costs when there is no reason to expect that the resulting information will be of practical consequence to the administration of the estate or the protection of the interests of the parties.

*Illustrations:*

4.6 When an asset is held under circumstances that make it clear that it will not be sold (e.g., a residence held for use of a beneficiary) the fiduciary's estimate of value would be acceptable in lieu of an appraisal.

4.7 Considerations such as a pending tax audit or offer of the property for sale may indicate the advisability of not publishing the fiduciary's best estimate of value. In such circumstances, a statement that value was fixed by some method such as "per company books", "formula under buy-sell agreement", "300% of assessed value" would be acceptable, but the fiduciary would be expected to provide further information to interested parties upon request.

V. GAINS AND LOSSES INCURRED DURING THE ACCOUNTING PERIOD SHALL BE SHOWN SEPARATELY IN THE SAME SCHEDULE.

*Commentary:* Each transaction involving the sale or other disposition of securities during the accounting period shall be shown as a separate item in one combined schedule of the account indicating the transaction, date, explanation, and any gain or loss.

Although gains and losses from the sale of securities can be shown separately in accounts, the preferred method of presentation is to present this information in a single schedule. Such a presentation provides the most meaningful description of investment performance and will tend to clarify relationships between gains and losses that are deliberately realized at the same time.

VI. THE ACCOUNT SHALL SHOW SIGNIFICANT TRANSACTIONS THAT DO NOT AFFECT THE AMOUNT FOR WHICH THE FIDUCIARY IS ACCOUNTABLE.

*Commentary:* Transactions such as the purchase of an investment, receipt of a stock split or change of corporate name do not alter the total fund for which a fiduciary is accountable but must be shown in order to permit analysis and an understanding of the administration of the fund. These can be best shown in information schedules.

One schedule should list all investments made during the accounting period. It should include those subsequently sold as well as those still on hand. Frequently the same money will be used for a series of investments. Therefore, the schedule should not be totalled in order to avoid giving an exaggerated idea of the size of the fund.

A second schedule (entitled "Changes in Investment Holdings" in the Model Account) should show all transactions affecting a particular security holding such as purchase of additional shares, partial sales, stock splits, change of corporate name, divestment distributions, etc. This schedule, similar to a ledger account for each holding, will reconcile opening and closing entries for particular holdings, explain changes in carrying value and avoid extensive searches through the account for information scattered among other schedules.

# MODEL ESTATE ACCOUNT

IN THE COURT OF COMMON PLEAS OF __________
COUNTY, PA.
ORPHANS' COURT DIVISION
FILE NO. 98765

FIRST AND FINAL ACCOUNT OF
William C. Doe, Executor
For
ESTATE OF JOHN DOE, DECEASED

| | |
|---|---|
| Date of Death: | 11/14/05 |
| Date of Incapacity, if any: | None |
| Date of Executor's Appointment: | 11/24/05 |
| Date of First Complete Advertisement: | 11/27/05 |
| Accounting for the period: | 11/24/05 to 11/30/06 |
| † Gross Estate: | $__________ |

Purpose of Account: The Executor offers this account to acquaint interested parties with the transactions that have occurred during the Administration.

It is important that the Account be carefully examined. Requests for additional information, questions or objections can be discussed with:

[Name of Counsel]
[Address]
[Address]
[Phone Number]
Supreme Court I.D. No. ________

† Some local rules require inclusion of this item.

SUMMARY OF ACCOUNT

| | *Pages* | | |
|---|---|---|---|
| PRINCIPAL | | | |
| Receipts | 3–4 | | $160,488.76 |
| Net Gain on Sales or Disposition | 5 | | 2,662.00 |
| | | | $163,150.76 |
| Less Disbursements: | | | |
| Debts of Decedent | 6 | $ 485.82 | |
| Funeral Expenses | 6 | 1,375.00 | |
| Administration Expenses | 6 | 194.25 | |
| Family Exemption | 6 | 3,500.00 | |
| Federal, State & Local Taxes | 7 | 5,856.83 | |
| Fees and Commissions | 7 | 11,689.64 | −23,101.54 |
| Balance before Distributions | | | $140,049.22 |
| Distributions to Beneficiaries | 8 | | −52,630.00 |
| Principal Balance on Hand | 9 | | $ 87,419.22 |
| For Information: | | | |
| Investments Made | 10 | | |
| Changes in Holdings | 11 | | |
| INCOME | | | |
| Receipts | 12 | | $ 2,513.40 |
| Less Disbursements | 13 | | −178.67 |
| Balance before Distributions | | | $ 32,334.73 |
| Distributions to Beneficiaries | 14 | | −2,334.73 |
| Income Balance on Hand | | | $ .00 |
| COMBINED BALANCE ON HAND | 15 | | $ 87,419.22 |

Verification

PRINCIPAL RECEIPTS

*Assets Listed in Inventory*
*(Valued as of Date of Death)*

| | |
|---|---|
| Real Estate: | |
| Residence | |
| 86 Norwood Road | |
| Philadelphia, PA | $ 50,000.00 |
| Common Stocks | |
| 50 Shs. Best Oil Co. | 5,000.00 |
| 1,000 Shs. Central Trust Co. | 50,850.00 |
| 151 Shs. Electric Data Corp. | 1,887.50 |
| 200 Shs. Home Telephone & Telegraph Co. | $ 25,000.00 |
| 200 Shs. XYZ Corporation | 6,000.00 |
| Personal Effects | |
| Furniture—1 antique chair | 55.00 |
| Furniture—1 antique highboy | $ 2,000.00 |
| Furniture—1 antique side table | 60.00 |
| Jewelry—1 pearl necklace | 515.00 |
| Mutual Funds | |
| 50 Shs. Fabulous Mutual Fund | 1,833.33 |
| | $ 143,200.83 |
| Cash in possession of decedent | 42.54 |
| FORWARD | $ 143,243.37 |

| | | |
|---|---|---|
| FORWARD | | $ 143,243.37 |
| First National Bank—checking account | | 516.93 |
| Prudent Savings Fund Society—savings account | | 2,518.16 |
| | | $ 146,278.46 |
| ADJUSTMENTS TO INVENTORY | | |
| Increased value of common stock upon audit of Federal Estate Tax Return: | | |
| RECEIVED AS: | | |
| 200 Shs. XYZ Corporation | $ 6,000.00 | |
| SHOULD BE: | | |
| 200 Shs. XYZ Corporation | 10,000.00 | 4,000.00 |
| SUBSEQUENT RECEIPTS | | |
| 2/22/06 Proceeds of Sale—Best Oil Co., rights to subscribe received 2/15/06 | | 50.00 |
| 3/12/06 Fabulous Mutual Fund, capital gains dividend received in cash | | 32.50 |
| 5/11/06 Refund of overpayment of 2005 U.S. individual income tax | | 127.80 |
| 9/25/06 From Richard Rose, Ancillary Administrator, net proceeds on sale of oil and gas leases in Jefferson Parish, Louisiana | | 10,000.00 |
| TOTAL PRINCIPAL RECEIPTS | | $ 160,488.76 |

PRINCIPAL GAINS OR LOSSES ON SALES
OR OTHER DISPOSITIONS

| | | | *Gain* | *Loss* |
|---|---|---|---|---|
| 02/07/06 | 100 Shs. Home Telephone & Telegraph Co. | | | |
| | Net Proceeds | 14,025.00 | | |
| | Acquisition Value | 12,500.00 | $ 1,525.00 | |
| 03/15/06 | 1,000 Shs. Central Trust Co. | | | |
| | Net Proceeds | 27,467.00 | | |
| | Acquisition Value | 25,425.00 | 2,042.00 | |
| 03/15/06 | 200 Shs. XYZ Corporation | | | |
| | Net Proceeds | 9,000.00 | | |
| | Acquisition Value | 10,000.00 | | $ 1,000.00 |
| 05/21/06 | 35 Shs. Electric Data Corp. | | | |
| | Net Proceeds | 530.00 | | |
| | Acquisition Value | 437.50 | 92.50 | |
| 07/20/06 | $10,000 U.S. Treasury Bonds, 3% due 07/01/2009 | | | |
| | Net Proceeds | 10,000.00 | | |
| | Acquisition Value | 9,997.50 | 2.50 | |
| TOTALS | | | $ 3,662.00 | $ 1,000.00 |
| | NET GAIN TRANSFERRED TO SUMMARY | | | $ 2,662.00 |

DISBURSEMENTS OF PRINCIPAL

| | | | | |
|---|---|---|---|---|
| DEBTS OF DECEDENT | | | | |
| 01/25/06 | John T. Hill, M.D. | | | |
| | Professional services | | $ 250.00 | |
| 01/25/06 | Thomas Pharmacy | | | |
| | Prescriptions | | 23.82 | |
| 02/01/06 | Sanders Hardware | | | |
| | Purchases per bill dated 12/15/06 | | 56.00 | |
| 04/12/06 | PA Department of Revenue | | | |
| | Balance Final Life Period Income Tax | | 156.00 | $ 485.82 |
| FUNERAL EXPENSES | | | | |
| 01/10/06 | Smith Funeral Home | | | |
| | Services | | $ 1,200.00 | |
| 02/15/06 | Jones Memorials | | | |
| | Grave marker | | 175.00 | 1,375.00 |
| ADMINISTRATION EXPENSES | | | | |
| 11/14/05 | Register of Wills | | | |
| | Probate fees | | $ 72.00 | |
| 02/22/06 | Henry Smith | | | |
| | Appraisal of jewelry and antiques | | 50.00 | |
| 11/16/06 | Arden, Miles & Solomon | | | |
| | Disbursements | $ 56.00 | | |
| | Various miscellaneous affidavits, registered mail, toll telephone charges and other costs | 16.25 | 72.25 | 194.25 |
| FAMILY EXEMPTION | | | | |
| 05/15/04 | Janet Doe | | | 3,500.00 |
| | FORWARD | | | $ 5,555.07 |

| | | | | |
|---|---|---|---|---|
| FEDERAL, STATE & LOCAL TAXES | | | | |
| 02/12/06 | Register of Wills, Agent PA inheritance tax, payment on account | $ 2,105.26 | | |
| | Less 5% discount | −105.26 | $ 2,000.00 | |
| 03/13/06 | Register of Wills, Agent PA inheritance tax | $ 2,501.33 | | |
| | Less payment on account 02/12/06 | −2,105.26 | 396.07 | |
| 08/13/06 | Internal Revenue Service Federal estate tax | | 2,663.29 | |
| 11/15/06 | Internal Revenue Service U.S. fiduciary income tax for fiscal year ending 07/31/06 (allocable to capital gains) | | 283.84 | |
| 11/23/06 | Internal Revenue Service Deficiency in Federal Estate Tax | $ 505.24 | | |
| | Interest 08/14/06 to 11/24/06 | 8.39 | 513.63 | 5,856.83 |
| FEES AND COMMISSIONS | | | | |
| 11/16/06 | Albert Schryver, Esq. Fee as Guardian ad litem | | $ 375.00 | |
| 11/16/06 | William C. Doe | | 6,314.64 | |
| 11/16/06 | Arden, Miles & Solomon Attorney's fees | | 5,000.00 | 11,689.64 |
| | TOTAL DISBURSEMENTS OF PRINCIPAL | | | $ 23,101.54 |

DISTRIBUTIONS OF PRINCIPAL TO BENEFICIARIES

| | | | |
|---|---|---|---|
| | TO: Janet Doe, in satisfaction of gift under Article FIRST of Will | | |
| 12/01/05 | Jewelry — 1 pearl necklace | $ 515.00 | |
| 12/01/05 | Furniture — 1 antique highboy | 2,000.00 | |
| 12/01/05 | Furniture — 1 antique side table | 60.00 | |
| 12/01/05 | Furniture — 1 antique chair | 55.00 | $ 2,630.00 |
| | TO: Janet Doe, in satisfaction of gift under Article SECOND of Will | | |
| 12/01/05 | Residence<br>86 Norwood Road<br>Philadelphia, PA | | 50,000.00 |
| | TOTAL DISTRIBUTIONS OF PRINCIPAL TO BENEFICIARIES | | $ 52,630.00 |

PRINCIPAL BALANCE ON HAND

| | *Value at 11/30/2006* | *Fiduciary Acquisition Value* |
|---|---|---|
| Bonds | | |
| $40,000 U.S. Treasury Bills due 12/14/2006 | $ 39,300.00 | $ 39,300.00 |
| Common Stocks | | |
| 50 Shs. Best Oil Co. | 4,500.00 | 5,000.00 |
| 1,000 Shs. Central Trust Co. | 32,168.76 | 25,425.00 |
| 116 Shs. Electric Data Corp. | 1,684.000 | 1,450.00 |
| 200 Shs. Home Telephone & Telegraph Co. | 16,000.00 | 12,500.00 |
| Mutual Funds | | |
| 50 Shs. Fabulous Mutual Fund | 4,016.17 | 1,833.33 |
| | $ 97,668.93 | $ 85,508.33 |
| CASH (AUTOMATICALLY INVESTED) | 1,910.89 | 1,910.89 |
| TOTAL PRINCIPAL BALANCE ON HAND | $ 99,579.82 | $ 87,419.22 |

PRINCIPAL INVESTMENTS MADE

| | | |
|---|---|---|
| 02/01/06 | $10,000 U.S. Treasury Bonds, 3% due 07/01/2009 | $ 9,997.50 |
| 09/14/06 | $40,000 U.S. Treasury Bills due 12/14/2006 | 39,300.00 |
| TOTAL PRINCIPAL INVESTMENTS MADE | | $ 49,297.50 |

CHANGES IN PRINCIPAL HOLDINGS

| | | | *Account Value* |
|---|---|---|---|
| Central Trust Co. | | | |
| | 1,000 Shs. | Inventoried at | $ 50,850.00 |
| 01/15/06 | 1,000 Shs. | additional received in 2-1 split—par reduced to $2.50 | 0.00 |
| | 2,000 Shs. | | $ 50,850.00 |
| 03/15/06 | 1,000 Shs. | Sold | −25,425.00 |
| | 1,000 Shs. | | $ 25,425.00 |
| Electric Data Corp. | | | |
| | 151 Shs. | Inventoried at | $ 1,887.50 |
| 05/21/06 | 35 Shs. | Sold | −437.50 |
| | 116 Shs. | | $ 1,450.00 |
| Home Telephone & Telegraph Co. | | | |
| | 200 Shs. | Inventoried at | $ 25,000.00 |
| 02/07/06 | 100 Shs. | Sold | −12,500.00 |
| | 100 Shs. | | $ 12,500.00 |
| 03/30/06 | 100 Shs. | additional received in 2–1 split—par reduced to $5 | 0.00 |
| | 200 Shs. | | $ 12,500.00 |

RECEIPTS OF INCOME

| | | |
|---|---|---|
| Best Oil Co. | | |
| Dividend 50 Shs. | | |
| 01/02/06 to 10/02/06 | | $ 20.00 |
| Central Trust Co. | | |
| 01/15/06 – Dividend 2,000 Shs. | $ 600.00 | |
| Dividend 1,000 Shs. | | |
| 04/13/06 to 10/15/06 | 900.00 | 1,500.00 |
| Electric Data Corp. | | |
| Dividend 151 Shs. | | |
| 12/29/05 to 03/30/06 | $ 30.20 | |
| Dividend 116 Shs. | | |
| 06/29/06 to 09/28/06 | 23.20 | 53.40 |
| Fabulous Mutual Fund | | |
| Dividend 50 Shs. | | |
| 03/14/06 to 09/12/06 | | 140.00 |
| Home Telephone & Telegraph Co. | | |
| 02/01/06 – Dividend 200 Shs. | $ 225.00 | |
| Dividend 200 Shs. | | |
| 05/01/06 to 11/01/06 | | |
| (after stock split) | 450.00 | 675.00 |
| U.S. Treasury Bonds, 3% due 07/01/2009 | | |
| 06/29/06 – Interest $10,000 | $ 150.00 | |
| Less: accrued interest paid | | |
| on purchase 02/1/06 | −25.00 | 125.00 |
| TOTAL RECEIPTS OF INCOME | | $ 2,513.40 |

DISBURSEMENTS OF INCOME

| | | |
|---|---|---|
| 11/15/06 | Internal Revenue Service | |
| | U.S. fiduciary income tax for fiscal | |
| | year ending 07/31/06 (allocable to income) | $ 53.00 |
| | To be paid: | |
| | William C. Doe | |
| | Executor's income commission | |
| | 5% on $2,513.40 | 125.67 |
| | TOTAL DISBURSEMENTS OF INCOME | $ 178.67 |

DISTRIBUTIONS OF INCOME TO BENEFICIARIES

| | | | |
|---|---|---|---|
| | TO: Sharon Doe | | |
| 11/16/06 | Cash | $ | 1,167.36 |
| | TO: William C. Doe, Trustee under Article FOURTH (A) for Walter Doe | | |
| 11/16/06 | Cash | | 1,167.37 |
| | TOTAL DISTRIBUTIONS OF INCOME TO BENEFICIARIES | $ | 2,334.73 |

_______________________________

William C. Doe, Executor of the
Will of John Doe, Deceased

VERIFICATION

WILLIAM C. DOE, Executor of the Will of JOHN DOE, Deceased, hereby declares under oath that he has fully and faithfully discharged the duties of his office; that the foregoing First and Final Account is true and correct and fully discloses all significant transactions occurring during the accounting period; that all known claims against the Estate have been paid in full; that, to his knowledge, there are no claims outstanding against the Estate; that all taxes presently due from the Estate have been paid; and that the grant of Letters Testamentary and the first complete advertisement thereof occurred more than four months before the filing of the foregoing First and Final Account.

This statement is made subject to penalties of 18 Pa. C.S. Section 4904 relating to unsworn falsification to authorities.

_______________________________

WILLIAM C. DOE

Dated: ______________________

## § 15.8 ALLOCATION OF INCOME—CHANGING FRACTION

Whenever distributions have been made on account of distributive shares during the period of the estate administration, the allocation of income among the distributees can become unfair unless income is adjusted to reflect changes of the principal shares held for the distributees, and this is especially true as the undistributed assets fluctuate in value. Consequently when equity demands it, personal representatives have employed the changing fraction method of accounting.

In *Greenfield Est.*, 484 Pa. 141, aff'g 28 Fiduc. Rep. 314, it was held that the executors properly "used the 'changing fraction' method of allocation, which allocated appreciation to the electing spouse on the basis of her actual share of the principal fund . . . . Adoption of the fixed fraction rule of convenience for estates with prolonged periods of administration would permit those receiving discretionary advances of their distributive shares to speculate at the expense of those whose full interests . . . remain in the common fund."

See also *Lewis Est.*, 26 Fiduc. Rep. 510 and *Corson Est.*, 1 Fiduc. Rep. 2d 146.

## § 15.9 COMBINATION OF ACCOUNTINGS

PEF 3501.2 permits annexation of a trustee, agency or guardianship account to a personal representative's account. The official comment explains:

> This section parallels Section 7188 [now 7799.1] and covers the case of a trust that terminated in favor of the decedent's estate, a guardianship for a deceased incompetent or ward, and a power of attorney under which the agent held funds at the death of the principal. Although agents do not often file accounts, Section 3501.2 provides a possibly useful procedure

> if an agent desires to do so. Section 3501.2 relieves the fiduciary of the piggybacked account from liability to persons who are entitled to notice of the filing of the account of the personal representative and who receive notice of the annexation, to the same extent as if the piggybacked account had been filed and confirmed separately.

PEF § 5163.1 and § 5533.1 were repealed by Act 182 of 1984, effective October 12, 1984. The following comment was made:

> "Sections 5163.1 and 5533.1 are repealed. Their substance is covered in Sections 304 and 3533 insofar as they relate to responsibility for administration of the distributed property after it is turned over to the receiving fiduciary. It is arguable that the repealed sections would also provide protection for prior acts of administration even though no disclosure of the facts was made. This result seems undesirable. A fiduciary who wishes such protection may file his account or piggyback it onto the account of the receiving fiduciary under Sections 7188 [now 7799.1] or 3501.2"

Pursuant to PEF 7188 [now 7799.1] a personal representative's accounting may be annexed to a trustee's account with similar effect. The Joint State Government Commission comment explains its impact:

"*Comment:* Trustees may receive assets from other fiduciaries as a 'pour-over' under the will of the settlor who created the trust or as an addition from the estate or trust of another decedent or donor. It has been suggested that when no account has been filed for the precedent estate or trust, the receiving fiduciary may assume liability for the administration of the paying fiduciary. This section will provide the receiving fiduciary with a method of presenting the account of the precedent estate or trust to the beneficiaries of his trust and obtaining the same protection he would have received if an account had been filed for the precedent estate or trust. It will also provide a method for obtaining simultaneous approval of an executor's account and the division into marital and residuary shares of a trust to which the probate estate is added without necessity for a separate account of each fund. No attempt is made to deal with the rights of creditors of the precedent estate since they would not be a concern to the receiving fiduciary; Section 3532 gives protection to the executor of a 'pour-over' will against unknown creditors; if there are known creditors, the filing of an account of the precedent estate would probably be indicated."

For combination of trustees' accounts, see *Fiduc. Rev.* Aug. 1977 and Aug. 1978.

For "piggy-backing" the accounting of an incompetent's estate to the personal representative's account, see *Murphy Est.*, 1 Fiduc. Rep. 2d 160.

For combining of executor's account with trustee's account, see *Hutchins Trust,* 29 Fiduc. Rep. 2d 323; *Fiduc. Rev.* Oct. 1981.

## § 15.10 OBJECTIONS TO ACCOUNTS— CONFIRMATION OF ACCOUNTS

Local rules govern the filing of objections[1] to accounts: Sup. Ct. O.C. Rule 6.10. When a co-executor wishes to object to an item in the account he may do so by a notation opposite the item to which he objects: *Steen Estate*, 2 Fiduc. Rep. 495.

The right to file objections is available only to parties in interest and may relate to any item in the account,[2] either

§ **15.10**

**1.** Objection, not exception, is the proper term: *Banks Est.*, 1 Fiduc. Rep. 404.

**2.** The objection should be such that, if sustained, it would have a definite monetary result: *Thompson v. FitzGerald*, 4 Fay. 71, *aff'd*, 344 Pa. 90.

because of failure to include assets or because of wrongful or inaccurate disbursements. See Section 16.4.

For the use of discovery procedures in the Orphans' Court with respect to objections to an account, see *McClatchy Est.*, 85 Montg. 19, dismissing preliminary objections to interrogatories, and holding that there is no requirement that the objectors to an account establish a *prima facie* case before being entitled to file interrogatories. "There can be no doubt that the person attempting to prove an account incorrect must sustain the burden of establishing his position": *Dunn Est.*, 54 D. & C. 2d 760.

When there are no objections, or when the objections are overruled and no exception is taken,[3] it is the usual practice of the courts, by express decree or automatically by rule, to confirm the account without further proceedings.[4] Once the account has been confirmed absolutely, review will be granted on petition within five years[5] and then only if one of the following is shown: (1) a manifest error of law, (2) new matters which have come up subsequent to the confirmation, or (3) the discovery of new evidence that could not have been discovered previously by the use of diligence and care: *Coulter Est.*, 379 Pa. 209. See Section 16.28.

## § 15.11 STATUS REPORT

Effective for decedents dying after July 1, 1984, Supreme Court Orphans' Court Rule 6.12 required the personal representative or estate counsel to file a report of the status of administration. Rule 6.12 was repealed and new

**§ 15.10**

**3.** See Supreme Court O.C. Rule 7.1.

**4.** For additional attorney fees and expenses of successful defense against surcharge action, see *Crawford Est.*, 2 Fiduc. Rep. 2d 229; *Fiduc. Rev.* July 1981, p. 3.

**5.** See PEF 3521; *Stotesbury Est.*, 387 Pa. 591. For computation of five-year period, see *Taylor Est.*, 11 Fiduc. Rep. 149. For extension of five-year period in case of fraud, see 5 Hunter, O.C. Commonplace Book (2d ed.), Review § 8(d).

Rule 6.12 was adopted, effective for decedents dying on or after July 1, 1992. New Rule 6.12 is as follows:

RULE 6.12 STATUS REPORT BY PERSONAL REPRESENTATIVES

(a) Report of uncompleted administration. If administration of an estate has not been completed within two years of the decedent's death, the personal representative or counsel shall file at such time, and annually thereafter until the administration is completed, a report with the Register of Wills showing the date by which the personal representative or counsel reasonably believes administration will be completed.

(b) Report of completed administration. Upon completion of the administration of an estate, the personal representative or his, her or its counsel shall file with the Register of Wills a report showing:

(1) completion of administration of the estate;

(2) whether a formal account was filed with the Orphans' Court;

(3) whether a complete account was informally stated to all parties in interest:

(4) whether final distribution has been completed; and

(5) whether approvals of the account, receipts, joinders and releases have been filed with the Clerk of the Orphans' Court.

(c) Form of report. The report required by this Rule shall be in substantially the prescribed form.

(d) No fee. No fee shall be charged for filing the report required by this Rule.

(e) Copy of rule. Upon the grant of letters, the Register shall give a copy of this Rule to each personal representative and his, her or its counsel.

(f) Failure to file a report. After at least ten (10) days prior notice to a delinquent personal representative and counsel, the Clerk of the Orphans' Court shall inform the Court of the failure to file the report required by this Rule with a request that the Court conduct a hearing to determine what sanctions, if any, should be imposed.

See Appendix 8 for form of status report revised in 2006.

# Chapter 16

# DISTRIBUTION

---

---

## § 16.1 IN GENERAL

Distribution, the final step in the administration of the estate, must be made with the utmost care if the personal representative is to avoid liability. Although it is the final step, problems of distribution should remain in the foreground during the entire administration of the estate if administration is to be successfully accomplished. See especially Chapters 2, 7, 8, 9, 10. The distribution of real estate is discussed in Section 9.8, and is dealt with only incidentally in this chapter. For set-off of a distributee's obligation to the estate, see Section 6.16.

If the decedent died testate, his will furnishes the basis for distribution, subject to the sufficiency of assets of the estate (see Section 16.16) and rights which the surviving spouse may elect to assert (see Chapter 8). If he died intestate, Chapt. 21 of the PEF Code will control the scheme of distribution. See Section 16.8. The right of all distributees—creditors, legatees, heirs or next of kin—in event of contest are determined at audit, when the auditor or auditing judge hears objections to the account, testimony in support of claims and arguments on any question relating to distribution. See Section 16.4.

It is stated frequently that the primary duty of the personal representative is to reduce the decedent's personal estate to cash so that claims can be paid and distribution facilitated, but in many instances this course cannot be followed properly. For example, it would be improper for the personal representative to sell any real property specifically given in the will unless necessary to pay a creditor or other superior claim.[1] So also he should not sell an item which has been specifically bequeathed or which a distributee wishes to receive in kind, unless it must be sold to protect parties having superior rights: *Minichello Est.*, 368 Pa. 639; *Polanco Est.*, (*No. 1*), 2 Fiduc. Rep. 124, annot. *Fiduc. Rev.* March 1952; cf. *Vandergrift Est.*, 406 Pa. 14. If he is to assume no risk whatsoever, the personal representative should make no distribution of any kind except that approved by the court. See Sections 16.4, 16.26. Nevertheless, there are situations in which it is possible for the personal representative to make distribution or partial distribution in advance thereof. Reference should be made to the discussion of distribution of small estates under PEF 3102. See Section 2.4.

The Supreme Court Orphan's Court Rules (6.9 and 6.11) require that a statement of proposed distribution, or a request that distribution be determined by the court or by an auditor, shall be filed by the personal representative and that no account shall be confirmed or distribution approved without an adjudication or decree of distribution. When distribution has been made according to an account confirmed by the court, the personal representative is relieved of liability with respect to property so distributed: PEF 3533.

If the gross real and personal estate of the decedent does not exceed $25,000 in value, the personal representative, after the expiration of one year from the grant of letters, may present his petition to the court with an annexed account showing the administration and proper distribution of the estate. Upon proof of notice to all known parties in interest, the court may order his discharge from future liability: PEF 3531; *Goldberg Est.*, 4 Fiduc. Rep. 264.

---

§ **16.1**

**1.** The PEF Code recognizes the limitation on a personal representative's power to sell real estate specifically devised without joinder of the devisee (3351) unless expressly authorized by the court (3353).

# DISTRIBUTION OF DECEDENTS' ASSETS*

**ORDER OF AVAILABILITY OF ASSETS: PEF Code 3541**

*(Without distinction between real and personal property*

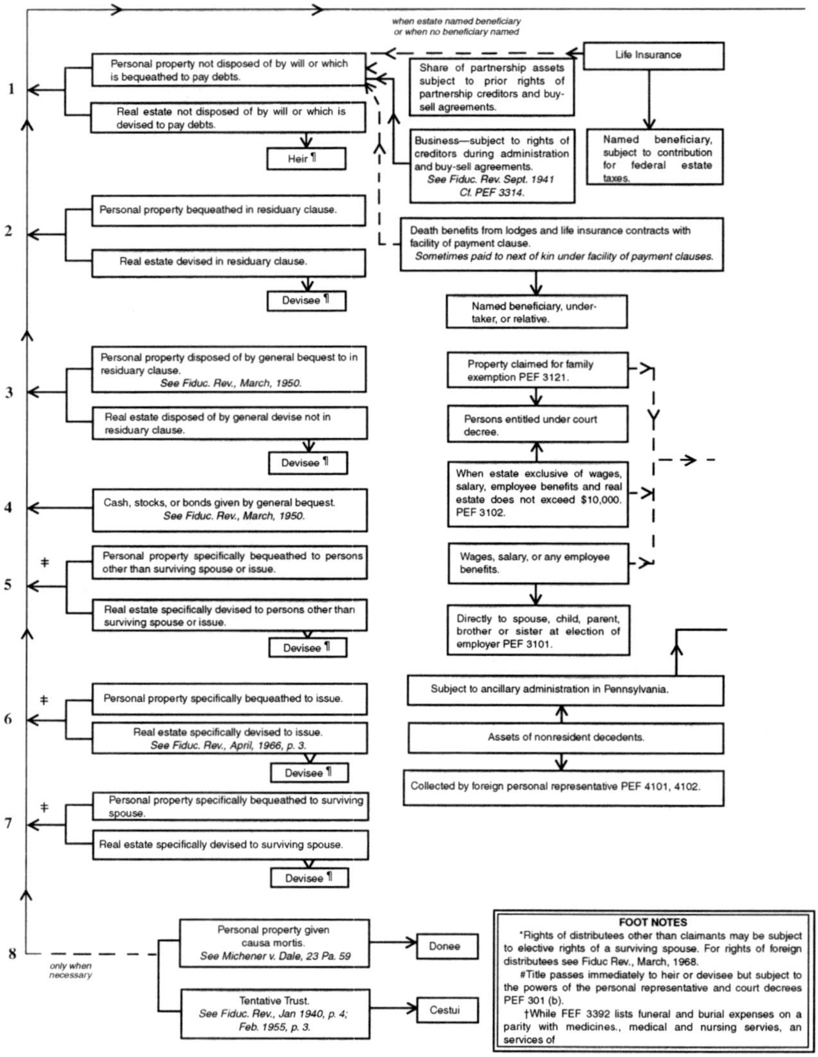


**FIDUCIARY REVIEW, April 1975*

**ORDER OF PRIORITY IN DISTRIBUTION:
PEF Code 3392 and 3541.**

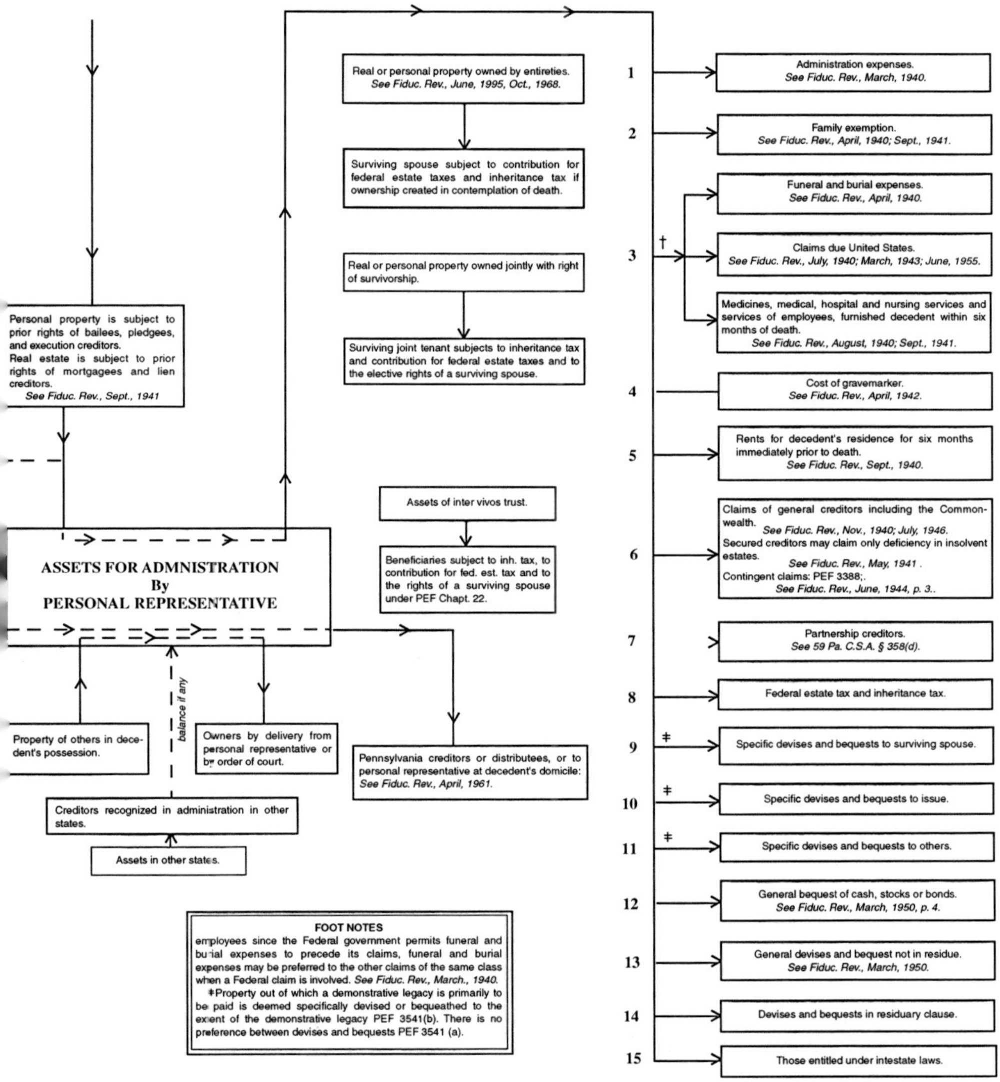


**FOOT NOTES**

employees since the Federal government permits funeral and burial expenses to precede its claims, funeral and burial expenses may be preferred to the other claims of the same class when a Federal claim is involved. *See Fiduc. Rev., March., 1940.*

‡Property out of which a demonstrative legacy is primarily to be paid is deemed specifically devised or bequeathed to the extent of the demonstrative legacy PEF 3541(b). There is no preference between devises and bequests PEF 3541 (a).

## § 16.2 RISK DISTRIBUTION

If a personal representative makes a voluntary distribution—that is, one that is not directed by the court—he not only assumes the risk of having distributed to the wrong person but he is liable personally for all lawful unsatisfied claims against the estate: PEF 3532; Sup. Ct. O.C. Rule 6.11(b). Thus, if he makes such a voluntary distribution under a will which is later set aside, or under the intestate laws and a will is later probated (PEF 3133), the personal representative may be responsible to other distributees entitled to such property. Difficulties can arise with respect to determining the proper date of interpretation. See e.g., *Burstin Est.*, 436 Pa. 163, annot. *Fiduc. Rev.* Dec. 1969; *Marks Est.*, 435 Pa. 155, annot. *Fiduc. Rev.* Aug. 1969.

The personal representative is prohibited by PEF 5703 from making any distribution of the property of a presumed decedent except under a decree of court. See Section 16.5.

Although the law gives the personal representative little, if any, protection against distributions voluntarily and improperly made to distributees, full protection is given him against creditors (except those having liens of record at the decedent's death) who have failed to give notice of their claims within one year of the first complete advertisement of the grant of letters: PEF 3532. This provision enables the personal representative to make a risk distribution in order to save the expense of formal accounting, without liability to creditors who have not given the specified notice.

PEF 3532(c) provides that:

"The personal representative may file with the clerk receipts, releases and refunding agreements which he may have received from persons to whom he has made a risk distribution, or from other parties in interest. Receipts, releases and refunding agreements so filed shall be indexed under the name of the estate. Their acceptance shall not be construed as court approval of any act of administration or distribution therein reflected."

This should provide a ready record of what is frequently done when court approval of informal administration is not considered necessary.

For problems of recovery in case of error in risk distribution, see *The Fiduciary Bank, Trustee v. Tiernan & Lynagh*, 25 Fiduc. Rep. 475, annot. *Fiduc. Rev.* Oct. 1975; 249 Pa. Super. 216, annot. *Fiduc. Rev.* Sept. 1977, rev'd 487 Pa. 484, by a per curiam order which leaves lingering doubts about the proper form and validity of receipt, release and refunding agreement; *Kessler Est.*, 25 Fiduc. Rep. 398.

For problems when overdistribution has been made to a nonresident claimant, see *Schumann Est.*, 27 Fiduc. Rep. 617, annot. *Fiduc. Rev.* Jan. 1978, p. 3.

When distribution is made to some distributees but not to all equally entitled, the "changing fraction" method of adjusting income may be appropriate. See *Greenfield Est.*, 28 Fiduc. Rep. 314, aff'd 484 Pa. 141; *Lewis Est.*, 26 Fiduc. Rep. 510.

For distributions directly to the ultimate distributee, see *Annear Trust*, 26 Fiduc. Rep. 438.

PEF Code Section 304 which is derived from section 2 of the Uniform Fiduciaries Act has been added. It provides:

> A person who, in good faith, pays or transfers to a fiduciary any money or other property, which the fiduciary as such is authorized to receive, is not responsible for the proper application thereof by the fiduciary, and any right or title acquired from the fiduciary in consideration of the payment or transfer is not invalid in consequence of a misapplication by the fiduciary.

While this new section is a duplication in part of what is now found in 7 PS § 6361, it is appropriate in the PEF Code because of its broader application to all fiduciaries and to all transfers regulated in the PEF Code. Its addition is the occasion for the repeal of Sections 5163.1 (Distribution to personal representatives) and 5533.1 (Account of personal representative of deceased incompetent). Their repeal is explained in the official comment as follows:

> *Comment:* Sections 5163.1 and 5533.1 are repealed. Their substance is covered in Sections 304 and 3533 insofar as they relate to responsibility for administration of the distributed property after it is turned over to the receiving fiduciary. It is arguable that the repealed sections would also provide protection for prior acts of administration even though no disclosure of the facts was made. This result seems undesirable. A fiduciary who wishes such protection may file his account or piggyback it onto the account of the receiving fiduciary under Sections 7188 or 3501.2.

## § 16.3 ENFORCEMENT OF DISTRIBUTION BY CREDITORS AND DISTRIBUTEES

Creditors should give prompt written notice of their claims (see § 10.1)[1] and, if they are not admitted or reduced to judgment in another court, should prosecute them at the audit of the account of the personal representative (see § 16.4; PEF 3383, 3384, 3386). If they have given proper notice, they will be entitled to notice of the filing of the account and of its call for audit or confirmation: PEF 3503. Beneficiaries, heirs and next of kin known to the accountant as entitled to an interest in the estate are entitled to such notice whether or not they have given written notice of their claims: PEF 3503; Sup. Ct. O.C. Rule 6.3.

---

§ **16.3**

**1.** PEF 3384(b) lists several circumstances which can be considered the equivalent of notice. Creditors must be careful, however, to see that a personal representative is appointed so that notice is given before the statue of limitations runs against them or before real estate is sold more than one year after the decedent's death: PEF 3385; cf. *Kerr v. Chanutin,* 24 Fiduc. Rep. 379; *Johnston, Admrx. v. Johnston, Executrix,* 71 D. & C. 2d 745. But see *Fiduc. Rev.* April 1956, regarding the protection to creditors by filing a notice of claim with the clerk of orphans' court division. See Section 10.12.

When the estate is small (PEF 3102) or is claimed for the family exemption (PEF 3122, 3123), it may be possible for the claimant to enforce an early distribution (see Chapters 2, 7). However, in the normal case distribution can be enforced only by requiring the personal representative to file an account after six months from the first complete advertisement of the original grant of letters: PEF 3501.1; Sup. Ct. O.C. Rule 6.4. See Section 15.1. In special circumstances, as when the personal representative has failed to give prompt notice of the grant of letters, the court is empowered to direct an earlier accounting, but it is unlikely that distribution would be directed before expiration of the six-month period from the advertisement of the grant of letters: cf. *Hayden Est.*, 28 Dist. 39. See Section 15.1.

The court will not direct a legacy to be paid or order distribution except following an accounting. See Section 15.1; *Shuck Est.*, 13 Fiduc. Rep. 488. Once there has been an accounting and an additional asset is discovered after the final distribution thereunder, the court may order direct distribution of the after-discovered asset to the distributee: *Plogstert Est.*, 350 Pa. 474.

When the administration of the estate is likely to be prolonged, the payment of claims against the estate may be authorized, even though litigation is pending in other courts (see Section 10.7; PEF 3387-3389; *Sawdey Est.,* 7 Erie 99) or assets have not been reduced to a form which makes distribution possible (cf. PEF 762).

## § 16.4 AUDIT

All accounts of the personal representative shall be filed with the clerk of the orphans' court division for audit and confirmation on dates fixed by the court by general rule or special order (PEF 3502). The clerk is required to advertise the time when accounts will be presented to the court. The advertisement must appear in the county legal publication, if any, and in at least one nonlegal newspaper at least once a week during the two weeks immediately preceding the time fixed for presentation of the accounts to the court: PEF 745.

The day of audit is the last day for the presentation of claims (see Chapter 10), and is the day for suggesting the distribution which should be made. The procedure to be followed is governed by local rules and varies widely throughout the Commonwealth, depending largely on whether or not there is a separate orphans' court division: PEF 3511. When hearing or argument is required, or the appointment of an auditor is requested, a hearing date usually is fixed for a time which is agreed upon by the court (or the auditor) and the parties.

In counties where there is a separate orphans' court division, the court is alert to protect the interests of those entitled under the will or intestate laws, whether or not they appear in person or by counsel. However, creditors whose claims are not admitted by the personal representative and to whom constructive or written notice of the audit has been given must appear and prove their claims or they may lose whatever rights they might have in the distribution: cf. *Scott Est.*, 7 Fiduc. Rep. 495; *Emig Est.*, 7 Fiduc. Rep. 497. See Chapter 10. They do not, however, by the audit and distribution, lose their possible rights in funds accounted for thereafter: *Wilson Est.*, 9 Fiduc. Rep. 253.

In counties having no separate orphans' court division and when there is no dispute requiring appointment of an auditor, it is customary for the local court by rule to require that statements of proposed distribution be filed for all accounts showing a balance, either at the time of filing the account, at the time of audit or by a specified time thereafter. See Section 15.10. These schedules, by express decree or automatically by rule, are approved by the court or by the clerk, unless objections are filed thereto within the time fixed by rule of court. If there is any dispute concerning the accuracy of the account, payment of any claim or the proposed distribution, the account will be referred to an auditor appointed by the court: PEF 3512. For auditors' duties, see Sup. Ct. O.C. rule 8; *Ream Est.*, 9 Leb. 307, aff'd 413 Pa. 489; *Pearson Est.*, 15 Fiduc. Rep. 552.

In counties having a separate orphans' court division, the court audits all accounts, "Without expense to the parties, except when all parties in interest in a pending proceeding shall nominate an auditor whom the court may in its discretion appoint": PEF 3511. In Philadelphia and Allegheny counties, which have more than one judge assigned to the orphans' court division, it is customary for the accounts to be divided and for a separate list of accounts to be assigned to each judge.

Where there is a separate orphans' court division, the usual procedure is to present to the court a "petition for distribution," a "petition for adjudication" or a "statement of proposed distribution." For forms, see 8 Dunlap-Hanna, Pennsylvania Forms § 76.07. Supreme Court Orphans' Court Rule 1.3 adopts forms "which shall be acceptable in all jurisdiction in addition to forms otherwise approved or mandated for use pursuant to local rules." Included is a form of petition for adjudication for Decedent's Estates set forth in Appendix 13. The essential facts for the adjudication are recited therein, and the auditing judge's attention is directed toward questions of law upon which he must rule. If a statement of proposed distribution is included, it is customarily the last clause of the petition. The petition should recite the name of the surviving spouse, if any, and whether or not there has been an election to take against the will. It should also set forth the names of legatees and their respective interests, and it should state the names of unpaid creditors and the amounts claimed or due them. The petition is usually on a printed form with marginal instructions for counsel. These should be followed carefully since the facts required to be recited are an essential basis for the court's adjudication. In many counties, there is no hearing at routine audits, and the personal representative's recital of facts in his petition and his affidavit thereto, in absence of contest, are accepted as establishing the essential facts. In some counties, however, the personal representative takes the stand on audit day to verify the facts alleged in his petition.

Usually the petition for distribution presented to the court on the day of audit supplies the court with sufficient information to make awards in its adjudication. Compare the use of the "audit memorandum" in Philadelphia County: *McEachern Est.*, 7 Fiduc. Rep. 650; *Moll Est.*, 7 Fiduc. Rep. 652. Counsel for the personal representative customarily supplies the court with such additional papers as the inheritance tax receipt or certificate showing the status of such tax; copy of the inventory; copy of the will and codicils, if any, certified by the attorney to be accurate; original letters testamentary or of administration; proofs of publication of estate notices of grant of letters; copy of spouse's election, if any, to take under or against the will; assignments, copies of notice letters and such other papers as should become a part of the court's permanent record. If not required, in some instances, as when the court is called upon to decide a question of law, it is advisable that there be handed to the court, for inclusion in the record, copies of the letters of notice informing the parties of the question involved and of the solution which the personal representative will recommend to the court: cf. *Draper Est.*, 6 Fiduc. Rep. 105. Audit may be postponed until adequate notice of a possible distribution question is given to distributees: *Simonin Trust*, 26 Fiduc. Rep. 434.

In a situation involving the inheritance tax charitable exemption, the charitable gifts will have been reported in the inheritance tax return and the tax computed accordingly. If the exemption is denied and the accountant wishes to contest that action, he should proceed under Section 9186 of the Inheritance and Estate Tax Act. 72 P.S. 9186. See Section 13.14. Presumably an assessment of tax disallowing the charitable exemption, notice of the filing of which has been given prior to the audit and which has not been the subject of proper action under that section, may not be questioned at audit.

All counsel should file appearance slips giving the names of parties represented. Counsel for the personal representative may submit at audit a statement of additional receipts and disbursements supplemental to the account, which the court can allow in the adjudication. Usually such items are minimal and can be listed on counsel's appearance slip. When such items are numerous, as when there has been a long delay occasioned by continuance of the audit, a supplemental account may be filed. See *Fiduc. Rev.* Jan. 1982, Dec.

1982, p. 4. Frequently, however, the additional receipts[1] and disbursements are reflected in the schedule of distribution directed by the court in the adjudication. For deduction of such "last minute" expenses for inheritance tax purposes, see Inheritance and Estate Tax Act, § 9138, 72 P.S. 9138.

## § 16.5 DETERMINATION OF DISTRIBUTEES

Determination of the distributees of the decedent's estate involves consideration of a number of matters which are dealt with in Sections 16.7–16.26, and reference should be made thereto in conjunction with the ensuing discussion.

Questions relating to the determination of heirs and next of kin and to the construction of wills frequently arise at audit of the account: *Crawford Est.*, 8 Fiduc. Rep. 169. Although the register of wills passes initially on what constitutes the will (see § 4.4), it is the court which construes the will and awards the estate accordingly. Thus, the rights of all distributees are determined at audit. The personal representative will often have to determine whether it will be advisable to seek the appointment of a guardian and trustee *ad litem* to represent unborn, unascertained and minor beneficiaries with respect to questions of distribution. It has been held that testamentary direction prohibiting appointment of a guardian and trustee *ad litem* is invalid: *Hiester Trust*, 16 Fiduc. Rep. 303.

In the event of intestacy, the identity and shares of heirs and next of kin usually are established with a minimum of difficulty. See Section 16.8. In most instances, they can be set forth accurately in the statement presented to the court at audit or in the proposed schedule of distribution when there is no audit. Since the Commonwealth now receives the estate before next of kin more remote than children of first cousins (PEF 2103(6)), the difficulty of tracing relatives of the dece-

§ 16.4

1. Receipts should be confined to income and gains on conversions and not include after-acquired assets, because as to such assets, creditors who did not present their claims at audit have not received the required statutory notice. Cf., however, *Plogstert Est.*, 350 Pa. 474.

dent is not as great as it was formerly (see *Verrall Est.*, 12 Fiduc. Rep. 129). However, problems can still arise, and when the identity of the parties is not clear, the rules of evidence, including presumptions, become important. For a review of many of the applicable rules relating to pedigree, see *Garrett Est.*, 372 Pa. 438, annot. *Fiduc. Rev.* Feb. 1953; *McClain Est.*, 481 Pa. 435, annot. *Fiduc. Rev.* March 1979; *Fiduc. Rev.* Oct. 1965; *Weiss Est.*, 2 Fiduc. Rep. 2d 86; *Schultz Est.*, 13 Fiduc. Rep. 540; *Makarus Est.*, 16 Fiduc. Rep. 620.

For employment of genealogist, see *Atkinson Est.*, 2 Fiduc. Rep. 2d 79. For employment of deposition to establish relationship, see *Rogers Est.*, 30 Fiduc. Rep. 537, annot. *Fiduc. Rev.* Jan. 1981.

When the decedent dies testate, one of the more important duties of the court is to determine the rights of the parties under the will as probated. This usually is incident to the adjudication or decree of distribution, and normally the court is unwilling to construe a will or determine the rights of a legatee or claimant prior thereto. Occasionally, however, when a definite service can be rendered the parties by so doing, a declaratory judgment will be rendered; cf. *Keefer Est.*, 351 Pa. 343, annot. *Fiduc. Rev.* May 1945; *Carter Will*, 435 Pa. 492.

A decree of court is required for the distribution of the estate of a presumed decedent: PEF 5701. Cf. Sections 3.3, 4.2. In awarding distribution of such an estate, the court will require that a refunding bond, with or without security and in such form and amount as the court shall direct, be executed by each distributee and filed with the clerk. The bond contains the condition that, if it shall later be established that the presumed decedent was in fact alive at the time of distribution, the distributee will return the property received by him upon demand, or, if it has been disposed of, will make restitution therefor as the court shall deem equitable: PEF 5703. New Section PEF 5706 added in 2002 permits the Court to determine immediately that a person presumed dead as a result of the September 11, 2001 terrorist attack died on September 11, 2001.

In addition to the distribution of the estates of presumed decedents, the court must also determine whether distributees have predeceased or survived the decedent. See Section 16.13. This determination can be difficult if the decedent and the distributee died in the same accident. However, the Uniform Simultaneous Death Act, PEF Chapt. 85 (annot. *Fiduc. Rev.* July 1941, 20 A.L.R.2d 235), is helpful in this regard. It provides, inter alia, that "Where the title to property or the devolution thereof depends upon priority of death and there is no sufficient evidence that the persons have died otherwise than simultaneously, the property of each person shall be disposed of as if he had survived, except as provided otherwise in this chapter": PEF 8501. For discussion of survivorship problems as they affect distribution, see Bregy, Intestate, Wills and Estates Acts of 1947, pp. 165–167. See also *Christensen Est.*, 8 Fiduc. Rep. 382. In instances other than simultaneous death, the court, in absence of positive proof, must establish whether a distributee predeceased the decedent. This can be found from an unexplained absence of seven years before the decedent's death or from an exposure to a specific peril. See Section 3.3; PEF 5701; *Fiduc. Rev.* Nov. 1945; *Wheelock Est.*, 5 Fiduc. Rep. 553; for forms, see 8 Dunlap-Hanna, Pennsylvania Forms Chapter 86.

When the distributee survived the decedent, but died thereafter, the deceased distributee's share is awarded to his personal representative, unless the will provides otherwise. See Section 16.13; cf. *Fiduc. Rev.* July 1955. However, in *McCredy Est.*, 17 Fiduc. Rep. 405, annot. *Fiduc. Rev.* July 1967, p. 3, the executor's renunciation of an interest in an estate to reduce death taxes was approved. See Section 16.6.

When any distributee is a minor or an incapacitated person, distribution is made to his guardian. However, when the minor's net estate does not exceed a value of $25,000, distribution in the discretion of the court may be made directly to the minor or to the parent or other person maintaining the minor, without the appointment of a guardian or the entry of security, and the court may require that the funds be deposited in a savings account in such fashion that they cannot be withdrawn until the minor is of age or until prior order of court: PEF 5101, 5102; cf. *Volk Est.*, 16 Fiduc. Rep. 156; *Kurtz Est.*, 18 Fiduc. Rep. 8. Similarly, when an incapacitated person's net estate has a value of $25,000 or less, it may be received and held or disposed of by the person or institution maintaining the incapacitated person without the appointment of a guardian or the entry of security: PEF 5505; see *Fiduc. Rev.* Nov. 1956. In addition, guardianship for a minor or incapacitated person can be avoided regardless of the amounts involved when the court directs deposit of the sum involved in sequestered bank accounts, provided the amount deposited in any one savings institution does not exceed the amount to which the accounts are insured by a Federal governmental agency: PEF 5103, 5505(3).

When the distributee is a nonresident trustee, minor or incapacitated person, distribution is governed by PEF 4112. In *McMullin Trust*, 490 Pa. 502, annot. *Fiduc. Rev.* Sept. 1980, the court accorded full weight and comity to an Iowa court's determination that the donee, a resident of Iowa, had validly and effectively exercised a power under the will of her husband who had earlier died a resident of Pennsylvania.

Distribution may be made through the imposition of a constructive trust, as where a beneficiary's deceit has prevented revocation of the testator's will: *McCloskey Est.*, 9 Fiduc. Rep. 629. Cf. 28 N.C.L. Rev. 111, regarding constructive and resulting trusts of proceeds of co-ownership United States savings bonds.

A difficult question is raised by a gift which is made "to A or her estate." In *Goddard Est.*, 14 Fiduc. Rep. 593, it was held that such a gift was one in the alternative and the property was awarded to the fiduciary of the estate of the sister who predeceased testatrix. The court refused to interpret the words as words of limitation which would result in an intestacy in the testatrix' estate, but instead interpreted the phrase "or her estate" as words of substitution. The Supreme Court reversed (in a related case, 18 Fiduc. Rep. 460) finding that there was an intestacy: *Braman Est.*, 435 Pa. 573, annot. *Fiduc. Rev.* Jan. 1970.

A trust may be terminated under PEF 6102, at its inception, upon the audit of the executor's account: *O'Neill Est.*, 7 Fiduc. Rep. 451.

For discussion of extrinsic evidence and identity of distributees, see *Fiduc. Rev.* Dec. 1957, p. 3; Oct. 1958; Oct. 1965; Oct. 1973, p. 3. For identification of "person who takes care of her last," see *Stauffer Trust*, 2 Fiduc. Rep. 2d 181, annot. *Fiduc. Rev.* July 1982, p. 3.

The problem of identifying the proper distributee frequently arises with respect to charitable beneficiaries where the testator has failed to use the proper name of the charity. See, for example, *Berks County Tuberculosis Society Appeal*, 418 Pa. 112, annot. *Fiduc. Rev.* May 1965.

Problems may also arise where the will creates an annuity and the question is the manner in which funds should be set aside in distribution, the amount thereof, and the nature of the assets so set aside: see *Wasserman Trust*, 19 Fiduc. Rep. 404.

PEF 2514(1.1) provides that "A will shall be construed to apply to all property which the testator owned at his death, including property acquired after the execution of his will." For the time of ascertaining the class where the gift is to a class, see PEF 2514(5), 6114(2); *Fiduc. Rev.* Nov. 1947, April 1979.

PEF 2521 provides that, "A provision in a will or trust purporting to penalize an interested person for contesting the will or trust or instituting other proceedings relating to the estate or trust is unenforceable if probable cause exists for instituting proceedings." An *in terrorem* clause will be enforced where no probable cause exists for filing a will contest. *Tercha Est.*, 2 Fiduc. Rep. 3d 158, annot. *Fiduc. Rev.* Mar. 2012, p. 1.

## § 16.6 RENUNCIATIONS AND DISCLAIMERS

Chapter 62 of the PEF Code has given statutory recognition of the right of distributees to disclaim their interests in property which would have devolved to them by whatever means: *Fiduc. Rev.* Oct. 1976. This privilege is employed frequently to reduce the burden of Pennsylvania inheritance tax (*Lieberman Est.*, 1 Fiduc. Rep. 2d 281, annot. *Fiduc. Rev.* Aug. 1981, p. 2), as well as to bypass claims of creditors: *Clark Est.*, 488 Pa. 1; *Sousa Est.*, 30 Fiduc. Rep. 355, annot. *Fiduc. Rev.* Oct. 1980, p. 4; *Fenner Est.*, 3 D. & C. 3d 421. However, disclaimers are not effective to defeat federal tax liens. *Drye v. U.S.* (12/7/99), annot. *Fiduc. Rev.* Feb. 2000. See *Bernecker Est.*, 654 A.2d 246 and 27 Pa. Bulletin 4115 for Pennsylvania Department of Revenue policy regarding disclaimers of non-probate assets.

By 1982 amendment to PEF 6202, the court may authorize an attorney-in-fact (granted the power to do so in a durable power of attorney) to disclaim an interest of the incapacitated person. This authority had originally been limited to guardians of minors and incapacitated persons and to personal representatives.

Subsequent amendments permit a testator to authorize his executor to disclaim without court approval (6202), and to permit a donee under "a third party beneficiary contract (including beneficiaries of life insurance and annuity policies and pension, profit-sharing and other employee benefit plans)" (6201) to disclaim by the procedure there prescribed (6204(b.1)). The amendment to 6205 is explained in the official comment, which states that it "is intended to obviate the need to insert into marital trust/residuary trust wills a clause such as: 'A disclaimed portion of the marital trust shall pass to the residuary trust, and be held thereunder as if my wife were living.' "

A surviving co-tenant may disclaim interests in bank accounts and certificates of deposit held in tenancy by entirety within nine months of the death of the first co-tenant (TAM 9529001, 9612002), but interests in bonds only within nine months of transfer to tenancy by entirety. TAM 9529001. See annotation *Fiduc. Rev.* July 1996 questioning applicability of PEF 6301 et seq. to husband and wife bank accounts.

The decision in *McCutcheon Est.* (Pa. Super.), 699 A.2d 746, annot. *Fiduc. Rev.* Dec. 1997, created some uncertainty regarding the effect of disclaimers in intestate estates because of its interpretation of the words ". . . all persons claiming through or under [disclaimant]" to preclude "any issue or heirs, direct or collateral, of the disclaimant from sharing in the disclaimed property." PEF 6205 was amended to reverse this result and restore the usefulness of disclaimers as a post-mortem planning device.

## § 16.7 INCORPORATION BY REFERENCE; INDEPENDENT LEGAL SIGNIFICANCE; POUR-OVER

Regarding the effect of these concepts upon determination of distributees and distribution of the estate, see PEF 2515; *Clark Est.*, 7 Fiduc. Rep. 73, annot. *Fiduc. Rev.* March 1957; Aker, Law of Wills in Pennsylvania § 1.9; Pour-over Provisions in Pennsylvania, 62 Dick. L. Rev. 346; Pour-overs—Recent Developments, 57 Mich. L. Rev. 81; 98 Trusts & Estates 949 (pour-over wills); 45 Cornell L.Q. 135 (pour-over); 59 Mich. L. Rev. 1276 (pour-over to amended trust). See *Clapphanson Est.*, 9 Fiduc. Rep. 328, for incorporation by reference of a later-revoked will of another.

Where the residue of the estate has been given to trustees of a revocable inter vivos trust of a certain date, which was in fact later replaced by another trust agreement supplanting the designated one, the estate will be awarded to the trustee under the original agreement "as modified by" the later trust agreement: *Gould Est.*, 17 Fiduc. Rep. 569.

## § 16.8 INTESTATE DISTRIBUTION

If the decedent died without leaving a valid will, distribution will be made to the surviving spouse, if any, and to the heirs and next of kin in accordance with the provisions of Chapter 21 of the PEF Code.[1]

The real and personal estate of a decedent, not disposed of by will or otherwise, passes as follows:

*Surviving spouse* (PEF 2102):

---

§ **16.8**

**1.** See Chart, Appendix 5. Persons who fail to survive decedent by five days are excluded: PEF 2104(10).

(1) If there is no surviving issue or parent of the decedent, the entire intestate estate.

(2) If there is no surviving issue of the decedent but he is survived by a parent or parents, the first $30,000 plus one-half of the balance of the intestate estate. Act No. 26 of 2003 provided that the surviving spouse would receive 100% of any compensation award paid pursuant to the Air Transportation Safety and System Stabilization Act where decedent dies as a result of the September 11, 2001 terrorist attacks.

(3) If there are surviving issue of the decedent all of whom are also issue of the surviving spouse, the first $30,000 plus one-half of the balance of the intestate estate.

(4) If there are surviving issue of the decedent one or more of whom are not issue of the surviving spouse, one-half of the intestate estate.

(5) In the case of partial intestacy any property received by the surviving spouse under the will shall satisfy pro tanto the $30,000 allowance under paragraphs (2) and (3).[2]

*Others* (PEF 2103): Subject to the rights of the surviving spouse, the estate is distributable to other heirs and next of kin in the following order of preference:

(1) Issue of the decedent, children of deceased issue taking by representation;

(2) Parents and survivor, by entireties;

(3) Issue of parents, children of deceased issue taking by representation;

(4) Grandparents, who receive their shares in pairs, maternal and paternal, limited right of representation where both on one side are deceased and at least one on the other side survives;

(5) Uncles and aunts, and children and grandchildren of deceased uncles and aunts by representation, except that

---

**§ 16.8**

**2.** The allowance is $20,000 in estates of persons dying prior to Sept. 9, 1980.

children of a first cousin take nothing unless there is no relative as close as a first cousin;

(6) Commonwealth of Pennsylvania, in default of all persons described above.

Among lineal descendants and descendants of brothers and sisters, there is an unlimited right of representation; that is, issue of such descendants take the parent's share per stirpes. Of course, where all of the issue are of the same degree of consanguinity to the decedent they take per capita: PEF 2104(2). The rules of descent applicable to shares descending to issue of the decedent or of others taking from him in different degrees are set forth in PEF 2104(1). Full discussion of the intestate laws may be found in Bregy, Intestate, Wills and Estates Acts of 1947.

A spouse who fails to support or deserts for one year or more forfeits any intestate share (PEF 2106(a)), as does a parent who fails to support or deserts for one year or more. PEF 2106(b). *See Krichmar Est.*, 1 Fiduc. Rep. 3d 411 where wife left the residence at her husband's request for her own safety and no desertion was found. Also see *Bortz Est.*, 2 Fiduc. Rep. 3d 342, annot. *Fiduc. Rev.* Oct. 2012, p. 4, where wife who did not live with husband for most years of their forty-year marriage was determined not to be a deserter. However, where decedent is neither a minor nor a dependent child, no forfeiture occurs and the father who filed to support is entitled to his intestate share. *In re Kistner*, 858 A.2d 1226. Forfeiture also occurs when a person is a slayer. PEF 2106(c).

See *Hoff Est.*, 14 Fiduc. Rep. 119, where the court "finds that in view of the fact that the husband of the decedent has been absent for more than seven years, the presumption is that he did not survive and if he did survive, that he has forfeited his right under the intestate law, and will make awards to the collateral heirs."

Where natural relatives of an adopted decedent began a proceeding to revoke the adoption (there being no adoptive relatives as close as first cousins), and then reached a compromise with the Commonwealth, the estate was awarded in accordance with the compromise: *Landell Est.*, 7 Fiduc. Rep. 273.

The Commonwealth must choose whether to claim by escheat or as an intestate heir: *Moll Est.*, 7 Fiduc. Rep. 652. On the subject of participation by the Commonwealth in distribution of estates, see *Fiduc. Rev.* Nov. 1964, p. 3; March 1968; May 1968, p. 4; *Fiduc. Rev.* June 1983, p. 3. The Disposition of Abandoned and Unclaimed Property Act (27 P.S. § 1; see *Fiduc. Rev.* Jan. 1972, p. 4) repealed Fiscal Code Article XIII, so that Section 1314 does not apply after December 31, 1971. Distributions due absentees and unclaimed property are now governed by PEF 3540, and by amendment to the Escheat laws: 72 Pa. C.S. § 1301.1 et seq., annot. *Fiduc. Rev.* Aug. 1980, p. 2.

Note that the Commonwealth is not an "heir" within the meaning of federal law regarding estates of intestate veterans who die in veterans' hospitals: *United States v. Oregon*, 366 U.S. 643; *Skriziszouski Est.*, 382 Pa. 634; *Maguire Est.*, 7 Fiduc. Rep. 701; cf. *Tamaszwicz Est.*, 8 Fiduc. Rep. 553; *Ayres Est.*, 7 Fiduc. Rep. 374. Nor is a reference to next of kin of a life beneficiary (who died in 1958) intended to include the Commonwealth in the will of a decedent who died in 1895; the term refers to cousins once removed: *Cope Est.*, 10 Fiduc. Rep. 92.

In the settlement of an intestate's estate, account will have to be taken of advancements or settlements made by the decedent in his lifetime to or upon any of his heirs, children or grandchildren,[3] see *Fiduc. Rev.* Nov. 1957, p. 4. The rule has been applied for distributions made during the incompetency under court order: *Spencer Est.*, 2 Fiduc. Rep. 2d 332, annot. *Fiduc. Rev.* Oct. 1982, p. 3. An "advancement" is a gift made by anticipation, in whole or in part, of what it is supposed the next of kin of the decedent would be entitled to on the latter's death, and the advancement therefore must be taken into consideration so that the total share of the distributee shall not exceed the share received by each of the other persons who take equally from the decedent, and for this reason is charged against the heir's share of the estate, but only if declared in

---

**§ 16.8**

**3.** Although PEF 2109.1 states that any "heir" is to be charged with advancements, the doctrine has in the past been applied only to the decedent's children and grandchildren.

writing by the decedent or acknowledge in writing by the heir to be an advancement: PEF 2109.1. See *Fiduc. Rev.* Dec. 1944; 1 Hunter, O.C. Commonplace Book (2d Ed.), Advancements.

If the decedent left a will which does not dispose completely of his estate, the intestate laws are applicable to that undisposed-of portion. However, under these circumstances the doctrine of advancements apparently has no application: Brégy, Intestate, Wills and Estates Acts of 1947, pp. 955–956. See *Smith Trust*, 21 Fiduc. Rep. 312, annot. *Fiduc. Rev.* June 1971, regarding what is in fact an "undisposed of" share.

PEF 2104(11) was added in 2002 to provide for distribution where an intestacy occurs at this termination of a valid prior estate, designating those who would be heirs living at the time of the termination of the prior estate. The provision is the same as concepts for PEF 2514(4) regarding class members and gifts under wills.

## § 16.9 SURVIVING SPOUSE AND PRETERMITTED CHILDREN

During the entire administration of the estate, and especially at the time of distribution, special consideration must be given to the rights of the surviving spouse.[1] Reference should be made to Chapter 8, which sets forth the rights of the surviving spouse to retain or claim a family exemption superior to the rights of all other distributees, and to the intestate shares, summarized in Section 16.8.

Property specifically devised or bequeathed to or for the benefit of a surviving spouse is the last to abate when funds are needed to satisfy the rights of claimants. See Section 16.16. The right to choose particular personal property in satisfaction of the allowance has not existed since the enactment of the Intestate Act of 1947 (*Fiduc. Rev.* March 1952), and a 1956 amendment took away the right to choose partic-

---

§ 16.9

1. A common law spouse's status is not supplanted by that of an innocent "second" spouse: *Larry Est.*, 29 Fiduc. Rep. 298, annot. *Fiduc. Rev.* Oct. 1979, p. 4. For proof of marriage, see *Neiderhiser Est.*, 27 Fiduc. Rep. 329; *Riley Est.*, 2 Fiduc. Rep. 2d 219.

ular real property in satisfaction thereof. However, the right to choose particular property for the family exemption remains except as it conflicts with specific testamentary gifts: PEF 3121. See Chapter 7; *Fiduc. Rev.* June 1953, p. 3.

The Attorney General is entitled to notice of *all* proceedings involving charitable trusts: Sup. Ct. O.C. Rule 5.5; *Pruner Est.*, 390 Pa. 529; *Garrison Est.*, 391 Pa. 234. Clearly this includes notice of the filing of an election to take against the will, which reduces charitable bequests therein: see *Fiduc. Rev.* April 1958.

If the decedent married after the execution of his will, the surviving spouse automatically (*Doney Est.*, 10 Fiduc. Rep. 29) is entitled to the share of the estate to which he or she would have been entitled had the decedent died intestate (PEF 2507(3)); see Section 16.8; cf. *Fiduc. Rev.* April 1959, p. 3. The fact that an after-married spouse has a greater share in the estate under PEF 2507(3) than would be her one-third elective share under PEF 2203(a) does not violate the equal protection and due process clauses of the U.S. Constitution. *Long Est.* (Pa. Super.), 600 A.2d 619. See *Fiduc. Rev.* Jan. 1991. The surviving spouse will be deprived of any benefit under the decedent's will if the decedent was divorced from such spouse after execution of the will or if he or she participated in the unlawful slaying of the decedent: PEF 2507(2), 2507(5). Similarly, a prenuptial or postnuptial agreement may preclude the widow-sole legatee from taking under the will: *Fratoni Est.*, 413 Pa. 594.

See Chapter 8 regarding election against the will and inter vivos transfers by a surviving spouse.

If the decedent failed to provide in his will for a child born or adopted after the execution thereof, such child is entitled to receive out of the estate not passing to the surviving spouse the share which the child would have received if the decedent had died unmarried and intestate and owning only that portion of his estate not passing to the surviving spouse: PEF 2507(4).

This rule, however, has no application if it appears from the will that the failure to provide for the child was intentional: see *Connell Est.*, 14 Fiduc. Rep. 251; *Arnold Est.*, 7 Fiduc. Rep. 531; *DeSolms Est.*, 6 Fiduc. Rep. 463. *DeBias Est.*, 15 Fiduc. Rep. 2d 58.

Regarding after-born and after-adopted children, see *Trattner Est.*, 394 Pa. 133, annot. *Fiduc. Rev*. Jan. 1959. *Tafel Est.*, 449 Pa. 442, annot. *Fiduc. Rev*. Dec. 1972, held that children of testator's son, adopted after testator's death, were "issue." This change in the prior law was announced as the presumption to be applied in the absence of proof of testator's contrary intent, and is probably applicable only to minor adoptees. See Section 16.10.

The decree of a foreign court establishing the status of an adopted child will be recognized in Pennsylvania under the principle of comity: *Christoff Est.*, 411 Pa. 419.

Regarding the time for ascertaining class members, see *Fiduc. Rev*. April 1959, PEF 2514(5) 6114(2).

## § 16.9A MINORS

The Pennsylvania Uniform Transfers to Minors Act, PEF Chapter 53, provides a simplified method for making gifts or other transfers to minors. However, the custodian's powers give the ability to use PUTMA assets improperly, such as the father-custodian who used funds for his personal obligations. *Schultz v. Schultz*, 15 Fiduc. Rep. 2d 387. The same father also invested and lost one-half of the funds in the commodities market (copper futures), but was not required to re-pay the funds lost by his good faith attempt to increase the fund.

PEF 5305(a) sets forth the authority of a personal representative to make an irrevocable transfer to a custodian as authorized in the will.

Transfers under Chapter 53 made pursuant to a will, trust or life insurance beneficiary designation may be delayed until age 25 rather than age 21 as related to life time gifts. This provision obviates the necessity of creating a trust for such beneficiaries.

## § 16.10 ADOPTEES

With the Supreme Court's decision in *Tafel Est.*, 449 Pa. 442, annot. *Fiduc. Rev.* Dec. 1972, Pennsylvania disavowed its earlier decisions making a distinction between the rights of natural children and adopted children in the estates of Pennsylvania decedents. The difficulties which remain are in the application of res judicata in the disposition of remainder interests and in the interpretation of wills and trust instruments executed prior to *Tafel* (11/17/72); also as to the interest of an adoptee in the estates of members of his natural family.

While an adopted child for most purposes becomes a member of the adopting family (*Fiduc. Rev.* April 1974, p. 4) and is no longer considered a child of his natural parents (*Fiduc. Rev.* Oct. 1953, p. 3), this distinction does not apply when his family relationship is undisturbed as when his natural parent has married his adopting parent or the family relationship continued after adoption: PEF 2108, 2514(7), 6114(4); *Block Trust*, 1 Phila. 587; *Rickert Est.*, 30 Fiduc. Rep. 13.

For instances where earlier decisions in the same estate have barred an adoptee and his descendants from sharing in distribution under res judicata see: *Holton Est.*, 493 Pa. 584; *Tower Est.*, 463 Pa. 93, annot. *Fiduc. Rev.* Aug. 1975; 2 Fiduc. Rep. 2d 109. Where it has been no bar, see: *Fownes Trust*, 465 Pa. 182, annot. *Fiduc. Rev.* Aug. 1975; *Fownes Trust*, 3 Fiduc. Rep. 2d 179, annot. *Fiduc. Rev.* May 1983; *DeRoy Est.*, 481 Pa. 403, annot. *Fiduc. Rev.* Dec. 1978; *Sewell Est.*, 487 Pa. 379, annot. *Fiduc. Rev.* Feb. 1980 (the trustee being surcharged for erroneous post-Tafel income distributions despite intervening audit excluding adopted child); *Biddle Est.*, 487 Pa. 616, annot. *Fiduc. Rev.* March 1977.

While a person cannot become a member of an adopting family as an adult for the purpose of changing devolution of property, this prohibition may not be applicable where a parent-child relation had existed for many years during minority: *Buzby Est.*, 30 Fiduc. Rep. 5.

The use of words such as "born" (*Riley Trust*, 30 Fiduc. Rep. 51), "issue" (*Bower Trust*, 30 Fiduc. Rep. 323), and "of the blood" (*Farmers Trust Co. v. Bashore*, 498 Pa. 146), do not necessarily exclude adoptees; cf. *Sykes Est.*, 477 Pa. 254.

The current applicable statutory provision is the *Adoption Act of 1980*, 23 Pa. C.S. § 2101 et seq., annot. *Fiduc. Rev*. Dec. 1980. Adoptees who are of age and of sound mind upon request are entitled to certified copies of their original birth certificates: *Attorney General Opinion*, 8 D. & C. 3d 104.

PEF 3539 was added in 1984 to give needed protection to personal representatives who continue a pattern of distribution after a law change that would require a different pattern. The official comment reads:

> *Comment:* Changes in the position of adopted and illegitimate children have created problems about the extent to which a fiduciary should be expected to disrupt the ongoing administration of a fund to protect himself against possible liability to unknown claimants. *Estate of Sewell*, 487 Pa. 379, 409 A.2d 401 (1979), suggests the further difficulty a fiduciary may face if his file contains information about the possible existence of such persons that was irrelevant when received but would have been perceived as important after the law changed.

## § 16.11 ILLEGITIMATES

Prior to *Trimble v. Gordon*, 430 U.S. 762, annot. *Fiduc. Rev*. June 1977, 23 Villa. L.R. 405, the illegitimate under Pennsylvania case and statutory law had progressed from the common law status of a *nullius filius* to the status of being the child of his mother and a member of her family, but an impenetrable barrier existed to recognition as a child of the father. Since *Trimble v. Gordon*, the equal protection clause of the Fourteenth Amendment to the United States Constitution has become a solid stepping stone to the recognition of the illegitimate as a child of the father and as a member of the father's family: *Browning Est.*, 28 Fiduc. Rep. 1; *Flum v. Lichtenfeld*, 2 Fiduc. Rep. 2d 158. However, it is essential that the new status be authenticated properly and that the possibility of fraudulent claims be avoided.

The child of an unwed mother is no longer "illegitimate" and is now referred to as a child "born out of wedlock." By Acts 46, 288 and 303 of 1978, all children are recognized as legitimate regardless of the marital status of their parents. However, as described in an annotation of those Acts in the January 1979 issue of *Fiduciary Review*, substantial requirements are set forth for establishing a status in the father's family. See PEF 2107. Also, new sections 3538 and 7183(14) of the PEF Code protect personal representatives and trustees, who, in good faith and without knowledge of their existence, have made distributions excluding children born out of wedlock. As reported in the December 1980 issue of *Fiduciary Review*, page four, Act 163 of 1980 includes a provision for the father of a child born to an unmarried mother to acknowledge paternity of their child.

Cases which highlight the necessity of establishing and preserving evidence of paternity include *Hardiman Est.*, 30 Fiduc. Rep. 561; *Fleming Trust*, 30 Fiduc. Rep. 545; *In re Mengel*, 287 Pa. Super. 186. They also demonstrate that the recent statutory aids for the child born out of wedlock do not preclude comparable treatment in pre-statutory cases: *Klaber Est.*, 2 Fiduc. Rep. 2d 167, where the natural father died prior to these Acts; cf. *Hoffman Est.*, 2 Fiduc. Rep. 2d 95; *Scott Est.*, 2 Fiduc. Rep. 2d 334. For proof of paternity other than the lawful husband of the mother, see *Leider v. Leider*, 434 Pa. 293, annot. 9 Duquesne L.R. 129. For effect of illegitimate's delay in asserting claim, see *Maule Est.*, 29 Fiduc. Rep. 543. For equitable adjustments after paternity has been established, see *Dulles Trust*, 494 Pa. 180, annot. *Fiduc. Rev.* August 1981, p. 3. See generally, 23 Villa. L.R. 405.

## § 16.12 FOREIGN DISTRIBUTEES

Since the Act of February 23, 1791, 68 P.S. §§ 22 et seq., Pennsylvania has recognized the right of aliens to dispose of and receive Pennsylvania property by will or descent. No distinction is made between nationals of enemy or friendly countries except as they may reside in enemy-occupied territory: *Gregg Est.*, 266 Pa. 189, *cert. denied*, 252 U.S. 588.

Domicile, not citizenship, is the test which determines whether Pennsylvania law will control the disposition of a decedent's personal property. The principles of conflict of laws control here; it was formerly under PEF 2114, 2520, repealed in 1976 by Act 135. Real property located within the state passes under Pennsylvania law regardless of the decedent's domicile. If the decedent was domiciled in a foreign country, there may be a Pennsylvania administration (*Caputo Est.*, 57 Pitts. 584), but the foreign, rather than Pennsylvania, law then controls ultimate distribution of personalty (*Stapay Est.*, 12 D. & C. 16). When there are foreign distributees, special notice of the account frequently is required: cf. *Kelsey Est.*, 1 Fiduc. Rep. 267. For adequacy of notice to person in military service outside of the continental United States, see *Steingrabe, Minor*, 26 Fiduc. Rep. 540. Special notice to consular officials may also be required by general rule of court or special order: cf. *Mellon Est.*, 46 D. & C. 287.

Act 39 of 1980 prohibits acquisition of an interest in Pennsylvania agricultural land exceeding 100 acres by a nonresident alien, except for devise or inheritance in the case of a Class A transferee. One who is not within the class A category is given three years to divest himself of such interest.

Regarding claims by the United States Attorney General as successor to the Alien Property Custodian, see *Flehinghaus Trust*, 7 Fiduc. Rep. 595. And see *Kolovrat v. Oregon*, 366 U.S. 187. In *Zschernig v. Miller*, 389 U.S. 429, annot. *Fiduc. Rev.* March 1968, the United States Supreme Court struck down an Oregon statute restricting distribution to iron curtain countries and residents thereof and in the process of so doing pointed to Pennsylvania law and decisions as also unconstitutional. The basis for the court's decision was that such statutes are improper "intrusion by the State into the field of foreign affairs which the Constitution entrusts to the President and the Congress." It is to be noted that despite the Supreme Court's decision, it does not follow necessarily that persons residing in foreign countries who claim to be distributees automatically will receive their distributive shares, since the burden will still rest upon them to establish their existence and identity as heirs or legatees. See *Bjarsch v. Di Falco*, 314 F. Supp. 127 (USDC NY 1970) finding that New York statute restricting distribution to foreign distributees was not unconstitutional, despite *Zschernig v. Miller*. Where citizen of Cuba died without known heirs, funds were paid to Commonwealth without escheat "until the question of who is legally entitled to the funds is resolved." *Bayuk Trust*, 28 Fiduc. Rep. 454, annot. *Fiduc. Rev*. Oct. 1978, p. 3.

In *Kwiedarawicz Est*., 19 Fiduc. Rep. 568, it was held that "A finding that a claimant has not established his identity, if there is any evidence to sustain it, is just as repugnant to the reasoning of *Zschernig v. Miller*, supra, as a finding that the claimants will not have the actual benefit, use, enjoyment or control of the funds." See also *Fiduc. Rev*. March 1972.

## § 16.13 DECEASED DISTRIBUTEES—LAPSED AND VOID GIFTS

When a distributee predeceases the decedent, the personal representative of the former is not entitled to the distributive share which he would have received if living, unless the will makes it plain that survivorship of the decedent was not a condition precedent to his taking. Unless the testator's will makes an alternative provision for his estate, or gives the donee a power which the donee has exercised in favor of his estate, either the share lapses or, if the distributee bears a stated relation to the decedent, it passes to his surviving issue under the anti-lapse provisions: PEF 2514 (9-11); *Fiduc. Rev*. Dec. 1948; Nov. 1957, p. 3; April 1979; *Vanderkraats Est*., 27 Fiduc. Rep. 2d 327. For distribution of undisposed share of estate to residuary legatees, see *Welsh Trust*, 29 Fiduc. Rep. 583. PEF 3540 provides for the distribution of shares due absentees and shares of possible distributees.

A problem sometimes arises where a distributee is missing but his death prior to the decedent has not been established. See for example *Czerwonka Est*., 17 Fiduc. Rep. 148, where the share of a son missing for more than seven years prior to his mother's death was awarded to her other children upon their giving refunding bonds without security. Entireties property will be divided equally if the order of their deaths cannot be established: *Specht v. Hartman*, 20 D. & C. 3d 735.

Unless the decedent has provided otherwise in his will (see *Fiduc. Rev.* July 1955) the share of a distributee who survived the testator but died thereafter is distributable to his personal representative (see Section 16.5). When the amount to be awarded is less than $25,000, the court is empowered under PEF 3102 to make award directly to the person or persons entitled to his estate. If distribution is long delayed, as when an undisposed-of remainder falls into a decedent's estate, and it is unlikely that rights of creditors will be prejudiced, the court will award the share of a deceased distributee directly to those who ultimately will be entitled thereto, after making sure that inheritance tax in the intervening estate is paid or provided for: see *Fiduc. Rev.* Feb. 1941; *Hemsley Trust*, 28 Fiduc. Rep. 495, annot. *Fiduc. Rev.* Oct. 1978, p. 2.

When a deceased distributee who survives the decedent and then dies is a nonresident, the situation is governed by PEF 4111.

## § 16.14 ADEMPTION AND SATISFACTION

Occasionally specific personal or real property which the decedent has bequeathed or devised to named individuals is not among his assets when he dies or its form has changed. When the testator does not own such property at his death, either because he has sold it or given it away in his lifetime, or its form has changed substantially, a legacy or devise is said to have been "adeemed," with the result that it is not available for distribution to the distributee named in the will. No ademption occurred when the airplane and Rolex watch of decedent were destroyed in the crash which caused his death and his son was entitled to the insurance proceeds received for those assets. *Sagel Est.*, 25 Fiduc. Rep. 2d 348, annot. *Fiduc. Rev.* Sept. 2005, p. 3. Ademption is not a question of intention but results from a change in form which makes the property different from that described in the will: see *Horn Est.*, 317 Pa. 49; *Gibson Est.*, 57 Pa. Super. 283; 74 Harv. L. Rev. 741. If, however, a testator has given a general legacy, for example, a "gold watch," and made it clear that he has no specific watch in mind, the legatee is entitled to *a* watch, whether or not one is found among the testator's assets, and in the latter event the executor is under a duty to procure one. Ademption also is avoided when it is determined that testator intended the legatee to have the proceeds of the conversion of that which was originally given: see *Fiduc. Rev.* July 1946, June 1952, p. 3; Jan. 1957, Jan. 1963; *Bireley Est.*, 30 Fiduc. Rep. 522; *Ferer Est.*, 2 Fiduc. Rep. 2d 134. See *Irwin Est.*, 10 Fiduc. Rep. 241, annot. *Fiduc. Rev.* May 1960, p. 3; *Fiduc. Rev.* Dec. 1976; Feb. 1981, regarding ademption by occurrences during incompetency. In *Schofield Est.* (Pa.), 477 A.2d 473, 302 Pa. Super. 554, aff'g 1 Fiduc. Rep. 2d 188, annot. *Fiduc. Rev.* June 1981, a specific devise of real estate was not saved from ademption by PEF 2514 (16.1) where there was no adjudication of incompetency prior to death. In response to this case, clause (16.1) of PEF Code 2514 (Rules of Interpretation) was amended to clarify its application to the estate of an adjudicated incapacitated person only. A new clause (16.2) was added to deal with non-ademption when the principal is incapacitated but not adjudicated. It reads:

(16.2) *Nonademption; Agent.* If an agent, during the time that his principal is incapacitated within the meaning of section 5501 (relating to meaning of incapacitated person), sells or exchanges property of the principal which is specifically devised or bequeathed, the specific legatee or devisee has the right to the net sale price or the property received in exchange. For the purposes of this paragraph, a sale or exchange of property made by any attorney-in-fact shall be deemed to have been made during the time that the principal is incapacitated, unless shown to the contrary. This paragraph does not apply if it is shown that for a period of at least one year subsequent to the sale or exchange the principal was not an incapacitated person within the meaning of section 5501.

As to the nonademption of the balance of specific devises and bequests, see PEF 2514(18); *Martin Est.*, 29 Fiduc. Rep. 117, annot. *Fiduc. Rev.* April 1979, p. 3.

A legatee or devisee may be excluded from distribution in another not uncommon situation. A general legacy or a gift of the residue may be "satisfied" by a gift during the testator's lifetime. If the decedent bequeaths $5000 to his son, and if, subsequent to the execution of the will but before his death, he gives the son $4000 to set him up in business, the legacy may be found to have been satisfied to that extent by this "advance," and the son may be entitled only to $1000. The purpose of the doctrine is to secure equality among children. Whether or not satisfaction has taken place depends on the testator's intention. There is a presumption of satisfaction when the testator stood in loco parentis to the legatee and when the property given inter vivos is of the same kind as that bequeathed in the will. See *Fiduc. Rev.*, Nov. 1955; *Lemly Est.*, 28 Fiduc. Rep. 155.

Regarding extrinsic evidence and satisfaction of legacies, see *Fiduc. Rev.* Dec. 1957, p. 4. A testator may also "satisfy" a debt by bequeathing to his creditor a sum equal to or exceeding the debt: *Steelman Est.*, 8 Fiduc. Rep. 586. Regarding satisfaction and co-ownership of United States bonds, see *Hollenbaugh Est.*, 402 Pa. 256. See annotation dealing with satisfaction of a legacy in *Fiduc. Rev.* Oct. 2005, p. 4.

## § 16.15 CHANGES IN SECURITIES

It frequently occurs that a testator bequeaths "my 100 shares" or "100 shares" of X Corp. stock, but due to a stock split or dividend there are more than 100 shares in his estate at his death. Whether the legatee will receive all the shares, or merely 100 shares, depends upon the interpretation of testator's intention. See *McFerren Est.*, 365 Pa. 490; *Woodward Est.*, 407 Pa. 638, annot. *Fiduc. Rev.* Sept. 1962, p. 3; 4 Hunter's O.C. Commonplace Book (2d ed.), Legacies and Devises 3. See also *Watson Est.*, 15 Fiduc. Rep. 120, annot. *Fiduc. Rev.* Feb. 1965, p. 3; *Greathead Est.*, 428 Pa. 553, annot. *Fiduc. Rev.* Jan. 1968; *Marks Will*, 435 Pa. 155, annot. *Fiduc. Rev.* Aug. 1969; *Rice Est.*, 22 Fiduc. Rep. 409, annot. *Fiduc. Rev.* Sept. 1972; cf. *Thomas Est.*, 457 Pa. 546, annot. *Fiduc. Rev.* Nov. 1974, p. 3. To clarify the testator's presumed intention, PEF 2514 was amended in 1976 to add:

"(17) *Change in securities.*—If the testator intended a specific bequest of securities owned by him at the time of the execution of his will, rather than the equivalent value thereof, the legatee is entitled only to:

(i) as much of those securities as formed a part of the testator's estate at the time of his death;

(ii) any additional or other securities issued by the same entity thereon and owned by the testator by reason of a stock dividend, stock split or other action by the entity, excluding any acquired by exercise of purchase options for more than a fractional share; and

(iii) securities of another entity received thereon or in exchange therefor and owned by the testator as a result of a merger, consolidation or reorganization of the entity or other similar change."

See *Fiduc. Rev.* Dec. 1976; *Philbin Est.*, 808 A.2d 584, annot. *Fiduc. Rev.* Jan. 2003, p. 3.

## § 16.16 ORDER OF ABATEMENT

PEF 3541 sets forth the rules applicable to the distribution of an estate when there are insufficient assets to pay all claims and distributees:

"(a) *General rules.* Except as otherwise provided by the will, if the assets are insufficient to pay all claimants and distributees in full, the shares of distributees, without distinction between real and personal estate, shall have priority of distribution in the following order:

(1) Property specifically devised or bequeathed to or for the benefit of the surviving spouse;[1]

---

**§ 16.16**

**1.** *Dormer Est.*, 1 Fiduc. Rep. 2d 199, annot. *Fiduc. Rev.* Nov. 1981, p. 3.

(2) Property specifically devised or bequeathed to or for the benefit of the decedent's issue;[2]

(3) Property specifically devised or bequeathed to or for the benefit of other distributees;

(4) Property disposed of by will in the form of a general bequest of cash, stocks or bonds;

(5) Property disposed of by general devise or bequest and not included in a residuary clause;

(6) Property devised or bequeathed in a residuary clause;

(7) Property not disposed of by the will.

(b) *Demonstrative legacies.*[3] Property out of which a demonstrative legacy is primarily to be paid shall be deemed to be specifically devised or bequeathed to the extent of such demonstrative legacy."

The term "issue" as used in (a)(2) includes all lineal descendents and is not limited to those who would take in the event of intestacy: *Thornton Est.*, 420 Pa. 521, annot. *Fiduc. Rev.* April 1966, p. 3.

PEF 2514(19) and 6114(7), in identical wording, provide a rule of presumed intention for wills and inter vivos trusts, reading:

"*Employee benefits.*—Benefits received by a trust under a Federally qualified profit sharing, pension or stock bonus plan shall not be available for the payment of obligations of the decedent or of his estate."

---

§ **16.16**

**2.** See *Fleischut Est.*, 2 Fiduc. Rep. 2d 17; *Tenos Est.*, 1 Fiduc. Rep. 2d 382, annot. *Fiduc. Rev.* Nov. 1981, p. 2.

**3.** A "demonstrative legacy" is a general legacy charged upon specific property but payable even if the legacy is adeemed, provided the estate contains sufficient other property not specifically bequeathed.

See additional references in Section 10.13.

See generally, 4 Hunter, O.C. Commonplace Book (2d ed.), Legacies and Devises, §1(j); *see Fiduc. Rev*. Apr. 2011, p. 1.

## § 16.17 INTEREST OR INCOME ON LEGACIES

The right of debtors to interest on their claims is discussed in Section 10.6. A decree awarding distribution without interest to which neither exceptions nor appeal was filed was final and not subject to review under PEF 3521: *Litostansky Est.*, 499 Pa. 321. The rights of distributees to interest or income on their legacies or distributive shares have been a source of confusion and litigation in the past, but PEF 3543 now provides with considerable precision the interest or income to be allowed on distributive shares:

"(a) *Pecuniary legacy*. A pecuniary legacy bequeathed in trust shall bear interest at the rate of 5%[1] per annum from the death of the decedent until the payment of the legacy, and when not in trust shall bear interest at the rate of 5%[1] per annum from one year after the death of the decedent until the payment of the legacy.[2]

(b) *Specific legacy or devise*. A specific legatee or devisee shall be entitled to the net income from property given to him accrued from the date of the death of the decedent.

(c) *Demonstrative legacy*. A demonstrative legacy shall bear interest from the death of the decedent until the payment of the legacy at the rate earned by the property out of which it is primarily payable, and to the extent that it is

**§ 16.17**

**1.** A 3% rate was in effect prior to January 1, 1981.

**2.** See *Banes Est.*, 27 Fiduc. Rep. 580., annot. *Fiduc. Rev*. Dec. 1977, p. 2, where gift to charity in trust received interest only after one year from death. See *Tose Est.*, 482 Pa. 212, where assets were insufficient to pay the legacies in full and *Passmore Trust*, 3 Fiduc. Rep. 2d 132, where distribution was delayed by litigation. Legatee who refuses unconditional tender of cash bequest loses right to interest thereon thereafter: *Kehr Est.*, 2 Fiduc. Rep. 2d 216.

not paid from that source, shall bear interest at the rate of 5% per annum from one year after the death of the decedent until the payment of the legacy.

(d) *Residuary legacy or devise.* All income from real and personal estate earned during the period of administration and not payable to others shall be distributed pro rata among the income beneficiaries of any trust created out of the residuary estate and the other persons entitled to the residuary estate.

(e) *Future date.* A legacy payable at a future date, unless earlier set aside as a separate trust, shall not bear interest or income until three months after the date fixed for payment or delivery.

(f) *Relationship.* Interest or income shall be paid on distributive shares with no distinction because of the relationship of the distributee to the decedent.

(g) *Testamentary provisions.* All rules set forth in this section are subject to the provisions of the decedent's will."

See generally, 4 Hunter, O.C. Commonplace Book (2d ed.), Legacies and Devises, 14; *Fiduc. Rev.* July 1966, p. 3, Feb. 1971. See PEF 7799(1) for income on trust payments.

Problems of apportionment between income and principal must be determined before the above rules are applicable. Such problems are beyond the scope of this book. However, many of them, as to events occurring after May 3, 1945, are governed by the Principal and Income Acts of 1945 and 1947, now PEF Chapt. 81. See *Fiduc. Rev.* May 1972, Aug. 1973, p. 3; *Wasserman Trust*, 22 Fiduc. Rep. 375.

## § 16.18 ASSIGNMENTS AND ATTACHMENTS

The court, in making distribution, will recognize the rights of attaching creditors and assignees of distributees. In fact, at least one court has gone so far, when the decedent left real estate, as to require that a search be made to determine whether a distributee had any judgment creditors: see *McCormick Est.*, 1 Fiduc. Rep. 225. However, distribution will not be delayed because of an unliquidated claim against a distributee (*Rupert Est.*, 26 Fiduc. Rep. 535) and a creditor of a distributee has no valid objection to award of real estate to another distributee when the value at which real estate was awarded was correct: *Hoy Est.*, 25 Fiduc. Rep. 623. In *Gaulbert Est.*, 14 Fiduc. Rep. 247, a fund was awarded back to the executors to insure its preservation where the distributees' shares had been levied upon by United States for income tax deficiencies which were not yet finally determined. For a general discussion of the rights and remedies of creditors of a distributee, see *Fiduc. Rev.* April 1955; March 1957, p. 3; Oct. 1957.

*See Lebanon Plaza Associates LLC v. Grumbine*, 28 Fiduc. Rep. 2d 474 for procedure to garnish sole legatee's interest in decedent's estate which was not yet settled. However, the civil division judge recognized the jurisdiction of the orphans' court division to direct payment.

A legatee's assignments need not be recognized in distribution where the will contains a spendthrift provision, but the attachment of his interest for delinquent income taxes nevertheless is valid: *Scott Est.*, 7 Fiduc. Rep. 218. In the absence of such a provision, an assignment of a vested remainder will result in distribution to the assignee upon the life beneficiary's death (*Kenney Est.*, 7 Fiduc. Rep. 585), but possibly not a contingent future interest: *Sessler Trust*, 19 Fiduc. Rep. 178; cf. *Braman Will*, 435 Pa. 573, annot. *Fiduc. Rev.* Jan. 1970.

Alimony and child support claim of wife to reach pecuniary bequest to her husband-beneficiary, where PEF 6112 did not apply, was nevertheless reachable by her under the equity doctrine requiring "clean hands" which doctrine was made applicable by the fact that the legatee was a fugitive from a bench warrant in Monroe County. *Griffin Est.*, 17 Fiduc. Rep. 2d 227, annot. *Fiduc. Rev.* Oct. 1997, p. 4.

Where an assignment of a distributive share is found to be in fraud of creditors, a subsequent attachment will be preferred in distribution. Thus, in *Haas Est.*, 15 Fiduc. Rep.

554, the attachment in 1964 of a son's intestate share by a wife on a judgment for support order arrearages was preferred in distribution over the son's 1963 assignment to his sister, which was found to be fraudulent against the wife.

In *Menkovskaya Est.*, 10 Fiduc. Rep. 510, the Pennsylvania estate of a Russian decedent was awarded to a Pennsylvania assignee in partial satisfaction of a claim, where the sole heir (a Russian) had assigned her interest to the claimant, and the latter had made no agreement to transmit the funds to Russia: cf. *Kurz Est.*, 14 Fiduc. Rep. 168.

Several cases involving the sale of a distributee's interest in an estate have exhibited the court's fear that improprieties may be involved, and have contained warnings to the personal representative who honors questionable assignments before audit. See *Eldridge Est.*, 8 Fiduc. Rep. 191, and *Coffey Est.*, 8 Fiduc. Rep. 192, both annotated in *Fiduc. Rev.* May 1958, p. 3; cf. *McIlwain Est.*, 27 D. & C. 619; 171 A.L.R. 351. It should also be noted that an insolvent distributee's assignment may be fraudulent as to his creditors: *Centrella Est.*, 10 Fiduc. Rep. 344.

In *Walters Est.*, 8 Fiduc. Rep. 644, an assignment by a charity of its $5000 legacy for $4000 was condemned as tantamount to a breach of trust and was honored only to the extent of $4000 in distribution: cf. *Jeffers Est.*, 7 Fiduc. Rep. 522, *rev'd on another grounds*, 394 Pa. 393. The assignment of an expectancy in an estate prior to the death of decedent must disclose a transaction that is not unconscionable or inequitable: *Walker Est.*, 28 Fiduc. Rep. 243, annot. *Fiduc. Rev.* Aug. 1978, p. 3. In *Miller Est.*, 19 Som. 20, an assignment of an intestate share fraudulently procured by the administrator was set aside. But see *Nichols Est.*, 11 Fiduc. Rep. 163, holding that an assignment of a claim for $5000 and agreement to pay an additional $10,000 after final adjudication was not champertous.

Regarding the impropriety of making distribution checks payable to the attorney for the distributees, in the absence of a power of attorney or instructions given by such distributees, see *Thilow Est.*, 13 Fiduc. Rep. 348. See *England*

*Est.*, 21 Fiduc. Rep. 383, for evidentiary problems where there were several assignments and a dispute existed as to the date of one of them.

For additional discussion of creditors of a distributee, see *Fiduc. Rev.* Oct. 1957. See generally, 1 Hunter, O.C. Commonplace Book (2d ed.), Assignments.

## § 16.19 AVOIDANCE OF TRUST

In accord with current developments in our statutory (PEF 6102 and 6110) and case law (*Whelan Est.*, 22 Fiduc. Rep. 221; *Cheston Est.*, 12 Fiduc. Rep. 118) permitting the termination of trusts which are impractical of fulfillment, it is frequently possible to arrange for the funds to be awarded in a manner which will more appropriately accomplish the intention or presumed intention of the decedent. For instances when requests for avoidance of the trust have been denied, see *Oberhuber Est.*, 30 Fiduc. Rep. 604, annot. *Fiduc. Rev.* Jan. 1981, p. 2; *Bass Est.*, 1 Fiduc. Rep. 2d 388.

Termination of an ill-advised inter vivos trust including real estate was directed properly by the orphans' court division as authorized by PEF 6110(c), which is applicable to a trust executed prior to its effective date. The college which is the sole beneficiary of the trust which was to continue for 45 years had standing to seek termination of the trust which had no specific purpose. *Robison Family Trust*, 453 Pa. Super. 688, aff'g 15 Fiduc. Rep. 2d 367.

## § 16.20 DECLINED BURIAL TRUST

Decedent's legacy for perpetual cemetery care may be so small that his named trustee declines to act. In such case, the legacy has been awarded to the perpetual endowment fund of the cemetery: *Ward Est.*, 7 Fiduc. Rep. 100; cf. *Wood Trust*, 7 Fiduc. Rep. 541. For a discussion of legislation regarding cemetery trusts and administrative difficulties, see *Fiduc. Rev.* Nov. 1959; March 1962, p. 3.

## § 16.21 CAPACITY OF DISTRIBUTEE

Regarding a form of award to a corporate distributee enabling the court to exercise continuing jurisdiction of such charity, see *Wanamaker Trust*, 7 Fiduc. Rep. 486; cf. PEF 711(21); *Balch Est.*, 21 D. & C. 2d 97; *Jeanes Trust*, 2 Fiduc. Rep. 2d 298. For jurisdiction of orphan's court division over non-profit corporations and cemetery trusts, see *Fiduc. Rev.* June 1975. For exercise of that jurisdiction, see *Scranton Surface Protective Ass'n Special Fund*, 487 Pa. 39; *In re The Edwin Forest Home*, 2 Fiduc. Rep. 2d 104.

If the will purports to create a trust but designates trustees not capable of acting (for example charitable trusts naming a savings bank as trustee which bank is not qualified so to act) it may be appropriate to award the trust fund directly to the charities to maintain it in trust: *Biehl Est.*, 15 Fiduc. Rep. 285.

See also *Gerhart Est.*, 34 D. & C. 2d 39, and cf. *Cowperthwaite Trust*, 15 Fiduc. Rep. 85. Where the will creates a trust, and the trustee is not physically or mentally capable of acting, the trustee will not be permitted to undertake his duties; the court's power of removal includes the power of refusal: *Groesch Est.*, 13 Fiduc. Rep. 65.

For animal as object of testamentary gift, see Section 6.5, supra.

## § 16.22 SLAYERS

Under Chapter 88 of the Probate, Estates and Fiduciaries Code, "any person who participates, either as a principal or as an accessory before the fact, in the willful and unlawful killing . . . shall [not] in any way acquire any property or receive any benefit as the result of the death of such decedent": §§ 8801, 8802. See *Kravitz Est. (No. 2)*, 14 Fiduc. Rep. 393, *aff'd* 418 Pa 319, annot. *Fiduc. Rev*. Aug. 1965, p. 1. The remaining sections of Chapter 88, Sections 8803–8815, set forth the manner in which such property shall be distributed.

For distribution of proceeds of sale of entireties property, see *Ulatoski Est.*, 29 Fiduc. Rep. 27, annot. *Fiduc. Rev.* Mar. 1979, p. 4.

See in general, *Fiduc. Rev.* Aug. 1970, March 1976, April 1977; *DeMatteo Est.*, 1 Fiduc. Rep. 2d 57.

See also *Chase Est.*, 17 Fiduc. Rep. 2d 187, annot. *Fiduc. Rev.* June 1987 where intoxicated driver's accident resulted in death of wife. Although not a wilful slayer, he could not participate in her estate since he would be unjustly enriched. Contra *Marsh Est.*, 25 Fiduc. Rep. 2d 217, where the conviction of vehicular homicide because of an accident while driving under the influence of alcohol which resulted in wife's death was held not to bar husband from sharing in his wife's estate.

Conviction of murder is conclusive proof of liability in a wrongful death and survival action: *Allison Est. v. Sharp*, 96 York 1. However, son acquitted of killing mother by reason of insanity could share in her estate. *Ford Est.*, 18 Fiduc. Rep. 2d 324.

## § 16.23 DIVORCE

Under PEF 2507(2) as to wills and PEF 6111.1 as to all conveyances, all provisions in favor of or relating to a spouse theretofore made become ineffective upon divorce. This provision does not apply to a beneficiary designation on a life insurance policy, since no conveyance is involved: *Equitable Life Assurance Society v. Stitzel*, 299 Pa. Super. 199; *Manhattan Life Ins. Co. of N.Y. v. Evanek*, 587 F. Supp. 479.

In 1994, PEF 6111.2 was amended to make it clear that upon divorce all beneficiary designations of employee benefits and life insurance shall be "construed as if such former spouse had predeceased" the deceased spouse. Although the amendment was stated to apply to beneficiary designations whenever made, it was held by the Pennsylvania Supreme Court that it cannot be applied retroactively to a beneficiary designation made prior to its effective date. The designation of decedent's former wife as beneficiary was not altered by their divorce: *Parsonese v. Midland Nat'l Ins. Co.*, 550 Pa. 423; *Mager v. State Employees' Retirement Board*, 849 A.2d 287.

ERISA preempts PEF 6111.2 so payment to decedent's divorced wife whose designation as beneficiary of his life insurance policy was not changed after divorce was proper. *Sauers Est.*, 32 A.3d 1241. *See Fiduc. Rev.*, June 2008, p. 1 for annotation of Superior Court decision (971 A.2d 1265).

Since divorced wife-beneficiary waived life insurance proceeds subject to ERISA as a part of the divorce action, the estate may sue her for the proceeds received by her. *Kenisnger Est. v. URL Pharma Inc.*, 674 F.3d 131 (U.S. Ct. of Ap., 3rd C., 3/20/12).

Effective as to decedents dying on or after January 28, 2005 during the course of divorce proceedings, the surviving spouse no longer is entitled to an elective one-third share of the assets enumerated in PEF 2203(a) if grounds for divorce have been established under 23 Pa. C.S. § 3323(g). See annotation *Fiduc. Rev.* Feb. 2005, p. 4. Cf. *Timulak v. Timulak*, 26 Fiduc. Rep. 2d 161, where neither party filed the affidavit under § 3323 (g) and the divorce action abates and determination of economic rights proceeds under PEF Code. *See Halterman v. Halterman*, 28 Fiduc. Rep. 2d 138, annot. *Fiduc. Rev.* Apr. 2008, p. 1, where wife died before signing an affidavit of consent and this provision didn't apply.

## § 16.24 EQUITABLE ELECTION

A distributee often is required to make a choice between the benefit provided under the will or other instrument and the retention of property owned or acquired by him from another source. See 2 Hunter O.C. Commonplace Book (2d ed.), Election in Equity. A frequent occasion requiring the exercise of a choice is in connection with life insurance: cf. *Stalnaker Est.*, 1 Fiduc. Rep. 2d 377, annot. *Fiduc. Rev.* Nov. 1981, p. 4, affirmed (Pa. Super.), 479 A.2d 612.

## § 16.25 TANGIBLE PERSONAL PROPERTY

When it has not been possible to make an early distribution or sale of tangible personal property (see Section 6.7), because of disputed claims of ownership (cf. *Baker Est.*, 495 Pa. 522, annot. *Fiduc. Rev.* Nov. 1981; *Rudy Est.*, 2 Fiduc. Rep. 2d 250) or uncertainty of solvency of the estate, the court under PEF 3534 may direct a disposition thereof by distribution in kind among the distributees or by sale.

## § 16.26 ADJUDICATION

After the audit in a county having a separate orphan's court division, the auditing judge in due course will file his adjudication, including a decree of distribution and a confirmation of the account. The adjudication first sets forth such facts as the date of the decedent's death, whether he died testate or intestate, the date of the granting of letters, the payment of inheritance taxes and the terms of the will or (in the event of intestacy) the names of the decedent's heirs and next of kin. Questions of law, if involved, are discussed and a decision thereon is made. The adjudication then directs the payment of claims and awards distribution to those entitled. The auditing judge however, may require the filing of a schedule of distribution. See Section 16.27. If any distribution has already been made by the personal representative, the awards will be stated to be subject to such prior distribution.

The adjudication becomes final unless exceptions thereto are filed with the clerk within the period prescribed by Supreme Court Orphans' Court Rule 7.1(a) (twenty days). After it has become final it may be reviewed in some circumstances. See Section 16.28. If exceptions are filed, they must set forth specifically the alleged errors of the auditing judge, and in due course they will be argued before the court en banc. However, exceptions to the adjudication will be dismissed where no objections have been filed to the account or the schedule of distribution submitted at the audit, and the exceptions were not supported by any newly discovered evidence: *Verdelli Est.*, 17 Fiduc. Rep. 192. The court's opinion, sustaining or dismissing the exceptions, is a final decree, but an appeal therefrom may be taken to the Superior Court. The Orphans' Court must decide exceptions within one hundred twenty days after the filing of the initial exception. O.C. Rule 7.1(f).

In counties having no separate orphan's court division, the auditor's report takes the place of the auditing judge's adjudication.

## § 16.27 SCHEDULE OF DISTRIBUTION

In many instances it is not practical for the court to make definitive awards in the adjudication because of the numerous adjustments and calculations required, especially when assets are to be distributed in kind or when real estate is to be awarded in distribution. In such circumstances, the adjudication will direct the filing of a schedule of distribution. Preparing such a schedule is a matter of reducing to dollars and cents, or to specific assets, the awards made or to be made to claimants and distributees. If required, it should be prepared without delay: cf. *Hickling Est.*, 27 Dist. 652. Even if not required, the personal representative may wish to request an order for the filing of a schedule as an added protection to himself in making distribution. The schedule should show any real estate, securities, cash and other assets which each distributee will receive. Insofar as real estate is concerned, it should be described by metes and bounds, disclose the nature of the title awarded and give a short recital of the source of title into the decedent. In many respects, it performs the same function as a deed from the decedent to the heir or devisee: see PEF 3536. A suggested schedule of distribution will be accepted by most courts at the time of audit. In some counties it is required that it be filed concurrently with the filing of the account. If this is done, the time for final distribution can be accelerated.

When distribution is to be made in kind or in other than fractional shares, it should be approved by all parties in interest or their counsel: *Evans Est.*, 30 Dist. 253. The auditing judge will then approve it as a matter of course. If all parties have not signified their approval, written objections to the schedule may be filed within the time fixed by local rules. If no objections are filed, the schedule becomes absolute and a part of the adjudication.

A schedule of distribution usually is supplementary to the adjudication. It should therefore begin with the balance shown by the adjudication. When the balance for distribution includes assets which fluctuate in value, as in the case of marketable securities, it is necessary to have a reappraisement as of a time close to actual distribution, which should be shown in the schedule of distribution.

The failure to file a schedule of distribution ordered by the Orphans' Court in 1964 was the basis for continued jurisdiction to require the personal representative of the deceased executor, who had moved to Florida prior to this death, to file a second account. *Kravitz Est. (No. 2),* 26 Fiduc. Rep. 2d 406.

Where executor's account reflects a disbursement from principal of a "Reserve for legal fees and closing costs," the schedule of distribution must "reflect the accurate disposition" of the amount reserved. "Major items, and most certainly fees [requested in the petition for adjudication and reserved in the account or on counsel's appearance slip] must be the subject of notice to interested parties—normally in the notice of audit letter": *Prince Est.*, 3 Fiduc. Rep. 2d 160. For objections to schedule of distribution, see *Brickajlik Est.*, 30 Fiduc. Rep. 553. For inclusion of receipts and disbursements subsequent to audit, see *Grote Trust* (*No. 2*)., 2 Fiduc. Rep. 2d 360, annot. *Fiduc. Rev.* Dec. 1982, p. 4. For refusal to reopen account, adjudication and schedule of distribution seven years after approval of schedule of distribution, see *Thomas Est.*, 495 Pa. 93.

For more detailed discussion of the procedure in counties having no separate orphans' court, see Section 16.4.

For forms relating to schedules, see 8 Dunlap Hanna, Pennsylvania Forms 76.10-6.

## § 16.28 REVIEW OF ADJUDICATION

The adjudication of the court or the report of an auditor becomes conclusive upon the parties if no exceptions thereto are filed within the time permitted by rule of court: *Hall Est.*, 36 D. & C. 582; Sup. Ct. O.C. Rules 6.11, 7.1. When errors are discovered in the adjudication or report, they can be corrected within the time fixed for filing exceptions; even after the expiration of such time, the court on its own motion, or upon petition, will correct obvious errors without the necessity of a formal review: *Sloan Est.*, 254 Pa. 346; *Gerlach Est.*, 364 Pa. 207; Sup. Ct. O.C. Rules 2.1; *Jurkowitz Est.*, 359 Pa. 570. This is an inherent right under the common law and a statutory right under the Judicial Code (42 Pa. C.S. § 5505): *Hendel Est.*, 30 Fiduc. Rep. 99, aff'd 496 Pa. 401.

Even after final confirmation of the account, a petition to review any part thereof, or of an auditor's report, or of the adjudication, or of any decree of distribution, may be filed with the court within five years of such final confirmation: PEF 3521. See *Taylor Est.*, 11 Fiduc. Rep. 149. For forms, see 8 Dunlap-Hanna, Pennsylvania Forms § 76.09. The personal representative is protected as to any property distributed by him in accordance with a decree of court before the filing of the petition. Review is a matter of grace and is granted sparingly, usually only on the basis of after-discovered evidence which could not have been obtained previously: *Fiduc. Rev.* June 1970, p. 2; *Cipriotti Est.*, 451 Pa. 91; 5 Hunter, O.C. Commonplace Book (2d ed.), Review.

The court or master considering the petition may include in his adjudication or report findings of fact and of law as to the entire controversy, in pursuance whereof a final order may be made: PEF 3521. This provision is intended to avoid the cumbersome duplication of evidence when a review is granted.

## § 16.29 DISTRIBUTION BY THE PERSONAL REPRESENTATIVE

If no exceptions are filed to the adjudication within the period prescribed by Supreme Court O.C. Rule 7.1 (a) (see

Section 16.26), the personal representative can proceed to distribute the estate in accordance with the decree of the court. If exceptions have been filed, he should consider waiting for one month after the court's decision thereon because of the possibility of an appeal. It should be noted, however, that the filing of exceptions to the adjudication should not necessarily postpone distribution as to persons whose interests are not affected by the exceptions. See PEF 793 re effect of appeal.

If there has been no formal accounting and audit because the personal representative has decided to proceed under PEF 3102, 3531 or 3532, he should be careful to comply with the provisions thereof so as not to make himself personally liable for an improper distribution. See Sections 2.4, 16.1, 16.2.

See annotation "Review—What Actions Are Reviewable?" for discussion of Section 3521 of the Probate, Estates and Fiduciaries Code. *Fiduc. Rev.*, Mar. 1999, p. 3.

## § 16.30 SATISFACTION OF AWARDS-RECEIPTS AND RELEASES

The personal representative is relieved of all liability with regard to real or personal property distributed in conformity with a court decree or in accordance with a rule of court after confirmation of an account: PEF 3533; *Frick Est.*, 1 Fiduc. Rep. 2d 129; *Gallagher Est.*, 30 Fiduc. Rep. 488. But see Section 10.4 regarding claims of the United States. Nevertheless, he is not required to make distribution except upon the execution of a receipt by the distributee. If such receipt is not forthcoming, the personal representative may avoid responsibility by payment of the fund into court: see 42 Pa. C.S. § 3561; *Gehman Est.*, 51 D. & C. 237. Except when the court directs it (cf. PEF 5703), the personal representative is not entitled to a refunding bond when distribution is directed by the court (PEF 3533). However, when the personal representative makes a distribution without benefit of court decree, he would be well advised to demand a refunding bond to protect himself from the hazard thus voluntarily assumed. Cf. *Fiduc. Rev.* Sept. 1977; *Fidelity Bank, Trustee v. Tiernan and Lynagh*, 487 Pa. 484. For forms of refunding bond, see 8 Dunlap-Hanna, Pennsylvania Forms § 76.13.

The personal representative is not personally liable for interest except when he has committed a breach of trust, and then only in the discretion of the court at the rate fixed by the court, "not exceeding the legal rate": PEF 3544.

## § 16.31 ENFORCEMENT OF AWARDS

PEF sections 781 through 786 specify the methods by which all orders and decrees of the court may be enforced. These include (1) attachment of the person, (2) sequestration of real or personal property, (3) execution on personal property, (4) attachment execution and (5) execution on real estate. Of the methods therein listed, the distributee's most effective method of enforcing distribution of an award is the attachment of the person of the personal representative if he is available.

The attachment is usually preceded by a petition for an order to pay (*Wilczinski Est.*, 40 D. & C. 179; cf. *Yeisley Est.*, 358 Pa. 200), but an order to pay is premature when a schedule of distribution has been ordered but has not been filed (*Reimel Est.*, 23 Dist. 675; cf. *Ruane Est.*, 26 Dist. 320). When the occasion requires, as when the personal representative is absconding, there is no reason why the court should not issue its writ peremptorily. Provision is made in PEF 3545 for the filing with the prothonotary of transcripts of balances due by the personal representative. Such balances, when filed, constitute a judgment against the personal representative.

PEF 3545 is not applicable to a decree awarding assets in kind, so that judgment may not be entered therefor: *Montague v. Earnest*, 186 Pa. Super. 210.

For an example of attachment of the person by orphans' court division, see *Lang, Incapacitated Persons (No. 2)*,

16 Fiduc. Rep. 2d 218, annot. *Fiduc. Rev.* Aug. 1996, p. 4, and see also *Lang, Incapacitated Persons* (*No. 3*), 16 Fiduc. Rep. 295, where appeal from dismissal of habeas corpus petition alleging that incarceration of guardian-son was illegal and that orphans' court lacked subject matter jurisdiction over incapacitated parents' missing funds was denied.

## § 16.32 ENFORCEMENT AND CONTROL OF CHARITABLE GIFTS

Consistent with the holding of *Cavill Est.*, 459 Pa. 411, annot. *Fiduc. Rev.* Feb. 1975, 80 Dick. L. Rev. 152, the statutory requirements nullifying charitable gifts (PEF 2507(1) and 6118) made within 30 days prior to death have been repealed. This change in the law presented our courts with the question of the distribution of remainders currently distributable which, except for the 30-day rule, would have been vested when earlier adjudications determined them to be invalid. In *Heilig Est.*, 29 Fiduc. Rep. 265, annot. *Fiduc. Rev.* July 1979, it was ruled that the holding in *Cavill* could not be applied retroactively to defeat the rights of an assignee who had given value for a remainder interest based on the opinion of an attorney who had relied on an adjudication which recited that "a charitable bequest in such circumstances is invalid" unless all the beneficiaries agreed otherwise. To like effect is *Fridenberg Trust*, 1 Fiduc. Rep. 2d 70, where a fund of $100,000 had been set aside to support an annuity and the award of the remainder to the heirs in a 1943 adjudication was held res adjudicata. On the other hand, *Barnholser Trust*, 29 Fiduc. Rep. 423, annot. *Fiduc. Rev.* Oct. 1979, p. 3, ruled that charitable gifts in the will of a 1931 decedent payable at the death of a life beneficiary were valid despite the lack of witnesses. The 1933 adjudication in that case recited that the "charitable bequests given in remainder would *appear* to be void under the Wills Act."

In *Pruner Est.*, 390 Pa. 529, and *Garrison Est.*, 391 Pa. 234, the standing of the Attorney General to represent the public in proceedings involving charities was recognized. Notice must be given to the Attorney General in proceedings involving charities, prominent among which would be the audit of an account when a present distribution is to be made to unnamed charities or to a charitable corporation to be formed, proceedings involving a claim that charitable bequests are invalid, and those involving an election by a surviving spouse which will reduce a charitable bequest: see *Fiduc. Rev.* April 1958. In the absence of a contrary local rule, notice is not required with respect to pecuniary charitable legacies of $25,000 or less which have been or will be paid in full: Sup. Ct. O.C. Rule 5.5.

Action of the Attorney General in behalf of charity has taken the form of objection to compensation claimed by fiduciaries and their attorneys[1] (*Serfass Est.*, 27 Fiduc. Rep. 648), and participation in compromises: cf. *Mitchell Est.*, 2 Fiduc. Rep. 2d 178, annot. *Fiduc. Rev.* June 1982, p. 3.

Usually the Attorney General and the court act in concert in making certain that the public's interest in charities is adequately represented and asserted. And, if the Attorney General is not timely in his actions the court may appoint a trustee ad litem to so act: *Shelly Will*, 484 Pa. 322.

Trusts have been reformed to qualify as charitable remainder unitrusts deductible for federal estate tax purposes: *Ray Trust*, 27 Fiduc. Rep. 476, annot. *Fiduc. Rev.* Oct. 1977 and Act 136 of 1996 amended the Charitable Instruments Act of 1971 to authorize the trustees or directors of charitable organizations "acting alone, without the approval of any member, any court, any donor, or any beneficiary" to amend the governing instrument to insure that gifts qualify as charitable deductions and the charitable organization qualifies for tax exemption.

The Attorney General has represented the public's interest in the combination or termination of charitable trusts to avoid wasteful administration (see *Fiduc. Rev.* Aug. 1977,

---

§ **16.32**

**1.** Compensation can be awarded out of principal whenever the court determines it to be appropriate: PEF 7185(b); *Fiduc. Rev.* Nov. 1979, p. 3.

Dec. 1979, p. 3) as authorized by PEF 6110, and also when application of charitable funds cy pres is sought: *Fiduc. Rev.* May 1974, p. 3; *Eckhart Trust*, 1 Fiduc. Rep. 2d 393, annot. *Fiduc. Rev.* Dec. 1981.

See *Riddle Est.*, 7 Fiduc. Rep. 176, for power of the Attorney General to enforce formation of a charitable corporation in accord with the testator's will: see also 105 U. of Pa. L. Rev. 1044; 73 Harv. L. Rev. 433; *Fiduc. Rev.* Sept. 1974. See Section 16.21 for court's retention of jurisdiction when awards are made to charitable corporation. See *Fiduc. Rev.* Oct. 1969, dealing with problems which arise with respect to honorary trusts, cemetery trusts and charitable trusts under the rule against perpetuities and with respect to excess funds.

## § 16.33 RESERVATION OF FUND FOR CONTINGENCIES

PEF 3387–3389 list instances in which the court may order the personal representative to withhold from distribution sums to meet specified claims. These include claims certain to become due (3387), not certain to become due (3388), and subject to litigation in other courts (3389).[1] See Section 10.7. The court may also direct reservation of funds by the personal representative pending an investigation of the possible existence of distributees: see *Fiduc. Rev.* Sept. 1944; May 1957.

Compare the situation with respect to setting aside of funds in distribution in order to secure payments of annuities created under the will: *Wasserman Trust*, 19 Fiduc. Rep. 404.

A frequent occasion for the reservation of funds at the time of distribution is to meet anticipated claims of the United States Government for taxes, as to which the personal representative might be personally liable without regard to whether or not he was making distribution under court decree. When funds are reserved for any such purpose, the form

---

**§ 16.33**

**1.** See *Franks Est.*, 25 Fiduc. Rep. 646 (distribution suspended), and *Rust Est.*, 29 Fiduc. Rep. 365 (reserve unnecessary), involving litigation in other courts.

of the court's award may be important. For example, in *Harbison Est.*, 365 Pa. 468, annot. *Fiduc. Rev.* Dec. 1950, p. 3, when a fund to meet federal taxes had been awarded to the personal representative "for future accounting," it was held that an omitted creditor who first presented his claim eight months after the decree of distribution was entitled to participate in the fund to the extent it was not needed to pay the tax claim. At the same time, it was indicated that if an absolute award had been made of the excess not required for taxes, the dilatory creditor would not have had a claim as against such surplus. Language of the award sufficient to foreclose such dilatory creditor might be as follows: "To accountants as a reserve for such additional federal and Pennsylvania taxes as may be determined to be due, any unexpended balance thereof remaining to be distributed to the residuary beneficiaries A and B": cf. *U.S. v. Rose* (CA-3), 346 F.2d 985.

## § 16.34 DISCHARGE OF THE PERSONAL REPRESENTATIVE

A personal representative who has concluded his duties and made distribution of the estate to the parties entitled may be discharged (together with his surety, if any) by the court from future liability as a personal representative: PEF 3184. His accounting, subject only to its review (see § 16.28), is a protection against liability for past actions. If the surety alone is discharged, the personal representative continues without surety, but he is not permitted to receive further assets until a new bond is filed with the register: PEF 3184. The discharge is accomplished by petitioning the court and submitting satisfactions of awards.

It is advantageous for an administrator or other personal representative who has given bond with surety to secure discharge of his surety. It is usually inadvisable for a personal representative to petition for discharge because, if additional assets are found, or it is discovered that some additional paper must be signed with regard to assets already delivered, he continues able to act for the estate without incurring the trouble and expense of securing letters d.b.n.

For forms, see 8 Dunlap-Hanna, Pennsylvania Forms § 76.12 and Pennsylvania Probate, Estates and Fiduciaries Code Annotated (3rd Ed. Aker).

## § 16.35 DISTRIBUTION BY PENNSYLVANIA ANCILLARY PERSONAL REPRESENTATIVE

The balance remaining after administration in Pennsylvania (see Sections 3.8, 10.15) may be transmitted to the decedent's domiciliary personal representative (*Middleby Est.*, 249 Pa. 203; *Hazel Est.*, 11 Fiduc. Rep. 169, annot. *Fiduc. Rev.* April 1961), or distributed to foreign creditors or legatees (see *Wolfe v. Lewisburg Trust Co.*, 305 Pa. 583, 590; *Bertin Est.*, 245 Pa. 256; *Mamoto Est.*, 43 D. & C. 331), or may be distributed in part and transmitted in part (*Hough Estate*, 3 Dist. 187). See *Thaw Est.*, 13 Fiduc. Rep. 308, aff'd 414 Pa. 347, regarding distribution by a Pennsylvania corporate executor appointed by a nonresident's will for her Pennsylvania property. It may not be transmitted to another ancillary administrator: *Baldwin Ap.*, 81 Pa. 441. See 21 Am. Jur., Executors and Administrators, §§ 884–889.

## § 16.36 ABANDONED AND UNCLAIMED PROPERTY

Fiduciaries should be alerted to the possibility that decedents may have failed to keep track of assets owned by them. Pursuant to the Disposition of Abandoned and Unclaimed Property Act, 72 P.S. § 1301.1, *et seq.*, after prescribed time periods (for example, bank deposits, seven years), funds held are to be reported to the Secretary of Revenue, who is required to publish listings of owners of abandoned and unclaimed property in a newspaper in the county or in the Pennsylvania Bulletin. Ultimately unclaimed funds are to be paid to the Department of Revenue.

Fiduciaries may find that individuals whose estates they are administering have interests listed in these publications. One of two beneficiaries objected to payment of 15%

finder's fee to claimant who brought existence of unclaimed property to the executor's attention. Claimant did not comply with 72 P.S. § 1301.11 (g) (1–4) which required a signed agreement concerning fees. Court awarded one half of the claimed fee because the other beneficiary did not object. *Miller Est.*, 30 Fiduc. Rep. 2d 391.

See also PEF 3540, which provides for payment of assets of absentees to the Department of Revenue.

## § 16.37 POWER OF ATTORNEY GIFTS

Much litigation has occurred after use of powers of attorney to make gifts. One power of attorney authorized daughter to make unlimited gifts, including gift of $96,545.27 to herself as trustee for her son, which gift was made after the donor of the power had lapsed into a coma one day before death. "The grant of the power of attorney expressly allowing unlimited gifts, coupled with the clear conviction of several disinterested witnesses that the decedent wanted to provide a college education for his grandson, satisfies the respondent's burden to prove that the gift was fair and beyond suspicion." *White Est.*, 16 Fiduc. Rep. 2d 272.

Wife's power of attorney to her daughters by her first marriage incorporated by reference all powers in PEF Code Chapter 56 and, therefore, daughter's change of beneficiary on decedent's life insurance policies from second husband to daughters was upheld under *Reifsneider Est.*, 531 Pa. 19, 610 A.2d 958. Amendments to PEF Code Chapter 56 do not apply to pre-existing power of attorney. *In re Weidner* (Pa.) 938 A.2d 354, *rev'g* Superior Court, 895 A.2d 11.

Numerous other cases invalidated some or all gifts. *Dolezal v Volpe*, 27 Fiduc. Rep. 2d 356, annot. *Fiduc. Rev.* Dec. 2007, p. 4; *DeMitis Est.* 28 Fiduc. Rep. 2d 105 annot. *Fiduc. Rev.* March 2008, p. 3; *Kuehn Est.*, 29 Fiduc. Rep. 2d 374; *Est. of Loretta Frances Wolf*, 29 Fiduc. Rep. 2d 4; *Brodsky Est.*, 29 Fiduc. Rep. 2d 57, annot. *Fiduc. Rev.* Mar. 2009,

p. 1; *Makuch Est.*, 28 Fiduc. Rep. 2d 323, annot. *Fiduc. Rev.* Oct. 2008, p. 3; *Slomski Est. v. Thermoclad Co. et al.*, 956 A.2d 438, annot. *Fiduc. Rev.* Nov. 2008, p. 1. *See* annotation re impact of confidential relation on power of attorney gifts. *Fiduc. Rev.* Dec. 2009, p. 3.

Act 39 of 1999 makes extensive changes to Chapter 56 of the PEF Code dealing with power of attorney, including new Section 5601.2 setting forth special rules for gifts. See annotation *Fiduc. Rev.* Dec. 1999.

# Chapter 17

# WILL CONTESTS



## § 17.1 INTRODUCTION

A contest to determine whether or not a writing is the will of the decedent may involve as many as three separate hearings de novo: first, on caveat before the register prior to the probate of the will; again, before the court on appeal from the register's decree of probate or refusal to probate; and finally, before the court sitting with a jury. A contestant attempting to upset a will ordinarily assumes a heavy burden of proof, and, proportionately speaking, few contests are successful. For this reason, and because the proceedings can be lengthy and costly, settlement should be encouraged whenever possible. Provisions designed to encourage settlements are included in PEF 3323, 5144(10), 5521(16), 7133(10).

A will contest is begun by a caveat before probate or by an appeal from probate. A caveat[1] is a proceeding to challenge the validity of the testator's will; it is begun by filing a writing which requests the register not to probate the will without giving notice to the caveator.[2] A telephone call to the

**§ 17.1**

**1.** "Caveat," literally translated from the Latin means "let him beware."

**2.** Parties to caveat proceedings are called "caveators" and "proponents."

register is not equivalent to filing of a written caveat: *Buck Est.*, 14 Fiduc. Rep. 201. The effect of the filing of a caveat is to delay probate until the register determines the issues raised by the caveat, or the caveat is abandoned. See Section 17.5. Any decree of the register may be appealed to the orphans' court division by a party aggrieved thereby. See Section 17.6. If on appeal the court finds from the record that there is an issue of fact, it may then order a jury trial: PEF 776, 777; 1 Hunter, O.C. Commonplace Book (2d ed.), Contests of Wills § 7. Otherwise, the court must hear the evidence de novo, unless all parties appearing in the proceedings agree that the case be heard on testimony taken before the register: PEF 776. At any stage of the proceedings, the court, in its discretion, may impanel a jury to decide any question of fact, but the jury verdict will be advisory only: PEF 777(c); *Fiduc. Rev.* Aug. 1961, p. 3. The award of a jury trial upon an appeal from probate is an interlocutory order and is not reviewable by the court en banc or by appeal: *Murray Will*, 404 Pa. 120, annot. *Fiduc. Rev.* Aug. 1961, p. 3. Of course, a refusal to award a jury trial is a final order. Any party in interest may appeal a final order or decree of the court to the Superior Court: 42 Pa. C.S. § 5105.

A will contest is a proceeding in rem which, if notice has been given to all interested parties,[3] is conclusive as to all the world: *Mangold v. Neuman*, 371 Pa. 496. The death of a party to a contest does not result in abating the action or impairing the jurisdiction of the court to proceed to a final decree: *Stewart Est.*, 358 Pa. 434. For the procedure to be followed in a will contest hearing, see *McCarthy Will*, 2 Fiduc. Rep. 2d 410. See also Aker, Law of Wills in Pennsylvania §§ 9.2, 10.2.

The Pennsylvania Rules of Civil Procedure regarding depositions and discovery are applicable to the orphans' court division (*Doran Estate*, 12 D. & C. 2d 167; cf. *Commonwealth*

---

§ **17.1**

**3.** A party who has no notice is not barred from later action: *Miller Est.*, 159 Pa. 562. However, omission of joinder of a party in interest is not, by itself, necessarily reversible error: *Thomas Will*, 349 Pa. 212. See the discussion of pleadings and service to obtain jurisdiction of the parties in *Conley Est.*, 8 Fiduc. Rep. 427.

*v. Barnes Foundation (No. 2)*, 11 Fiduc. Rep. 29; 74 Harv. L. Rev. 940; *Fiduc. Rev.* Feb. 1962), although it has been held that contestants are not entitled to take legatees' depositions until they show a prima facie case (*Evans Will*, 8 Fiduc. Rep. 431; *contra: Erb Estate*, 11 Fiduc. Rep. 630). See *Fiduc. Rev.* Feb. 1971, p. 3; *Fecera Est.*, 24 Fiduc. Rep. 12. See in general, 1 Hunter O.C. Commonplace Book (2d ed.), Contest of Wills, § 7(a) et seq.; Aker, Law of Wills in Pennsylvania § 8.1 et seq.

On May 8, 1998 the Pennsylvania Supreme Court adopted its Rules of Evidence which became effective October 1, 1998. The Rules of Evidence are to be cited Pa. R.E. [see Rule 101(b)] and are published at 28 Pa. Bulletin 2369. The rules in proposed form were the subject of an article in the May, 1997 issue of *Fiduciary Review* which should be read in conjunction with an article in the August 1998 issue.

## § 17.2 PARTIES IN INTEREST

As used in this chapter, the term "party in interest" denotes one who has legal standing to engage in a will contest: see PEF 908(a); 42 Pa. C.S. § 5105; Pa. R.A.P. 342, 501. One whose share in the estate would be greater if the purported will is not probated is a proper party contestant, whereas one who stands to lose if the will is not probated is a proper party proponent: *Kreider Est.*, 85 D. & C. 443; *Leathem Est.*, 54 D. & C. 73; *Boland Estate*, 99 Pa. Super. 321. Any person named in a testamentary writing[1] may appeal a decree refusing probate of it. See generally, *Fiduc. Rev.* May 1963, p. 3.

The Attorney General may be a necessary party in, and (except for pecuniary legacies of $25,000 or less which have been or will be paid in full) is entitled to notice of, proceedings involving charitable gifts: Sup. Ct. O.C. Rule 5.5; *Pruner Est.*, 390 Pa. 529; *Garrison Est.*, 391 Pa. 234; *Fiduc. Rev.* April 1958.

**§ 17.2**

**1.** Except the executor, who may not appeal: PEF 908(a); see Section 17.3.

When the interest of a contestant is challenged, the validity of that interest may be determined before any further issue may be considered: *Rogers Est.*, 154 Pa. 217. The burden is on the contestant to show that he is a "party in interest": *Kreider Est.*, 85 D. & C. 443. A person who would receive a smaller share of the estate if successful is not a party in interest entitled to contest a will: *Terregino Est.*, 17 Crawford 359. Preliminary objections may be filed, even though a citation had not yet issued, to the status of the appellant from probate as a proper party: *Cameron Est.*, 11 Fiduc. Rep. 41. Some examples of "parties in interest" who may contest a will are:

(1) Heirs at law, who would share in the estate in the absence of the will: *Rogers Est.*, 154 Pa. 217; *Whitaker Est.*, 10 W.N.C. 106; *Heffner Will*, 17 Fiduc. Rep. 572. They need not account for all other possible next of kin to continue their contest of the will: *McClain Est.*, 30 Fiduc. Rep. 232. Intestate heirs who stipulated two earlier wills were valid have no standing to contest probate of a document. *Whelan Will*, 23 Fiduc. Rep. 2d 124. Intestate heir has no standing where the will makes an alternate disposition if the residuary legatee did not survive testator. *Burger Est.*, 852 A.2d 385.

(2) A beneficiary under a prior otherwise unrevoked will: *Ash Will*, 351 Pa. 317; *McCarty Will*, 355 Pa. 103; 47 Va. L. Rev. 901.

(3) A beneficiary under a later will: *Boland Est.*, 99 Pa. Super. 321.

(4) The guardian or guardian ad litem (*Hornsey Will (No. 2)*, 1 Fiduc. Rep. 2d 332) of a minor (see *Posey Est.*, 52 D. & C. 127) or of an incompetent (*Furda Will*, 40 Wash. 72) if the ward is a proper party contestant.

(5) An escheator appointed by the Commonwealth: *Cassidy Est.*, 54 D. & C. 647; *Smith Est.*, 23 D. & C. 519; cf. *Springer Est.*, 5 Fiduc. Rep. 528, annot. *Fiduc. Rev.* Oct. 1955, p. 4.

(6) For status of the Commonwealth as a party in interest, see *Tierney Will*, 10 Fiduc. Rep. 310. For the status of

the Attorney General representing charity, see *Cain Will*, 1 Fiduc. Rep. 2d 152, annot. *Fiduc. Rev.* May 1981, p. 3.

(7) One who would take in default of the exercise of a power of appointment: *Hurst Will*, 406 Pa. 612; *Coleman Est.*, 4 Dist. 105.

(8) A surviving spouse who would receive a greater amount under an earlier or a later will (*Boland Est.*, 99 Pa. Super. 321), or whose right to the spouse's allowance in the event of intestacy is involved (*Sherman Est.*, 5 Fiduc. Rep. 497, annot. *Fiduc. Rev.* Sept. 1955). Otherwise, the surviving spouse is not a party in interest.[2]

(9) After-born or after-adopted children.

(10) A trustee named in a testamentary writing.

(11) The register of wills of the county alleged to be the testator's principal residence, where the will has been probated elsewhere: *Burke Est.*, 1 Fiduc. Rep. 260; *contra: Cameron Est.*, (*No. 2*), 12 Fiduc. Rep. 586.

## § 17.3 ROLE OF THE PERSONAL REPRESENTATIVE

If letters have been granted to a personal representative before a contest is initiated, he has power to continue administration until the contest results in voiding his authority to act. In other words, an appeal from probate does not suspend his powers or prejudice his acts: PEF 793, 908(c), 3329, 3357. This rule is to avoid prejudicing the estate by holding the administration in abeyance pending the outcome of a will contest. However, the personal representative should not make any distribution until the contest is resolved.

A personal representative, as such, is not a "party in interest" eligible to initiate a will contest, and he may not ap-

**§ 17.2**

**2.** There is no inconsistency between electing to take against a will and challenging its validity on appeal from probate: *Butler Est.*, 3 Fiduc. Rep. 104.

peal from a decree refusing probate: PEF 908(a); *Fleszar Will*, 8 Fiduc. Rep. 99. However, if there are two wills, the executor of the later one can appeal from the probate of the earlier one, and the executor of the earlier one cannot contest the appeal; see *Gulden Will*, 3 Fiduc. Rep. 627, annot. *Fiduc. Rev.* Dec. 1953, p. 3; cf. *Thompson Will*, 416 Pa. 249; *Underdown Will*, 24 Fiduc. Rep. 311.

The personal representative is a necessary party defendant to an appeal from probate: *Evans Will*, 8 Fiduc. Rep. 431. However, active participation in defense of the will involves a personal risk to the executor, since it is a general rule that if he does engage in a will contest he has no authority to charge to the estate the fees of legal counsel incurred in such contest but must look for remuneration to those who authorized him to participate therein: *Faust Est.*, 364 Pa. 529, annot. *Fiduc. Rev.* June 1950, p. 3;[1] cf. *Coffin Est.*, 16 Fiduc. Rep. 627.

## § 17.4 GROUNDS FOR WILL CONTESTS

(1) *Mental incapacity*. PEF 2501 requires that a person be of "sound mind" to make a will. One has a "sound mind" if he has full and intelligent knowledge of the act that he is engaged in, a knowledge of the property he possesses and an intelligent understanding of the dispositions he desires to make of it and the persons and objects he desires to be the recipients of his bounty: *Snyder Est.*, 279 Pa. 63.

Sickness or old age, peculiar beliefs or opinions and incapacity to do business (and even an adjudication of incompetence: *Bartnikowski Will*, 2 Fiduc. Rep. 2d 118; *Hastings Est.*, 479 Pa. 122) do not of themselves prove incapacity: *Rife Will*, 59 York 169. Testamentary capacity is presumed. Clear and convincing proof is required to set aside a will drawn by an attorney and proved by subscribing witnesses:

---

**§ 17.3**

**1.** An executor of a will later invalidated may, however, recover from the estate any administrative expense incurred by him prior to such invalidation: see *Royer Ap.*, 13 Pa. 569.

*Protyniak Will*, 427 Pa. 524. After proof of execution by two witnesses, the burden of proof as to incapacity is on the contestant: *Sturgeon Will*, 357 Pa. 75. Regarding monomania, see *Sommerville Will*, 406 Pa. 207; *Mason Will*, 20 Fiduc. Rep. 499. Regarding insane delusions, see *Duross Will*, 395 Pa. 492; *Agostini Est.*, Pa. Super., 457 A.2d 861.

Senile dementia is the most common mental weakness alleged by contestants in attempting to show lack of testamentary capacity. Characteristics of behavior generally found in a person suffering from senile dementia are: delusions, usually of infidelity or of persecution by those close to the person; general mental confusion and lack of orientation in time or space and in his personal relationships; loss of memory as to significant facts about himself, his family and his possessions; deterioration of the emotions, marked by little response to such occurrences as a family tragedy or public calamity but by a major response to anything pertaining to himself; substantial changes in his respect for social conventions; excessive anger or irritability; neglect of personal cleanliness or general care of his person; bizarre mannerisms; intense feelings of impoverishment, anxiety and depression.[1] If many of these characteristics are manifested by the testator at the time he makes his will, considerable doubt may be cast on his testamentary capacity and hence on the validity of his will.

Regarding the relative weights of testimony by an attorney[2] and a subscribing witness and attending physicians not present at the execution of the will, see *Spirof Will*, 11 Fiduc. Rep. 433; *Cohen Will*, 21 Fiduc. Rep. 186; *Fiduc. Rev.* May 1958. In *Crumling Will*, 9 Fiduc. Rep. 4, a codicil executed by an adjudicated incompetent was admitted to probate where the subscribing witnesses (psychiatrist, physician and legal adviser-scrivener) testified to decedent's capacity. Desiring to revise her will and P.O.D. account beneficiaries, a person adjudicated incapacitated petitioned for review and it was determined she had testamentary capacity. The possible

§ **17.4**

**1.** Strecker, Basic Psychiatry 80–84 (1952); Strecker, Ebaugh and Ewalt, Practical Clinical Psychiatry 103–113 (1951).

**2.** For attorney–client privilege, see *Fiduc. Rev.* April 1983.

impact of this decision on a future will contest was not determined. *German, Incapacitated Person*, 28 Fiduc. Rep. 2d 459, annot. *Fiduc. Rev.* Dec. 2008, p. 1.

(2) *Undue influence.* Undue influence, to affect the validity of a will or a part thereof, must be such as to subjugate the mind of a testator to the will of the person exerting the influence. To establish this, there must be proof of some threats, misrepresentations, inordinate flattery or some physical or mental coercion employed to destroy the free agency of the testator: *Quein Will*, 361 Pa. 133. These influences must be proved to have operated as a present constraint at the time of the making of the will: *Williams v. McCarroll*, 374 Pa. 281; *King Will*, 369 Pa. 523. It is impossible to say what combination of parts makes out a case of undue influence. Influence or persuasion is permissible; for the influence to be "undue" it must operate so as to substitute the will of another for the authentic will of the testator.

There is generally a presumption of the absence of undue influence: *Quein Will*, 361 Pa. 133. If undue influence is alleged to have been exerted on a testator who was well and strong at the time, it can only be supported by proof of fraud or coercion to prevail: *Plege Est.*, 340 Pa. 529. However, if there is evidence that the testator was infirm in body and mind and that the beneficiary was a stranger to the blood or standing in a confidential relationship to the testator, a presumption as to undue influence will arise: *Phillips Est.*, 244 Pa. 35. In these circumstances, the burden is on the proponents to show that the testator made the will with understanding and on his own volition and that the circumstances were open and fair: *Williams v. McCarroll*, 374 Pa. 281. For shifting of the burden of proof and of going forward with evidence, see *Clark Est.*, 461 Pa. 52; *Ziel Est.*, 467 Pa. 531; *Cleaver Will*, 1 Fiduc. Rep. 2d 403, annot. *Fiduc. Rev.* Nov. 1981, p. 3; *Younger Est.*, Pa Super., 461 A.2d 259, annot. *Fiduc. Rev.* July 1983.

If the circumstances are such that undue influence and mental incapacity are so closely interwoven that it is difficult to separate them in conducting a judicial inquiry, both of these questions must be included in the issue submitted to the jury: *Lewis Will*, 364 Pa. 225; *Lawrence Est.*, 286 Pa. 58.

To the extent that *Younger Est.* (Pa. Super.), 461 A.2d 259, holds that the Code of Professional Conduct has the force of substantive law, "it is disapproved." However, the attorney-scrivener-beneficiary's departure from ethical standards bars him from relief in equity under the "clean hands" doctrine and the action of the orphans' court, in entertaining the appeal of the attorney from refusal to probate the will, is reversed. *Pedrick Est.* (Pa. Supreme), 482 A.2d 215. Query whether this case identifies an additional ground for relief in will contests, since the court did not rely on undue influence or other grounds mentioned in this section.

"The effect of *Pedrick* is to return the law on undue influence to its pre-*Younger* state. Accordingly, a presumption of undue influence does not arise where an attorney drafts a will under which he or his family is a beneficiary." If there is no weakened intellect, "there is no presumption placing the burden on the attorney-scrivener to show by clear and convincing evidence that the gift arose from the will of testator and not from undue influence of the attorney." *McDonnell Will*, 5 Fiduc. Rep. 2d 225.

A will gift of more than one-third of a million dollar estate to the attorney-scrivener was not set aside where there was confidential relationship and substantial benefit, but no weakened intellect of the decedent. In addition, the equitable doctrine of clean hands set forth in *Pedrick* did not preclude the attorney-scrivener from sharing in the estate. *Younger Est.* (Pa. Super.), 508 A.2d 327.

See *Fiduciary Rev.*, Dec. 1998, p. 4 for an annotation concerning undue influence and substantial benefit. The annotation points out that two recent cases have found no substantial benefit when the benefit in the will under attack is compared with the decedent's preceding will. In *Ciaffoni Will*, 18 Fiduc. Rep. 2d 177, the court found a one-sixth share of $200,000 did not constitute a substantial benefit. More recently, in *Gower Will*, 18 Fiduc. Rep. 2d 388, the court found no substantial benefit where decedent revised his will to increase respondent's share from zero to one-fifth and to reduce contestant's from one-fifth to zero. No substantial benefit existed where proponent received 40% of the estate and contestant received 60%. *Revenson Est.*, 27 Fiduc. Rep. 2d 385.

In most cases in which undue influence is alleged, a confidential relation between the testator and a beneficiary is averred. As stated in *Leedom v. Palmer*, 274 Pa. 22, 25, "Confidential relation is not confined to any specific association of the parties; it is one wherein a party is bound to act for the benefit of another, and can take no advantage to himself. It appears when the circumstances make it certain the parties do not deal on equal terms, but, on the one side there is an overmastering influence, or, on the other, weakness, dependence or trust, justifiably reposed; in both an unfair advantage is possible. When these circumstances appear, the law presumes the transaction void, unless the party claiming the benefit of such transaction shows affirmatively that no deception was used and the act was the intelligent and understood act of the grantor, fair, conscientious and beyond the reach of suspicion." The relation is most commonly found between trustee and beneficiary, lawyer and client, guardian and ward, and principal and agent. See generally 1 Hunter, O.C. Commonplace Book (2d ed.), Contest of Wills § 12(a).

Proof of undue influence, if it existed, should be collected to establish such matters as the dominant personality of the person charged with the undue influence, his opportunity to exert pressure, the procurement by him of the draftsman of the instrument, his supervision of the work done, his seizure and retention of the writing and his denial of access by others to the testator. In general, the contestant should try to develop whatever facts establish the overmastering of the mind, intention and will of deceased. See generally, 42 U. of Pitts. L.R. 225.

The Superior Court opinion in *Basile and Clavin v. H & R Block, Inc.*, 777 A.2d 95 by Judge Johnson contains a helpful review of Pennsylvania case law on the test for proving a confidential relation. See annotation in *Fiduc. Rev.* Apr. 2002, p. 1.

(3) *Improper execution of the will.* Wills are subject to attack on the ground that (a) execution thereof does not com-

ply with provisions of the Wills Act or (b) the will is a forgery. Either the text of the will or the signature may be attacked: see *Lare Will*, 352 Pa. 323.

Due execution is a question of law for the court: *Cohen Will*, 356 Pa. 161; cf. *Ruoff Ap.*, 26 Pa. 219. Credibility of proof as to whether or not the will is genuine may be a question for the jury: PEF 777(c); cf. *Lare Will*, 352 Pa. 323; *Maganuco Est.*, 1 Fiduc. Rep. 188. When there is proof of due execution by two witnesses, a heavy burden rests on the contestant to prove forgery: *Pochron Will*, 367 Pa. 306; *Elias Will*, 429 Pa. 314; *Cline Will,* 433 Pa. 543.

As to what constitutes a signature, see *Fiduc. Rev.* March 1949. Compare *Pavlinko Will*, 394 Pa. 564, annot. *Fiduc. Rev.* Feb. 1959, p. 3, 107 U. of Pa. L. Rev. 1237, where husband and wife mistakenly executed wills prepared for the other. Compare *Coyne Will*, 349 Pa. 331, rev'g 45 Lack. 21, annot. *Fiduc. Rev.* June 1944; *Glace Will*, 413 Pa. 91. On execution by mark, see *Fiduc. Rev.* June 1960, p. 3, May 1964, Nov. 1977, p. 4; *Torhan Will*, 401 Pa. 529. See also Brégy, Intestate, Wills and Estates Act of 1947, p. 2206. Regarding the requirement that the signature be at the end of the will, see *Kretz Est.*, 410 Pa. 590; *Fiduc. Rev.* Nov. 1962; *Weiss Will*, 21 Fiduc. Rep. 1, annot. *Fiduc. Rev.* Jan. 1971, aff'd 444 Pa. 126; *Knupp Will*, 428 Pa. 409, annot. *Fiduc. Rev.* Jan. 1968, p. 3; *Flynn Will*, 2 Fiduc. Rep. 2d 124, annot. *Fiduc. Rev.* May 1982 (error in employing "self proved" procedure). See chart in *Fiduc. Rev.* Sept. 1976, p. 4, concerning the execution, revocation, alteration and modification of wills under the PEF Code.

Execution of a codicil by an agent under a power of attorney is improper, since an agent cannot sign a testamentary document. *Pendergrass Will*, 30 Fiduc. Rep. 2d 430, annot. *Fiduc. Rev.* Oct. 2010, p. 3.

When the court, after hearing, either sustains or dismisses an appeal alleging that the will was not executed in compliance with the Wills Act, the order is a definitive, final and appealable order: *Henry Est.*, 290 Pa. 537. Thus, a petition for rehearing without a stay order does not stop the running of the appeal period.[3]

If there is a suspicion of forgery, a party in interest will do well to have the instrument examined by handwriting experts at an early date: *Jones Will*, 19 Fiduc. Rep. 55. There has been, in this area, marked scientific improvement to the point that the expert opinions of competent handwriting experts are gaining the confidence of the courts: cf. *Kadilak Will*, 405 Pa. 238; *Cruciani Est.*, 986 A.2d 853 and *Zachry Will*, 30 Fiduc. Rep. 2d 157, annot. *Fiduc. Rev.* June 2010, p. 3; *Shupe Will*, 21 Fiduc. Rep. 230; *Politis Will*, 19 Fiduc. Rep. 110. Regarding cross-examination of a handwriting expert, see 13 Rutgers L. Rev. 306; and see 22 U. of Pitts. L. Rev. 675.

(4) *Fraud.* A ground of contest closely related to undue influence and improper execution is fraud, that is, where the will or some part thereof has been procured by deception rather than coercion or forgery. Such fraud consists of two kinds: fraud in the inducement and fraud in execution: Aker, Law of Wills in Pennsylvania § 9.5. An illustration of fraud in the inducement is *Nicoll Est.*, 8 West. 41, in which a sister and mother, in order to procure a will in their favor, succeeded by misrepresentations in poisoning the testator's mind against his son. Fraud in execution arises, for example, when the testator's signature to a testamentary paper is obtained by misrepresenting to him that the paper is a power of attorney: see *Thomas Will*, 349 Pa. 212. For inadequacy of petition alleging forgery, see *Holleran Will*, 29 Fiduc. Rep. 32. There are few instances in which a will is attacked solely on the ground of fraud. The charge is frequently conjoined with allegations of undue influence or improper execution. For evidence in support of forgery, see *Fiduc. Rev.* Sept. 1956, p. 4. For successful contest on ground of forgery alone, see *Brubaker Will*, 2 Fiduc. Rep. 2d 129. See *Roos Est.*, Pa. Super., 451 A.2d 255, aff'g 1 Fiduc. Rep. 2d 117, for award of attorney fee to attorney-scrivener who totally without foundation was accused of fraud and undue influence.

---

§ **17.4**

**3.** See Section 17.7.

## § 17.5 CAVEAT

A caveat to probate can be filed only before the will is probated. See Section 17.1. Initially, it is generally an informal writing setting forth the name of the decedent, the date and place of his death, the interest of the caveator and a request that he be heard before any action is taken by the register. While initially informal, it must nevertheless be in writing, and a telephone call to the register is insufficient: *Buck Est.*, 14 Fiduc. Rep. 201. Its effect is to delay probate and grant of letters until the contest is determined or abandoned; it also, therefore, delays administration unless the register decides to appoint an administrator pendente lite during this period. See Section 3.2; PEF 3160. Such an appointment cannot be made after certification to the court except by leave of court: PEF 907. Within ten days of the filing of the caveat or of the petition for probate, whichever is later, the caveator must post a bond which may be set at any figure from $500 to $5000: PEF 906(a). The caveat may be withdrawn at any time and will be considered abandoned if no bond is filed within the ten-day period: PEF 906(b). A request to permit a caveat nunc pro tunc will be denied: *Dewey Will*, 2 Fiduc. Rep. 2d 204, annot. *Fiduc. Rev.* Sept. 1982, p. 3.

If the caveator wishes to proceed with the contest, he should then file a formal caveat alleging facts sufficient to warrant a refusal to probate the will. The caveat should include the names of all parties in interest both under the alleged will or wills and under the Intestate Act. For form of caveat, see Partridge-Remick, O.C. Practice § 4.03. Thereafter, the register will call for a preliminary hearing to inquire into the basis of the complaint.

After the preliminary hearing the register may decide either to hear and determine the case or to certify the entire record to the court for hearing and determination therein. Before certification, there must be at least a preliminary hearing: PEF 907. See *Fiduc. Rev.* Feb. 1961, p. 2; July 1976. If the register decides to determine the case himself, the court on its own motion, or on petition of any party in interest, may require certification at any stage of the hearing before the register: PEF

907. For procedure and form of certification, see Aker, PEF Code Annot. § 907; Partridge-Remick, O.C. Practice §§ 4.04, 4.05; Aker, Law of Wills in Pennsylvania § 9.2G.

When the evidence has been heard, the register may dismiss the caveat and probate the will, or he may enter a decree refusing probate, or he may certify the entire record to the court. The decree of the register may be appealed to the court by a party in interest within one year: PEF 711(18), 908(a); Aker, PEF Code Annot. § 908.

## § 17.6 APPEALS FROM DECREES OF THE REGISTER

An appeal from any decree of the register must be perfected within one year, but the court, on petition of a party in interest, may set the time limit at three months: PEF 908(a); cf. *Thomas Est.*, 19 Fiduc. Rep. 184. The time limit may be waived in cases of forgery (*Culbertson Estate*, 301 Pa. 438), or of uncertainty of the probate record (*Rockett Will*, 348 Pa. 445). The time limit has been waived upon discovery of a later will: see *Fiduc. Rev*. Jan. 1959, p. 3. Failure to give notice under Rule 5.6(a) to a son required a waiver of the one-year time limit since the false certification of notice to all required parties was a fraud on the Register. *Schulman Will*, 21 Fiduc. Rep. 2d 310, annot. *Fiduc. Rev*. Sept. 2001, p. 3. See annotation in the March 1987 issue of *Fiduciary Review* concerning effect of Judicial Code amendment relating to minors on the one-year limitation for appeal from probate. Abuse of discretion by the Register must be shown to set aside the appointment of a fiduciary. *Dennis Est.*, 1 Fiduc. Rep. 3d 288, annot. *Fiduc. Rev*. Aug. 2011, p. 4.

Under PEF 3138, the register may open the probate record within three months of death to receive proof of later wills or codicils and may amend the probate record after such notice as he deems advisable, but with at least ten days notice to the petitioner who presented the probated instrument if the earlier petitioner has not requested probate of the later instrument. Confusion created by court decisions which interpreted PEF Code § 3138 to limit the time for appeal to three months was eliminated by amendment of PEF Code § 908, effective September 5, 2006, which clarified the one-year time limit as the appropriate period. See annotation of *Wolfe Will*, 27 Fiduc. Rep. 2d 11, annot. *Fiduc. Rev.* March 2007, p. 3.

A will contest is a proceeding in rem which operates directly upon the will to determine the condition or status of the estate of the decedent as testate or intestate and to vest the property in his heirs at law or in the beneficiaries named in the will. This is so even though the legatees, devisees and personal representatives are necessary parties defendant. Hence, all legatees named in the challenged will and all heirs or next of kin under the intestate law must be joined in the contest. Only one appeal can be taken. Those who are not notified of the appeal are, however, not barred from an appeal, and any party in interest who chooses to do so may intervene: *Miller Est.*, 159 Pa. 562. An appeal cannot be dismissed or withdrawn without notification to all the heirs: *Davis Est.*, 8 D. & C. 298; cf. *Thomas Will*, 349 Pa. 212.

An appeal from probate is addressed to the court, but it is filed with the register of wills. An appeal bond is not required but the court "upon cause shown" may require a bond to cover the costs or charges which may be decreed against him: PEF 908(b); cf. *Shelly Est.*, 463 Pa. 430, for effect of bond requirement prior to Act 135 of 1976. Upon the appeal, the register certifies the record to the court. The contestant then petitions the court to cite all parties in interest, whether beneficiaries under the will or heirs at law, to show cause why the appeal should not be sustained: *Cohen Will*, 356 Pa. 161.[1] The petition must set forth facts sufficient to enable preparation of an answer.[2] Once an appeal is perfected, it must be prosecuted with diligence, or it will be dismissed: *Megargel Est.*, 349

---

§ 17.6

1. Whether the parties at interest are cited as a matter of course or whether the appellant must petition the court to have them cited is determined by local rules: cf. 10.1B of Montgomery County Orphans' Court Division.

2. A "substantial dispute" exists when the evidence would sustain a verdict either way: *DeLaurentiis Est.*, 323 Pa. 70; *Buben Will*, 3 Fiduc. Rep. 443. For sufficiency of pleadings, see *Fiduc. Rev.* Feb. 1962, p. 3; *Thompson Will*, 416 Pa. 249; *Yesner Will*, 1 Fiduc. Rep. 2d 90; *Jaczszyn Will*, 25 Fiduc. Rep. 393; for forms thereof, see Partridge-Remick, O.C. Practice § 4.09.

Pa. 14. However, an appeal which has been dismissed may be reinstated if good cause is shown: *Kelchner Est.*, 326 Pa. 472.

If the citation is granted by the court, either as of course or after petition filed, service of the citation and of the petition must be effected. It may be served by any adult person or by the sheriff. Deputized service or service by publication is also available: PEF 765, 768.

The respondents (proponents) have 20 days after they are served with citation in which to file an answer, and then the petitioner (contestant) has 20 days in which to file a reply. Thereafter, the case is ready for hearing: Pa. O.C. Rule 3.2. If the contestant wants a jury trial, he should make a demand in writing at least ten days before the initial hearing, or ten days before trial if initial hearing is dispensed with: PEF 777(d); see *Fiduc. Rev.* Aug. 1961, p. 3. The court is the trier of fact unless a jury trial is ordered.[3] As stated in Section 17.1, the court must hear the testimony de novo unless the parties agree that the court act on the basis of testimony before the register. If the proponents wish to challenge the standing of the contestant as a "party in interest," they should do so by preliminary objection, and that issue may be taken up first by the court. See Section 17.2.

After the answer has been filed, the pleadings will normally be closed, and the proponents and contestants should decide whether it may be expedient to take depositions or commissions of ill, aged or dying witnesses. The pretrial devices of discovery, examination and inspection of documents should also be considered at this time by counsel: PEF 774; see *Doran Est.*, 12 D. & C. 2d 167; *Carmichael Trust*, 19 Fiduc. Rep. 484; *Fiduc. Rev.* Feb. 1962.

## § 17.7 TRIALS IN ORPHANS' COURT

(1) *Proponent's prima facie case*. All a proponent need prove to establish his prima facie case is due execution of the

**§ 17.6**

**3.** It is usually to the advantage of a contestant to obtain a jury trial because a jury is more likely than the court to set aside the will.

will. This is accomplished by introducing the probate record of the register and the affidavits of subscribing witnesses: *Plotts Est.*, 335 Pa. 81; *Szmahl Est.*, 335 Pa. 89; *Ash Will*, 351 Pa. 317. Further proof should be withheld until the time of rebuttal. If no testimony is offered by the contestant, the probate record stands as a binding judicial decision in rem.

Proof of execution raises the presumption that the testator knew the contents of the will, and it is only where fraud or undue influence "is charged and proved" that evidence of such knowledge is necessary: *Hoffman Est.*, 8 Fiduc. Rep. 609, aff'd 394 Pa. 391. See *Fisher Will*, 10 Fiduc. Rep. 577, where the subscribing witness appeared unsuccessfully as a contestant and attempted to repudiate statements in the attestation clause of the will. For burden of proof, see *Ziel Est.*, 467 Pa. 531. For appropriate practice in proof of execution of will and the shifting of the burden of going ahead with the evidence, see *McCarthy Will*, 2 Fiduc. Rep. 2d 410. See Section 17.4, supra.

(2) *Contestant's case*. After the proponent has offered the record and decree of probate and rests his case in chief, the burden of going forward with the evidence shifts to the contestant to overcome the prima facie case established: *Jack Est.*, 22 D. & C. 2d 409.

Although entry of a compulsory nonsuit was earlier considered improper in a will contest (*Jervis Will*, 443 Pa. 226, annot. *Fiduc. Rev*. Aug. 1971, p. 3), it now is authorized expressly when the contestant fails to carry the burden of overcoming the presumption of validity of the will: PEF 779.

The subscribing witnesses are "court" witnesses and may be freely examined and cross-examined by both parties without either being bound by any adverse testimony: *Plotts Est.*, 335 Pa. 81. The attendance of the subscribing witnesses should be required by the court upon the request of proponent or contestant. In some circumstances, the court should summon the scrivener: *Kline Est.*, 322 Pa. 374.

The contestant may build his proof through direct evidence or through expert testimony, as well as by cross-examination of the proponent's witnesses. If the contestant produces evidence which, if uncontradicted, would support a verdict against the will, the proponent's prima facie case has been overcome, and the burden of going forward shifts back to the proponent: *Keen Est.*, 299 Pa. 430, 440; *Szmahl Est.*, 335 Pa. 89; *Plotts Est.*, 335 Pa. 81; *Geho Est.*, 340 Pa. 412, 415, 416.

(3) *Proponent's rebuttal.* If the proponent has done what is customary and merely has established the will, he will have a substantial rebuttal. If the contestant has offered proof that the signature is a forgery, the proponent should call lay and expert witnesses to prove its genuineness. If the contestant has introduced evidence attempting to establish undue influence or fraud, the proponent should call lay witnesses to disprove or nullify the effect thereof. If the contestant has offered proof of lack of testamentary capacity, the proponent should call lay and expert witnesses to prove the contrary. In this connection, it is well to remember that a showing by the proponent that the testator had "business ability" goes a long way to disproving lack of testamentary capacity and is especially effective if it can be shown that the contestant's witnesses had business dealings with the decedent or accepted gifts from him during the period it is alleged he was incompetent: *Ash Will*, 351 Pa. 317; cf. *Hall Will*, 402 Pa. 212, 220.

(4) *Competency of witness.* The Act of 1887, P.L. 158, 28 P.S. § 322, expressly provided that all persons shall be fully competent witnesses in will contests. This is now controlled by 42 Pa. C.S. § 5930: see *Schreckengost Est.*, 77 Pa. Super. 235.

For medical testimony in will contests, see *Fiduc. Rev.* June 1976, p. 2; 47 *Pa. Bar Ass'n Q.* 567 (Oct. 1976).

Where a latent ambiguity existed, parol evidence including testimony of the attorney-scrivener is admissible: *Thompson Est.*, 25 Fiduc. Rep. 254.

For right of discovery and limitation on physicians' privilege, see *Kohr Est.*, 26 Fiduc. Rep. 419. See *Fiduc. Rev.* May 2002, p. 1 for annotation of *McNeil v. Jordan (No. 2)*, 22 Fiduc. Rep.2d 81, concerning discovery in the Orphans' Court.

(5) *Appeal from verdict*. A party in interest has thirty days in which to appeal from the court's decree accepting or rejecting the jury verdict, or from a decree of the court refusing a jury trial: *Fiduc. Rev*. Oct. 1970; *Luckenbach v. Luckenbach*, 443 Pa. 417. Action by the lower court is appealable within thirty days unless exceptions are filed within twenty days. O.C. Rule 7.1. Under Pa. R.C.P. No. 227.1, effective January 1, 1984, a motion to remove a nonsuit in a will contest should be filed before an appeal to the Superior Court. *Duffy Will* (O.C. Div. Bucks), 4 Fiduc. Rep. 2d 183. All appeals from the orphans' court division must be taken to the Pennsylvania Superior Court: 42 Pa. C.S. § 742. After the appeal to an appellate court has been taken, the court cannot act further in the estate until the appeal has been disposed of and the records returned to the register (*Taubel Est*., 9 Fiduc. Rep. 597; *Fisher Est*., 73 Mont. 574), unless permission is granted by the appellate court to so act.

(6) *Effect of verdict*. Under PEF 777(c) it is clear that a jury verdict in will contests is advisory only, and that the court has broad discretion in determining whether to award a jury trial: see *Fiduc. Rev*. Aug. 1961, p. 3. Since the verdict of the jury is advisory only, the proponent is not entitled to a new trial because of any error in the trial proceedings: *Fickert Est*., 461 Pa. 653; *Kornblatt Will*, 26 Fiduc. Rep. 169, annot. *Fiduc. Rev*. March 1976, p. 3. Even prior to September 12, 1961, (when the wording now found in PEF 777(c) was enacted), the court had a measure of control over jury verdicts in will contests as well as in cases where jury trial had not been a matter of right. If the court was not satisfied with the verdict, it could set it aside, grant a new trial "or enter such other judgment as satisfies its conscience." See *Fiduc. Rev*. Jan. 1954; May 1954, p. 4; May 1955, p. 4.

(7) *Effect of judge's determination of fact*. See *Masciantonio Est*., 73 Montg. 410, rev'd 392 Pa. 362, annot. *Fiduc. Rev*. May 1958, *opinion on remand*, 8 Fiduc. Rep. 487, rev'd 396 Pa. 16, where the Supreme Court initially reversed the decision of the judge sitting without a jury, by in effect treating his opinion as if it was erroneous instructions to a jury, and eventually ordered that the issue be tried before a jury. And see *Hall Will*, 402 Pa. 212, annot. *Fiduc. Rev*. Feb. 1961.

## Appendix 1

# ATTORNEY'S CHECK SHEET OF EXECUTORS' DUTIES*

---

### Basic Data

Estate of ........................................
Executors ................ ........................
  Address .............. ........................
  Phone ................ ........................
Burial instructions followed ........................
Domicile .............. Place of death ....................
Date of death .................. Soc. Sec. No. ............
Age ............ Birthdate ........ Place ............
Cause of death ........... Duration of last illness ..........
Will Dated ................. Codicils ..................
Marriage or birth since date of will ....................
Witnesses ................ ........................
  Paid ................. ........................
Estimated personalty $ ........... Realty $ ..............
Letters granted ................ Rec'd ....................
Will No. ................ Court No. .....................

### Early Administration

Perishable assets processed ............................
Family exemption paid ................................
Advertising: Legal ........... Newspaper .................
Proofs of publ. rec'd ...................................
Notified corporations ......... Other legatees ...............
Ordered gravemarker ...................................
Postmaster advised re disposition of mail .....................

---

*This check sheet, which is reprinted from *Fiduc. Rev.* May 1954, does not attempt to be all-inclusive. Its principal value is in refreshing the attorney's mind, when the estate originates, of the essential information required and initial steps to be taken in the settlement of the estate.

See Estate Settlement Timetable, Appendix 2.

Safe deposit box opened, contents listed . . . . . . . . . . . . . . . . . . . .
Copies of prior inc. tax ret. . . . . . Pers. prop. tax . . . . . . . . . . . . . .
Assembled back check books, stmts. and cks. . . . . . . . . . . . . . . . . .
Estate bank account opened—
Securities placed in estate name or name of nominee of corporate fiduciary . . . . . . . . . . . . . . . . . . . . . . . . . . . . . . . . . . . . . . .
Appraisers . . . . . . . . . . . . . . . . . . . . . . . . . . . . . . . . . . . . . . . . .
Inventory filed . . . . . . . . . . . . . . . Supplemental . . . . . . . . . . . . . .
Spouse's election filed . . . . . . . . . . . . . . Recorded . . . . . . . . . . . .
Are distributions subject to apportionment of death taxes? . . . . . .
Is property outside of will subject? . . . . . . . . . . . . . . . . . . . . . . .
Gifts within one year . . . . . . . . . . . . . . Other gifts . . . . . . . . . . . . .

**Assets** (/, applicable; X, processed and in hands of executor; (X) distributed)

*Intangibles:*

Cash . . . . . . . . Deposit a/ cs . . . . . . . . . Savings a/ cs . . . . . . . . .
Stocks . . . . . . . . . Bonds . . . . . . . . Death benefits . . . . . . . . . . . .
Life Ins. . . . . . Soc. Sec. benefits: Est. . . . . . Others . . . . . . . . . .
Veterans' benefits . . . . . . . . . . . Brokerage a/ cs . . . . . . . . . . . . . .
Collateral under loan . . . . Mortgages . . . . . . . Notes . . . . . . . .
A/cs receivable . . . . . . . . . . . Business interests . . . . . . . . . . . . . .
Contracts . . . . . . . . . . . . .Claims in litigation . . . . . . . . . . . . . . . .
Interests in fiduciary a/cs . . . . . . . . . . . . . . . . . . . . . . . . . . . . . . .
Powers of appointment . . . . . . Fire and other ins. Pols. . . . . . . . .
Jointly-held property . . . . . . . . . . . . . . . . . . . . . . . . . . . . . . . . . .

*Tangible Personalty:*

Appraised . . . . . . . . . . . . . . . . Safeguarded . . . . . . . . . . . . . . . . .
Released for disposal by tax authorities . . . . . . . . . . . . . . . . . . . . .
Public liab. ins. . . . . . . . . . . Fire ins., etc. . . . . . . . . . . . . . . . . . .
Automobile . . . . . . . Furniture . . . . . . Jewelry . . . . . . . . . . . . .
Other . . . . . . . . . . . . . . . . . . . . . . . . . . . . . . . . . . . . . . . . . . . .

*Real Estate and Related Items:*

Appraised . . . . . . Insured . . . . . . . . . . Safeguarded . . . . . . . . . . .
Title papers assembled . . . . . Tax and/or title search . . . . . . . . . .

Utilities: Paid . . . . . . . . . . . . . . . . shut off . . . . . . . . . . . . . . . . . . . .
Ancillary administrator . . . . . . . . Exemplified copy of will filed in other states . . . . . . . . . . . . . . . . . . . . . . . . . . . . . . . . . . . . . . . . . .
Tenants notified to pay executors . . . . . . . . . . . . . . . . . . . . . . . .
Legal description in schedule of distribution . . . . . . . . . . . . . . . . . .
Excerpt recorded . . . . . . . . . . . . . . . . . . . . . . . . . . . . . . . . . . . .
Existence of environmental liability determined . . . . . . . . . . . . . .

**Liabilities** (/, applicable; X, determined; (X), paid)

Funeral . . . . . . . . . . Gravemarker . . . . . . . . . Doctors . . . . . . . . .
Hospital . . . . . . . . . . Notes . . . . . . . . . . Current bills . . . . . . . . . .
Rent (leases terminated) . . . . . . . . . . . . . . Wages . . . . . . . . . . . . .
Utilities . . . . . . . . . . . . . . . . Real estate taxes . . . . . . . . . . . . . . . .
Mortgage . . . . . . . . . . . . . . . . Appraisers' fees . . . . . . . . . . . . . . .
Counsel fee . . . . . . . . . . . Executors' commissions . . . . . . . . . . . . .
Liability as fiduciary: Acct. filed . . . . . . . Adjudicated . . . . . . . . . .

**Taxes** (/, filed; X, paid; (X), closed)

*Pers. Prop.:* Decedent's . . . . . . . . . . . . . . Estate's . . . . . . . . . . . . . .
*Income:* Life period . . . . . . . . . . . . Fiduciary . . . . . . . . . . . . . . . . . .
Request for prompt assessment . . . . . . . . . . . . . . . . . . . . . . . . . . .
*Inheritance:* Discounted . . . . . . . . . . . . Final . . . . . . . . . . . . . . . .
apportionment completed . . . . . . . . . collected . . . . . . . . . . . .
*Federal Estate:* (date of death or option) . . . . . . . . . . . . . . . . . . . . . .
Apportionment completed . . . . . . . . . collected . . . . . . . . . . . .
Copy filed with Register . . . . Form 712 re life ins. . . . . . . . . .
Request for discharge of personal liability

**Later Administration**

Estimated net estate $ . . . . . . . residuary est. $ . . . . . . . . . . . . . .
Registered securities transferred . . . . . . . . . . . . . . . . . . . . . . . . . . .
Funds raised for adm. expenses, debts, taxes and legacies . . . . . . .
Remaining investments conform to terms of will . . . . . . . . . . . . . .
retention approved by legatees . . . . . . . . . . . . . . . . . . . . . . . . . .
*Court a/c:* Prepared . . . . . filed . . . . . . . . . notices to parties in interest . . . . Veterans admin. . . . Dept. of Revenue (inmate of state inst.) . . . . . . . . . . . . . . . . . . . . . . . . . . . . . . . . . . . . . . . . . . . . .
*Statement of Prop. Distribution:* Prepared . . . . . . . . Audit . . . . . . .
Postponed audit . . . . Adjudication nisi . . . . Absolute . . . . . .

**APPENDIX 1**

*Schedule of Distribution:* prepared . . . . . . . . . filed . . . . . . . . . . . .
Notice to parties . . . . . . approved . . . . . . . absolute . . . . . . .
*Releases* obtained . . . . . . . . . . . . . . . . filed . . . . . . . . . . . . . . . . . . .
*Reserves* released . . . . . . . . . . . . . . . . paid . . . . . . . . . . . . . . . . . . .

| BENEFICIARIES | | | | |
|---|---|---|---|---|
| NAME | ADDRESS | SOC. SEC. NO. | RELATIONSHIP | SHARE |
| | | | | |
| | | | | |
| | | | | |
| | | | | |
| | | | | |
| | | | | |
| | | | | |
| | | | | |
| | | | | |
| | | | | |
| | | | | |
| | | | | |
| | | | | |
| | | | | |
| | | | | |
| | | | | |
| | | | | |

## Appendix 2

# ESTATE SETTLEMENT TIMETABLE†

---

## FOR IMMEDIATE ATTENTION

### Entry Into Safe Deposit Box

Arrange to comply with requirements of Inh. & Est. Tax Act, Part XII.

### Petition for Letters

Usually after funeral: *Comfort Est.*, 12 Pa. C.C. 571.

File with Register of Wills: PEF 3151. Enter bond, if required: PEF 3171. If 21 years have elapsed obtain prior court approval: PEF 3152.

### Advertise Grant of Letters

As soon after grant of letters as possible: PEF 3162.

First complete advertising starts running of period after which account may be filed (PEF 3501.1) or distribution made at risk of personal representative: PEF 3532.

### Consider Termination of Consent Under IRC Subchapter S

If continuation of election is not desirable, consider joining action of majority to terminate election: IRC 1362(d).

### Give Notice of Assumption of Fiduciary Duties

To District Director of IRS at domicile of decedent (IRC 6903; Reg. 301.6903-1(b)) to prevent valid assessment by mailing to decedent's last known address despite lack of receipt thereof by executor: IRC 6903, 6901(g). Use IRS form 56.

---

†This chart is based on a chart originally in *Fiduc. Rev.* Sept. 1952, which was prepared in collaboration with Edward M. David, Esquire, of the Philadelphia Bar. Section references except as otherwise indicated are to the PEF Code. The timetable includes statutory and regulatory requirements, and is not intended to be an all-inclusive checklist of administrative duties. For small estates and dispositions independent of grant of letters see PEF 3101, 3012, 3121-3126. For notice to Attorney General when charitable interests are involved; see *Fiduc. Rev.* April 1958.

### Obtain Permission to Distribute or Sell Household Goods and Personal Effects

When estate subject to Federal estate tax, from District Director, IRS; Reg. 20.2031-6(c).

### Apply (Form SS-4) to IRS for Employer Identification Number

Use on estate income tax return Form 1041 and furnish to dividends and interest payors: *Fiduc. Rev.* Nov. 1962, p. 4.

## FOR EARLY ATTENTION

### Apply for Monthly Social Security Benefits

Prior to end of 12 months immediately succeeding month in which insured died: 42 USCA 402j(1).

### Apply for Lump-Sum Death Payment Under Social Security Act

Within 2 years after death of insured individual, except in cases of certain veterans dying outside U.S. whose bodies are returned for interment in which case within 2 years of such interment: 42 USCA 402i. Claim is barred thereafter. Benefit is lesser of three times primary insurance or $255. See Section 6.10.

### Apply for Federal Burial and Other Benefits for Veteran

Within 2 years after death, to Veterans' Administration, for benefits: 38 USCA 902, 904.

### Apply for County Burial Benefit and Grave Marker for Veteran or Widow of Veteran

Within one year after death.
To County Commissioners: 16 PS [Deceased Service Persons] 1909-1913, 5109-5113, 8062-8065.

### Consider Transfer of Securities to Name of Personal Representative

Or to nominee of corporate fiduciary for prompt sale.

### Inform Surviving Spouse of Elective Rights and Spouse, Children or Parents of Right to Family Exemption

## WITHIN THREE MONTHS

### Make Payment on Inheritance Tax

Within 3 months after date of death, to Register.

To obtain 5% discount: Inh. & Est. Tax Act, 9142.

### Pay Inheritance Tax on Remainder Interest or Succeeding Estate Where Decedent Had Life Interest

If tax had not been pre-paid, pay within 3 months after remainderman comes into actual possession: Inh. & Est. Tax Act of 1961, 506, 712; cf. 713, 714, 651. (See new *Pa. Inheritance and Estate Tax* (Grossman and Smith 2002), 9142.

To Register of Wills of county where donor of life interest was domiciled.

To prevent charging of interest: Inh. & Est. Tax Act, 9143.

### File Personal Property Tax Affidavit

For school purposes in certain counties: 24 PS 581.10 and 581.40.

As procedural requirement in additional counties to show date of acquisition of taxable property.

### Given Written Notice to Beneficiaries and Intestate Heirs

Within 3 months after grant of letters, as required by Sup. Ct. O. C. Rule 5.6.

### Given Written Notice of Gift to Corporation or Association

Within 3 months of grant of letters, stating date of death, county where will probated and that it is beneficiary: PEF 3330.

### Given Written Notice to Commonwealth or Subdivision

Within 3 months of grant of letters, to Department of Revenue or proper officer of subdivision—when recipient has claim for maintaining in institution person who has died therein: PEF 3393.

## ANY TIME AFTER FOUR MONTHS

### File Account

After expiration of 4 months after first complete advertisement of grant of letters: PEF 3501.1.

May be cited to file account 6 months: PEF 3501.1.
Distribution or sale within 6 months will affect alternate valuation for Federal estate tax: IRC 2032.

### Give Written Notice of Filing of Account and of Audit

At least 10 days prior to audit: Sup. Ct. O. C. Rule 5.3; local rules may require earlier notice.
To unpaid claimants and all persons interested as beneficiaries and next of kin: Sup. Ct. O. C. Rule 6.3.
Send copies of account and notice of audit to Department of Revenue: PEF 3393, Sup. Ct. O. C. Rule 6.7; to the Attorney General: Sup. Ct. O. C. Rule 5.5; and to U.S. Veterans' Administration when circumstances require it: Sup Ct. O. C. Rule 6.8.
For method of notice see Sup. Ct. O. C. Rule 5 and local rules: PEF 768.

### File Statement of Proposed Distribution

According to local rules: PEF 3513; Sup. Ct. O. C. Rule 6.9.

### File Schedule of Distribution

According to local rules: See Sup. Ct. O. C. Rule 6.9.

### Record Decree Awarding Real Estate

Or excerpt therefrom.
In each county where real estate lies: PEF 3536.

### File Satisfactions of Awards

After payment of legacies, with Clerk: See local rules.

## WITHIN SIX MONTHS

### File Election to Take Under or Against Will

Within six months of probate, unless extended.
With Clerk and personal representative and, if there is real estate, with the Recorder in county where real estate lies: PEF 2210; cf. 2211(b).

## WITHIN NINE MONTHS

### File Inventory

Unless time for filing of inheritance tax return is extended, file inventory in accordance with PEF 3301(c).

**File Inheritance Tax Returns**

Within nine months after death, with Register: Inh. & Est. Tax Act, 9136(d) and (f). Extension of 6 months may be granted in discretion of Secretary of Revenue: Inh. & Est. Tax Act, 9136(d). Objections to matters relating to Pa. Inheritance taxes must be made within 60 days by filing written protest with Department of Revenue, notifying Register of election to have matter determined at audit, or appealing to Court: Inh. & Est. Tax Act 9186(a).

**Arrange for Payment of Inheritance Tax on Future Interests**

By compromise of rate of tax: Inh. & Est. Tax Act, 9116(e).

By appeal from rate of tax fixed by assessment: Inh. & Est. Tax Act, 9186(b).

**Pay Balance of Inheritance Tax**

Within nine months after date of death, to Register: Inh. & Est. Tax Act, 9142.

To prevent charging of interest: Inh. & Est. Tax Act, 9143.

**File Certificate of Payment of Inheritance Tax**

With Register of other counties where real estate is located: Inh. & Est. Tax Acts, 9152.

**File Federal Estate Tax Return**

Within nine months from date of death [IRS 6075(a)], unless extension up to six months granted by District Director: IRC 6081; Reg. 20.6081-1.

With District Director at domicile of decedent: IRC 6091(b).

If gross estate of U.S. resident exceeds the exemption equivalent at time of death: Reg. 20.6018-1(a).

Consider application to District Director for prompt audit under IRC 2204. Cf. *Fiduc. Rev.*, Oct. 1943.

**Pay Federal Estate Tax**

Within nine months of death, regardless of date of filing return, unless District director extends the time: IRC 6161, 6165, 6503(d), and Regs. thereunder. See also IRC 6166 for installment payment of tax.

### File Copy of Federal Estate Tax Return With Register

Within 1 month after filing original with IRS: Inh. & Est. Tax Act, 9145(b). Thereafter file copy of IRS changes.

## AFTER NINE MONTHS

### Family Exemption

If exemption is claimed from real estate, obtain decree and record in county of real estate within one year of death or before recording of lien or sale: PEF 3126(b).

### Alternate Election for Payment of Inheritance Tax on Future Interest (where decedent had died prior to 12/13/82)

Consider election prior to termination of prior estates to pay tax on value of future interest determined as of date of filing election: Inh. & Est. Tax Act of 1961, 714; *Fiduc. Rev.* May 1976.

## ANY TIME AFTER ONE YEAR

### Distribution Without Audit—At Risk of Personal Representative

After one year from first complete advertisement of grant of letters—without liability to claimants who have given no notice and have no lien: PEF 3532.

## AT TWO YEARS AFTER DEATH

### File Status Report

Two years after death with the Register of Wills (See Rule 6.12, Appendix 8, *infra*) for decedents dying after July 1, 1992.)

## BY DATE—MATTERS NOT RELATED TO DATE OF DEATH OR GRANT OF LETTERS

### Feb. 15—File Personal Property Tax Return

Each year by date specified (72 PS 4843.1a) in county where decedent was domiciled at death, regardless of executor's domicile: 72 PS 4841, if required.

File for decedent, if living on January 1; otherwise, file for estate. Note returns no longer required in most countries

**Apr. 15—File Federal Income Tax Return for Decedent's Lifetime**

By April 15 of year following year of death [IRC 6072, 6012(b)(1)] unless extension is granted: IRC 6081.

With District Director at executor's residence or principal place of business: IRC 6091(b)(1).

**Apr. 15—File Pennsylvania Income Tax Return for Decedent's Lifetime**

By April 15 of year following year of death: 72 PS 7330 and 7331(e). Use Form PA 40.

**Apr. 15—File Federal Fiduciary Income Tax Return**

With District Director at executor's residence or principal place of business: IRC 6091(b)(1). File within 3½ months after end of fiscal year.

Not required if gross income is under $600, and no beneficiary is a non-resident alien: IRC 6012(a)(3) and (5).

Consider application to District Director for prompt assessment of all tax upon income during decedent's lifetime or during period of administration under IRC 6501(d). Cf. *Fiduc. Rev.*, Oct. 1943.

**Apr. 15—File Pennsylvania Fiduciary Income Tax Return**

Use form PA-41. File within 3½ months after end of fiscal year.

**Federal and Pennsylvania Income Tax Returns for Decedent's Lifetime**

No amended declaration of estimated income is required, nor are payments of estimated tax required after death, but if joint estimated return, survivor liable for installments unless survivor files amended declaration.

If joint return with surviving spouse would have been filed except for decedent's death, fiduciary and surviving spouse may file federal joint return for year of decedent's death. Pennsylvania requires deceased tax-payer and spouse to file separate returns for year of death. Thereafter, surviving spouse and fiduciary file separate returns.

### Fiduciary

File first for year of decedent's death, including income received from time of death to end of year, and yearly thereafter through year of final distribution (special rules apply if fiscal year chosen).
Pay estimated federal income taxes quarterly for years commencing more than two years after decedent's date of death.
Pay estimated Pennsylvania personal income tax quarterly for years ending two or more years after decedent's date of death.

## WITH RELATION TO ADVERSE ACTION

### File Caveat

With Register before probate—file bond within ten days thereafter: PEF 906.

### Appeals From Decree of Register

Within one year, unless court sets shorter time.
File bond if required: PEF 908.
One-year limitation does not apply when will a forgery (*Culbertson Est.*, 301 Pa. 438) or a nullity (*Taylor Est.*, 306 Pa. 7) or there is uncertainty of the probate record: *Rockett Will*, 348 Pa. 445; cf. *Fiduc. Rev.* Jan. 1959, p. 3.

### Creditor's Claims

Give personal representative written notice (PEF 3384) before accounting and within 1 year of death (PEF 3383, 3385, cf. 3352, where period is one year from first complete advertisement of grant of letters), and if not paid theretofore present claim at audit: PEF 3386.
If no personal representative, enforce grant of letters (PEF 3155(4)) to prevent statute of limitations barring claim: cf. PEF 3383.
Give Clerk in county where letters were granted written notice (PEF 3384) of claim against real estate within one year of death (PEF 3383, 3385 and 3532) *and* if personal representative does not file account within five years of death, petition to compel accounting (PEF 3532).

Judgment, a lien at death, must be revived within year of death or within five years from inception or last revival, whichever is later: PEF 3382.

See *Fiduc. Rev.* Oct. 1949, Nov. 1949, April 1956.

**File Exceptions to Adjudication or Schedule of Distribution**

Time limit set by Sup. Ct. O. C. Rule 7.1.

**Appeal to Superior Court: 42 Pa. C.S. 742.**

Within 30 days after entry of order: 42 Pa. C.S. 5105, 5571; Pa. RAP Rules 342, 501.

**Terminate Any Liability of Personal Representative to Corporate Surety**

As soon as administration of estate is completed.

By discharge after confirmation of final account and distribution (PEF 3184; Sup. Ct. O. C. Rule 12.7) or without discharge by agreement with surety company—to terminate further liability for bond premiums and to obtain partial refund of premiums paid for second or later year.

**Give Notice of End of Fiduciary Duties by Letter**

To District Director of IRS when duties terminate under state law: IRC 6903.

**Notice to Internal Revenue Service for Early Audit or Discharge of Tax Lien**

Consider request to IRS at office where tax returns are on file for audit and discharge of decedent and fiduciary for *all* federal taxes (e.g. income, gift) except estate tax: IRC 6501(d).

When federal estate tax return is filed, consider request for determination of tax and discharge of fiduciary: IRC 2204(a).

# Appendix 3

## CHECK LIST—DECEASED VETERANS' ESTATES
## **Federal Benefits**

| | Insurance | Burial | Headstones, Flags | Education |
|---|---|---|---|---|
| *Vietnam Era* Aug. 5, 1964 to May 7, 1975 | Insurance follows veteran's beneficiary designation. If none named, goes to his estate in a lump sum. Beneficiary (other than estate) may have choice of method of receiving payment: 38 USCA 1917(d). | U.S. may make payment toward burial, plot allowance and transport of body where death is due to nonservice-connected causes. For death due to service-connected disability the amount could be as much as $1500: 38 USCA 2302, 2303 and 2307. Personal representative makes claim if estate paid for funeral, otherwise other payor. Claim must be made within two years of burial: 38 USCA 2304. A veteran, his spouse, minor child and possibly unmarried adult child may be buried in a national cemetery: 38 USCA 2402. Special provisions apply to interment in national cemeteries. | U.S. will furnish: (1) a flag to drape veteran's casket: 38 USCA 2301. (2) a headstone for veteran's grave (or eqivalent reimbursement for the cost thereof): 38 USCA 2306. | Benefits for education of widows and certain children if veteran died in service or from service-connected disability: 38 USCA 3501 et seq. |
| *Korea* June 27, 1950 to Jan. 31, 1955 | Same as Vietnam | Same as Vietnam | Same as Vietnam | Same as Vietnam |
| *World War II* Dec. 7, 1941 to Dec. 31, 1946 | Same as Vietnam | Same as Vietnam | Same as Vietnam | Same as Vietnam |
| *World War I* | Same as Vietnam | Same as Vietnam | Same as Vietnam | Same as Vietnam |
| *Peacetime Service Only* | Same as Vietnam | Same as Vietnam for burial in national cemetery. No provisions for burial expenses unless receiving disability pension or discharged by reason of a disability: 38 USCA 2402. | 1. No flag unless one enlistment term served or service-connected disability: 38 USCA 2301. 2. Headstone, same as Vietnam. | No provisions |
| *Dying in Service* | Death and indemnity compensation to widow (1311), certain children (1313, 1314) and parents (1315) for service-connected death. See 28 USCA 1310–1317. | All expenses paid. | Same as Vietnam. | Same as Vietnam |

| Monthly Payments | Miscellaneous | Pennsylvania Benefits |
|---|---|---|
| *1. Service Connected Death*<br>Widows, children and parents are entitled to Dependency and Indemnity Compensation or Death Compensation if veteran died from service-connected or compensable disability: 38 USCA 1310 et seq.<br>*2. Non-Service Causes*<br>Widows and children are entitled if veteran died with, or entitled to, a pension based upon a service-connected disability, or if veteran died having met length of service requirements set out in 38 USCA 1521: 38 USCA 1541-1543.<br>Pensions are limited to widows with limited annual income: 38 USCA 1521, 1541.<br>V.A. also has discretion to disallow a claim where claimant has adequate assets: 38 USCA 1543. | Widows and children may get payments from V.A. which are equivalent of Social Security, had veteran been fully insured, if veteran not insured and dies from service-incurred injury or disease: 38 USCA 1312, 1322.<br>Accrued pensions payable, in order, to (1) widow, (2) children, (3) dependent parents—do not become part of veteran's estate: 38 USCA 5121.<br>Unremarried widows and widowers of veterans who died in war or from service-incurred causes entitled to same loan rights as veteran: 38 USCA 3701(b)2.<br>Veterans' funds are free of claims of Commonwealth for support of deceased incompetent veteran: *Jones Est.*, 15 Fiduc. Rep. 397. | *The Following Apply to Veterans of All Wars:*<br>1. Burial—may get partial payment from county through County Commissioners. Apply within one year of death, unless death occurred while in the service: 16 PS 1908, 1909, 5108, 5109, 8061, 8062. Same for widows: 16 PS 1910, 5110, 8063.<br>2. Gravemarkers and headstones for veterans available through County Commissioners: 16 PS 1913, 5113, 8065.<br>3. Pension (and tuition credit for children) allowed for dependents of soldiers killed while in active service: 51 Pa.C.S.A. 3502, 3503.<br>4. Widows of war veterans and wives of deceased or disabled soldiers entitled to preference in Civil Service examinations and promotions: 51 Pa.C.S.A. 7108.<br>5. Certain children (including adopted children: 25 Fiduc. Rep. 425) of veterans who served during any war or armed conflict, eligible for admission to Scotland School and maintenance therein until 19 years old: 24 PS 2695.<br>6. Certified copies of birth and death records are issued to veterans and their dependents *without cost* by the Division of Vital Statistics, 51 P.C.S.A. 9201. Also one certified copy of Certificate of Release From Active Duty free of charge (1996). |
| Same as Vietnam | Same as Vietnam | |
| Same as Vietnam | Same as Vietnam | |
| Same as Vietnam | No loan or social security provisions. | |
| Widows, children and dependent parents entitled if veteran died from injuries incurred or aggravated in peacetime service: 38 USCA 1310-1317. | No loan provisions. Social Security same as Vietnam if peacetime service after 1940. Accrued pensions same as Vietnam. | |
| Same as Vietnam for service-connected death: 38 USCA 1310-1317. | No loan provisions. Equivalent of Social Security payments same as Vietnam.<br>If death on active duty occurs after Dec. 31, 1956, the survivors are entitled to receive an amount equivalent to Social Security benefits: 38 USCA 1312. | |

## APPENDIX 3

# FEDERAL BENEFITS FOR VETERANS' FAMILIES

The Veterans' Administration (VA) administers some benefits for certain spouses, children, and parents of veterans.

To file a claim, it will be necessary to identify the veteran. If the veteran, in turn, had ever filed a VA claim and the veteran's file number ("C" number) is known, the file number serves as identification.

Otherwise, it will be necessary to establish the veteran's identity by submitting the veteran's full name and a copy of discharge from service or military service number, branch of service, and dates served.

The VA advises keeping the above information, and the veteran's government insurance number, in a safe, convenient location. Also, a statement regarding burial preference (location and type of burial) should be included in the veteran's personal papers.

If not already on record in VA files, the following documents will be required for claims.

(a) The veteran's death certificate for all claims where the veteran died outside of service or outside of a VA hospital.

(b) The veteran's marriage certificate where the claim is made for the surviving spouse or children.

(c) The children's birth certificates, whether claim is made in the child's own right or by the surviving spouse.

(d) The veteran's birth certificate if the parents of the veteran wish to establish eligibility.

### Immediate Death Benefits

The immediate benefits following the death of the veteran—a burial flag and burial in national cemeteries—can be secured with the aid of the funeral director handling the veteran's funeral. The funeral director's requests are usually sufficient to alert the VA insurance division so that an insurance claims form is sent to the veteran's beneficiary without inquiry on the beneficiary's part.

### GI Insurance

If the funeral director has not alerted the VA at the time of the veteran's death, families in the eastern half of the United States should send their insurance claim to the VA Regional Office and Insurance Center. Be sure to send the complete name of the veteran and number of the policy or, if the number is unknown, identify the veteran by file number, military serial number or the branch and dates of military service, and date of birth.

### Servicemen's Group Life Insurance (SGLI)

### Veteran's Group Life Insurance (VGLI)

Designated beneficiaries of those deceased persons covered by SGLI or VGLI may submit their claim to the Office of Servicemen's Group Life Insurance. They should send the full name of the insured member together with other identifying information such as military serial number, branch of service, dates of military service, Social Security number and dates of birth and death. Claim forms may be secured from the nearest VA office, or by writing to the Office of Servicemen's Group Life Insurance at the above address.

### Burial Expense Reimbursement

The funeral director will also assist in filing for *Reimbursement of Burial Expenses*.

### Compensation

If the veteran's death was service-connected, the surviving spouse and minor children may be eligible for *Dependency and Indemnity Compensation*.

### Pension

Nonservice-connected death may entitle the surviving spouse and veteran's minor children to *Pension* payments.

### Parent's Compensation

In certain cases, parents may be eligible for *Dependency and Indemnity Compensation*.

### Children's Benefits—Restoration or Entitlement to, Upon Termination of Child's Marriage.

Entitlement to benefits payable to or on behalf of a child which has been denied or terminated by reason of the child's marriage may be restored if the marriage is terminated by death or dissolved by a court decree.

### Children's Education

Children of veterans who die or become permanently and totally disabled because of service-connected disabilities or of service personnel who are missing in action or prisoners of war may be eligible for *Dependents' Educational Assistance*.

### Surviving Spouse's Education

Surviving spouses of veterans who died as the result of service-connected disabilities are eligible for educational assistance.

### Spouse's Education

Spouses of veterans who are permanently and totally disabled because of a service-connected disability and spouses of servicepersons who are missing in action or prisoners of war are eligible for educational assistance.

### Home Loans for Surviving Spouses

Unremarried surviving spouses of veterans of any period of service occurring since September 16, 1940, whose deaths were service-connected, are eligible for a GI *home loan*.

### Home Loans for Spouses

Spouses of service personnel who are missing in action or prisoners of war are eligible for a GI *home loan*.

### Death Gratuity

Paid by the Armed Services to surviving spouses, children—and if designated by the deceased—to parents, brothers or sisters.

# Appendix 4

# POST-DEATH TAX PLANNING CHECKLIST*

## Affecting Both Income and Estate Taxes†

1. *Commissions.* When beneficiary is also executor or administrator consider whether he should waive commissions in writing (see Rev. Rul. 66-167, 64-225 and 56-472) and save personal income tax, or take commissions and save estate income tax or death taxes: see *Fiduc. Rev.* Aug. 1966, p. 4.

2. *Commissions, counsel fee and other expenses of administration.* (a) Consider whether to take all or part as estate income tax deductions or all or part as estate tax deductions (IRC §642(g)). (b) If decision favors income tax deductions, consider spacing payment to derive maximum income tax advantage. (c) As alternative to both (a) and (b) consider whether to take all or part as income tax deduction in final tax year of estate administration in order to create excess deductions which may be distributed to beneficiary as personal income tax deductions if estate passes outright (IRC §642(h)).

3. *Decedent's medical expenses.* Consider whether to have (a) surviving spouse pay and deduct on personal income tax return (IRC §213(a)); (b) estate pay and deduct on federal estate tax return (IRC §2053(a)(3)); or (c) estate pay within one year of death and deduct on decedent's income tax return for period when incurred (IRC §213(c)). The portion not deductible for income tax purposes is not an allowable estate tax deduction: Rev. Rul 77-357.

4. *Stock in close corporation.* Consider redemption on non-dividend basis (generally within 3 years and 90 days of filing return, IRC §303(b)) of stock, which is included in decedent's gross estate and

*Based upon a chart appearing in *Fiduc. Rev.*, Sept. 1983.

†Whenever an election can be made which will benefit income at the expense of principal, appropriate adjustments may be required: see *Bell Est.*, 7 Fiduc. Rep. 1, aff'd 393 Pa. 623, annot. *Fiduc. Rev.* Nov. 1958. Certain deductions can be taken for both federal estate and income tax purposes: IRC §691(b).

amounts to at least 35 per cent of adjusted gross estate, not exceeding sum of death taxes, with interest, and deductible funeral and administration expenses (IRC §303).

5. *Employee benefit-plan payments.* Consider rights of surviving spouse under Retirement Equity Act of 1984.

**Affecting Income Taxes:**

1. *Joint return.* Consider filing joint return, for year of decedent's death, with surviving spouse. IRC §6013. See *Fiduc. Rev.* July 1959.

2. *Choice of tax year.* Consider choosing fiscal year other than calendar year (IRC §441), for estate income tax purposes to make possible postponing tax to distributees (see §662(c)), or ultimate tax-free distribution (IRC §662(a)(2)) and to allow short first and last years.

3. *Exemption.* Consider fact that estate has separate annual income tax exemption of $600 (IRC §642(b)), which exemption is not reduced although the first and last years are short ones (IRC §443(c)). See Reg. 1.641(b)-3 about allowable duration of administration.

4. *Distribution of income during administration.* Weight relative merit of accumulating some or all income thus taxable to estate and currently distributing some or all income thus taxable to distributee. Distribution may be made within 65 days after end of fiscal year. IRC §662. *Caution:* Any distribution is deemed a distribution of income unless it be a bequest of a specific sum of money or of specific property payable in not more than three installments. IRC §663(a)(1). However, see Regs. 1.663(c) re separate share rule. It would seem that payment of the family exemption will not be treated as an income distribution. See Reg. §1.661(a)-2(e). For treatment of distribution in satisfaction of pecuniary formula marital deduction gift, see Casner, *Estate Planning*, p. 87 (3d Ed.). See *Salesky Est.*, 15 Fiduc. Rep. 213. Consider distributions during administration where the charitable beneficiary is involved.

When will creates several testamentary trusts, consider early distribution thereto in order to create additional taxable entities. See IRC §§643(c), 661–662.

When decedent's last return is joint with surviving spouse, consider distributing enough income to spouse to take maximum advantage of relative rates.

5. *United States savings bond interest.* Consider election to accrue interest on United States savings bonds in decedent's final income tax return. IRC §454(a). See *Fiduc. Rev.* March 1960, p. 3.

6. *Income in respect of decedent.* Consider prompt distribution of right to such income to beneficiary with potentially lost deductions or in lower bracket. IRC §691(a)(2). Deduction also available to beneficiary for estate tax attributable to such income. IRC §691(c).

7. *Sales during administration.* In the case of assets which appreciate after decedent's death, consider distribution as against sale and subsequent distribution of proceeds, weighing applicable income tax rates of estate and of legatee, and existence of offsetting capital losses. 26 Temple L.Q. 240. *Caution:* Further considerations are applicable when distribution is to pecuniary legatees. *Kenan v. Comm'r*, 114 F.2d 217; cf. *Guthrie*, 42 B.T.A. 696; *Ewing*, 40 B.T.A. 912; Rev. Rul. 56-270, 1956-1 C.B. 325; Rev. Rul. 60-87, 1960-1 C.B. 286.

8. *Closing estate.* Schedule closing so that beneficiaries receive maximum amount of accumulated income tax-free (IRC §662) and obtain advantage of maximum deductions (IRC §642(h)).

**Affecting Estate Tax:**

1. *Election against will.* Consider such action by surviving spouse, within six months of probate (PEF 2210(b)), to secure advantage of marital deduction if not otherwise available. 14 U. of Pitts. L. Rev. 224.

2. *Renunciation.* Consider prompt renunciation of legacy by surviving spouse (in whole or in part: PEF 6201; *Bronstein Est.*, 3 Fiduc. Rep. 585) to decrease size of her potential estate. Renunciation of legacy before any benefit is received incurs no gift tax. *Brown v. Routzahn*, 63 F.2d 914. Also, where spouse is the co-trustee and trustees have right of invasion, consider having spouse renounce power to avoid having non-marital share taxed in spouse's estate.

3. *Disclaimer.* Consider disclaimer by beneficiary, before time for filing return, which results in property passing to charity or to surviving spouse. IRC §2518. Same applies to termination of power to consume or invade, or appoint to another, before it is exercised. IRC §2055(a). For methods of disclaimer see PEF 6103(b); 6204. See also

*Fiduc. Rev.* Oct. 1975, p. 2, Oct. 1976.

4. *Alternate valuation date.* Consider within 9 months of decedent's death (IRC §2032(c)) whether to value assets for federal estate tax at date of death or as of six months thereafter (IRC §2032(a)). Consider effect of basis on future capital gains and losses, and on depreciation. See *Fiduc. Rev.* Sept. 1959, p. 2. Note that since 1984 alternate valuation date cannot be used to increase total basis of estate assets.

5. *Special use valuation.* Consider advantages of special use valuation for family farm or closely-held business property: IRC §2032A.

6. *Jointly-owned property and property transferred inter vivos.* When large part of taxable estate consists of property not part of administered estate, consider paying IRC §2053 expenses before date for filing estate tax return. IRC §2053(c)(2).

7. *Payment of tax.* Use eligible government bonds at par to satisfy part or all of tax due. IRC §6312; Reg. 301.6312; 31 C.F.R. 306.28. Such bonds, when redeemable at par value in payment of estate tax, are taxable at such value regardless of their fair market value. See *Fiduc. Rev.* March 1969, p. 4. Bonds issued after March 3, 1971 do not quality for such use: (PL 92-5) and all eligible bonds have been redeemed.

8. *Closely-held business.* Consider installment payment of taxes: IRC §6166.

9. *Pennsylvania inheritance tax discount.* Consider foregoing 5 per cent discount for payment within three-month period when additional Pennsylvania tax will be payable in any event to equal federal credit, thus allowing use of funds in interval.

# Appendix 5

# INTESTATE DESCENT IN PENNSYLVANIA

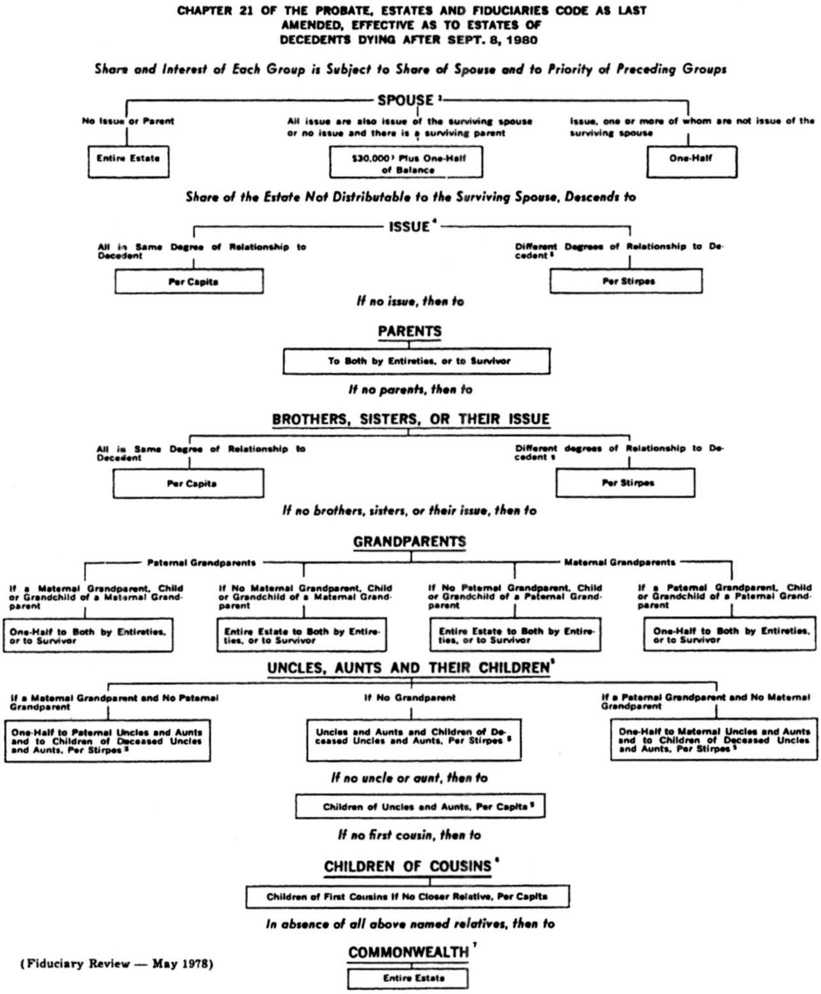


(Fiduciary Review — May 1978)

## ANNOTATIONS

1. To inherit each heir must survive decedent by five days, but Commonwealth cannot benefit by such a divesture: PEF 2104(10). No distinction is made between descent of real and personal property: PEF 2101; between whole and half blood: PEF 2104(3); between citizen and alien: PEF 2104(8); or concerning the source of ownership: PEF 2104(5). Persons begotten before decedent's death take as if born in his lifetime: 2104(4). Persons related to decedent through two lines of relationship take one share only, which is the larger share: PEF 2104(9). Married parents and grandparents receive shares by entireties, others as tenants in common: PEF 2104(7). Only the interest of the decedent passes: PEF 2104(6). Shares of heirs are subject to advancements when the advancement is evidenced by a contemporaneous writing of the decedent or acknowledged in writing by the heir: PEF 2109.1. Shares may be lost by a wilful and unlawful killing: PEF 2106(c).

2. The surviving spouse's statutory share is given in lieu of common law dower and curtesy and applies to present and future estates: PEF 2105. (See 1957 P.L. 969, discussed in *Fiduc. Rev.*, August 1957). The respective intestate rights of widower and widow are the same. The family exemption of $3,500 is, of course, a separate and unrelated matter. A surviving spouse's share may be lost by wilfully neglecting or refusing to perform the duty to support the other spouse, by wilfully and maliciously deserting the other spouse for one year or upwards or by a wilful and unlawful killing of the other spouse: PEF 2106.

3. The $30,000 is allowed whether the intestacy is entire or partial, but in the case of partial intestacy any amount received under the will is in pro tanto satisfaction of the allowance: PEF 2102(5). It is a vested right which does not have to be claimed. When payable from real estate, the allowance is awarded in distribution as are other distributive shares: PEF 2110. Intestate share given by will [PEF 2514(4)] or by inter vivos transfer [PEF 6114(1)] does not always include the spouse's allowance. For estates of decedents dying after Sept. 8, 1980, see Act 118 of 1980, increasing allowance to $30,000.

4. Illegitimates, in absence of "marriage" of parents (see Act of 1959, P.L. 1916, annot. *Fiduc. Rev.*, March 1960), are considered issue in the family of the mother (PEF 2107) and may also be issue of

a natural father: *Trimble v. Gordon*, 430 U.S. 762, annot. *Fiduc. Rev.*, June 1977; *Browning Est.*, 28 Fiduc. Rep. 1. Adopted children are considered issue of the adopting parents and not issue of natural parents unless a family relationship has been maintained, and except that the status of a natural parent married to an adopting parent does not change: PEF 2108.

5. The shares going to persons in different degrees of relationship to decedent are calculated by dividing the entire share so descending "into as many equal shares as there shall be persons in the nearest degree of consanguinity to the decedent living and taking shares therein and persons in that degree who have died before the decedent and have left issue to survive him who take shares therein. One equal share shall pass to each such living person in the nearest degree and one equal share shall "pass" per stirpes to the issue of each such deceased person but not so as to include persons more remote than children of first cousins: PEF 2104 (1 & 2).

6. Children of first cousins do not share if there is a living closer relative: PEF 2104 (1 & 2). See *Fiduc. Rev.*, March 1966, p. 4.

7. The Commonwealth will not share as a statutory heir if another heir survived decedent and died within the five-day period of PEF 2104(10).

# Appendix 6

# AUDIT NOTICES

---

FORM OF NOTICE TO BENEFICIARIES WHO ARE AFFECTED BY THE BALANCE IN THE ACCOUNT.

Herewith is a copy of the account of Bank [at this point further identify the account]. Also enclosed is a copy of the will [or deed of trust] of [or you have heretofore received a copy of the will-or deed of trust-of].

The original of the enclosed account was filed in the office of the Clerk of the Orphans' Court of Montgomery County and will be called for audit on Monday, October 2, 2000 at 10:00 a.m. in the Orphans' Court Division of the Court of Common Pleas of Montgomery County, Court House, Airy and Swede Streets, Norristown, Pennsylvania.

If, after reviewing the account you have any questions, we will be pleased to answer them. You may attend the audit if you desire, but, it will not be necessary for you to do so.

If you have any objection to any transaction shown in the account or omitted from the account you must file with the Clerk of the Orphans' Court Division objections thereto in writing in conformity to Montgomery County Orphans' Court Division Rules prior to audit, or appear in person or by counsel and present your written objections to the court at audit. In absence of written objections, the court may assume you have no objection to the account.

[At this point, state the purpose of the account or make an otherwise appropriate statement, having in mind the following provision from Montgomery County Local Rule.]

> ". . . the accountant's interpretation of any dispute, or fairly disputable question, known to the accountant, together with a copy of the instrument or material parts thereof containing any provision which forms the basis of the dispute, and a statement that if the person notified does not agree with the accountant's interpretation, he must appear at the audit in person or by

counsel to present his contention, under penalty for failure to appear that the court will assume that he agrees with the accountant's interpretation; and unless shown in the account the amount of any commission claimed by the accountant and the amount of any attorney's fee claimed as due the accountant's attorney."

FOR NOTICE TO CLAIMANTS THE FORM CAN BE ADJUSTED APPROPRIATELY, HAVING IN MIND THE FOLLOWING PROVISION IN MONTGOMERY COUNTY LOCAL RULE.

"In the case of notice to a claimant, the accountant's understanding of the nature of the claim; whether the claim is admitted or contested; if admitted, whether it will be paid in full or in part, and, if contested, that an appearance in person or by counsel must be made at the audit to press any such claim."

FOR NOTICE TO LEGATEES OR DONEES OF PECUNIARY OR SPECIFIC GIFTS, THE NOTICE SHOULD BE SIMILAR TO THAT GIVEN TO CLAIMANTS AND INCLUDE AN APPROPRIATE EXCERPT FROM THE WILL OR DEED OF TRUST.

# Appendix 7

## SHORT-CUTS—STATUTORY PROVISIONS —PROTECTION OF FIDUCIARIES

(All number references are to sections of the Probate, Estates and Fiduciaries Code)

| | Decedents' Estates | Minors' Estates* and Incapacitated Persons' Estates | Trusts |
|---|---|---|---|
| *When existence of a fiduciary is not essential as to probate assets* | Payments by employer to family up to $5,000: 3101(a)<br>Payments of deposit account to family up to $3,500: 3101(b)<br>Payments not exceeding $3,500 from deceased patient's care account to funeral director by facility where decedent was a patient receiving medical assistance: 3101(c)<br>Personal property to $25,000 distributed under court decree: 3102<br>Family exemption ($3,500 value) retained; or obtained under court decree: 3121<br>Motor vehicle may be transferred: see *Pa. Fiduc. Guide*, § 2.2(2).<br>U.S. savings bonds may be reissued: see *Pa. Fiduc. Guide*, § 2.2(3). | When estate of minor or incapacitated person has net value of $25,000 or less guardian is not essential: 5101; 5505(1)<br>Parent, person or institution may act for minor or incompetent when estate has net value of $25,000 or less: 5102; 5505(2)<br>Funds not exceeding amount insured by a federal government agency in any one institution may be deposited in a sequestered savings account: 5103; 5505(3). No limit upon number of accounts in different institutions.<br>When an action in which a minor or incapacitated person is a party is compromised, settled or discontinued, the procedural rules have provisions similar to those of the PEF Code: Pa. R.C.P. 2039 and 2206 as to minors, and 2064 and 2206 as to incapacitated person. | In some circumstances trusts can be terminated before their inception: for example when the estate is too small (*O'Neill Est.*, 7 Fiduc. Rep. 451) or the funds can be deposited in a restricted savings account (*Fellner Est.*, 20 Fiduc. Rep. 253). |

***Short-cuts—Statutory Provisions—Protection of Fiduciaries—Cont.***

| | Decedents' Estates | Minors' Estates* and Incapacitated Persons' Estates | Trusts |
|---|---|---|---|
| *When bond or security not required (absent decree requiring bond)* | No bond is required of a resident individual personal representative (3174(b), guardian of a minor (5122(a)), guardian of an incapacitated person (5515) or trustee (7762(a)) appointed by or in accord with a governing will or other instrument. No bond is required of a corporate personal representative (3174(a)), guardian of a minor (5122(b)), guardian of an incapacitated person (5515) or trustee (7762(c)). Security for the bond of an individual distributee may be waived by the court when awarding assets of estate of a presumed decedent: 5703. | | |
| | No bond is required of a resident administrator who "is either the sole residuary legatee or next of kin or is the nominee of all residuary legatees or next of kin who are adult and sui juris." | | |
| | No bond is required of a named nonresident personal representative excused in will from giving bond or of a nonresident co-personal representative who agrees assets will remain with resident co-personal representative: 3174. | | |
| *Advertisement* | A personal representative is required to advertise the grant of letters: 3162. It is a prerequisite for filing an account (3501.1) and for protecting | There is no requirement for the advertisement of the appointment of a guardian of a minor or of an incapacitated person, or of the existence of trusteeship, except that PEF 7755(c) requires advertisement if no personal representative is appointed within 90 days after settlor's death. | |

***Short-cuts—Statutory Provisions—Protection of Fiduciaries—Cont.***

| | Decedents' Estates | Minors' Estates* and Incapacitated Persons' Estates | Trusts |
|---|---|---|---|
| | against claims of creditors (3532) but sometimes is omitted when risks are assumed. | | |
| *Inventory* | A personal representative (3301-3305) and guardian of a minor (5142) and of an incapacitated person (5521(b)) are directed to file an inventory. They can be compelled to file the inventory after expiration of three months, but filing of an inventory frequently is omitted without penalty unless required in connection with an accounting. | | There is no requirement that a trustee file an inventory. |
| *Accounting* | An accounting by a personal representative (3501.1), guardian of a minor (5161), guardian of an incapacitated person (5531) and of a trustee (7797), to be advertised and audited by the court, is optional but may be required. | | |
| | When the estate of a deceased minor or of a deceased incapacitated person comes to the decedent's estate duplicate auditing of accounting can be avoided without risk: 3501.2. When estate assets pour over | The guardian of a minor or of an incapacitated person is relieved of all liability with respect to property delivered to the personal representative of his deceased ward when the guardian's account is annexed to the personal representative's account in accordance with 3501.2. | Trustee who receives property from a personal representative or another trustee and annexes a copy of the account of such other fiduciary to his |

## *Short-cuts—Statutory Provisions—Protection of Fiduciaries—Cont.*

| | Decedents' Estates | Minors' Estates* and Incapcitated Persons' Estates | Trusts |
|---|---|---|---|
| | to a trust without an estate accounting, risk to distributees (but not claimants) can be avoided without duplicate accounting: 7799.1. The risk to claimants may be avoided under 3532. | (For piggybacking of accounts see *Fiduc. Rev.*, Oct. 1981. For receipts and disbursements after audit, see *Fiduc. Rev.*, Dec. 1982, p. 4.). | accounting and gives notice thereof to the parties entitled can protect all such fiduciaries against claims of distributees as though separate accounts had been filed and confirmed: 7799.1. |
| *Record of risk distributions* | The personal representative (3532(c)), the guardian of a minor (5163), the guardian of an incapacitated person (5533) and trustee** "may file with the clerk receipts, releases and refunding agreements which he may have received from persons to whom he has made a risk distribution, or from other parties in interest. Receipts, releases and refunding agreements so filed shall be indexed under the name of the estate. Their acceptance shall not be construed as court approval of any act of administration or distribution therein reflected." | | |

*This chart does not deal with estates of minors under the Uniform Transfers to Minors Act: Chapter 53 of the Probate, Estates and Fiduciaries Code. This chart based on chart contained in *Fiduc. Rev.*, Feb. 1979.

**The reference to 3532(c) in deleted 7183 was omitted from new 7799.2, apparently in error, so there is no express statutory authorization for a trustee to file such documents.

## Appendix 8

# Pa. O.C. Rule 6.12 STATUS REPORT

REGISTER OF WILLS OF ________________ COUNTY, PENNSYLVANIA

Name of Decedent: ________________________________________

Date of Death: ________________________ File Number:__________

Pursuant to Pa. O.C. Rule 6.12, I report the following with respect to completion of the administration of the above-captioned estate:

1. State whether administration of the estate is complete: . . . . . . . . . . . . . . . . . . . . . . . . . . . . . . . . . . . . . . . ❑ Yes ❑ No

2. If the answer is No, state when the personal representative reasonably believes that the administration will be complete: __________

3. If the answer is No. 1 is Yes, state the following:

a. Did the personal representative file a final account with the Court? . . . . . . . . . . . . . . . . . . . . . . . . . . . . . . . . . . . . . . . ❑ Yes ❑ No

b. The separate Orphans' Court No. (if any) for the personal representative's account is: ____________________

c. Did the personal representative state an account informally to the parties in interest? . . . . . . . . . . . . . . . . . . . . . . . . . . . ❑ Yes ❑ No

d. Copies of receipts, releases, joinders and approvals of formal or informal accounts may be filed with the Clerk of the Orphans' Court and may be attached to this report.

*Date*____________ ________________________________________

*Signature of Person Filing this Form*

Capacity: ❑ Personal Representative ❑ Counsel

________________________________________

*Name of Person Filing this Form*

________________________________________

*Address*

________________________________________

________________________________________

*Telephone*

# Appendix 9

# REAL ESTATE—HEIRS AND DEVISEES

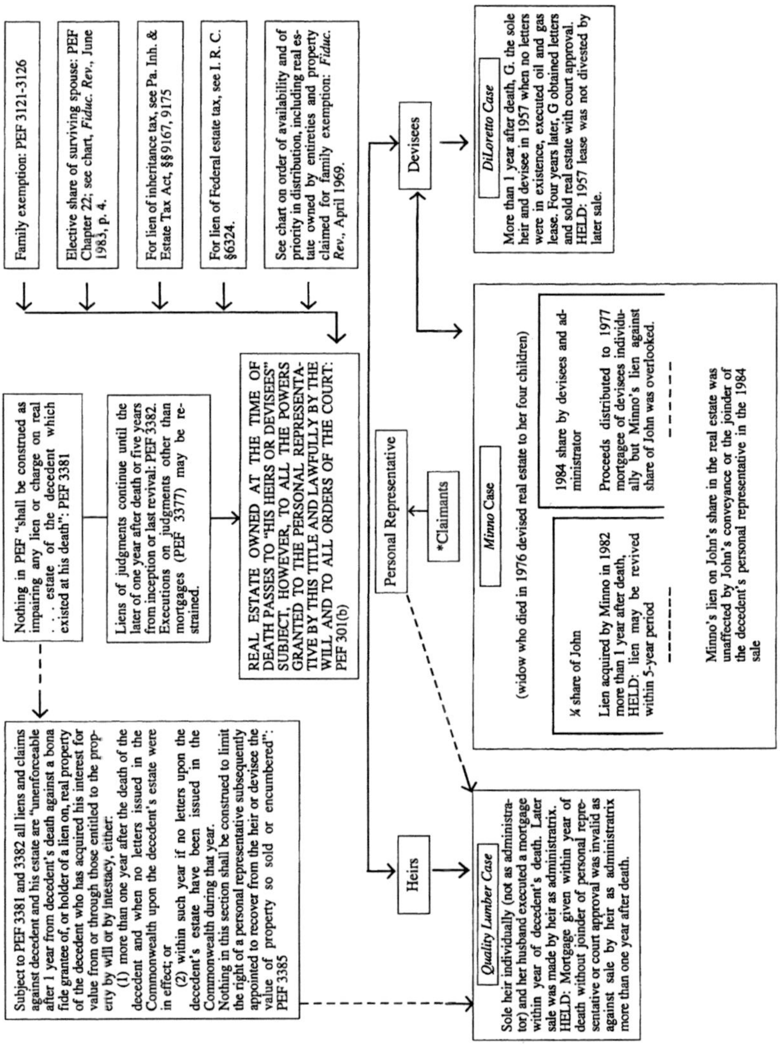


*For rights of claimants against the personal representative and distributed personal and real property, see PEF 3532 and *Fiduciary Review,* June 1988.

## Appendix 10

# IMPORTANT NOTICE

# NOTICE OF ESTATE ADMINISTRATION PURSUANT TO Pa.O.C. Rule 5.6

THIS NOTICE DOES NOT MEAN THAT YOU WILL RECEIVE ANY MONEY OR PROPERTY FROM THIS ESTATE OR OTHERWISE

*Whether you will receive any money or property will be determined wholly or partly by the decedent's will. If the decedent died without a will, whether you will receive any money or property will be determined by the intestacy laws of Pennsylvania.*

BEFORE THE REGISTER OF WILLS, COUNTY OF
________________, PENNSYLVANIA

IN RE: ESTATE of ______________________________, Deceased,

File Number ________________

TO: ______________________________________________ (Beneficiary)

______________________________________________ (Address)

______________________________________________

Please take notice of the death of the Decedent and the grant of Letters to the personal representative(s) named below. The Decedent died on the day of ________________, __________,a resident of ______________________ County, PA.

The Decedent died: _________ testate (with a will) or _________intestate (without a will)

You may have a beneficial interest in the estate as follows:

______________________________________________

(If additional space is needed, use separate sheet)

The name(s), address(es) and telephone number(s) of all personal representatives appointed are:

NAME ADDRESS TELEPHONE

______________________________________________

______________________________________________

If the Decedent died testate, the will has been filed with Office of the Register of Wills of ______________________ County.

If the Decedent died intestate, a Petition for the Grant of Letters of

Administration was filed with the Office of the Register of Wills of
______________________ County.

The Register's address is ________________________________________
_________________________, and telephone number is______________.

A copy of the Will or Petition may be obtained by contacting the Register of Wills and paying the charges for duplication.

*Date*____________

________________________________
*Signature of Person Filing this Form*

________________________________
*Name of Person Filing this Form*

Capacity: ❑ Personal Representative
❑ Counsel for Personal Representative

________________________________
*Address*

________________________________

________________________________
*Telephone*

## Appendix 11

# CERTIFICATION OF NOTICE UNDER Pa. O.C. Rule 5.6(a)

REGISTER OF WILLS
____________________, COUNTY, PENNSYLVANIA

Name of Decedent: ____________________________________________

Date of Death: ________________________ File Number:__________

Date Letters Granted: __________________________________________

To the Register:

I certify that Notice of Estate Administration required by Pa.O.C. Rule 5.6(a) of the Orphans' Court Rules was served on or mailed to the following beneficiaries of the above-captioned estate on __________________, ______:

| Name | Address |
| --- | --- |
| ____________________ | ______________________________________ |
| ____________________ | ______________________________________ |
| ____________________ | ______________________________________ |
| ____________________ | ______________________________________ |
| ____________________ | ______________________________________ |
| ____________________ | ______________________________________ |
| ____________________ | ______________________________________ |

*(If additional space is needed, use separate sheet)*

Notice has now been given to all persons entitled thereto under Rule 5.6(a) except: ________________________________________________________

________________________________________________________________

*Date*____________ ____________________________________________

*Signature of Person Filing this Form*

Capacity: ❑ Personal Representative ❑ Counsel

____________________________________________

*Name of Person Filing this Form*

____________________________________________

*Address*

____________________________________________

____________________________________________

*Telephone*

## Appendix 12

# FORM OF NOTICE TO DEPARTMENT OF PUBLIC WELFARE RE MEDICAL ASSISTANCE PAYMENTS

Department of Public Welfare
Bureau of Financial Operations
3rd Party Liability Section—Casualty Unit
P.O. Box 8486
Harrisburg, PA 17105

Re: Estate of Mary Doe
SSN #000-00-0000

Gentlemen:

This office represents John Doe, executor of the will of the above decedent, who died on August 21, 1995. She was residing at Pennsylvania Rest Home, Main Street, Norristown, PA 19401.

As provided by the Public Welfare Code § 1412, please forward a statement of the Department's claim for medical assistance.

Very truly yours,

Certified Mail, R.R.R.

____________________________

Samuel Attorney

# Appendix 13

# DECEDENT'S ESTATE

COURT OF COMMON PLEAS OF
____________________ COUNTY, PENNSYLVANIA
ORPHANS' COURT DIVISON

ESTATE OF ____________________________, DECEASED

No. ________________

**PETITION FOR ADJUDICATION / STATEMENT OF PROPOSED DISTRIBUTION PURSUANT TO Pa. O.C. Rule 6.9**

*This form may be used in all cases involving the Audit of the Account of a Decedent's Estate. If space is insufficient, riders may be attached. Attach the spouse's election, if any; the papers required under items 8–19 inclusive; and any instrument pertinent to the adjudication.*

***INCLUDE ATTACHMENTS AT THE BACK OF THIS FORM***

Name of Counsel: ______________________________________________

Supreme Court I.D. No.: ________________________________________

Name of Law Firm: _____________________________________________

Address: _____________________________________________________

Telephone: ___________________________________________________

Fax: _________________________________________________________

1. Name(s) and address(es) of Petitioner(s):

   *Name:* __________________________ __________________________

   *Address:* __________________________ __________________________

   __________________________ __________________________

   Identify any executors or administrators who have not joined in the Petition for Adjudication and Statement of Proposed Distribution and Account and state reason:

   ______________________________________________________________

APPENDIX 13

Estate of ________________________________________, Deceased

Is this the first accounting by this fiduciary? . . . . . . . . . ❑ Yes ❑ No

If not, identify prior accountings, the accounting periods covered, and the date of adjudication of the prior accounting.

________________________________________________________________

________________________________________________________________

2. Decedent died on ______________________________.

❑ Letters Testamentary *or* ❑ Letters of Administration were granted to Petitioner(s) on ___________________________.

Date of Will (*if applicable*): ________________________________________

Date(s) of Codicil(s) (*if applicable*): ________________________________

Date of probate (*if different from date Letters granted*): _____________

Was a bond required? ❑ Yes ❑ No If yes, state amount: _________

Are proofs of advertising of the grant of Letters attached? . . . . . . . . . . . . . . . . . . . . . . . . . . . . . . . . . . . . ❑ Yes ❑ No

Date of advertising of the grant of Letters: _______________________

________________________________________________________________

3. Was decedent survived by a spouse? . . . . . . . . . . . . . . . ❑ Yes ❑ No

If yes, name of the surviving spouse: ________________________________

4. Has the surviving spouse filed to take an elective share? . . . . . . . . . . . . . . . . . . . . . . . . . . . . . . . . . . . . . . . . . ❑ Yes ❑ No
*(See Section 2201 et seq. of the Probate, Estates and Fiduciaries Code)*

If yes, date of election: ________________________________________

5. In the case of an intestacy, state the names of the decedent's surviving children or surviving issue of deceased children *(if none, so state)*:

________________________________________________________________

________________________________________________________________

________________________________________________________________

Estate of ________________________________________, Deceased

6. Did decedent marry after execution of Will or Codicil(s)? .......................................... ❑ Yes ❑ No

   Were any children born to decedent after execution of Will of Codicil(s)? .......................................... ❑ Yes ❑ No

   If yes, give names and dates of birth:

   | *Name:* | *Date of Birth:* |
   |---|---|
   | ______________________________ | ____________ |
   | ______________________________ | ____________ |
   | ______________________________ | ____________ |
   | ______________________________ | ____________ |

7. If required by the Medical Assistance Estate Recovery Act, 62 P.S. § 1412, was a request for a statement of claim sent to the Department of Public Welfare? .............................. ❑ Yes ❑ No

8. Written notice of the Audit as required by Pa.O.C. Rules 6.3, 6.7, and 6.8 has been or will be given to all parties in interest listed in item 9 below, all unpaid creditors and all claimants listed in item 10 below. In addition, notice of any questions requiring Adjudication as discussed in item 14 below has been or will be given to all persons affected thereby.

   A. If Notice has been given, attach a copy of the Notice as well as a list of the names and addresses of the parties receiving such Notice.

   B. If Notice is yet to be given, a copy of the Notice as well as a list of the names and addresses of the parties receiving such Notice shall be submitted at the Audit together with a statement executed by a Petitioner or counsel certifying that such notice has been given.

   C. If any person entitled to Notice is not *sui juris* (e.g., minors or incapacitated persons), Notice of the Audit has been or will be given to the appropriate representative on such party's behalf as required by Pa. O.C. Rule 5.2.

Estate of ______________________________________, Deceased

D. If any charitable interest is involved, Notice of the Audit has been or will also be given to the Attorney General as required under Pa. O.C. Rule 5.5. In addition, the Attorney General's clearance certificate (or proof of service of Notice and a copy of such Notice) must be submitted herewith or at the Audit.

9. List all parties (charitable and non-charitable) of whom Petitioner(s) has/have notice or knowledge, having or claiming any interest in the estate as beneficiaries under the Will or Codicil(s) or as intestate heirs if there is a complete or partial intestacy:

A. State each party's relationship to the decedent and the nature of each party's interest(s):

| *Name and Address of Each Party in Interest* | *Relationship and Comments, if any* | *Interest* |
|---|---|---|
| | | |
| | | |
| | | |
| | | |

Estate of ______________________________________, Deceased

B. Identify each party who is not *sui juris* (*e.g.*, minors or incapacitated persons). For each such party, give date of birth, the name of each Guardian and how each Guardian was appointed. If no Guardian has been appointed, identify the next of kin of such party, giving the name, address and relationship of each.

C. State why a Petition for Guardian/Trustee *Ad Litem* has or has not been filed for this Audit (*see Pa. O.C. Rule 12.4*).

D. If distribution is to be made to the personal representative of a deceased party, state date of death, date and place of grant of Letters and type of Letters granted.

10. Other than the claim for the family exemption, list the names of all known claimants and the amount of their claims and state whether each claim is admitted.

| *Name and Address of Each Claimant* | *Amount of Claim* | *Claim Admitted?* | *Will Claim Be Paid in Full?* |
|---|---|---|---|
| | | ❑ Yes<br>❑ No | ❑ Yes<br>❑ No |
| | | ❑ Yes<br>❑ No | ❑ Yes<br>❑ No |
| | | ❑ Yes<br>❑ No | ❑ Yes<br>❑ No |
| | | ❑ Yes<br>❑ No | ❑ Yes<br>❑ No |

Estate of ________________________________________, Deceased

If the estate is insolvent, attach a schedule setting forth the order of preference under 20 Pa.C.S. § 3392 and the proposed payments.

11. Was family exemption claimed? . . . . . . . . . . . . . . . . . . . ❑ Yes ❑ No

Was family exemption allowed? . . . . . . . . . . . . . . . . . . . ❑ Yes ❑ No

Family exemption claimant's name and relationship:

*Name:* ______________________________ *Relationship:* ______________

12. The amount of Pennsylvania Transfer Inheritance Tax and additional Pennsylvania Estate Tax paid, the date(s) of payment(s), and the interest(s) upon which paid, are as follows:

| *Date:* | *Payment* | *Interest* |
|---|---|---|
| ____________________ | ____________________ | ____________________ |
| ____________________ | ____________________ | ____________________ |
| ____________________ | ____________________ | ____________________ |

13. On the date of death, was the decedent a fiduciary (personal representative, trustee, guardian, agent under power of attorney) or surety on the bond of a fiduciary? . . . . . . . . . . . . . . . . . ❑ Yes ❑ No

If yes, provide the name of the estate, indicate whether an account has been filed and confirmed absolutely and all awards performed, or, in the alternative, how the decedent's estate will be discharged for the decedent's fiduciary administration of the estate.

14. A. Describe in detail any questions requiring adjudication and state the position of the Petitioner(s) as to each question:

B. Has notice of the question requiring adjudication been given to the parties identified in Paragraph 9 above? . . . . . . ❑ Yes ❑ No

Estate of ______________________________________, Deceased

15. If Petitioner(s) has/have knowledge that a share has been assigned, renounced, disclaimed or attached, provide a copy of the assignment, renunciation, disclaimer or attachment, together with any relevant supporting documentation.

16. Had the decedent been adjudicated an incapacitated person? . . . . . . . . . . . . . . . . . . . . . . . . . . . . . . . . . . . . . . . . ❑ Yes ❑ No

    If yes, attach a copy of the Order if available; otherwise state the Court, term, number, date, and name of Hearing Judge.

17. A. List or attach a separate list of additional receipts and disbursements since the closing date of the Account.

    B. Has notice of the additional receipts and disbursements been given to the parties identified in Paragraph 9 above? . . . . . ❑ Yes ❑ No

18. If a reserve is requested, state amount and purpose.

    *Amount:* ________________________________________

    *Purpose:* ________________________________________

    ________________________________________

    ________________________________________

    If a reserve is requested for counsel fees, has notice of the amount of fees to be paid from the reserve been given to the parties in interest? . . . . . . . . . . . . . . . . . . . . . . . . . . . . . . . . . . . . . . ❑ Yes ❑ No

    If so, attach a copy of the notice.

19. Is the Court being asked to direct the filing of a Schedule of Distribution? . . . . . . . . . . . . . . . . . . . . . . . . . . . . . . . . . ❑ Yes ❑ No

    As to real estate only? . . . . . . . . . . . . . . . . . . . . . . . . . . ❑ Yes ❑ No

## APPENDIX 13

Estate of ________________________________, Deceased

Wherefore, your Petitioner(s) ask(s) that distribution be awarded to the parties entitled and suggest(s) that the distributive shares of income and principal (residuary shares being stated in proportions, not amounts) are as follows:

A. Income:

| *Proposed Distributee(s)* | *Amount / Proportion* |
|---|---|
| ________________________ | ____________ |
| ________________________ | ____________ |
| ________________________ | ____________ |

B. Principal:

| *Proposed Distributee(s)* | *Amount / Proportion* |
|---|---|
| ________________________ | ____________ |
| ________________________ | ____________ |
| ________________________ | ____________ |

Submitted By:
*(**All** petitioners **must** sign.*
*Add additional lines if necessary):*

________________________________
Name of Petitioner:

________________________________
Name of Petitioner:

Estate of ________________________________________, Deceased

**Verification of Petitioner**

(Verification must be by **at least one** petitioner.)

The undersigned hereby verifies * [that *he/she* ______ is *title* __________ ____________________ of the above-named *name of corporation* ____________ ________________________________ and] that the facts set forth in the foregoing Petition for Adjudication / Statement of Proposed Distribution which are within the personal knowledge of the Petitioner are true, and as to facts based on the information of others, the Petitioner, after diligent inquiry, believes them to be true; and that any false statements herein are made subject to the penalties of 18 Pa.C.S. § 4904 (relating to unsworn falsification to authorities).

_________________________________________

Signature of Petitioner

***Corporate petitioners must complete bracketed information.***

**Certification of Counsel**

The undersigned counsel hereby certifies that the foregoing Petition for Adjudication/Statement of Proposed Distribution is a true and accurate reproduction of the form Petition authorized by the Supreme Court, and that no changes to the form have been made beyond the responses herein.

_________________________________________

Signature of Counsel for Petitioner

# INDEX

**[References Are to Sections]**

**– A –**

[References Are to Sections]

## – C –

**– M –**

## – P –

[References Are to Sections]

## – R –

## – T –